About the Author

Christine A. Hult, Ph.D., is an emeritus faculty member of the English Department at Utah State University. Dr. Hult also served as an Associate Dean in the College of Humanities, Arts, and Social Sciences at Utah State University. She received her Ph.D. from the University of Michigan in English and Education. Dr. Hult has written several successful writing textbooks, including: *The New Century Handbook*, fifth edition; *The New Century Pocket Guide for Writers*, third edition (with Thomas Huckin); and *Researching and Writing across the Curriculum*, third edition. Her research interests include computers in the writing classroom, writing in the disciplines, program and teacher assessment, and women in academia. She was selected as the D. Wynne Thorne Researcher of the Year at Utah State University in 2004. She is past editor of the Council of Writing Program Administrator's journal, *WPA: Writing Program Administration,* and is active in numerous professional organizations (speaking at conferences, chairing panels and programs, and leading workshops), including the National Council of Teachers of English, the Conference on Computers and Writing (conference chair, 1996), the Council of Writing Program Administrators (conference chair, 1987), the Alliance for Computers in English Studies, the National Science Foundation's Advance Project, and the Conference on College Composition and Communication.

i

Also from Visible Ink Press

The Handy African American History Answer Book
by Jessie Carnie Smith
ISBN: 978-1-57859-452-8

The Handy Anatomy Answer Book, 2nd edition
by Patricia Barnes-Svarney and Thomas E. Svarney
ISBN: 978-57859-542-6

The Handy Answer Book for Kids (and Parents), 2nd edition
by Gina Misiroglu
ISBN: 978-1-57859-219-7

The Handy Art History Answer Book
by Madelynn Dickerson
ISBN: 978-1-57859-417-7

The Handy Astronomy Answer Book, 3rd edition
by Charles Liu
ISBN: 978-1-57859-190-9

The Handy Bible Answer Book
by Jennifer Rebecca Prince
ISBN: 978-1-57859-478-8

The Handy Biology Answer Book, 2nd edition
by Patricia Barnes Svarney and Thomas E. Svarney
ISBN: 978-1-57859-490-0

The Handy Chemistry Answer Book
by Ian C. Stewart and Justin P. Lamont
ISBN: 978-1-57859-374-3

The Handy Civil War Answer Book
by Samuel Willard Crompton
ISBN: 978-1-57859-476-4

The Handy Dinosaur Answer Book, 2nd edition
by Patricia Barnes-Svarney and Thomas E. Svarney
ISBN: 978-1-57859-218-0

The Handy Geography Answer Book, 2nd edition
by Paul A. Tucci
ISBN: 978-1-57859-215-9

The Handy Geology Answer Book
by Patricia Barnes-Svarney and Thomas E. Svarney
ISBN: 978-1-57859-156-5

The Handy History Answer Book, 3rd edition
by David L. Hudson, Jr.
ISBN: 978-1-57859-372-9

The Handy Hockey Answer Book
by Stan Fischler
ISBN: 978-1-57859-569-3

The Handy Investing Answer Book
by Paul A. Tucci
ISBN: 978-1-57859-486-3

The Handy Islam Answer Book
by John Renard Ph.D.
ISBN: 978-1-57859-510-5

The Handy Law Answer Book
by David L. Hudson Jr.
ISBN: 978-1-57859-217-3

The Handy Math Answer Book, 2nd edition
by Patricia Barnes-Svarney and Thomas E. Svarney
ISBN: 978-1-57859-373-6

The Handy Military History Answer Book
by Samuel Willard Crompton
ISBN: 978-1-57859-509-9

The Handy Mythology Answer Book,
by David A. Leeming, Ph.D.
ISBN: 978-1-57859-475-7

The Handy Nutrition Answer Book
by Patricia Barnes-Svarney and Thomas E. Svarney
ISBN: 978-1-57859-484-9

The Handy Ocean Answer Book
by Patricia Barnes-Svarney and Thomas E. Svarney
ISBN: 978-1-57859-063-6

The Handy Personal Finance Answer Book
by Paul A. Tucci
ISBN: 978-1-57859-322-4

The Handy Philosophy Answer Book
by Naomi Zack
ISBN: 978-1-57859-226-5

The Handy Physics Answer Book, 2nd edition
By Paul W. Zitzewitz, Ph.D.
ISBN: 978-1-57859-305-7

The Handy Politics Answer Book
by Gina Misiroglu
ISBN: 978-1-57859-139-8

The Handy Presidents Answer Book, 2nd edition
by David L. Hudson
ISB N: 978-1-57859-317-0

The Handy Psychology Answer Book
by Lisa J. Cohen
ISBN: 978-1-57859-223-4

The Handy Religion Answer Book, 2nd edition
by John Renard
ISBN: 978-1-57859-379-8

The Handy Science Answer Book, 4th edition
by The Carnegie Library of Pittsburgh
ISBN: 978-1-57859-321-7

The Handy Supreme Court Answer Book
by David L Hudson, Jr.
ISBN: 978-1-57859-196-1

The Handy Technology Answer Book
by Naomi Balaban and James Bobick
ISBN: 978-1-57859-563-1

The Handy Weather Answer Book, 2nd edition
by Kevin S. Hile
ISBN: 978-1-57859-221-0

Please visit the "Handy" series website at www.handyanswers.com.

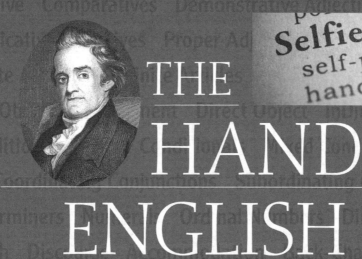

THE
HANDY
ENGLISH
GRAMMAR
ANSWER
BOOK

Christine A. Hult, Ph. D.

VISIBLE
INK
PRESS

Detroit

THE HANDY ENGLISH GRAMMAR ANSWER BOOK

Visible Ink Press®
43311 Joy Rd., #414
Canton, MI 48187–2075
Visible Ink Press is a registered trademark of Visible Ink Press LLC.

Most Visible Ink Press books are available at special quantity discounts when purchased in bulk by corporations, organizations, or groups. Customized printings, special imprints, messages, and excerpts can be produced to meet your needs. For more information, contact Special Markets Director, Visible Ink Press, www.visibleinkpress.com, or 734–667–3211.

Managing Editor: Kevin S. Hile
Art Director: Mary Claire Krzewinski
Typesetting: Marco Di Vita
Proofreaders: Barbara Lyon, Cheryl Ruffing
Indexer: Shoshana Hurwitz

Cover images: Image of Noah Webster is public domain; all other images courtesy of Shutterstock.

Cataloging-in-Publication Data is on file at the Library of Congress.

Printed in the United States of America

10 9 8 7 6 5 4 3 2 1

Contents

Photo Credits

Acknowledgements

I wish to thank those who have made this book possible, including my colleagues in the English and education professions, my co-author of the "New Century Handbook" series, Thomas Huckin, and all of the many researchers and writers in the fields of grammar, linguistics, and composition whose work has informed my own over the years. I am very grateful for the students who have allowed me to use their work as models for other students. I also wish to thank the publishing team at Visible Ink Press for inviting me to write this book and for helping me to shape it into what we all hope will be a useful guidebook to English grammar for many different audiences. Finally, a huge thank you to my husband, Nathan Hult, who supports me in whatever I do.

Introduction

When I thought about writing a handy guide to English grammar, I thought first about the potential readers of such a book, and what their questions might be. I thought about students who may be considering attending college or who might be preparing for the SAT or ACT college entrance tests. Or college students, either new to college or returning after some time away from school, who needed a quick refresher about grammatical principles and rules. I thought about English as a Second Language learners who might be preparing for the TOEFL or who just needed a handy guide to the English language. I also envisioned adult readers who might need such a guide to help them with a writing task on the job or even to write an announcement or an invitation correctly.

To make the book as useful as possible to a variety of readers, I divided it into the following parts: Brief History of the English Language (an overview of the origins of English and of language change), Grammar Basics (important grammatical terms and concepts, including sentence structure, spelling, punctuation, mechanics, correctness), and Writing for Various Purposes (academic writing; science, social science, arts, humanities, business writing, writing in the electronic age, writing in English as a Second Language). In the appendices, I include much more information about grammar: for example, irregular verb forms, idioms, and misused homophones and other potential grammar snares. Complete model papers from academic fields and from non-school settings are also included in the appendices, as well as expanded examples of bibliographic formats from a variety of fields.

As I wrote the book, I was conscious to make it useful to teachers—both secondary school and college teachers—as well as to students. I made sure the book would interface smoothly with the Common Core State Standards for English Language Arts and Literacy. In particular, the key shifts in 2014 toward "regular practice with complex texts and their academic language," are reflected in the content I chose to include in this book. The standards' new emphasis on evidence-based writing along with the ability to inform and persuade, and the use of "informational texts to build content knowledge," fits right in with the content included in *The Handy English Grammar Answer Book*.

Finally, this book will quickly give you the answers to your grammar queries: "Do I use *who* or *whom*?" "Should it be *its* or *it's*?" Not only will you get the answer, but you will understand why a particular choice is preferred over another, giving you the power to make your writing say what you mean and mean what you say.

THE ROOTS OF MODERN ENGLISH

How did language begin?

Human beings have always been fascinated by the origin of language. All religions and mythologies include in their creation stories the beginning of language. The Jewish Talmud says, "God created the world by a Word, instantaneously, without toil and pains." The Christian Bible says, "In the beginning was the Word." According to Judeo-Christian tradition, God gave Adam the power to name everything. Similar beliefs exist throughout various cultures and religions: in ancient Egypt, speech originated with the god Thoth; for the Babylonians, it was the god Nabu; for Hindus, speech comes from the goddess Sarasvati. Language is what makes human beings uniquely human.

Anthropologists believe that human beings have existed for at least one million years, and perhaps as long as five million years. Yet the earliest written records, writings of the Sumerians of 4000 B.C.E., are barely six thousand years old. In studying the history of languages, scholars have come to believe that many developed from a single language. However, we will probably never be able to determine exactly when human language began. Humankind's ability to acquire language is a unique genetic quality. No one needs to teach us language; we learn it as children through the language spoken in our environment.

Is the history of language cultural?

The history of language is a history of cultures. Political, social, and cultural events in the world affect language development. This is especially true of English. What we know today as the English language developed over many centuries and is the result of historical events in England. These include Roman invasion and occupation of Britain as early as the first century C.E.; the island's introduction to Christianity in the sixth century; Scandinavian incursions; and French influences thrust upon the people by the eleventh-century Norman Conquest. Each of these major political events shaped the

1

> ## Wild Children
>
> There are many cases of children who have been raised "in the wild" without any human interaction. In all of these cases, upon being found in France, the children had never learned language. Victor, "the wild boy of Aveyron," who was found as a teenager in 1798, is one of two famous examples. François Truffaut documented Victor's case in the film *The Wild Child*. Victor had somehow been left in the woods as a very young boy and managed to survive. In a similar case, two feral children, called Amal and Kamala, were found in India in 1920, supposedly raised by wolves. Without exposure to language as children, these three never learned to speak.

English language. Further, the influences on the English language of Latin, Scandinavian, and French are considerable. More recently, expansion of the British Empire, with its global reach of commerce and industry, has affected the development of English and helped make it the international language it is today.

What is the relationship between a language and its speakers?

We can hardly separate the language a people speak from the people themselves. A language lives as long as a people actively speak it as their native tongue. Its significance is proportional to the political, economic, social, commercial, and cultural influence of its people. In the twenty-first century, English, French, Spanish, and German are widely spoken and learned as second languages by speakers all over the world. In contrast, for example, Serbian and Sudanese are seldom learned by those in other ethnic groups or nations. Sometimes a language continues to be influential long after the political power of its speakers has faded. An example is the Greek language, which is still widely studied because of the classical civilization from which it sprung. The modern form of Greek, as it is spoken today, is largely neglected in favor of its classical form.

How important is the English language?

English is the third most-spoken language as a native tongue, following Mandarin Chinese and Spanish. It is the first language spoken in the United Kingdom, the United States, Canada, Australia, Ireland, and New Zealand, among other countries. English is an official language of the European Union and many Commonwealth countries, and one of six official languages of the United Nations. English is spoken as a first language by approximately 335 million people. In contrast, Mandarin Chinese is spoken as a first language by approximately 850 million people, more than double the number of native English speakers. All over the world, however, English is widely learned as a second language, with approximately 500 million people speaking it in this capacity. While the number of speakers is an obvious indicator of a language's importance, the political status of the nations using it is inextricably linked to that importance—their influence...

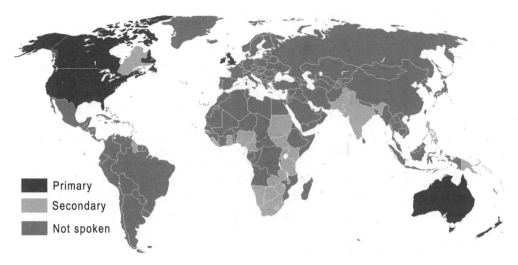

This political map shows where the English language is the primary official language (black) and where it is an official language but not the primary language (light grey).

their influence on international affairs, their economic power, and their contributions to world civilization.

Should English be considered a world language?

More scientific research is published in English than in any other language, and English has become the international language of business and commerce. Some aspects of English that make it relatively easy to learn are: its origin as a mixture of languages; its openness to assimilating words from other languages; its inflectional simplicity, in that it eliminates elaborate adjective inflections and personal endings of verbs; and its use of natural gender rather than grammatical gender, which contrasts with French, for example, wherein each noun is categorized as either masculine or feminine, affecting the choice of verbs, determiners, and the like.

What are some common English words that are derived from other languages?

Common Words from Other Languages

Language of Origin	Examples
Arabic	alcohol, algebra, coffee, cotton, hashish, Muslim, nadir
Dutch	brandy, cruller, golf, duck, landscape, measles, selvage, uproar, wagon, wildebeest
Greek	acme, acrobat, anthology, barometer, catarrh, catastrophe, chronology, elastic, magic, tactics, tantalize
Italian	balcony, canto, duet, granite, opera, piano, pizza, umbrella, volcano
Native American	chipmunk, hominy, moose, raccoon, skunk

3

Common Words from Other Languages

Language of Origin	Examples
Persian	borax, caravan, check, chess, dervish, divan, khaki, jasmine, lemon, lilac, mogul, pajamas, paradise, shawl, sherbet, turban
Russian	steppe, vodka,
Scandinavian	geyser, sky, troll,
Spanish	alligator, cargo, cigar, cork, guerilla, guitar, hammock, mosquito, plaza, renegade, rodeo, salsa, sherry, stampede, tornado, vanilla

Other languages from which English has borrowed include: Bengali, Chinese, Hebrew, Hindi, Hungarian, and Malay. Other nations from which English has borrowed words include: Australia, Brazil, Java, Polynesia, Tahiti, and countries found in West Africa.

What are the roots of modern English?

English is a Germanic language that was first spoken in medieval England. *Old English* is a collection of dialects that were brought to the eastern coast of Great Britain by Germanic settlers (also called Anglo-Saxons) around the fifth century C.E. The word *English* is the modern spelling of *englisc*, the name used by the Angles and Saxons for their language. English was also influenced greatly by Viking invasions in the ninth and tenth

The Anglo-Saxon people migrated from what is now Germany to England around the fifth century, and their language evolved into what is known as Old English, which was heavily influenced by its Germanic origins.

centuries C.E. When the Normans conquered England in the eleventh century, English began to borrow from Norman French and was therefore heavily influenced by the Latin-derived Romance languages. It became, in the eleventh century, what has been termed *Middle English*. The relationship between German and English is easy to see in many of its vocabulary words: *milch* and *milk, brot* and *bread, fleisch* and *flesh, wasser* and *water* are a few examples. Similarly, Latin and English words show a connection: *pater* and *father, frater* and *brother*.

What is the Indo-European family of languages?

Linguists studying word derivations have been led to hypothesize that the languages of a large part of Europe and a portion of Asia were at one time identical. All of the European languages have been found to correspond with one another and even with Sanskrit, a language of ancient India. For example, the English word *father* corresponds to Dutch *vader*, Gothic *fadar*, Old Norse *faoir*, German *vater*, Greek *pater*, Sanskrit *pitar*, and Old Irish *aithir*. There is no written record of a common Indo-European language, but by comparing its descendants linguists are able to come up with a reconstruction of its probable vocabulary and inflections. Scholars believe that prior to their dispersal throughout Europe and East Asia (which occurred before the dawn of recorded history), the Indo-Europeans occupied the district east of the Germanic area stretching from central Europe to southern Russia to India.

Were there languages in England before English?

Presumably there were a number of languages and cultures occupying what is known today as the British Isles. Evidence suggests that the earliest people in the British Isles, called Paleolithic, lived during a time before the English Channel was formed, when the British Isles were a part of continental Europe. From archeological finds, we know that Paleolithic people lived in rock shelters and caves, fished, ate wild animals, and foraged for food. Unfortunately, we know nothing about the language of this race, although they have left drawings on the walls of caves. Paleolithic people were succeeded around 5000 B.C.E. by a race of people migrating north from the Mediterranean. This people's descendants can still be seen in today's dark-skinned, dark-haired inhabitants of Scotland, Ireland, and Wales. Their language has not survived. The first people in the British Isles whose language can be heard today are the Celts. The Celtic language, which is still spoken by many people in Ireland, Scotland, and Wales, is the first Indo-European language spoken in Britain and Ireland.

How did the language of the Anglo-Saxons become the English language?

The Celts of Britain and Ireland were gradually conquered by the Anglo-Saxons during the fifth and sixth centuries C.E., until 839, when England and Wales were under the overlordship of a Saxon chieftain named Egbert (802–839). At first, the Celts called their conquerors the *Saxons* from *Saxonia*. Eventually, though, the terms *Angli* and *Anglia* began to appear in Roman writings. In 601, Pope Gregory anointed Ethelbert the *rex An-*

glorum, or King of England. Gradually over this period, *Angli* and *Anglia* became the terms used in Latin texts to describe English and England. Those who were writing in the English vernacular and not in Latin, however, always termed their language *Englisc* (*English*). Scholars speculate that perhaps *English* and *England* won out because the people on the British Islands wanted to distinguish themselves from the Saxons who remained in Europe.

What is Old English?

The language used in Britain and Ireland from around 450 to 1150 C.E. is known as Old English. It developed from the dialects spoken by the Germanic tribes of Anglo-Saxons who gradually conquered the Celts residing in the British Isles. The English language that we know today evolved over about 1500 years. Although the divisions between time periods in the development of English are somewhat arbitrary, scholars have been able to recognize three main

An illustration of a Pict woman (one of the peoples of Celtic origin) covered in tattoos and armed for battle. The Celtic peoples settled the British Isles before the Anglo-Saxons arrived.

periods: Old English, Middle English, and Modern English. Because of the changes that have occurred over time, today's English speakers would have more trouble reading Old English texts than they would texts written in French or Italian. The main difficulties in reading Old English arise because some of the letters of the Old English alphabet have changed. Other differences between Old English and today's English include changes in spelling, pronunciation, vocabulary, and grammar. To read Old English requires years of specialized study. It is interesting to note that one of the major differences that is apparent to the modern reader is that Old English has none of the vocabulary words derived from Latin and French, which now make up about half of our modern English vocabulary. The vocabulary of Old English is almost totally Germanic. The Norman Conquest in the eleventh century brought the French language to the British Isles, and that is when Old English vocabulary words began to be replaced by words borrowed from French and Latin.

What is the "legal doublet" of English law language?

Common law in the British Isles was derived from Celtic law, while French law developed from Anglo-Norman law. The "legal doublet" grew up in English legal language to pair an Anglo-Saxon word with its Latin/French synonym to ensure understanding in legal documents. Some of the common phrases used in legal language today preserve both of the terms (which remain as synonyms), as in the following examples:

Aid and abet
Bind and obligate
Breaking and entering
Cease and desist
Covenant and agree
Deem and consider
Depose and say
Due and payable
Final and conclusive
Fit and proper
Full faith and credit
Furnish and supply
Goods and chattels
Heirs and successors
Hue and cry
Indemnify and hold harmless
Law and order
Legal and valid
Null and void
Over and above
Part and parcel
Perform and discharge
Sale or transfer
Sole and exclusive
Successor and assigns
To have and to hold
Terms and conditions
True and correct
Will and testament

There are even some legal triplets, as in the following examples:

Cancel, annul, and set aside
Convey, transfer, and set over
Ordered, adjudged, and decreed
Remise, release, and forever quit claim
Right, title, and interest
Signed, sealed, and delivered

What is Old English literature?

A page from the original *Beowulf* folio.

Most of the literature written in Old English is poetry, both Christian and pagan. The most famous poetic work in Old English literature is the *Beowulf* folk epic. It is the earliest surviving work of literature written in the vernacular. The story, set in Scandinavia, traces the exploits of the hero Beowulf, a young warrior who battles monsters and dragons ravaging the land. His exploits are an important window into the heroic ideals of early Germanic times. Here is what Beowulf says to the king before embarking on the dangerous task of slaying the monster: "Sorrow not…. Better is it for every man that he avenge his friend than that he mourn greatly. Each of us must abide the end of this world's life; let him who may, work mighty deeds ere he die, for afterwards, when he lies lifeless, that is best for the warrior." Beowulf slays both the monster Grendel and Grendel's mother in two horrific battles in Denmark. The victorious Beowulf then returns to Sweden where he rules peacefully for fifty years, until a dragon attacks his castle, and Beowulf is fatally wounded in the battle that ensues.

What happened to English during the Norman Conquest?

Toward the end of the Old English period, an event took place that influenced the English language more than anything else: the Norman Conquest of 1066. The fortunes of the English language changed dramatically when the Duke of Normandy (William the Conqueror), who ruled on the northern coast of France directly across from the English Channel, conquered England. A new French-speaking nobility came to London with William, because most of the English upper class had been killed on the battlefields. This new noble class primarily spoke French, and for the next 200 years the English upper classes spoke French. The language of the masses, however, remained English. The royal family, who were kings of England and France, spent more than half of their time on the Continent. Similarly, nearly all English landowners also owned land on the Continent, spent much of their time in France, and often intermarried with nobles from Europe. The upper classes were not hostile to the English language; rather, they preferred French, as it was the language used at court and in business and military affairs.

What is Middle English?

Scholars date the *Middle English* period from about 1150 to 1500. This period marked significant changes in the English language. The changes affected both English grammar and English vocabulary. The many word inflections found in Old English nearly disappeared over this time period, and thousands of words of Latin and French origin

At the Battle of Hastings on October 14, 1066, William II of Normandy defeated an English army led by Harold II, who died during the battle. The Norman victory was not only political, but also cultural, as French words and phrases mixed with Anglo-Saxon ones.

were adopted into English. At the start of this period, English is a foreign, Germanic language; at the end of this period, it is modern-day English. The word inflections in Old English contained that troublesome feature of language termed "grammatical gender." So, for example, the Old English word for "woman" was masculine, while the words for "wife" and "child" were neuter. Over time, the use of grammatical gender all but disappeared in English. Scholars note, however, that this grammatical change was not due to French influences, because French retained its system of grammatical gender. Typically, languages borrow words but not grammatical structure from other languages. English borrowed heavily from French vocabulary during the Middle English period. The two languages existed side-by-side in England, so it is not surprising that many French words were adopted into the English language. Because French was the language of social and political power, more French words were absorbed into the English language than the other way around.

How did we get to Modern English?

The English language has always shown a remarkable flexibility and adaptability when it comes to incorporating new vocabulary words. The events of the Renaissance, during

9

which English fought to be recognized as a valid written language in place of Latin, and the centuries following, during which English was spread worldwide by way of the British victories at sea, influenced the development of modern-day English. The growth of science and enterprise also played a part in bringing new vocabulary words to the English language. In every field of science in the last hundred or so years, there has been a tremendous need to invent new terms. These words, which often begin as specialized jargon, become absorbed into more general use. Some examples include *anemia, bronchitis,* or *appendicitis; homeopathic, osteopathy,* or *orthodontia; aspirin, penicillin,* or *morphine;* plus thousands more from medicine. The same story can be told of other sciences: from physics—*calorie, electron, ultraviolet, relativity*; from chemistry—*alkali, creosote, cyanide, radium, biochemical*; from psychology—*egocentric, extrovert, inhibition, psychoanalysis;* from space science—*launch pad, countdown command module, splashdown.* Further, the rise of journalism, both newspapers and magazines, influenced the spread and popularization of new vocabulary words among the English-speaking populace.

THE ENGLISH LANGUAGE AND LANGUAGE CHANGE

How has the English language changed?

Languages change constantly, in a number of different manners: in the way words are pronounced (phonology), in the way sentences are put together (syntax), in vocabulary (lexicon), and in meaning shifts (semantics). Numerous examples of English language changes abound in the linguistic literature, but English is not unique in this phenomenon. All languages change over time, but no one knows exactly why. A language's grammar is the sum of all the knowledge acquired by native speakers of the language. Thus, all parts of any language's grammar are subject to change over time.

How has the pronunciation of English words changed?

The sound system of a language is its phonology. The ways in which words are pronounced are not necessarily static. Changes occur. For example, the language sound /x/, a part of the English language in Chaucer's day, dropped out of use by the time of Shakespeare. The word *night* in Chaucer's time would have been pronounced [nixt]. Similarly, the word *drought* was pronounced [druxt]. In some words spelled with *gh*, the sound became not /x/ but /f/. These include *rough* and *tough*. Some dialects of British English, however, retain the sound of /x/ in some words spelled with the *gh*. In addition to losing sounds, the English language has also gained new sounds, particularly from borrowing sounds used in other languages. For example, the language sound /z/ as in *azure*, was not a part of English until several French words with this sound were incorporated into English. These include *azure, measure*, and *rouge*.

How has the way English sentences are put together changed?

The way that English sentences are put together, the syntax of English, has evolved over time. For example, in the fifteenth century, to change a sentence from a positive to a negative statement, one added the negative to the end of the sentence. Here is a sentence from Shakespeare:

I love thee not, therefore pursue me not.

In today's English syntax, we put the negation before the verb as in the following:

I do not love you, so do not pursue me.

Another change that has occurred is the syntactic rule governing comparative (e.g., *greater, more comfortable*) and superlative (e.g., *greatest, most comfortable*) constructions. The rule today says that we add *more* and *most* to form comparatives and superlatives of words three syllables or longer, rather than adding *-er* or *-est*, and we never use more or most with words to which *-er* or *-est* have been added. In the

Geoffrey Chaucer (1343–1400), author of *The Canterbury Tales,* pronounced words differently than they would be in William Shakespeare's day.

fifteenth century, comparatives and superlatives such as *more gladder, more lower, most royalest, most shamefullest* were perfectly grammatical. Similarly, we might notice that some syntactic changes are occurring today. For example, the syntactic rule governing the use of *who* and *whom* in English is gradually fading out of existence. At some point, English speakers and writers will no longer use *who* for subjective case and *whom* for objective case, but instead will probably use *who* for both, a practice many English speakers have already adopted.

How has the vocabulary of English changed?

English vocabulary is extremely dynamic, and the lexicon of English is constantly changing. Words are added and subtracted, and the meanings of words are changed over time. When speakers start to use a new word, it may appear quite suddenly; in contrast, when words are lost, they seem to disappear gradually over several generations. New words can be coined to meet a specific purpose: *Xerox, Kleenex, Jell-O, Frigidaire, Vaseline* are all words that were coined for specific products that later evolved to refer to generic items. New words can also be created by compounding existing words. Some examples of compounding include *afternoon, bigmouth, egghead, offshore, pothole, railroad, sailboat, waterpipe,* etc. Other new words are created by blending two existing words, as in *motor + hotel = motel,* or *diskette + drive = disk drive.* Another way to create new words is to shorten a word: *prof* for *professor, nark* for *narcotics agent, doc* for *doctor.* The biggest source of new vocabulary, though, likely comes from borrowing words found in other languages. The English language has borrowed extensively over the centuries, and continues to be a heavy borrower. The word *algebra* was borrowed from Spanish, which in turn had borrowed it centuries earlier from Arabic. We can trace the history of the English-speaking peoples by looking at when new vocabulary words were introduced into the language and from which cultures: Scandinavian, Celtic, Dutch, German, French, Latin, and Native American. When English speakers moved to America, many Native American place names were adopted into English: *Erie, Huron, Michigan, Appalachia, Ozarks, Massachusetts,* etc.

How have the meanings of English words changed?

In addition to adding and subtracting words, languages can also change the meanings of words over time; linguists call these semantic changes. The meaning of a word can become broader, narrower, or entirely different. An example of the broadening of a word can be see in the Middle English word *dogge,* which meant a specific breed of dog, like the word *collie* in Modern English. Today, the meaning of *dog* has been broadened to include all dogs, not just a specific breed. Similarly, the word *holiday* originally meant holy day: that is, a day that held religious significance. Today the word has been broadened to include any day that is a break from work. The word *butcher* originally meant "slaughterer of bucks." Today's meaning includes anyone who works with any meat to prepare it for consumption. The meaning of words can also become narrower. One example is the word *meat,* as found in the King James Bible: "to you they shall be for

As English colonists began to interact with Native American tribes, the endemic vocabulary crept into that of the new settlers.

Change is a fact of life and language; it is neither good nor bad and it certainly is not corrupt. No one knows exactly why languages change. Linguists speculate that the ways in which children acquire language may contribute to language change. Children do not need to be taught the rules of their native language. Rather, they are genetically programmed to construct their own grammar as they hear the language spoken around them. As children learn the language, their system of grammar becomes increasingly complex, until they closely mirror the grammar of the adults they hear speaking. No child's grammar, however, is exactly like an adult's grammar, because each child constructs his or her own unique grammatical style. Children are exposed to numerous dialects, slangs, and individual speakers whose language styles may vary widely. The grammatical features a child is exposed to gradually fuse into his or her own grammatical system. For example, the older generation may already be using variable rules; at certain times they say "It is I," while at other times they say "It is me." The child hears both usages and may adopt the simpler version. If such a change is widespread among a generation of children, the grammar of the language will gradually change. The branch of linguistics that studies how languages change is called *historical and comparative linguistics*.

meat." In this context, meat signified all food, whereas today it has narrowed to the point where it almost always means animal flesh. The word *deer* once meant animal, and its German cognate *Tier* still does mean animal. In modern English, deer has been narrowed to a specific species of animal. The third kind of semantic change is meaning shift. An example comes from the Middle Ages, when the word *bead* originally meant prayer. Because prayers were recited using rosary beads, the meaning of bead changed to signify not the prayer itself, but the beads upon which people kept track of their prayers. The word *silly* used to mean happy in Old English; by Middle English, it meant naïve; and now, in Modern English, it means foolish.

How has the English language developed in America?

The colonists from England who settled in America in the seventeenth century brought their language to the New World. Over the subsequent years, many additional immigrants came from northern European countries, including Ireland, Germany, Norway, and Sweden; and later immigrants came from southern European countries, including Italy and the Slavic nations. In addition to the European influx, there was also the forced migration of Africans through the slave trade, and the immigration of peoples from Latin and South America. These immigrants largely assimilated into the country by learning the English language. The influences of their native languages on English were not particularly significant. Rather, the history of English in America began with those early colonists who essentially spoke the English of Shakespeare's generation. It is interesting to note that these colonists, even though they gradually dispersed throughout the American continent, retained contact with each other and essentially became a large, homogeneous population with a common language. As early as 1781, scholars noted that, unlike the English spoken in England, the English spoken in America was remarkably free of pronounced regional dialects. This uniformity of speech is probably due to the mobility that has always characterized the American people. It is unusual today to find an adult American living in the place that he or she was born. This mixing of people from all geographic regions has had a homogenizing effect on the English language in America.

How did Noah Webster affect the English language?

Noah Webster (1758–1843) was born in Hartford, Connecticut, and educated at Yale. He began a teaching career at a time when very few schoolbooks were available, so he determined to write and publish his own. *The American Spelling Book* became a standard for schoolchildren in America and sold more than 80 million copies. Subsequently, Webster wrote his *American Dictionary* (1828) by which he was determined to promote the American version of English as distinct from the British version of English.

He states in the preface "It is not only important, but, in a degree, necessary, that the people of this country, should have an American Dictionary of the English Language; for, although the body of the language is the same as in England, and it is desirable to perpetuate that sameness, yet some differences must exist." The differences between British and American spelling that we observe today are largely the result of Webster's efforts to Americanize English spelling. Where we write *honor* and *color*, British people write *honour* and *colour*. In a number of words, we use one consonant while the British employ two: *traveler/traveller, wagon/waggon*. Similarly, we prefer *s* to *c* in words like *defense* and *offense*, and write *ax, plow, tire, story, czar, jail*, and *medieval* for the British *axe, plough, tyre, storey, tsar, gaol*, and *mediaeval*. Versions of Webster's dictionary, revised and updated many times, are still in use today.

With the publication of his dictionary and spelling books, Noah Webster influenced American language, especially when it came to spelling.

What efforts have been made toward spelling reform?

Throughout its history, spelling has been a challenge for English speakers. The irregularity of English spelling was a problem that confronted writers at the time of Shakespeare, and it remains a problem today, particularly for second-language learners. In the nineteenth century, spelling reform societies were formed in both England and America. The joint Spelling Reform Association proposed the adoption of a long list of spelling changes, but on the whole, the public remained indifferent to these efforts, and attempts at spelling reform produced little in the way of actual results. There have been several attempts at reform in the twentieth century as well, including the British Simplified Spelling Society and the Swedish Regularized Inglish. Neither of these systems gained popular appeal. The English-speaking world has never been inclined to adopt wholesale changes in spelling; rather they seem to be content with gradual language changes over time.

Why are there variations of British English?

Geographical dispersion results in regional differences in a language. For English, regional separations within the British Isles and the dispersion of English-speaking communities throughout the world have resulted in regional dialects of English. When there is infrequent communication among communities of speakers of a common language, over the course of time, speakers develop distinctive dialects. Most of the regional variations in English occur in the way it is spoken, that is, in its phonology, but also somewhat in its distinctive vocabulary.

In addition to differences in pronunciation, British and American English differ in many of their vocabulary words. These differences generally strike one as quaint rather than as barriers to understanding. For example, the British call the trunk of a car the *boot*; they call the expressway the *motorway*; the elevator is called a *lift*; the garbage collector is the *dustman*; a railway baggage car is a *van*; a truck is a *lorry*; and the car hood is a *bonnet*. On the other hand, the British have often accepted Americanisms into common use: these include *telephone, phonograph, typewriter, ticker, blizzard, jazz*, and so on. In the written language of both British and American English, it is very hard to tell much of a difference. A case in point would be a scientific book written in the English language.

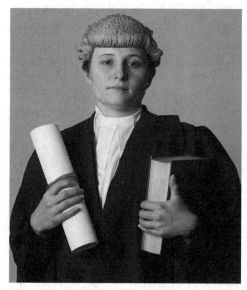

In England attorneys are called "barristers," while in the United States they are "lawyers." Geographical separations of people can, over time, result in diverging vocabularies.

16

> ## What is a dialect?
>
> A *dialect* is a mode of speech that is identified with a particular ethnic, social, or regional group. One example of an American English dialect is Black English Vernacular (BEV). One example of a regional dialect is northeastern or Bostonian English.

Within the British Isles, there are regional distinctions in the spoken dialects of those living in Ireland, Scotland, Wales, and even London. Distinct dialects of English are also spoken in former British colonies, including the United States, Canada, South Africa, Australia, and New Zealand. Grammatical variation tends to be less extensive.

What are the varieties of American English?

Within North America, most people would be able to distinguish Canadian, New England, Midwestern, and Southern varieties of English. Broad differences in regional dialects, particularly in pronunciation, are generally recognized by most speakers of English. (Other languages also contain different dialects.) It should be noted, however, that although there are some differences, by-and-large these differences are relatively minor. Speakers of different American dialects of English have little difficulty understanding one another. The differences are not defections from the general standard, but variations on it. For example, the regional dialect in New England, as characterized by Boston, has several distinguishing features of pronunciation: the retention of a rounded vowel in words like *hot* and *top*, which the rest of the country has unrounded to a shortened form of the *a* in *father*; the use of the broad *a* in *fast, path, grass*, etc.; and the loss of the *r* in *car, hard, yard*, etc. Speakers of other North American English dialects, however, will have no trouble understanding and being understood by Bostonians.

What are some examples of regional dialects?

Humorists have always poked fun at regional dialects. Mark Twain, in his *Life on the Mississippi*, said: "The educated Southerner has no use for an *r* except at the beginning of a word." The following are three guides to regional pronunciation:

Brooklyn, New York

Word	Definition
earl	a lubricant
oil	an English nobleman
tree	the numeral preceding four
doze	the ones over yonder
fodder	male parent

17

Southern American

Word	Definition
watt	primary color, as in "The flag is raid, watt, and blue."
height	not liking someone
pa	a dessert
bike	what you do to a pa
mine	principal or chief
mane	male person, as in "Ma best friend is ma mine mane."
rod	what you do in an automobile

Minnesotan

Word	Definition
abowt or aboot	in the area of something, as in "That deer was aboot 2 feet away."
-age	a suffix added to the end of a noun, as in "Look at all dat muddage on your truck."
ah-min-ah	I am going to, as in "If I find out you been lying to me, ahminah ground you."
bat-tree	"My car won't start because the bat-tree is dead."
bin	been, as in "It's sure bin a cold winter, eh?"
crick	a stream, as in "I went fishin' in da crick."
dem	them, as in "I went to da store and got dem new tires."

What is Black English vernacular?

Black English Vernacular (or BEV) is a dialect spoken by a segment of American blacks. The historical discrimination against blacks in ghettos and the existence of segregated schools served to isolate many American blacks and, where social isolation exists, dialect differences are intensified. Scholars differ as to the origins of BEV. One theory posits that it originated from black slaves having to learn English as a second language. The other theory posits that influences from African languages carried over into English. Both theories are probably true to some extent. There are systematic differences between Black English and Standard American English. For example, BEV has a phonological rule that can be stated as follows: delete the /r/ except before a vowel. This rule results in the following words being pronounced identically in BEV: *guard/god, nor/gnaw, sore/saw, poor/pa, fort/fought, court/caught*. The Black English dialect has many features that are also present in other dialects of southern English. These dialects no doubt grew up together in the slave-holding South in America. It is not true, however, that any dialect of English, and particularly BEV, is somehow inferior to any other dialect. They are just different. All dialects have their own systematic grammars and their own distinct lexical items.

What is "good" English?

A language is not a relic, like a historic building, that can be preserved intact. Rather it is a living organism, and the organism will differ depending on the social, political, and physical climate in which it flourishes. So, English, even American English, has many parallel voices. There is no such thing as one "good" English, particularly when we are referring to the spoken version. For example, in Pittsburgh someone might say, "The car needs washed." In a black neighborhood, someone might say "Leon not here; he be at work." In the American South, someone may say "We might could go" and be readily understood. All of these speakers are using "good" English within their particular context. The language spoken in one region may differ from that spoken in another.

When it comes to written English, however, there is a standard form, typically called SEE (Standard Edited English) or SWE (Standard Written English). Speakers and writers learn early on that there are different levels of appropriateness

In days gone by, English teachers may have demanded their students speak proper English. But what *is* good English? What is perfectly appropriate in one part of America may sound strange and even uneducated in another.

when it comes to language. We call these differences "registers." So there is the informal register, both spoken and written, that you might use with your friends, liberally sprinkled with slang words, abbreviations, and euphemisms.

There is also the more formal register, which you would use with your friends' parents or in the classroom for a formal assignment. Part of a child's learning of the language is distinguishing which register to use in which situation. While it might be appropriate to say *uh-uh* to a friend, it is more appropriate to say *"No, thank you"* to that friend's parent. Whereas it might be appropriate to write "c u l8er" in a text message to a friend, it would be more appropriate to write "I will see you in class later" in an email to your professor.

What is slang?

Slang is colloquial language, typically invented by a particular group as a way of forging common identity. Slang is created by the invention of new words, such as *barf* or *flub*; or by using old words for totally new meanings, such as *pot (marijuana)* or *rap (arrested for a crime)*. Using slang words in colloquial speech may be acceptable, depend-

This bluebird has a song vocabulary and dialect all its own.

The idea of animals that can talk is a very old one. Most human societies have legends wherein animals communicate. In Aesop's fables, animals all seem to talk. For Native Americans, coyote is an important character; in Africa, folk tales include a spider-man who is often the hero. Scholars agree that many animals and birds do have systems of communication. These are sometimes vocal, as in the case of communications between whales, but not always. For example, bees use dance to communicate, and wolves use facial expressions, tail movements, and growls to communicate with each other. Are these systems of communication the same thing as *language*? Linguists generally agree that the languages of animals differ from human languages in that they lack the creative element of human language. Our creative human languages allow us to formulate unique messages rather than simply to convey a fixed set of messages. An extensive study of animal language systems has convinced scholars that no animals, even higher-level primates like chimps, have the same creative capacity for language that humans do. Human children do not need to be taught language in any controlled way; they listen to the language being spoken around them and formulate their own grammar.

ing on the audience, but it is not acceptable in formal writing. In some cases, slang words may gradually become accepted into general use. For example, *freshman, dwindle, glib,* and *mob* were all previously unsavory slang words to prior generations. Other slang words simply fade away over time; for example, *skiddoo* and *chemise* are no longer in common use. I should point out, however, that using slang words in formal writing is not acceptable. You may want to check a dictionary if you are not sure whether a word has become commonly accepted or is still considered to be in the realm of slang.

Are there any language universals?

Scholars generally agree that some universal principles apply to all languages, regardless of where in the world the language originated. Following is a list of language universals from *An Introduction to Language* by Fromkin and Rodman (1974):

1. Wherever mankind exists, language exists.
2. There are no primitive languages—all are equally complex.
3. All languages change over time.
4. All human languages use sounds to express meaning.
5. All human languages use discrete, meaningful sounds (morphemes) that are then combined to produce whole thoughts (sentences).

6. All grammars contain phonological and syntactic rules.

7. There are similar grammatical categories in all languages, e.g., noun, verb.

8. There are universal semantic (meaning) concepts in every language, e.g., the ability to show positive or negative.

9. Speakers of all human languages are able to produce and understand an infinite set of sentences.

10. Any normal child born anywhere in the world is capable of learning the language to which he or she is exposed.

IMPORTANT GRAMMATICAL CONCEPTS AND TERMS

IMPORTANT GRAMMATICAL CONCEPTS

What is grammar?

In Chaucer's time, the Middle Ages, when educated people studied language, they studied Latin. In fact, to study grammar meant to study Latin. The two were so closely related that the term *grammar* became broadly used to refer to any kind of learning. This usage has continued into the present day, perhaps in a grandparent's reference to attending *grammar school* (meaning elementary school). In today's linguistic world, the study of grammar is the study of the language knowledge that exists in the minds of the speakers of a particular language. The grammar of a language is what native speakers know about the language; it is an internalized, unconscious set of rules that govern the way speakers communicate within that language. If you are a native speaker of a language, you possess expert knowledge of that language's grammar. Scholars study the grammar of a language from different points of view. Some study *historical grammar* to uncover how languages have changed over the centuries. Other scholars study *comparative grammar* to see how languages differ from or resemble each other. Still others create *descriptive grammars*, which are written to describe the unconscious set of rules that govern a language.

What is descriptive grammar?

When a scholar studies a language to understand it, that scholar attempts to describe the grammar that exists in the minds of the native speakers of the language. The result is a *descriptive grammar* of the language. A descriptive grammar does not try to tell speakers how to speak the language. Rather, a descriptive grammar tries to explain how it is possible for native speakers to both speak to others and be understood by others using the same language. A descriptive grammar will explain everything that a speaker knows about his or her language: its system of sounds (phonology), its system of meanings (semantics), and the rules by which sentences are formed (syntax). Scholars who produce descriptive grammars are primarily interested in finding out the laws that govern a language, not in making new laws.

What is prescriptive grammar?

A *prescriptive grammar* is one that prescribes what is the "correct," or what is the preferred, usage in a given situation. When most people think about learning grammar, they are usually thinking in terms of learning a prescriptive grammar. Most grammar textbooks would probably be termed prescriptive grammars. Their aim is not to teach you the grammar of the language you already know; rather their aim is to make explicit the linguistic knowledge that you have gained intuitively as you acquired your native language. Prescriptive grammar can be used as a teaching grammar for those learning a second language. It will tell the language learner explicitly what the underlying rules of the language are, rules that the native speaker already knows intuitively. As mentioned earlier, any language contains dialects characterized by differences in pronunciation, and likely, differences in grammar. If a speaker has learned one dialect, he or she may wish to study a prescriptive grammar in order to learn another. This is particularly important when there is one dialect that takes preference over another. In educational

Noam Chomsky (1928–) is considered the Father of Modern Linquistics, the study of the syntax, semantics, phonetics, and morphology of language.

settings, and in formal writing, there is a standard dialect, often termed Standard Edited English that many speakers of other English dialects need to learn.

What is functional grammar?

I have tried to achieve a balance between providing a descriptive grammar and a prescriptive grammar in this book. I term that balance a *functional grammar*. You need to know a certain amount of descriptive grammar, for example, the names for parts of speech, in order to be able to understand why a particular word or phrase is deemed correct or incorrect in a given sentence. There is no reason, however, that native speakers need to study a comprehensive descriptive grammar of the language they already speak, unless they are pursuing the science of linguistics. Instead, if you want to solve a particular grammar problem, or to write in what is considered the correct standard of English, you will need to learn a minimum amount of descriptive grammar and a modicum of prescriptive grammar. By studying functional grammar, you will learn *what* the prescribed standard is for educated people, as well as *why* that standard is preferred.

What is the study of linguistics?

The study of linguistics is the study of language in all its guises. Linguists work to find out, catalog, and describe all of the laws that make up a particular language. They also seek to discover commonalities in the laws of different languages and language families. Those laws that pertain to every language are called *language universals*, and when all the universals are put together, it becomes a *universal grammar*. For example, linguists have determined that there is a language universal that reveals both *consonants* and *vowels* in every human language, along with the rules that determine how these sounds are pronounced to form sentences. Linguists are interested in learning how language universals are expressed in a variety of languages, from Zulu, to Russian, to English, to Arabic. Linguists study human language to better understand the nature of human beings and their ways of communicating with each other. Linguists do not attempt to teach the grammatical rules to speakers of a language; instead they describe the rules that are already known by native speakers.

GRAMMATICAL TERMS

What are the eight parts of speech?

Words are divided into categories called "parts of speech," that are defined by the syntactic function of each word. The eight parts of speech are:

1. Noun: a word that names a person, place, thing, or idea.

2. Pronoun: a word that substitutes for a noun and refers to a noun.

3. Verb: a word in a sentence that expresses action, occurrence, or existence.

4. Adjective: a word used to modify a noun or pronoun.

5. Adverb: a word that modifies a verb, an adjective, another adverb, or in some cases the entire clause or sentence.

6. Conjuction: a connector word that shows relationships between ideas.

7. Preposition: a word that indicates a relationship between a noun or pronoun and some other part of the sentence.

8. Interjection: An *interjection* is a word that is considered to be independent of the main sentence and serves to add emphasis.

For more on parts of speech, see the Sentence Structure chapter.

What is an absolute phrase?

An *absolute phrase* is a noun phrase that is attached to a sentence, usually to explain something or to add some detail to the main clause. Here are some examples:

The weather being stormy, we decided to postpone our picnic.
He spoke with great emotion to his family, *his voice trembling*.
She left the committee meeting early, *her curiosity being satisfied*.

What are active and passive voice?

A sentence in which the subject is performing an action on a direct object is said to be in the *active voice*. *Voice* refers to the relationship between the subject and the verb. Active sentences will have a transitive verb, that is, a verb that takes a direct object. The

To say "Peter tossed the Frisbee® to Jill" is an example of the active voice; "The Frisbee® was tossed to Jill" is a passive voice sentence.

opposite of active voice is *passive voice*. In passive sentences, the subject receives the action rather than initiates the action. Here are some examples:

Mary threw the ball to Peter. [active]
The ball was thrown to Peter by Mary. [passive]
The soldiers shelled the village. [active]
The village was shelled by the soldiers. [passive]
The village was shelled. [It is possible in passive sentences to delete the *by* phrase, thus de-emphasizing the "passive" actor.]

What is agreement?

In grammatical terms, *agreement* refers to a verb having the same number (either singular or plural) as its subject. Similarly, a pronoun needs to have the same number and gender, and thus agree with, its noun antecedent. Following are examples of subject/verb agreement:

They intend to work all day long.
She intends to work all day long.
Those *dogs bark* all night and *bother* the neighbors.
The *dog barks* all night and *bothers* the neighbors.

Following are examples of pronoun/antecedent agreement:

Mark is extremely proud of *himself* for passing the exam.
Margaret is extremely pleased with *herself* for graduating from medical school.
They are both extremely proud of *themselves* for succeeding in graduate school.

What is ambiguity?

When a word or sentence can be interpreted in more than one way, it is said to have *ambiguity*. Following are some examples:

Ann is very *blue*.
Visiting relatives can be boring.
The police officer looked *hard*.

What is an appositive?

An *appositive* is a structure used to rename another structure. An appositive will either function as an adjective or as a noun. Here are some examples:

My father, *a realtor in Denver*, recently lost his job.
It is so nice *that you could come*.
We *students* are often misunderstood.

Saying "Visiting relatives can be boring" is ambiguous because it's not clear whether you mean that the relatives themselves are boring or that the act of visiting them is boring.

27

What is an article?

An *article* is a word that precedes a noun and signals whether the noun is indefinite or definite. The article *a* or *an* signals that a noun is indefinite, e.g., *a pony, a book, an apple* (referring to something in general); the article *the* signals that a noun is definite or particular, e.g., *the pony, the book, the apple* (referring to a specific item). Following are some examples:

Margarita has always wanted *a pony.*
The pony she likes best is a dapple-grey.
Give *the book* back to Henry.
He needs it for *a book report* in English class.
The apple doesn't fall far from the tree.
An apple a day keeps the doctor away.

What is an auxiliary verb?

An *auxiliary verb*, also called a helping verb, is a word that combines with a main verb to form a simple predicate. Auxiliary verbs include forms of *have* and *be*, as well as modals such as *will, shall, must*. Following are some examples:

The students *had left* by the time we arrived.
They *were going* to the library to study.
Perhaps they *will meet up* with us later.
He *must hurry* to make it to the meeting on time.

What is case?

Case is a feature of nouns and pronouns that signifies their relationship to other words in a sentence. Nouns have one case that denotes relationship, the *possessive case*, which signifies that something is in someone's possession: *Mary's mittens, the principal's note-book, their parents' guesthouse.*

Pronouns have three cases that denote relationships between the pronoun and other words in the sentence: *subjective, objective,* and *possessive case*. The subjective case is used when the pronoun is functioning as a subject of a sentence or clause. The objective case is used when the pronoun is functioning as an object receiving some kind of action. The possessive case is used when the pronoun shows ownership or possession of something. Following are some examples:

> *I* am the one you want. [subjective case: The pronoun serves as the subject.]

> Give the pencils back to *them*. [objective case: The pronoun serves as the object of the preposition *to*.]

> *Their* word is law. [possessive case: The *word* belongs to them.]

In the sentence "He handed the car keys to her" "He" is the subject, "car keys" is the object, and "her" is the indirect object.

What is a clause?

A *clause* is a syntactic structure with a subject and a predicate. Clauses are first categorized by whether or not they can stand alone in a sentence. A clause that can stand alone is termed an *independent clause* (or *main clause*). Here are some examples of independent clauses:

> *Many long-distance runners dream of winning a marathon; their training is geared to achieving this goal.* [two independent clauses]

> Since their training is geared to winning, *athletes sometimes are crushed when they come in second place.* [main clause; also called an independent clause]

A clause that cannot stand alone is called a *dependent clause* (or *subordinate clause*). Dependent clauses are named for the function that they are serving in a sentence. There are three types of dependent clauses: *adjective clause* (also called *relative clause* because it begins with a relative pronoun), *adverb clause,* and *noun clause.* Here are examples of dependent clauses by function:

> The lead swimmers, *who had already crossed the transition line*, were the first onto their bikes for the second stage of the triathlon. [adjective clause; also called a relative clause]

> The boat *that came all the way from Maine* crossed the finish line first. [adjective clause; also called a relative clause]

> *Because they had come such a long distance*, they were not favored to win. [adverb clause]

> *Although we wanted our team to win*, we were also cheering for the competition. [adverb clause]

> *Which boat will cross the finish line first* is anyone's guess. [noun clause]

What is a comma splice?

A *comma splice* is a faulty sentence wherein two independent clauses have been joined by a comma. The comma splice is not acceptable formal, edited English. Following are some examples of comma splices:

> Joe likes to work on antique cars, his brother Tim likes to work on motorcycles. [faulty; comma splice]

> Joe likes to work on antique cars. His brother Tim likes to work on motorcycles. [revised]

> Her grandson loves to watch the garbage trucks, anything with an engine fascinates the little tyke. [faulty; comma splice]

> Her grandson loves to watch the garbage trucks. Anything with an engine fascinates the little tyke. [revised]

What is a complement?

A structure that "completes" a sentence is called a *complement*. There are three types of complements that serve to complete a sentence: *subject complements, object complements*, and *verb complements*.

A *subject complement* is an adjective, adjective phrase, noun, or noun phrase that complements or elaborates on the subject of a sentence. The subject complement typically follows a linking verb. For example:

> Peter was chosen *squad leader on the football team*. [The phrase *squad leader on the football team* is the subject complement of the subject *Peter*.]

An *object complement* is an adjective, adjective phrase, noun, or noun phrase that complements or elaborates on the direct object of a sentence. For example:

> The movie made me *very angry*. [The phrase *very angry* is the object complement of the direct object *me*.]

A *verb complement* is an infinitive or participial phrase attached to a verb. For example:

> Mohamed likes *to run* marathons. [The infinitive phrase *to run* is the verb complement of the verb *likes*.]

What is a complete subject or a complete predicate?

The *complete subject* is the simple subject of a sentence plus any of its modifiers: For example:

> *Two of the earliest known primitive dinosaurs* were both fast-running carnivores.

The *complete predicate* is the simple predicate plus any objects, complements, or adverbial modifiers. For example:

> Scientists *have not named all dinosaur species that they have found.*

In the sentence "*Two of the earliest known primitive dinosaurs* were both fast-running carnivores," the italicized words compose the complete subject.

What is a complex sentence?

A *complex sentence* is a sentence that has an independent (or main) clause plus at least one dependent clause. For example:

Although the mighty dinosaurs were the dominant life form on Earth for millions of years, catastrophe awaited them.

What is a compound sentence?

A *compound sentence* has two or more independent clauses and no dependent clauses. For example:

The largest dinosaurs in the Jurassic tended to be plant eaters, and the best known examples ate leaves off the tops of trees.

What is a conditional sentence?

A *conditional sentence* indicates a condition or contingency and is made up of a subordinate clause (usually started with the word *if*) followed by a main clause. For example:

If I'm not there by noon, please start lunch without me.

What is a conjunction?

A *conjunction* is a connector word that shows relationships between ideas. There are *coordinating conjunctions, subordinating conjunctions,* and *adverbial conjunctions* (also called *conjunctive adverbs*).

31

Coordinating conjunctions are used between items that are parallel in meaning and grammatical structure. The coordinating conjunctions include words such as *and, but, or,* and *nor.* Here are some examples:

Wine *and* cheese always go together well.

Neither Lisa *nor* Nancy wanted to go on that strenuous hike with us.

Scientists can tell much from looking at dinosaur fossils, *but* they cannot determine sex.

Subordinating conjunctions are used to introduce a dependent clause and connect it to an independent clause. The subordinating conjunctions include words such as *although, because, if,* and *since.* Here are some examples:

When you say that wine and cheese go well together, the word "and" is the conjunction.

Because the toes of most dinosaurs were long and slender, they could grip the ground well.

If you are finished with those clothes, please give them to charity.

Adverbial conjunctions (also called *conjunctive adverbs*) are used to modify an entire sentence or clause while linking it in meaning to the preceding sentence or clause. Conjunctive adverbs include *however, therefore, furthermore, on the other hand, in general,* and *subsequently.* Following are some examples:

His opinion, *however*, differs radically from mine.

You might feel one way about the situation; *on the other hand,* I feel very differently.

Most four-legged dinosaurs had short foot bones and broad, stubby toes. *Therefore,* their footprints tend to be shorter and rounder.

Many Americans suffer from chronic health conditions due to obesity. *In general,* Americans are getting progressively more overweight.

What is a contraction?

A contraction is a reduced form of a word or pair of words. The reduction is indicated by an apostrophe; e.g., *cannot* becomes the contraction *can't,* and *will not* becomes the contraction *won't.* A frequently made punctuation error comes from confusing the contraction *it's* (it is) and the possessive pronoun *its.* Here is a correct example:

With the dog bone in *its* mouth, the poodle thinks *it's* in dog heaven. [correct]

What are coordination and subordination?

Coordination and *subordination* are two ways in which a simple sentence can be expanded. By using *coordination*, a writer can expand a sentence with two or more structures that are functioning as a unit. Any slot in the sentence, such as the subject, the verb, or the predicate, can be expanded by using coordination. Coordinating elements are signaled through the use of a coordinating conjunction (e.g., *and, but, or,* and *nor*), by using a semicolon, or by starting a new sentence and linking it to the previous sentence with a conjunctive adverb. Following are some examples of coordination:

Its and it's are often confused. In the case of this photo, the writer should have used the contraction it's.

Harvey *and* Leon like to play basketball on the weekends. [coordinated subjects]

Peggy planned to swim *and* run on Fridays to get ready for the triathlon. [coordinated infinitives]

We enjoy golfing on Saturdays, *but* they like to go for hikes in the mountains. [coordinated independent clauses joined with a coordinating conjunction]

Scientists believe the climate turned milder during the Jurassic period; lush, tropical vegetation began to grow. [coordinated independent clauses joined with a semicolon]

An increase in vegetation allowed dinosaurs to grow quite large. *Furthermore*, their long necks allowed them to reach food high up in the treetops. [coordinated sentences joined with a conjunctive adverb]

By using *subordination*, a writer can also show relationships between sentence elements. When two ideas in a sentence are not of equal importance, one may be subordinated to the other by making it into a dependent clause. Subordinate or dependent clauses are introduced by subordinating conjunctions (e.g., *although, because, if,* and *since*). Following are some examples of subordination:

Because we were late for the movie, we drove too fast and got a speeding ticket. [a subordinate clause and a main clause]

Since we didn't know what to expect from the concert, we brought along earplugs. [a subordinate clause and a main clause]

What is a correlative conjunction?

When conjunctions are used in pairs to express a relationship between the coordinated structures, they are called *correlative conjunctions*. Some examples include *both/and,*

33

either/or, neither/nor. When two sentence elements are connected by correlative conjunctions, they need to be in parallel grammatical form. Following are some examples:

> Changes in *both diet and exercise* are needed in order for a person to lose weight.

> *Either she goes or I go.*

> We noted that *neither the minister of First Gospel nor the liturgist from St. Peter's* attended the interfaith services this evening.

What are cumulative adjectives?

When adjectives are listed in a series, with each modifying the other, they are called *cumulative adjectives*. These adjectives in English typically must follow a certain order, and they are not separated by commas. Following are some examples:

> George was in love with his *big shiny new* truck.
> In the summer, Yolanda always carried her *small red decorative* parasol.

What is a dangling modifier?

An introductory verbal phrase that does not refer to the subject of the sentence is called a *dangling modifier*. In Standard Edited English, dangling modifiers are to be avoided. Here are some examples:

> *Crossing carefully*, the stoplight turned green. [faulty; dangling modifier]

> *After the stoplight turned green*, we crossed carefully. [corrected]

> *Seeing the bridge was out*, the truck took an alternate route. [faulty; dangling modifier]

> *When he saw the bridge was out*, the truck's driver took an alternate route. [corrected]

What is a determiner?

A determiner is a word such as *a, an, the, this*, or *that*. A determiner is used to initiate a noun phrase. For example:

> *The reason we are late* is our car wouldn't start.

> *This constant noise* will not be tolerated.

> *That we are going to the concert* is a sure thing.

When Sarah says she loves her *"big shiny new* truck" she is employing cumulative adjectives to describe the truck.

**What are some amusing examples
of misplaced modifiers collected by a sixth grade teacher?**

1. Napoleon wanted an heir to the throne, but since Josephine was a baroness, she could not bear children.

2. Strategy is when you don't let the enemy know you are out of ammunition, but keep on firing.

3. Twilight sleep means you set your clock three hours early.

4. A virgin forest is one where the hand of man has never set foot.

5. The general direction of the Alps is straight up.

6. A city purifies its water supply by filtering the water then forcing it through an aviator.

7. Most of the houses in France are made of Plaster of Paris.

8. The four seasons are salt, pepper, mustard, and vinegar.

9. The spinal column is a long bunch of bones. The head sits on the top and you sit on the bottom.

10. One of the main causes of dust is janitors.

What is an ellipsis?

When a writer wants to indicate that something has been left out of a quotation, he or she uses an *ellipsis*. These are three spaced periods used in place of the missing word or words. For example:

"The greenhouse effect … describes a warming phenomenon" (Barnes-Svarney and Svarney, p. 3).

What is an expletive?

In grammatical terms, an *expletive* is an introductory word (e.g., *it, there*) that opens a sentence but carries little meaning. An expletive may be useful if a writer wants to shift the stress of a sentence away from the subject (e.g., There's a fly in my soup). Expletives can be overused and should typically be avoided in formal writing. Here are some examples:

There are too many people on that committee. [faulty; expletive]

The committee is too large. [revised]

It was very cold in northern Alaska, even during the summer. [faulty; expletive]

Northern Alaska tends to be very cold, even during the summer. [revised]

Here is a paragraph with lots of expletives. They make the paragraph awkward and monotonous:

Your thinking expands in scope. *This* can be a profoundly liberating experience. *It* can take you beyond your limited preoccupations with yourself. *It* can put things in a larger perspective. *It* will certainly change the way you relate to others. [awkward paragraph]

What is a fragment?

Also called a *sentence fragment*, a *fragment* is a part of a sentence that has been mistakenly punctuated as if it were a complete sentence. Sentence fragments are not used in Standard Edited English. For example:

Before we go to England.

Because we love fish.

People of the faith.

What is a fused or run-on sentence?

A *fused* or *run-on* sentence is one in which two independent clauses are punctuated incorrectly as one sentence. For example:

The early atmosphere was composed mainly of water vapor, carbon dioxide, nitrogen, and hydrogen other gases were released by volcanoes. [faulty; fused sentence]

The early atmosphere was composed mainly of water vapor, carbon dioxide, nitrogen, and hydrogen. Other gases were released by volcanoes. [revised]

What is gender?

Grammatical *gender* in the English language is a feature of personal pronouns and certain nouns that distinguishes masculine (*he*), feminine (*she*), and neuter (*it*). Some nouns with gender distinctions include *waiter, waitress, actor, actress, girl, boy, man, woman, mare, ram.*

What are homophones?

Homophones are words that sound alike, but have different meanings. (See also Appendix C.) Here are some examples of homophones:

break/brake

sale/sail

too/to/two

red/read

lie/lye

What is an idiomatic expression?

An *idiomatic expression* is a phrase whose meaning cannot be predicted by the meaning of the individual words. (See also Appendix B.) It is the phrase that carries the meaning, not the words that make up the phrase. Idiomatic phrases are typically difficult for second language learners. Here are some examples:

> The old man *kicked the bucket* last week.

> The politician is *on the fence* about the reform measure.

> Marta is *over the moon* about her new job.

When you have a summer sale on sails the words "sale" and "sail" are homophones, words that sound alike.

What is an imperative?

An *imperative* is a verb or sentence in the form of a command. The subject of the command, often *you*, may be understood rather than stated. Here are some examples:

> *Go to bed* at once!

> *Don't worry; be happy.*

> Please *pick up* after yourself.

What is an infinitive?

An *infinitive* is a verb form that can be preceded by the preposition *to*, e.g. *to swim, to move, to live*. An infinitive phrase is a phrase that begins with an infinitive form of the verb. Following are some examples:

> We decided *to make our own pizza tonight.*

> The international students were determined *to make their mark on the world.*

What is an interjection?

An *interjection* is a word that is considered to be independent of the main sentence and serves to add emphasis. Here are some examples:

> *Ouch!* My hiking boots pinch.

> We love desserts and—*Oh!* that chocolate mousse was divine.

What is a modifier?

> A *modifier* is a word, phrase, or clause that adds detail to a sentence. Here are some examples:

Following a mass extinction, most plants would be wiped out.

No one really knows the size of dinosaur brains, *as they did not survive fossilization.*

What is nominalization?

Creating a noun from a verb is called *nominalization*, e.g., *fabricate* becomes *fabrication*, or *restore* becomes *restoration*. When writers use more nouns than verbs, they are said to be writing in a noun-heavy style. It is better to put the action into verbs whenever possible, rather than over-using nominalizations. Relying too heavily on nominalizations is likely to leave you with more passive sentences than active ones. Here is a paragraph with a noun-heavy style:

> People who know better make *a termination* to this dangerous cycle by stepping out of the interaction to make *a safe place* for the other person through *a talking point* about his or her Path to Action. *The performance* of this feat is accomplished by encouraging him or her into *a movement* away from harsh feelings and knee-jerk reactions toward *the location* of the root cause. In essence, *the retracing* of the other person's Path to Action is accomplished together. At *their encouragement*, the other person moves from his or her emotions to *the conclusion* and then *the observation*. [faulty; noun-heavy style]

Revising the paragraph and using action verbs makes for better writing:

> People who know better *cut* this dangerous cycle by *stepping out* of the interaction and *making* it safe for the other person *to talk* about his or her Path to Action. They *perform* this feat by encouraging him or her *to move* away from harsh feelings and knee-jerk reactions and toward *locating* the root cause. In

essence, they *retrace* the other person's Path to Action together. Through *encouraging*, the other person moves from his or her emotions to what *was concluded*, and then to what *was observed*.

What is a nonrestrictive or a restrictive element?

When a modifying noun phrase comments about the noun rather than defining or restricting its meaning, it is called *nonrestrictive*. Because it adds information, a nonrestrictive element can be excluded from the sentence without changing the essential meaning. Nonrestrictive elements are set off by commas. Following are some examples:

The dinosaurs, *who were a dominant life form for millions of years*, disappeared with scarcely a trace.

The officers, *who are hired to protect and serve*, also contribute in many other ways to the community.

A *restrictive element*, the opposite of nonrestrictive, serves to restrict the meaning of the sentence and is therefore not set off with commas. Following are some examples:

The dinosaurs *that evolved into birds* left a clear fossil record.

The police officer *who came to our rescue* lives in the next street.

What is an object?

An *object* in grammatical terms is a classification for a word that is receiving the action from a verb. There are different types of objects. These include direct and indirect objects, object complements, and objects of prepositions, as in the following examples.

A *direct object* is a noun, pronoun, or noun phrase that receives or completes the action of the verb in an active sentence. Here are some examples:

The children ate all *the cookies*.

The first baseman hit *the ball* into the outfield for a home run.

I enjoy *playing the piano* on Saturdays.

An *indirect object* is the recipient of some verbal action, whereas the direct object is the thing itself. For example, in the sentence *We gave our friends a ride home*, the indirect object is "our friends"; the direct object is "a ride."

What is number?

Number is a classification of a noun, pronoun, or verb as being singular or plural. Verbs must agree with their subjects in number; similarly, pronouns must agree with their antecedents in number.

An *object complement* is a noun, noun phrase, adjective, or adjective phrase that describes or elaborates on the direct object of a sentence, e.g., "The dinner made me *very full*."

The *object of a preposition* is the noun or pronoun, in the objective case, found in a prepositional phrase. For example:

They watched the speed skaters *at the ice rink*.

Give the pretzels *to him*.

What is parallel structure?

Parallel structure, or *parallelism*, is the use of a similar grammatical form for words or phrases that have a coordinate relationship with each other. For example:

The flora and the fauna are terms for *the plants and the animals* in an ecosystem.

What is a participle or a participial phrase?

A *participle* is a verb form ending in either *-ing* or *-ed/-en* that can also serve as an adjective, e.g., *earning* power or *earned* income; *falling* leaves or *fallen* leaves.

A *present participle* uses a form of *to be* plus the *-ing* added to the base form. For example:

She *is sewing*.

He *is writing*.

A *past participle* uses a form of *has* plus *-en* or *-ed* added to the base form. For example:

She *has fallen* on those steps before.

He *has favored* dogs over cats all his life.

A *participial phrase* is a phrase made up of a participle, present or past, plus any modifiers. For example:

I saw the car *speeding toward the edge of the cliff*.

The family *had fallen upon hard times*.

What is a particle?

A *particle* is a preposition or adverb added to a verb to form a phrasal verb. For example:

The dilapidated house *burned down*.

The race car *revved up* its engine.

A present participle uses a form of *to be* plus a verb with *-ing*, such as "She is sewing."

What are the parts of speech?

The *parts of speech* are the different categories into which words are classified according to their grammatical function in a sentence, e.g., nouns, pronouns, verbs, adjectives, adverbs, prepositions, conjunctions, verbals, and expletives.

What is person?

Person (first, second, or third person) is the way in which we classify pronouns. If a pronoun refers to the speaker, it is termed first person, e.g., *I, me, us*. If the pronoun refers to the person spoken to, it is termed second person, e.g., *you*. If the pronoun refers to someone or something being spoken about, it is termed the third person: *she, he, him, her, it, they*. Writers need to determine if they are going to write in the first person (using *I* and *we*), in the second person (referring to the reader directly as *you*), or in the third person (using *she, him, it, they*). Referring to yourself in the first person is generally not done in formal, academic writing. The third person is preferred because of its perceived objectivity.

What is a phrase?

A *phrase* is a group of related words that can be distinguished from a clause because a phrase does not have a complete subject and a complete predicate. Phrases can serve many functions in sentences, acting the role of nouns, verbs, or modifiers. Here are some examples of phrases:

> *over the top, into the wild, to the movies, on the mend* [prepositional phrases]

> *pick up, look over, see into, go away with* [verb phrases]

> *running down the road, throwing in the towel* [participial phrases]

What is a prefix?

A *prefix* is a word part that can be added to the beginning of a word, e.g., *re*furbish, *un*informed, *anti*dote, *dis*ingenuous.

What is a preposition and a prepositional phrase?

A *preposition* is a word that indicates a relationship between a noun or pronoun and some other part of the sentence. Some examples of prepositions include the following: *in, to, at, from, upon, above, below, into*, etc.

The preposition plus its object is called a *prepositional phrase*, e.g., *into the wild, over the moon, to the store*, etc.

What is a pronoun?

A *pronoun* is a word that substitutes for a noun and refers to a noun. There are several specific types of pronouns, as listed below:

An *indefinite pronoun* refers to one or more nonspecific persons, places, or things and does not require an antecedent, e.g., *anybody, anything.*

An *intensive pronoun* consists of a personal pronoun plus -self or -selves and is used for emphasis. For example:

We can do it *ourselves.*

An *interrogative pronoun* is a pronoun that introduces a question, e.g., *who, what, when, where, why, how.* For example:

How are they doing today?

Who made that delicious soup?

A *personal pronoun* is a pronoun that refers to one or more specific persons, places or things. For example, *she, he, it, they* are all personal pronouns.

A *possessive pronoun* is a pronoun that indicates possession and stands by itself (*hers, his, theirs, mine, yours*). For example:

That laptop is *hers*, not *yours.*

A *reciprocal pronoun* is a pronoun that refers to the separate parts of a plural antecedent. For example:

The girls made vows of loyalty to *one another.*

A *reflexive pronoun* is a pronoun that consists of a personal pronoun plus *-self* or *-selves* and refers back to the subject. For example:

Paul shot *himself* in the foot.

What is a sentence?

A *sentence* is a word or group of words based on one or more subject(s) and predicate(s). The written sentence begins with a capital letter and ends with terminal punctuation, e.g., a period, question mark, or exclamation point.

What is a sentence modifier?

A *sentence modifier* is a word, phrase, or clause that modifies the sentence as a whole. For example:

Walking quickly, the woman reached the convenience store before the storm.

After the flood, many people moved to higher ground.

What is a signal phrase?

A *signal phrase* is the introductory phrase that signals a quotation will follow. For example:

According to Fromkin and Rodman, "We learn the rules of the language without anyone teaching them to us and without being aware that we are learning such rules."

What is a split infinitive?

When an infinitive has other words between *to* and the verb, it is said to be a *split infinitive.* Some prescriptive grammarians say one should not split infinitives. To do so, however, is technically grammatical in English (though not in Latin, from which the rule was derived). In formal writing, it is better not to split infinitives, unless doing so makes an unwieldy expression. Here are some examples:

His mother told him not *to ever go* near that swamp. [split infinitive]

His mother told him not ever *to go* near that swamp. [revised]

Trekkies are admonished *to boldly go* where none have gone before. [split infinitive]

Trekkies are admonished *to go* boldly where none have gone before. [revised]

What is a subject?

A *subject* is a noun, pronoun, or noun phrase that indicates what a sentence is about. The subject typically comes before the main verb in a sentence. For example:

Mr. Ziglar spends an average of three hours each day reading.

What is slang?

Slang is nonstandard language using short, often colorful phrases and expressions. Slang is most commonly used by young people and by subcultures or special interest groups. It is not acceptable to use slang in formal writing. Slang expressions come in and out of favor rapidly.

That song is *sick*. [i.e., It's very good.]

Those guys are *all wet*. [i.e., They don't know what they are talking about.]

My exam was *a walk in the park*. [i.e., It was very easy.]

He will spend several hours polishing and incorporating new materials into his presentations.

The demand for power does not remain consistent at hydroelectric plants.

What is subjective or objective case?

A pronoun will be in the *subjective case* when it is being used as the subject in a sentence. The *objective case* is used when the pronoun is the object. For example:

Although *she* is retired, *she* is still called upon to give motivational speeches. [subjective case]

Her audiences always give *her* a warm reception. [objective case]

What is subjunctive mood?

Subjunctive mood refers to the grammatical form of a verb that is being used to express uncertainty. Verbs in subjunctive mood often are used in dependent clauses that begin with the words *if* or

Even though the famous *Star Trek* phrase tells explorers "to boldly go where no one has gone before," some grammarians would admonish them for using a split infinitive.

that. The subjunctive form is the base form of the verb. The subjunctive form of the verb *be* is expressed by *were*, or *be*, even for subjects that normally would take *was* or *is*. For example:

If I were to go along with you, you would need to promise me heightened security. [The subjunctive form uses *I were* instead of *I was*.]

We suggested *that an officer go* with them for added protection. [The subjunctive form uses *an officer go* instead of *an officer goes*.]

What is subordination?

Subordination makes one clause of lesser importance (i.e., subordinate) to another clause. A subordinate clause is also called a dependent clause. For example:

After we had surfed for many hours, we decided to take a lunch break. [subordinate clause]

What is a thesis statement?

A *thesis statement* is a sentence that explains the gist of what an essay is going to talk about. The thesis statement embodies the main point the writer is trying to make.

What are synonyms and antonyms?

Synonyms are words that are similar in meaning, such as *desire, wish for,* and *want.*

Antonyms are words that mean the opposite of one another, such as *good* and *evil,* or *fat* and *skinny.*

What is a topic sentence?

The *topic sentence* is the lead sentence of a paragraph. The topic sentence lets the reader know what the paragraph is going to be about and gives a brief overview of what is to come.

What is tone?

The *tone* of a piece of writing is the feeling or emotional impression the writer intends to leave with the reader. A writer achieves a particular tone through the grammatical and word choices he or she makes. A writer's tone can be passionate, objective, soothing, inflammatory, and so on.

What is usage?

Usage refers to an expert judgment about the correct use of a word or phrase. In many dictionaries, you will find usage notes that provide you with the dictionary author's expert opinion about how the word should be used appropriately.

What is voice?

Voice in writing refers to the form a transitive verb takes to indicate whether the subject is acting (active voice) or being acted upon (passive voice).

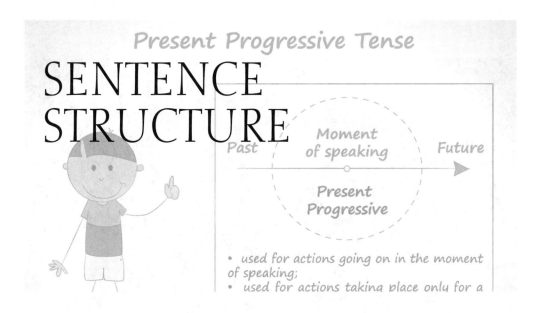

SENTENCE STRUCTURE

Past | Moment of speaking | Future

Present Progressive

- used for actions going on in the moment of speaking;
- used for actions taking place only for a

PARTS OF SPEECH

What is a noun?

A *noun* is a word that names a person, place, thing, or idea. There are several specific types of nouns, as described in the following questions and answers. Most nouns can take the plural (*boy/boys, book/books*) and possessive forms (*boy's book/boys' books*). Nouns often have characteristic endings, e.g., *-ion* (*action, compensation*), *-ment* (*content-ment, easement*), *-ness* (*happiness, gregariousness*).

Different types of nouns are discussed below.

An *abstract noun* is a word that describes some intangible concept, such as an emotion, idea, or quality. Some examples of abstract nouns include the following:

liberty, justice, despair, happiness, beauty, passion

In contrast, a *concrete noun* is a word that describes something that can be experienced through the five senses. Some examples of concrete nouns include the following:

car, symphony, sky, cloud, water, pencil, music

A noun that refers to a general item rather than to a unique item is called a *common noun*. The opposite of a common noun is a *proper noun*. Common nouns can refer to countable items, such as *house* or *book*, or they can refer to noncountable items, such as *water* or *oil*; common nouns may be concrete (*ball, tree*) or abstract (*democracy, indifference*). Unlike proper nouns, which are capitalized and refer to a specific item or individual (the Vatican, Sam), common nouns are set lower case.

A noun that refers to something that is a separate, countable entity is termed a *count noun*. Count nouns can be counted (e.g., one, two, or three dollars), and they can also be made plural (e.g., one dollar, two dollars, three dollars).

Kinds of Nouns

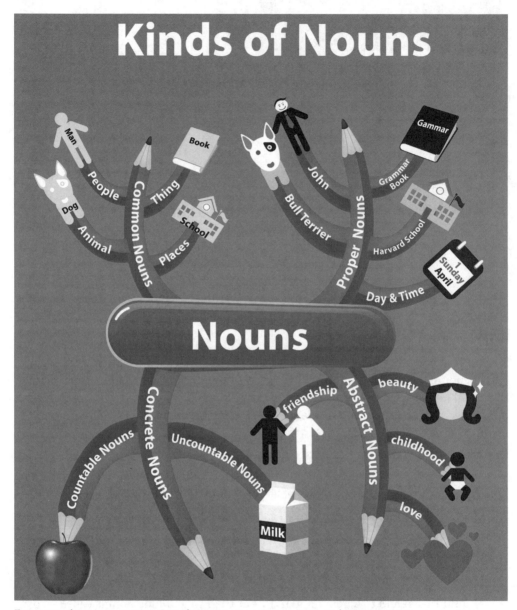

Four types of nouns are proper nouns, abstract nouns, concrete nouns, and common nouns.

A noun that refers to something that cannot be separated or counted is called a *noncount noun*. Some examples include *water, graciousness, honesty*, and *juice*. Typically, noncount nouns are not pluralized. There may be exceptions, however. For example, one could refer to the *headwaters* of the Mississippi river, wherein *water* becomes plural. Normally, one would not count water: one water, two waters. Instead, one might say one body of water, two bodies of water.

A *noun compound* is two or more nouns put together, with one noun being modified by the others, e.g., *income tax form, seven-year itch*.

What is an article?

Nouns are often preceded by an article such as *the* (called a definite article because it is referring to a specific noun: *the tree* means a specific tree) or *a, an* (called indefinite articles because they do not refer to a specific noun: *an apple* could be any apple). The indefinite article *a* is used when a noun begins with a consonant: *a book, a goat, a poster*. The indefinite article *an* is used when a noun begins with a vowel: *an orange, an idea, an opinion*.

What is a pronoun?

A pronoun is a word that can substitute for a noun. The most common pronouns are *he, she, I, me, you*, and *it*. Pronouns can be singular or plural: *it/they* or *I/we*. The noun being replaced by the pronoun is called the antecedent of the pronoun. For example, in the following sentence, Mark is the antecedent of the pronoun *he*: "*Mark said he was heading for the gym after work.*" The pronoun and its antecedent must be in agreement with each other in both gender and number.

A pronoun is a word that substitutes for a noun.

My *mother* said that *she* would support me in whatever career I chose. [The pronoun agrees with antecedent *mother,* feminine singular.]

My *parents* agreed that *they* would pay for my college tuition but not room and board. [The pronoun agrees with antecedent *parents*, plural.]

What are the different types of pronouns?

Here is a listing of the different types of pronouns and how they function in sentences:

1. Personal pronouns refer to specific persons, places, or things: "*I* gave the laptop to *her*."

   Singular: I, you, he, she, it; me, you, him, her, it; mine, yours, his, hers, its

   Plural: we, you, they; us, you, them; ours, yours, theirs

2. Indefinite pronouns refer to nonspecific persons, places or things: "*No one* has any interest in your problems."

   all, another, any, anybody, anyone, anything, both, each, either, everybody, everyone, everything, few, little, many, much, neither, no one, nobody, none, nothing, one, other, several, some, somebody, someone, something

3. Demonstrative pronouns point to a specific noun: "*This* cherry pie is delicious."

   this, that, these, those

4. Relative pronouns are used to introduce dependent clauses: "Maria is the one *who* should get the prize."

   that, what, which, who, whom, whose, whoever, whichever, whatever

5. Reflexive pronouns refer back to the subject itself as the object of an action: "He gave *himself* a black eye when he fell down the stairs."

   Singular: myself, yourself, himself, herself, itself

   Plural: ourselves, yourselves, themselves

6. Interrogative pronouns are used to introduce questions: "*Whose* money are you spending now?"

   who, whom, which, what, whose

7. Reciprocal pronouns refer to the separate nouns in a plural antecedent: "Feisal and Estella fell in love with *each other*."

   one another, each other

What is a verb?

A *verb* is a word in a sentence that expresses action, occurrence, or existence.

What are the pronouns according to case?

Person	Subjective	Objective	Possessive
First-person singular	I	me	my, mine
Second-person singular	you	you	your, yours
Third-person singular	he, she, it	him, her, it	his, her, hers, its
First-person plural	we	us	our, ours
Second-person plural	you	you	your, yours
Third-person plural	they	them	their, theirs
Relative and interrogative	who, whoever	whom, whomever	whose

What are regular verbs?

Most English verbs are what we call regular verbs. They are termed regular because they begin with a base form that is changed in a regular fashion, whether or not the verb is used to express a present or past action. For example, the verb *skip* becomes *skips* (present tense, "She *skips* classes often."); or *skipped* (past tense, "She *skipped* class last week.") in a regular fashion. That is, you add *-s* (or *-es*) to the base form for present tense, and *-d* (or *-ed*) to make the past tense and past participle. Regular verbs also form present participles in a regular way by adding *-ing: (skip* becomes *skipping*) to convey an ongoing action in the present (present participle, "She *is skipping* her way through school."). Below are some examples of regular verb forms.

Examples of Regular Verb Forms

Base Form	Present Tense	Past Tense	Past Participle	Present Participle
skip	skips	skipped	skipped	skipping
erase	erases	erased	erased	erasing
help	helps	helped	helped	helping
approve	approves	approved	approved	approving

What are irregular verbs?

Irregular verbs, in contrast to the regular verbs, do not form the past tense or past participle by adding *-d* or *-ed* to the base form. Instead, the verb itself changes form. ESL speakers will have to memorize the forms for irregular verbs. For example, the forms for the verb *begin* are as follows:

Base Form: *begin*, "We *begin* tomorrow."

Past Tense: *began*, "They *began* yesterday."

Past Participle: *begun,* "She *had begun* many days ago."

See Appendix A for examples of irregular verbs.

What is a linking verb?

A *linking verb* expresses a state of being and requires a subjective complement to complete the sentence. For example:

Peter *is wealthy*.

Dinosaurs *are extinct*.

My coffee *seems cold*.

What is a modal auxiliary verb?

A *modal auxiliary verb* is a verb that indicates necessity, probability, or permission. The modal verbs include *may, might, should, can*, and *could*.

What is a transitive verb?

A *transitive* verb is a verb that takes a direct object. For example:

The officer *gave my registration papers* back to me.

The short stop *hit the ball* over the fence for his first home run.

Politicians are infamous for using modal auxiliary verbs, such as *might* and *could* instead of commiting to a yes or no answer.

What is an intransitive verb?

An *intransitive verb* is a verb that does not take a direct object. For example:

My registration *has expired*.

Margaret's patience *has run out*.

What is verb tense?

A verb's *tense* tells you what time the verb's action takes place and shows time relationships within a sentence. There are several different verb tenses. Following are examples of the most commonly used tenses:

The *present tense* of a verb is used to express a general statement in the present time. For example:

Many birds *fly* south for the winter.

We typically *eat* pancakes on Saturdays.

The *past tense* of a verb is used to express time that occurred in the past. For example:

The birds *flew* south for the winter.

We *ate* pancakes last Saturday.

The *progressive tense* of a verb is used to show ongoing action. Progressive tenses use a version of the *to be* verb plus *-ing*. Following are some examples:

We *are going* to the store later today. [present progressive]

"The birds fly south for the winter" is in the present tense, and "The birds flew south for the winter" is in the past tense. *To fly* is also an irregular verb.

He *was just beginning* to shower when the doorbell rang. [past progressive]

She *will be going* to Mexico for the winter. [future progressive]

The *perfect tenses* of verbs combine the infinitive *to have* with the past participle of the verb, e.g., *to have finished, to have eaten*. The perfect tense is used for an action that occurs prior to the action expressed by the main verb. For example:

I have changed my email address, so now it is more secure. [present perfect tense]

Folks *have been griping* about my singing for years. [present perfect progressive tense]

Carson *had planned* on joining the ski team. [past perfect tense]

Mary Lou *had been hoping* to move to Nashville. [past perfect progressive tense]

What are the five forms that verbs can take in English?

English verbs, with the exception of *be*, all have five forms: base form, present tense, past tense, past participle, present participle. In English class, if you ever heard the phrase *verb conjugation*, it referred to putting the verb into these five forms. Here are some examples of two regular verbs (*walk* and *vote*) conjugated into their five forms:

What is a helping or phrasal verb?

Often a main verb is accompanied by a helping verb, formed from the verbs *be, do,* and *have.* For example, a verb form of *be* is used as a helping verb in this sentence: "I *am going* to the store later." Here are some other examples of verb phrases using helping verbs:"The birds *are flying* south for the winter." "She *has read* many novels this summer." "Martha *doesn't like* spinach."

Another way to make phrasal verbs is with helping verbs called modals. Modal verbs include *may, might, can, could, will, would, shall, should,* and *must.* Here are some examples of verb phrases using modal verbs: "Mario *might be able* to visit his family next weekend." "Democracy *will be adopted* in that country very soon." "We *shall overcome* someday."

Phrasal verbs are important in that they help a speaker or writer to indicate a question, a future or past tense, ongoing action in the present or past, or various conditions or qualifications of the main verb's action.

1. Base form: "I *walk* to the store every day." "They *vote* in every election."

2. Present tense, third-person singular, -*s*: "He/she/it *walks* on that road often." "Patsy only *votes* for local officials."

3. Past tense, -*ed*: "He/she/it *walked* past the driveway." "Peter *voted* for the president."

4. Past participle, helping verb *be* in one of its forms, plus -*ed*: "He/she/it *had walked* through the snow for many miles." "Mario *had voted* Republican for several years."

5. Present participle, helping verb *be* in one of its forms, plus -*ing*: "He/she/it *is walking* in an erratic fashion." "Amber *is voting* for someone from her town."

The base form of the verb, the form without the -*s*, is used with plural noun subjects (*birds fly*) and also with the pronouns *I, you, we,* and *they* in the present tense (*I walk*). When the subject of the sentence is *he, she, it* (*it walks*) or some other third-person singular subject (*a bird flies*), you need to add an -*s* or -*es* to the verb. For example, "Trees *grow* in the forest," uses the base form of the verb because *trees* is plural. If we use the singular, *tree,* we need to add -*s* to the verb: "A tree *grows* in the forest." Native English speakers know how to make these adjustments automatically, but ESL speakers may have some trouble remembering when to add the -*s* and when to leave it off.

What are participles?

Participles are forms into which verbs may be conjugated. As well as being used as verbs, participles can function as adjectives that describe or modify nouns or pronouns. The verb *drive* may be conjugated into the past tense *drove* and the past participle *driven.* Here is an example of the verb *drive* when used as a participle: "Snow White was as pure as the *driven* snow." In this sentence, *driven* functions as an adjective modifying *snow*, not as a verb. The real verb in this sentence is the linking verb *was* (which is the past tense of the verb *be*).

What are infinitives?

The base form of a verb is the infinitive form and may be preceded by the word *to*. For example, *to ride, to dig, to teach* are all infinitive forms of verbs. Sometimes, infinitives function in sentences as nouns, adjectives, or adverbs rather than as verbs. Here are some examples: "Mary's wish *to succeed* is admirable." "*To forgive* is *to forget*." "It is a sin *to steal*." Can you find the real verbs in each of these sentences?

What are gerunds?

Another type of fake verb is called a gerund. Gerunds are verbs that end in *-ing* and function as nouns in sentences. For example, the *-ing* (present participle) form of the verb *swim* is *swimming*. In the following sentence, *swimming* is used as a gerund (i.e., it functions as a noun rather than as a verb): "Robin's favorite sport is *swimming*." Compare the previous sentence with the following, in which swimming is used as a verb: "Robin *is swimming* every chance she gets."

What is an adjective?

An adjective is a word used to modify a noun or pronoun. Adjectives serve to either describe something or qualify something by adding more information. Typically in English, an adjective will come before the noun it is modifying (a *pink* carnation, the *deep* lake). Sometimes an adjective will fall on the opposite side of a linking verb from the noun it is modifying: "Mo's course of study is *challenging*." In this sentence, the noun phrase *course of study* is being further described by the predicate adjective *challenging*. Many adjectives take the same form as either the present or past participle of a verb, in other words, a "fake" verb (a *squeaking* wheel, a *torn* jacket, a *challenging* course of study).

Most adjectives have both comparative and superlative forms that are created by adding *-er*, and *-est* (*large, larger, largest* or *fast, faster, fastest*). When an adjective is longer than two syllables, the comparative and superlative are usually formed by placing either *more* or *most* before the adjective (*more determined, most determined*). Here are some sentences using comparative and superlative forms: "Marta is a fast runner. As a matter of fact, she is a faster runner than I am. She is by far the

A gerund is a word that ends in -ing when used in place of a noun; *swimming*, for example, is the gerund for the verb *swim*.

fastest runner on the cross-country team." "Sean is very *motivated* to get ahead in life. In fact, he is much *more motivated* than I am. He is the *most motivated* person I know."

A *demonstrative adjective* is one that points to a specific noun, e.g., *that* book, *those* apples.

An *indefinite adjective* is one that points to a non-specific noun, e.g., *some* people.

An *interrogative adjective* is one that raises a question about a noun. For example:

Whose book is it?

Which direction did he go?

What is an adverb?

An adverb is a word that modifies a verb, an adjective, another adverb, or in some cases the entire clause or sentence. Adverbs usually answer one of the following questions:

When? "She *almost* always runs at the gym after work."

Where? "The ponies live *together* in their stables."

How? "Race car drivers drive *very fast*."

How much? "Those earrings cost *a bundle* of money."

How often? "*Frequently*, philanthropists are asked to donate more money."

What is a conjunctive adverb?

Conjunctive adverbs, such as *however, thus, moreover*, and *consequently*, are used to modify an entire sentence or clause and link it in meaning to the previous sentence or clause. Here is an example of two sentences linked by a conjunctive adverb: "Many people are unable to balance a checkbook. *However*, they may be perfectly competent in other areas of their lives." Conjunctive adverbs always start a new sentence. They should not be joined to another clause with a comma. To do so results in an error that grammarians call a "comma splice."

What are some special adverbs?

Comparative and Superlative Adverbs

Adverb	Comparative	Superlative
early	earlier	earliest
fast	faster	fastest
hard	harder	hardest
late	later	latest
long	longer	longest

Adverbs with Irregular Forms

Adverb	Comparative	Superlative
badly	worse	worst
far	farther/further	farthest/furthest
little	less	least
much	more	most
well	better	best

What is a conjunction?

A conjunction is a word that functions as a link between two sentences or two parts of a sentence (clauses, phrases, or words). Conjunctions are used to show the relationship between the two parts, whether the parts are equal (coordinate) or unequal (one is subordinate to the other).

Coordinating conjunctions (*and, or, but, nor, yet, for, so*) connect the two parts, and show that they are parallel in meaning: "With your smart phone, you can search for information *and* play games."

Subordinating conjunctions (*because, since, if, although, unless, while*) are used to introduce a subordinate clause, i.e., a clause that is both grammatically subordinate and subordinate in meaning to the main clause. For example, in the following sentence, the phrase that comes after the subordinating conjunction is subordinate to (or dependent on) the main clause: "*Although* some people dislike the cold weather of winter, they may, at the same time, dislike the heat of summer even more." A subordinate clause must always be connected to a main, independent clause in the sentence. A sub-

When he had to make a choice between *either* eating healthy food *or* eating junk food, he was using *correlative conjunctions* to express his dilemma!

57

ordinate clause that is punctuated with end punctuation results in an error grammarians call a sentence fragment.

Correlative conjunctions (*either/or, neither/nor, both/and, not/but, not only/but also, whether/or*) are conjunction pairs that are used for placing extra emphasis on both elements of a coordinated sentence or sentence part. For example, in the following sentence, the correlative conjunctions both emphasize and show the relationship between the parts: "*Either* she goes *or* I go."

What is a preposition?

A preposition (e.g., *in, on, for, of, by*) is a word that precedes a noun or pronoun and its modifiers (collectively known as a substantive) in order to relate the substantive to a verb, adjective, or another substantive. The preposition and substantive that follows it form a prepositional phrase. Here are some examples of prepositional phrases: *off* the top, *in* the middle, *across* the bow, *between* us, *for* awhile, *by* the way.

Some prepositions are used in combination with each other: *because of, in regard to, according to*, etc.

Prepositions are also used in some phrasal verbs, such as *do over, put up with, burn down, burn up, turn off*, etc. There are literally hundreds of phrasal verbs in English with subtle shades of meaning—which makes them particularly challenging for ESL students. (*See also* Appendix D.)

What are some common English prepositions?

Here is a list of some of the most commonly used prepositions in the English language.

about	beyond	out
above	by	over
according to	concerning	past
across	down	since
after	during	through
against	except	to
along	for	toward
amid	from	under
among	in	underneath
around	into	until
at	like	up
before	near	upon
behind	next	with
below	of	within
beside	off	without
besides	on	
between	onto	

What is an interjection?

An interjection is an expression that shows an emotional response. Interjections should be used only in informal writing situations. Some examples of interjections include *"Holy Cow!" "Wow!" "Ouch!"*

WAYS IN WHICH SENTENCES ARE STRUCTURED

What is a sentence?

A sentence is the basic unit of English grammar. Forming a grammatically complete sentence requires both a subject and a predicate. Sentences are used to make assertions and commands, ask questions, and express wishes or desires.

What is a subject in a sentence and how do I find it?

The subject of a sentence is who or what the sentence is about. Subjects can be nouns, pronouns, or noun phrases. To see the underlying structure of the sentence, first find and exclude all prepositional phrases. Locating and excluding all prepositional phrases is a great way to find subjects and verbs. Neither the subject nor the verb will ever be in a prepositional phrase, so excluding any narrows down choices. The subject typically comes just before the verb. The simple subject is always a noun or pronoun. The complete subject includes the simple subject plus all of its modifiers. A compound subject includes two or more simple subjects. Here are some examples of subjects:

Margaret moderated the meeting. [simple subject; noun]

She needed to speak very loudly to be heard above the crowd. [simple subject; pronoun]

Everyone in attendance had a chance to speak at the meeting. [complete subject; noun plus modifier]

Even those who were against the motion were able to express their opinions. [complete subject; noun phrase plus modifiers]

Peter and José were violently opposed to the motion. [compound subject; two simple subjects]

What is a predicate in a sentence and how do I find it?

The predicate of the sentence contains the verb and tells us more about the subject. To find the predicate, first find the main verb and everything that follows it. The simple predicate is the verb itself plus any helping verbs. The complete predicate includes the verb, helping verbs, and any modifiers or objects of the verb. A compound predicate includes two or more verbs, each of which expresses the action of the same subject. Here are some examples of predicates:

She *needed to speak* very loudly to be heard above the crowd. [simple predicate; verb plus helpers]

Everyone in attendance *had a chance to speak at the meeting.* [complete predicate; verb plus modifiers]

Even those who were against the motion *were able to express their opinions.* [complete predicate; verb plus modifiers]

Peter *ranted and raved against the motion.* [compound predicate; two verbs for the same subject]

How is a sentence structured with a linking verb?

When a subject and predicate are joined with a verb that expresses a state of being rather than an action (*is, seems*), the verb is called a linking verb. For example, in the following sentences, a state-of-being verb links a subject with a predicate:

Alfred *is* a Sagittarius.

Rover *seems* restless.

Sentences that use a linking verb (standing alone) should not be confused with sentences that use a form of *to be* as a helping verb (paired with an action verb). Here are examples of helping verbs plus the main action verb:

Alfred *is painting* the fence today. [Contrast this with the linking verb in "Alfred *is* a painter."]

Rover *is running* all over the yard. [Contrast this with the linking verb in "Rover *is* a Labrador."]

How is a sentence structured with an action verb?

Many sentences are written with verbs in an active form, e.g., "She *shopped* in the mall." In fact, the liveliest writing uses primarily active sentences, wherein the subject of the sentence acts out something that is expressed by the verb in the predicate of the sentence. In other words, in active sentences, the subject performs action on something. Here are some examples of active sentences using action verbs:

Father *told* us a story about encountering a bear.

He *described* the incident in vivid detail.

The bear *approached* the tent while Father was sleeping.

What is a passive sentence?

A passive sentence is written using a form of the verb *be* and a past participle of a verb (e.g., The tent *was approached* by the bear). In a passive sentence, the subject of the sentence is passive; it is being acted upon rather than acting. The performer of the action in a passive sentence can often be included in a phrase introduced with *by*, e.g., *by the bear*.

In general, writers should favor active sentences over passive sentences, because they more directly show who is performing an action. Writing, "The bear approached the tent," is more effective than writing, "The tent was approached by the bear." Passive sentences, however, do have their uses, such as when a writer wants the subject to be hidden or de-emphasized:

"The bombs *were dropped* on the Vietcong." [by whom?]

"The wounds *were treated*." [by whom?]

What are objects that receive the action in a sentence?

A subject performs an action, a verb expresses that action, and a direct object receives the action. A direct object will always be a noun, pronoun, or noun phrase. "The teacher read *a story*."

An indirect object, as the name implies, is an object that is indirectly affected by the action of the verb. In the above sentence, if we add the recipients of the action (his students), they will become the indirect objects of the verb, e.g., "The teacher read *his students* a story." Direct and indirect objects are sometimes called verb complements.

When you say that a package was given to Jane, you are using the passive voice, but Jane *receives* a package is active voice.

A noun, noun phrase, adjective, or adjective phrase that elaborates on or further describes the direct object is called an object complement, e.g., "The story made the children *excited*."

In contrast, a subject complement is a noun, noun phrase, adjective, or adjective phrase that follows a linking verb and elaborates on the subject, e.g., "The children were *restless*." These are also called predicate nouns or predicate nominatives.

THE MANY DIFFERENT TENSES OF ENGLISH VERBS

What is verb tense and why is it important?

To express the time that the action or state of being takes place, English uses verb tenses. The three main tenses are past, present, and future. These main tenses are also called simple tenses. In addition, each tense can take on what grammarians call a verbal aspect, which is used to indicate the duration of the action or state of being. The three verbal aspects are progressive, perfect, and perfect progressive.

What are the simple verb tenses?

The three main, or simple, verb tenses are present, past, and future tense. Such verbs express actions or states of being at a particular point in time.

Present tense indicates an action is occurring now, is generally true, or is always happening. The present tense is the base form of the verb or the base form plus -*s*. Here are some examples of verbs in the present tense:

Trees *grow* in the forest.

Lincoln's life story *inspires* me.

Mary *eats* her baked potatoes with sour cream.

Georgie *walks* in a straight line.

Past tense indicates that something happened before the present time. The past tense of regular verbs is formed by adding -*d* or -*ed* to the base form. Here are some examples of verbs in the past tense:

Lincoln *wrote* the Gettysburg Address.

Mary *ate* a baked potato with dinner.

Georgie *walked* along the boardwalk last summer.

Future tense indicates that something will occur at some future time. The future tense is formed by the helping verb *will* plus the base form of the verb. Here are some examples of verbs in the future tense:

Lincoln *will be* one of our greatest Presidents.

Mary *will go* out to dinner tonight.

Georgie *will walk* along the boardwalk next summer.

How do I form present participles and past participles of regular verbs?

Present and past participles are simply forms of verbs. The present participle is formed by adding *-ing* to a regular verb, e.g., *asking, dreaming, dying*. The past participle is formed by adding *-d* or *-ed* to a regular verb, e.g., *asked, dreamed, died*.

How do I form past tense and past participles of irregular verbs?

Irregular verbs form past tense and past participles by changing the verb itself, rather than adding an *-ed* ending. Some examples include the following:

Base	Past	Past Participle
begin	began	begun
choose	chose	chosen
do	did	done
eat	ate	eaten
write	wrote	written

Irregular verbs are often confusing for ESL students. They simply have to be memorized. For a more complete list of irregular verbs, see Appendix A.

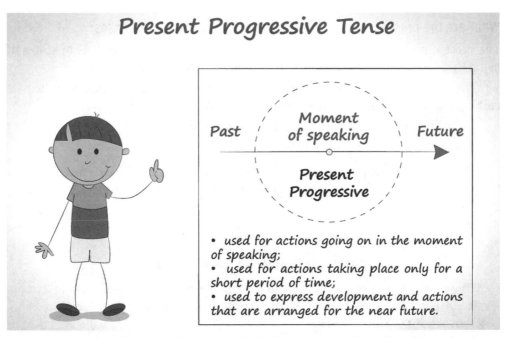

Present Progressive Tense

Past — Moment of speaking — Future

Present Progressive

- used for actions going on in the moment of speaking;
- used for actions taking place only for a short period of time;
- used to express development and actions that are arranged for the near future.

Present progressive tense uses the *-ing* form of the verb plus the present tense form of the helping verb *to be*.

What are the progressive verb tenses?

The progressive verb tenses are used to indicate the ongoing nature of an action or an ongoing process, whether the action is ongoing in the present, the past, or the future.

Present progressive tense uses the *-ing* form of the verb plus the present tense form of the helping verb *to be*. Here are some examples of verbs in the present progressive tense:

President Lincoln *is inspiring* to school children even today.

Mary *is eating* her baked potato and sour cream.

Georgie *is walking* in a straight line.

Past progressive tense uses the *-ing* form of the verb plus the past tense form of the helping verb *to be*. Here are some examples of verbs in the past progressive tense:

President Lincoln *was negotiating* with the Confederacy to secure a cease fire.

Mary *was eating* her baked potato when we dropped by her table to say hello.

Georgie *was walking* along the boardwalk when he slipped and fell.

The future progressive tense uses the helping verb *will be* along with the *-ing* form of a main verb to express ongoing action in the future. Here are some examples of verbs in the future progressive tense:

Lincoln *will be meeting* with his cabinet shortly.

Mary *will be eating* her baked potato as soon as she is served.

Georgie *will be walking* along the boardwalk this evening.

What are the present perfect and present perfect progressive tenses?

The present perfect and present perfect progressive tenses show actions or states of being that started in the past but are still going on in the present.

The present perfect is formed by using the helping verb *have* or *has* plus the past participle of a main verb. Here are some examples of present perfect verbs:

Fergus *has spent* all of the money he received from his father.

The photographer *has located* his subject.

The present perfect progressive is formed by combining *have been* or *has been* with the present participle of a main verb. Here are some examples of present perfect progressive verbs:

What are the perfect verb tenses?

The perfect tenses (present, past, and future perfect; and present, past, and future perfect progressive) are used to express time relationships between two different actions or states of being.

We often *have been fooled* in the past.

Yanghee *has been studying* English for many years.

What are the past perfect and past perfect progressive tenses?

The past perfect and past perfect progressive tenses place one action in the past in relationship to another action in the past.

The past perfect is formed by using the helping verb *had* plus the past participle of a verb. Here are some examples of past perfect verbs:

Before the crash, Bert *had thought* about taking another road.

The patient *had considered* the surgery for some time.

The past perfect progressive is formed by using the helping verb *had been* plus the *-ing* form of a verb. Use this tense when you wish to emphasize the repetitive nature of the past action. Here are some examples of past perfect progressive verbs:

Sarah *had been going* to basketball games for most of her life.

Before going abroad, Romero *had been thinking* about getting married.

What are the future perfect and future perfect progressive tenses?

The future perfect tense describes actions or states of being that will be completed at some point in the future, while the future perfect progressive tense describes actions or states of being that will be ongoing in the future.

The future perfect tense is formed by using *will have* and the past participle of a main verb. Here are some examples of future perfect verbs:

By next year, inflation rates *will have doubled*.

Susie *will have eaten* the entire cake before the party is over.

The future perfect progressive tense is formed by using *will have been* plus the *-ing* form of a verb. Use this tense when you wish to emphasize the continuous nature of the action. Here are some examples of future perfect progressive verbs:

By this time next month, I *will have been living* in my new house for a year.

When we reach Bombay, we *will have been traveling* in India for a month.

SPELLING CORRECTLY

GENERAL INFORMATION ABOUT SPELLING

Why are English words so hard to spell?

Words of the English language can be tricky to spell, because so many of them come from other languages, like French, German, Spanish, Greek, and Latin. In English, the same sound is not always represented by the same spelling. For example, the vowel sound in be*lieve* can also be spelled in several other ways: re*ceive*, *leave*, ma*chine*, *be*, *see*. Pronunciation and spelling are even more random with consonants. For example, we have ten spellings for the sound of *sh: shoe, sugar, mansion, nation, suspicion, ocean, nauseous, conscious, chaperone,* and *schist*. With practice, however, you can learn to spell in English. It is important to pay attention to correct spelling so as not to annoy your readers.

How do new media influence spelling?

New media, including social media sites (Facebook, Twitter, and the like) and constantly evolving hand-held devices (smart phones, tablets and so on) have changed the way we use the English language. An entire lexicon of words, phrases, acronyms, emoticons, and other types of abbreviations are constantly being invented and introduced into the English language. You will need to use a good dictionary to help you decide whether or not a word has been accepted into general use. Slang spellings used for text messaging—btw, pls, b4, fyi, 2nite—are not appropriate in formal or academic writing.

When and how should I use a spell checker?

Spell checkers that accompany word processors on computers, tablets, and smart phones can help you to avoid misspellings. You should always run a final spell check on any important document you write, or set the spell checker to routinely check as you are writing. Keep in mind, however, that spell checkers are far from perfect. The computer will flag potential errors, but it will not always offer the right solution, and it may miss several problems as well.

New technology and use of the Internet and social media sites have influenced how we spell, especially how younger people spell.

Autospellers on smart phones and tablets may substitute a word you had not intended, so be vigilant. Below is an example from a message written on a smart phone that I received recently.

> I have attached a PDF copy of the music and the female for you to make an individual copy if you need to.

(The autospeller on the phone substituted the word *female* for the word *file*.)

When your spell checker continually flags a word, such as a person's name or a place, you can add that word to your computer's spelling dictionary, so that it won't flag it in the future. For example, if I type my name, *Christine Hult*, in a document, I can add my name to the dictionary so the spell checker will recognize it in the future. With most spell checkers, you can customize the dictionary as you are writing.

Finding any misspellings that the computer's spell checker has missed is a more difficult problem. If the word is found in the spell checker's dictionary, it will not be flagged, even if the word is used incorrectly. For example, if you wrote "my physics coarse next semester will be difficult," the computer would not know that the word in this sentence should be *course* and not *coarse*. So, even though a spell checker can help, it will not solve all of your spelling problems.

How can I remember words that sound alike but are spelled differently?

Words that sound alike but are spelled differently are called homophones. The following joke pokes fun at uptight grammarians by using homophones: What did the therapist say to calm the upset grammarian? "There, their, they're...."

Misusing homophones is one of the most frequent causes of misspellings in English. Homophones used incorrectly cannot be detected by a spell checker. So, you need to study them yourself and memorize those that cause you problems. If you have words that you continually misspell, it is a good idea to start a personal spelling demon list and refer to it often. (*See also* Appendix E.)

What are some frequently misused homophones?

Below are some homophones that can confuse many people.

Homophone	Part of Speech/Meaning	Example
all ready	adjective: all prepared	I am *all ready* for today.
already	adverb: by this time	They have *already* left.
cite	verb: to quote	I always *cite* the author's work.
site	noun: a place	We went to the building *site*.
sight	noun: a view	The Grand Canyon is an awe-inspiring sight.
complement	verb: to complete	The color *complements* the decor.
compliment	verb: to praise	He *complimented* me on the decor.
discreet	adjective: tactful	She is always *discreet* with secrets.
discrete	adjective: distinct or separate	Each poem is a *discrete* chapter.
gorilla	noun: a large ape	*Gorillas* live in the jungle.
guerrilla	noun: rebel	The *guerillas* are fighting in Syria.
heard	verb: past tense of *hear*	We *heard* the gunfire.
herd	noun: group of animals	A *herd* of elk were grazing nearby.
hole	noun: gap or cavity	There is a large *hole* in the ground.
whole	adjective: complete	It takes up a *whole* block.
its	possessive pronoun	What is *its* title?
it's	contraction of *it is*	What if *it's* not any good?
loose	adjective: not tightly secured	My tooth is *loose*.
lose	verb: to fail to keep	I might *lose* my license.
patients	noun: people under treatment	The *patients* are resting in bed.
patience	noun: steadfastness	The nurse's *patience* is unflagging.
peace	noun: opposite of war	We need *peace* in the world.
piece	noun: segment or part	They ate a *piece* of humble pie.
plain	noun: flat piece of land	Buffalo lived on the *plain*.
	adjective: clear or evident	Their size makes them *plain* to see.
plane	noun: short for airplane	The *plane* will land in one hour.
presence	noun: opposite of absence	Your *presence* is requested.
presents	noun: gifts	Mary got *presents* on her birthday.
	verb: award something	May I *present* you with this prize?
principal	adjective: foremost	Our *principal* job is to keep order.
	noun: school leader	Jody is the *principal* of that school.
principle	noun: rule or standard	It's the *principle* of the thing.
stationary	adjective: not moving	The bus is *stationary*.
stationery	noun: writing paper	Her *stationery* has a monogram.
their	possessive form of *they*	*Their* house burned down.
there	adverb: in that place	Put the bike over *there*.
they're	contraction of *they are*	*They're* going cycling today.
threw	past tense of *throw*	He *threw* the snowball.
through	preposition	Walk *through* the door, please.
thru	informal preposition	"Come right on *thru*."

69

Homophone	Part of Speech/Meaning	Example
to	preposition	They go *to* the lake.
too	adverb: also	We like swimming *too*.
two	adjective and noun: *2*	They have *two* children.
weak	adjective: not strong	Today I feel very *weak*.
week	noun: seven-day period	Last *week* I felt stronger.
who's	contraction of *who is*	Guess *who's* coming to dinner.
whose	possessive form of *who*	*Whose* pony is that?
your	possessive form of *you*	*Your* uncle owns that pony.
you're	contraction for *you are*	*You're* the only one who rides.

GENERAL SPELLING RULES AND PATTERNS

How do prefixes affect spelling?

A prefix is a small small-word part that comes at the beginning of a word. Some examples include *pre-, re-, anti-*. Typically, when you add a prefix to the beginning of a word, the spelling stays the same: *anti-* plus *-freeze* becomes *antifreeze*; *pre-* plus *-meditated* becomes *premeditated*. Here are more examples of prefixes:

dis + service = disservice

mis + spell = misspell

re+ try = retry

un + necessary = unnecessary

Sometimes adding a prefix to a word results in an awkward spelling or an ambiguity. For example, adding the prefix *anti-* to *intellectual* would create a word that is difficult to read and pronounce. A hyphen solves this problem: *anti-intellectual*. If you are unsure about adding a hyphen, check your dictionary.

How do suffixes affect spelling?

A suffix is a small-word part that comes at the end of a word. Some examples include *-age, -ence, -ing, -tion*. When you add a suffix to a root word, you create a new meaning. Here are some examples of suffixes added to root words (notice that adding a suffix to the root word sometimes results in a change of spelling).

sense + itive = sensitive

sense + ual = sensual

sense + ory = sensory (When the root word ends in a silent *e* and the suffix starts with a vowel, drop the *e*.)

sense + less = senseless (When the root word ends in a silent *e* and the suffix starts with a consonant, do not drop the *e*.)

Duty + ful = dutiful (When the root word ends in a *y*, the *y* changes to an *i* if the letter preceding the *y* is a consonant.)

apply + ance = appliance

way + ward = wayward

boy + hood = boyhood (If the letter preceding the *y* is a vowel, the *y* stays the same.)

There is an exception to the rule of changing the *y* to an *i* with a suffix; that is, when adding the suffix -*ing*, the *y* stays the same in all cases. Some examples include the following:

paying, saying, frying, crying

How does changing an adjective into an adverb affect spelling?

To create an adverb from an adjective, add -*ly* to the adjective. The only exceptions are words that end in -*ic*, which typically use -*ally* instead of -*ly* (except for the word *publicly*). Following are some examples:

quiet + ly = quietly

evil + ly = evilly

sinful + ly = sinfully

basic + ally = basically

What are some English words that have letters that are not pronounced in casual speech?

Many English words include letters that are not pronounced in casual speech, and this can lead you astray when you are trying to spell them correctly. Often, these words have been derived from other languages, such as Spanish or French. Try to visualize the missing letters when attempting to spell a word containing silent letters. Here is a listing of some words that may prove troublesome. (*See also* Appendix F.)

address	hors d'oeuvres	recognize
candidate	interest	restaurant
different	library	surprise
doubt	parallel	trousseau
dumb	pneumonia	therefore
environment	privilege	tomatoes
foreign	probably	Wednesday
government	quantity	

fantastic + ally = fantastically

rustic + ally = rustically

How do I know whether to use *-able* or *-ible*?

When trying to decide whether to use the suffix *-able* or *-ible*, first take a look at the root word. If the root word can stand alone, use *-able*. If the root word cannot stand alone, use *-ible*.

like + able = likable

vary + able = variable

vis + ible = visible

divis + ible = divisible

Like many instances in the English language, however, there are a few exceptions to the above rule:

resist + ible = resistible

prob + able = probable

culp + able = culpable

When do I use a double consonant before a suffix?

This spelling rule is always confusing for students. When adding a suffix to a word, double the final consonant of the root word if both of the following are true:

a) the root word ends with a single accented vowel plus a consonant, and

b) the suffix begins with a vowel. Here are some examples:

plop + ed = plopped

What is the *i* before *e* rule?

You may have learned this rhyme in elementary school to help you remember the rule: "*i* before *e* except after *c* or when sounded like *ay*, as in *neighbor* or *weigh*." Here are some examples:

i before e	except after c	or when sounded like ay
achieve	receive	vein
field	ceiling	eight
believe	perceive	weight
wield	deceive	freight

stop + ed = stopped

trim + er = trimmer

tap + ing = tapping

remit + ance = remittance

Notice the following examples wherein the consonant is not doubled:

tape + ing = taping (root word ends in a vowel)

seem + ing = seeming (root word has two vowels before the consonant)

commit + ment = commitment (suffix does not begin with a vowel)

madden + ing = maddening (last syllable of root word is unaccented)

SPELLING NOUN PLURALS CORRECTLY

How do I make regular nouns plural?

Again, because of the many origins of the English language, there are several ways to make plurals from singular nouns. The most common way is to add *s* to the end of the noun. Here are some examples:

shovel, shovels

Some Commonly Misspelled Words

Below are some commonly misspelled words. Also please see Appendix F.

accidentally	calendar	lose	receive
accommodate	committee	jewelry	recommend
achieved	definitely	maintenance	seize
address	dependent	manageable	separate
apparent	develops	misspell	success
appropriate	environment	necessary	therefore
argument	exaggerate	noticeable	triathlon
athlete	exceed	occasionally	truly
athletic	February	occurred	until
basically	government	parallel	without
beneficial	heroes	quantity	

73

hour, hours

plate, plates

airplane, airplanes

How do I make regular nouns ending in *-s* and *-ch* plural?

To make words that end with *s, sh, ch, x,* or *z* plural, you need to add *es*. Here are some examples:

business, businesses

bush, bushes

church, churches

box, boxes

quiz, quizzes

How do I make regular nouns ending in a consonant plus *-y* plural?

For words that end with a consonant and a *y*, you will need to change the *y* to *i* before adding the *es*. Here are some examples:

raspberry, raspberries

anatomy, anatomies

tummy, tummies

posy, posies

How do I make irregular nouns plural?

Irregular plurals must be learned one at a time. Some nouns are the same whether singular or plural. Here are some examples:

deer, deer

moose, moose

species, species

In some cases, the spelling of the internal vowel is changed to make the plural:

man, men

woman, women

louse, lice

mouse, mice

die, dice

With some nouns that come from either Latin or Greek, the final *us, um,* or *on* must be changed to *i* or *a* to indicate the plural:

There is one big *raspberry* and four small *raspberries* in this example of a noun ending in *-y* in which the plural ends with *-ies*.

locus, loci

focus, foci

syllabus, syllabi

datum, data

medium, media

criterion, criteria

How do I make compound nouns written as single words plural?

When a compound noun is written as a single word, you simply add the *s* or *es* just as you would for any other noun. Here are some examples:

stovetop, stovetops

homerun, homeruns

database, databases

sourpuss, sourpusses

How do I make compound or hyphenated nouns plural?

When a compound noun is written as two or more words or is separated by a hyphen, add the *s* to the noun that is being modified. Here are some examples:

- toilet paper, toilet papers (The noun being modified is *paper*.)
- smart phone, smart phones (The noun being modified is *phone*.)
- mother-in-law, mothers-in-law (The noun being modified is *mother*.)
- attorney-at-law, attorneys-at-law (The noun being modified is *attorney*.)

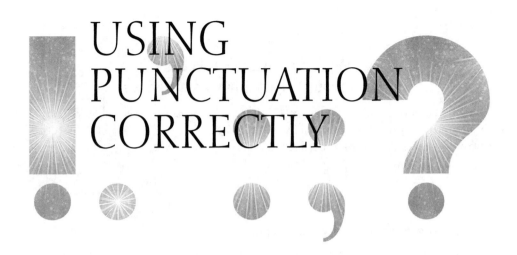

USING PUNCTUATION CORRECTLY

USING END PUNCTUATION CORRECTLY

What are the different types of end punctuation?

End punctuation consists of three types: periods, exclamation points, and question marks.

What are periods and how are they used at the end of sentences?

The most commonly used end punctuation for a sentence is the period, also know as the "full stop." A sentence that ends with a period is known as a declarative sentence, or statement. If the sentence ends with a quotation mark, as in the previous sentence, place the period inside the quotation mark. This is one instance in which British English differs from American English. In British English, the period typically is placed outside the quotation mark.

If the sentence ends with a parenthesis, the period is placed outside the parenthesis, unless the entire sentence is a parenthetical comment. (This is an example of a sentence that is used as a parenthetical comment.)

How are periods used in situations other than as end punctuation?

Periods are used with initials, abbreviations, and divisions. Here are some examples:

Use	Examples
Initials	Robert B. Parker, L. Ron Hubbard, Margaret A. Williams
Abbreviations	Dr., P.M., Feb., i.e., Inc.
Divisions	$45.50, 6.5 yards, 12.5 pints, christine.hult@usu.edu

77

What are some common misuses for periods?

Some people may think that a period is appropriate whenever there is a natural pause within a sentence, but this is not the case. The period should follow the grammatical structure of the sentence, not the pauses that readers make. If you put periods where they are not grammatically appropriate, you risk creating a sentence fragment.

The Burj Khalifa skyscraper in Dubai (United Arab Emirates) is currently the tallest structure in the world at more than 2,000 feet. Which surpasses the CN Tower in Canada. [sentence fragment]

Acronyms and other uppercase abbreviations often cause confusion in terms of the proper use of periods. No period is necessary in the following:

PhD
NY
USA
CIA
HTTP
COM
UN
NATO
USSR

Periods should not be used when a full sentence is found within another sentence (generally seen with quotations). Here is an example:

The Latin sentence *"Veni, vidi, vici"* was written by Julius Caesar in a letter to the Roman Senate.

Finally, periods should not be used after items in a formatted list, such as on a PowerPoint slide with bulleted lists, unless the items in the list are full sentences.

- pickles
- onions
- mustard
- ketchup

What are exclamation points and how are they used?

Writers use exclamation points to show strong feelings, such as astonishment or surprise. You should not use any other punctuation with an exclamation point. Some writers tend to use exclamation points too frequently. Take care to use them only in appropriately informal writing.

Please be careful!

Imagine my surprise at the news!

What are question marks and how are they used?

A question mark follows any sentence that is phrased as a direct question. These are known as interrogative sentences. Here are some examples:

Who is the author of *Jane Eyre*?

Why did you go along with them?

It's hard to be fair sometimes, isn't it?

Would you please pass me the sugar?

How do I use question marks with quotations?

When a direct quotation is a question and it falls at the end of the sentence, put the question mark inside the quotation mark, as in the following example:

The teacher asked me, "Why were you absent yesterday?"

If, on the other hand, you are asking an indirect question, leave out the quotation marks and question mark, as in this example:

The teacher asked me why I was absent yesterday.

How do I use question marks in a series?

When listing a series of items that are questions, use a question mark at the end of each. They do not need to be full sentences.

Do you think the investments will continue to grow? Lose money? Remain the same?

A sentence that is a direct question—interrogative sentence—should always end in a question mark.

79

USING COMMAS CORRECTLY

How do I use commas with an introductory phrase or clause?

An introductory phrase or clause gives background material, setting the stage with information about place or time. Such a phrase will not contain the subject of the sentence. To emphasize the section of the sentence that does contain the subject (and the verb)—in other words, the independent clause—precede it with a comma. This is especially important with an introductory clause that is lengthy. Here are a few examples:

> With 6.6 million square miles and 142 million people, Russia is Europe's largest and most populous country. [long introductory phrase]

> Blindly groping their way along the darkened trail, the hikers finally reached their campsite. [long introductory clause]

> Soon after starting, the engine began to make strange noises. [the comma helps to clarify the subject]

How are commas used to separate clauses with coordinating conjunctions?

Commas are used to separate independent clauses that are connected by a coordinating conjunction (*and, but, or, nor, for, so, yet*). This is the most common way that independent clauses in English sentences are combined. Here are some examples:

> A state must be an independent country, *and* it must have international recognition.

> Some western deserts receive little annual precipitation, *but* they are subject to flash flooding.

> Greenhouse gases from human activities are causing glaciers to melt, *so* we see them receding at unprecedented rates.

Is using a comma correctly really so important?

Let's eat, Grandma!

Commas may be the most frequently misused of all punctuation marks, so it is important to pay attention to a few basic principles regarding their use. Here's an example of a comma disaster:

"Let's eat, Grandma!"

"Let's eat Grandma!"

Commas can save lives!

Should I use a serial comma?

It depends. Omitting the final comma (the one before the last item in the series) is standard practice in journalistic writing. Including the final comma, however, may make the meaning of the sentence clearer. This final comma is known as the serial comma or Oxford comma. Here are examples of a sentence with and without the serial comma:

Great Britain is divided into highlands, lowlands, and flat plains. OR

Great Britain is divided into highlands, lowlands and flat plains.

How are commas used to separate phrases with coordinating conjunctions?

When phrases are used in a series with coordinating conjunctions, it is not necessary to use commas to link them:

There are about four million people in New Zealand but 56 million sheep.

Kiwi is a nickname for New Zealanders and a type of fruit found there.

How are commas used to separate items in a series?

If you have three or more items in a series, commas should separate each of the items:

Rome is situated on a series of hills: Capitoline, Quirinal, Viminal, Esquiline, Caelian, Aventine, and Palatine.

Do not place a comma after the last item in the series:

The Black Forest contains many vacations resorts, spa retreats, and wilderness trails for hikers.

How are commas used to separate coordinate adjectives?

Separating a series of adjectives with commas provides clarity:

The diked, drained, and reclaimed land found in the Netherlands is considered one of the seven wonders of the modern world.

How are commas used to set off nonessential or nonrestrictive elements?

The use of commas with interrupting clauses in a sentence can be confusing. When are commas necessary and when are they not necessary? It depends on the grammatical structure of the sentence. Some clauses are termed "essential" or "restrictive" because they are used to restrict the meaning of the clause they are modifying. In other words, taking out these clauses would result in a sentence without enough information. Notice that there are no commas used with restrictive clauses:

81

The yacht that was moored in the harbor was ready to set sail. [The yacht is restricted specifically to the one in the harbor, as opposed to the ones moored somewhere else.]

Other clauses are termed "nonessential" or "nonrestrictive," because they do not restrict the meaning of the clause and therefore could be removed from the sentence without changing the meaning. It is the nonessential clauses that should be set apart with commas. Here are some examples:

The Ottoman Empire, which included Eastern Europe, Western Asia, and Northern Africa, was also called the Near East. [The clause adds more information but does not restrict the meaning of the Ottoman Empire.]

Nigeria, which has a population of 177 million, is Africa's most populous country. [The nonrestrictive clause is separated from the main sentence by commas.]

How are commas used to set off conjunctive adverbs?

Some words are used as transitions to help readers follow the flow of ideas. The most common transition words are conjunctive adverbs, such as *however, therefore, thus, consequently, furthermore, in general, in other words*. Conjunctive adverbs should be separated from the rest of the sentence with commas, as in the following examples:

There are nearly 20,000 airports in the United States. *In general*, the busiest airport in the world is in Atlanta.

The next busiest, *however*, is Chicago's O'Hare International Airport.

How do I use commas correctly in dates?

When you are writing the month, day, year, as in the American formatting, set off the year with commas:

Ludwig van Beethoven was baptized on December 17, 1770, in Bonn, Germany.

When writing only the month and year, there is no need for a comma:

Ludwig van Beethoven was baptized in December 1770 in Bonn, Germany.

When writing the date in inverse order (day, month, year), there is no need for commas:

Ludwig van Beethoven was baptized 17 December 1770 in Bonn, Germany.

If you're having a party celebrating Beethoven's birthday, note that you use a comma when listing the month first (December 17, 1770), but you don't need a comma if you list the day first (17 December 1770).

How do I use commas correctly with an introductory signal phrase or speaker tag?

When you are writing a direct quotation, you will often let your reader know who is speaking by using an introductory signal phrase (also called a speaker tag). Put a comma between the signal phrase and the quotation itself:

According to Tucci and Rosenberg, "You should prepare for disaster by having a disaster supply kit."

How do I use commas correctly in addresses?

When writing out places and addresses, put commas before all of the elements except the ZIP Code:

Mario's new address is 4214 Santa Rosa St., Los Angeles, CA 90001.

Bon Jovi's mailing address is in New York, New York.

How do I use commas correctly with titles, degrees, and numbers?

Use commas to set off a person's degree, title, or the abbreviations for junior, senior, *I, II, III*, etc.:

Lisa Froelich, MD, is the psychiatrist she has been seeing.

Martin Luther King, Jr., was a great orator.

When using numbers of five digits or more, use commas to form three-digit groups. With four digits, the comma is optional:

There are approximately 1,192 islands within the Maldives. OR

There are approximately 1192 islands within the Maldives.

The Empire State Building cost $24,718,000 to build.

How do I use commas when directly addressing someone?

Indicate that you are directly addressing someone by setting off his or her name with commas:

Yes, Virginia, there is a Santa Claus.

What are some common misuses of commas?

Sometimes writers become overzealous in their use of commas and they end up with swarms of commas buzzing around in their sentences like swarms of bees. To make sure you do not place commas where they are not needed, heed the following rules:

1. Do not use a comma between two complete sentences.

   A fisherman discovered a very strange-looking fish, scientists determined that this lob-finned fish was not really extinct as previously thought. [faulty]

2. Do not use a comma between a subject and a predicate.

   Nelson Mandela, was an important South African leader. [faulty]

3. Do not use commas with restrictive elements.

   The countries, that had not yet gained independence in Africa, were divided up at the Berlin Conference. [faulty]

4. Do not use commas between cumulative adjectives.

   The suspect was seen wearing a large, black, floor-length, raincoat. [faulty]

5. Do not use a comma before a list.

   The four independent countries on the continent were, Egypt, South Africa, Ethiopia, and Liberia. [faulty]

6. Do not use a comma for two items in a series.

   Their dog was small, and cuddly. [faulty]

7. Do not use commas after a subordinating conjunction.

   Even though, Cameroon and Nigeria together contribute ten percent of the world's chocolate, Ghana alone produces twenty percent. [faulty]

8. Do not use a comma before parentheses or after a quotation mark or exclamation point.

   Almost all of the land in the country lies above 6,000 feet, (1,829 meters). [faulty]

   "Where have you been all this time?", [faulty]

USING SEMICOLONS AND COLONS CORRECTLY

What are the main functions of the semicolon?

A semicolon's main job is to link independent clauses, as in the following examples:

Because of the high temperatures in the Mediterranean region, evaporation of the Mediterranean Sea occurs more rapidly than in other bodies of water; more salt is left behind.

Because of the high temperatures in the Mediterranean region, evaporation of the Mediterranean Sea occurs more rapidly than in other bodies of water; therefore, more salt is left behind.

A semicolon is also used for punctuating a complex list that includes commas, as in the following example:

The five largest seas, in order, are: the South China sea, found in Asia; the Caribbean Sea, found in the tropics of the Western hemisphere; the Mediterranean sea, located in Europe; the Bering Sea, near Alaska; and the Gulf of Mexico, near Mexico and Cuba.

Colon? Semicolon? or perhaps a comma? When do you use these punctuation marks? Observing logical punctuation rules will help you to communicate.

What are some rules about using semicolons?

Overall, semicolon misuses involve writers using them when a comma is called for. To make sure you do not place semicolons where they are not needed, heed the following rules:

1. Be sure to place a semicolon outside of any quotation marks:

   Streams and rivers often flow in curves known as "meanders"; these S-shaped curves vary by the size and flow of the river. [correct]

2. Do not use a semicolon in place of a comma within sentences:

   The world's second largest lake; Lake Superior in North America; is a mere 31,700 square miles. [faulty]

3. Do not introduce a list with a semicolon instead of a colon:

   The Caspian Sea is surrounded by the following countries; Russia, Kazakhstan, Turkmenistan, Iran, and Azerbaijan. [faulty]

How do I use a colon with a quotation?

A colon may be used to introduce a quotation, if the sentence part that introduces the quotation is an independent clause, as in this example:

   In the *Handy Geography Answer Book*, Tucci and Rosenberg speculate about the next ice age: "Will there be another ice age? Yes, eventually the Earth will again cool and ice will cover land at higher latitudes and elevations."

How do I use a colon with an independent clause?

A colon may be used to set off an explanatory independent clause:

85

> ### What is the most common use for a colon?
>
> Colons have several specific uses. The most common one is to introduce a list, as in the following sentence:
>
> There are several famous river deltas in the world: the Nile River Delta, the Mississippi River Delta, the Ganges River Delta, and the Yangtze River Delta.

Skiing is like dancing: each move is reminiscent of a ballet.

How do I use a colon in a title?

A colon may be used to set off a subtitle from a title. This use of the colon is quite common in the titling of academic papers, for example:

"The Collapse of Discourse: Hyperreality in the Works of Pynchon"

How do I use a colon in salutations?

A colon is typically used in business letter salutations:

Dear Sir or Madam:

To Whom It May Concern:

How do I use a colon with numbers and Web addresses?

Colons may also be used with numbers (4:15 P.M.) and Web addresses (http://www.yahoo.com).

USING APOSTROPHES AND QUOTATION MARKS CORRECTLY

What are some exceptions to adding 's when showing possession?

1. It is not necessary to add the extra -s if it leads to an awkward pronunciation, as in the following examples:

   Jesus' teachings were often about peace-making.

   The Jones' car is always in the repair shop.

2. For a place name or company name, you may omit the apostrophe:

   Starbucks coffee is very popular these days.

   We like to dine at Herms Inn.

3. If the noun ends in *s*, it is proper to just add the apostrophe as in these examples:

The Yankees' third baseman was traded to another team.

Meredith is one of my parents' best friends.

How do I show possession with more than one noun?

Writers often have trouble with joint possession. The rule to remember is that you should generally add the apostrophe only to the last noun in joint possession. However, if you want to show separate possession, put an apostrophe after each of the nouns:

Obama and Biden's bid for a second term in the White House was successful.

Barbara and Mike's new house is quite lovely.

Julie's and Kathy's weddings both occurred in June.

Peter's, Greta's, and Martha's birthdays all fall on the same day.

How are apostrophes used in contractions?

You may use an apostrophe to indicate contractions or missing letters in words, particularly in casual writing. In more formal writing, however, it is best to spell out the entire word.

You should not use contractions in formal writing. OR

You shouldn't use contractions in formal writing.

They are going to the political rally after dinner.

OR

They're going to the political rally after dinner.

The '60s were the decade of sex, drugs, and rock-and-roll.

The boys were raised in the Chicago 'hood.

What is the most common use for apostrophes?

The apostrophe is most commonly used to indicate possession. The grammatical term *possession* refers to a relationship between two nouns in which one owns the other. To indicate possession, you will typically use an apostrophe and -*s* at the end of the noun, as in these examples:

That is Mary Beth's winter coat.

Tomorrow's forecast is for more rain.

My mother's friends always help her out when she is feeling ill.

The children's books are in a special section of the library.

87

When one says, "Obama and Biden's bid for a second term in the White House was successful," it is not necessary to place an 's after both names in the subject.

How are apostrophes used to mark plural forms for letters, symbols, numbers, and abbreviations?

You may wish to use an apostrophe to clarify the plural form of an unusual noun, as in the following examples:

There are four s's in Mississippi.

You should not use multiple @'s in your email address.

When forming the plural of abbreviations or numbers, however, you should not use an apostrophe:

Many PhDs are awarded to graduate students each year.

They have several IOUs outstanding.

The 1990s were a time of tremendous growth for personal computers.

She had five 20s in her wallet.

What are some common misuses of apostrophes?

1. Possessive pronouns.

Do not use an apostrophe to form the possessive of the pronoun *it*:

The horse had run away from it's pasture. [faulty]

The horse had run away from its pasture.

2. Non-possessive nouns

Do not use an apostrophe with nouns that are not showing possession:

Pedro loves all the features' that came with his new smart phone. [faulty]

Pedro loves all the features that came with his new smart phone.

3. Present-tense verbs

Do not use an apostrophe with present tense verbs that end in *-s*:

The addition of her name to the class roster appear's to be a mistake. [faulty]

The addition of her name to the class roster appears to be a mistake.

4. Nouns ending in a vowel or a y

Do not use an apostrophe with a plural noun that ends in a vowel or a y:

They were excited to see the colorful butterfly's fluttering around their back porch. [faulty]

They were excited to see the colorful butterflies fluttering around their back porch.

How do I use quotation marks correctly when directly quoting?

The most common use of quotation marks is to indicate a direct quotation. Quotation marks should be placed around any words, phrases, or sentences that you have taken from someone else's writing, as in the following examples:

One spectator called it "the game of the century."

In her book *Coming to Terms*, Patricia Lynne states, "Portfolios, I felt, would solve the worse of my two pedagogical dilemmas …" (Lynne 2).

The only time you would omit quotation marks when quoting is when the quotation itself is lengthy—generally defined as longer than four lines of text. Such a quotation is called a *block* quotation and is set off from the rest of the text by indenting it five spaces from the left-hand margin and without quotation marks, as in the following example. Notice that the end punctuation comes before the parenthetical citation with a block quotation.

Lynne sees portfolios as the answer to her grading dilemmas:

Portfolios, I felt, would solve the worse of my two pedagogical dilemmas—and at the time I was certain that the immutability of early semester grades was a bigger problem than a vague understanding of the criteria. I wanted to use portfolios during the second semester but was not allowed to; I was a TA and my mentor used a percentage-based system. (Lynne 2)

How do I use quotation marks when suggesting skepticism, sarcasm, or indicating shifts of tone?

Sometimes a writer may feel that a term is being widely misused by other writers and would like to indicate skepticism. Putting the term inside quotation marks is how this is done, but it's a device that should be used sparingly, as it can become a distraction for your readers if overused. Here is an example:

> Psychologists or therapists who claim to promote "family values" have anything but model families themselves.

Titles of songs such as the Rolling Stones' "Satisfaction" are placed within quotation marks.

Sometimes a writer may want to indicate sarcasm by including a term in quotation marks, as in the following:

> I notice that you always speak so "politely" to your mother! Not!

How do I use quotation marks when citing titles of short works?

Typically when you are referring to a song, poem, essay, book chapter, or other short work, the title should be enclosed in quotation marks, as in the following:

> The Rolling Stones' song "Satisfaction" is a rock-and-roll classic. The first snowfall of the year always made her think of "Stopping By Woods on a Snowy Evening" by Robert Frost.

What are some common misuses of quotation marks?

1. Indirect quotations

> Do not use quotation marks when you are quoting someone indirectly:
> My mother always said to clean up after myself.

2. Block quotation

> When directly quoting something that is four lines or more in length, do not use quotation marks. Use indentation to show that it is a block quotation.

3. Title of a paper

> When you are writing a paper, do not enclose your own title in quotation marks.

How do I combine colons and semicolons with quotation marks?

When a quotation ends with a colon or semicolon, place the punctuation mark outside the quotation mark, as in the following examples:

How do I combine commas and periods with quotation marks?

When the quotation ends with a period or a comma, American English calls for the quotation mark to follow the punctuation mark, as in the following. Notice that for a quotation within a quotation, the double quotation marks are changed to single quotation marks:

"The early amphibians' main problem," argue Barnes-Svarney and Svarney, "was support. In the water, a body is virtually 'weightless' because it is supported by the buoyancy of water."

Scientists believe "the climate turned milder in the Jurassic period": lush, tropical vegetation began to grow.

This gave rise to new dinosaur groups, "including the long-necked *sauropods* (plant eaters)"; the increase in the amount of vegetation allowed these animals to grow quite large.

Where do I put other punctuation marks when the quotation is part of a larger sentence?

Punctuation such as question marks, exclamation points, parentheses, and dashes should be placed according to the meaning of the larger sentence. If the punctuation mark is part of the quotation itself, it should be placed inside the quotation mark, as in this example:

The Tina Turner song "What's Love Got to do with It?" is still very popular today.

If the punctuation mark is part of the larger sentence, rather than part of the quotation, it should be placed outside the quotation mark, as in this example:

What do you think scientists know about the composition of *Coelophysis,* or "hollow form"?

When do I use single quotation marks?

Single quotation marks are used when a quotation falls within another quotation, as in this example:

Barnes-Svarney and Svarney note that "the *triceratops* ('three-horned face') was a *ceratopsian* that measured up to 30 feet (9 meters) long."

How do you incorporate direct quotations into sentences?

1. Use speaker tags or signal phrases to introduce a quotation and follow the tag with a comma:

91

As Barnes-Svarney and Svarney noted, "Some of the largest dinosaur trackways are called megatrack sites, where footprint-bearing rock can extend for hundreds or even thousands of miles."

2. Use standard grammar to introduce a quotation. If the sentence or phrase used to introduce the quotation is a not a complete sentence, do not use any punctuation:

Barnes-Svarney and Svarney maintain that "[d]inosaur trackways can tell us a few things about dinosaur behavior."

3. Use brackets or ellipses

When you are adding explanatory information to the quotation or changing any aspect of the quotation (such as changing an upper-case letter to a lower-case letter to make it fit your sentence (as in the above example), indicate the added information or change by including it within brackets. If you are omitting information from the quotation, indicate the omission by using an ellipsis:

The Dinosaur Freeway is a large trackway of dinosaur footprints extending along the Front Range of the Rocky Mountains.... In the Middle Cretaceous period [approximately 145 to 65 million years ago] this area was a coastal plain with a wide shoreline, a good source of water and food.

OTHER PUNCTUATION: PARENTHESES, HYPHENS, DASHES, BRACKETS, SLASHES, BULLET POINTS

When should I use parentheses?

Parentheses are most commonly used to indicate the insertion of extra information within a sentence. Take care, however, not to overuse parentheses, as they can become distracting for your readers and make it more difficult to follow your argument. Here is an example of a sentence that uses parentheses:

"Dinosaur trackways confirm that certain dinosaurs walked and ran on all four legs (quadrupeds) and others on two legs (bipeds)."

A second use for parentheses is around embedded numbers or lists:

Many scientists believe that gradual changes in Earth's environment (rather than a sudden catastrophic asteroid impact) played an important role in the extinction of dinosaurs, according to the following evidence: (1) although single-celled marine life showed a sudden decline, (2) other species declined gradually, and (3) a few groups showed no change.

When should I use a hyphen?

Hyphens are primarily used to show end-of-line word division. Most word processors automatically space lines to avoid breaking up a word. If, however, you cannot fit an entire word at the end of a line and have to continue it on the next, be sure to break it up by placing the hyphen between syllables. You should consult a dictionary to determine where to divide a compound word, that is, a word made up of two smaller words. Sometimes compound words need a hyphen, but they can be two separate words or one fused word. Since there are no firm rules about forming compounds, you need to consult your spell checker or dictionary. Here are some examples of compound words:

Pepsi-Cola®

twenty-twenty

self-control

Facebook

screen test

screensaver

You should hyphenate compounds acting as adjectives, as in the following:

Peter teaches third-grade reading.

He is up-to-date on all the latest reading techniques.

You should also hyphenate spelled-out fractions and numbers:

There are thirty-five elk out grazing in the field. That represents about one-half of the herd's entire population.

When should I use dashes?

Dashes are used to set off or highlight information more emphatically than parentheses. You should be sparing in the use of dashes, as they indicate an abrupt interruption to your thought process. A dash is created by either typing two hyphens together or by selecting the long dash (also called the *em* dash) from your character selection:

"Modern shark families developed at this time; bony fishes with symmetrical tails, the teleosts, diversified (they account for the great majority of modern fishes—over 20,000 species)."

The first American myth—the myth of the Chosen People—emerged among the Puritans in the colonial period.

When should I use brackets?

You should use brackets for clarifications or to insert editorial comments into quotations:

The "disease theory" of dinosaur extinction [which falls under the theory of gradualism] states that dinosaurs eventually died out because of disease.

93

In her letter to the editor, she wrote, "I was dismayed to read about your publications [sic] policy change regarding the placement of classified ads."

When should I use bullet points?

Bullet points are used for introducing itemized lists. Itemized lists using bullets are a powerful form of visual clustering. You can use bullet points or other symbols (such as diamonds, asterisks, or dashes) to indicate each point in the list. Here are some items to pay attention to when creating an itemized list:

- Punctuation with bulleted lists (Punctuate complete sentences in a list with a period, but punctuate phrases without a period.)

- Capitalization with bulleted lists (Generally begin each item in the list with a capital letter.)

- Grammatical parallelism with bulleted lists (Make sure that each item in the list is grammatically parallel, i.e., if one item starts with a noun, all items should start with a noun.)

USING MECHANICS CORRECTLY

USING CAPITAL LETTERS CORRECTLY

How do I use capital letters at the beginning of sentences?

Whenever you begin a sentence, the first word needs to be capitalized, as I have done in this sentence. The first word of each line of a poem is also typically capitalized, even if the poem's lines are not complete sentences:

> God in his wisdom made the fly
>
> And then forgot to tell us why — Ogden Nash (1902–1971)

Some poets, however, such as e. e. cummings (1894–1962), deliberately violate the capitalization rules:

> anyone lived in a pretty how town
> (with up so floating many bells down)
> spring summer autumn winter
> he sang his didn't he danced his did
>
> Women and men (both little and small)
> cared for anyone not at all
> they sowed their isn't they reaped their same
> sun moon stars rain
>
> —From "anyone lived in a pretty how town" (1940)

Should you use capital letters after a colon or within parentheses?

If a sentence follows a colon or a dash, the capital letter is optional, as in the following example:

How do I use capital letters with quotations?

When you introduce a quotation using an introductory signal phrase ending in a comma, colon, or dash, the first word of the quotation should be capitalized, as in this example:

> According to Cummings biographer Catherine Reef, "Friends begged Cummings to reconsider publishing these poems."

If the introductory signal phrase is not set off by a comma, colon, or dash, you should not capitalize the first letter of the quotation:

> Cummings biographer Catherine Reef stated that "friends begged Cummings to reconsider publishing these poems."

Many small business employers have strong objections to the government mandate of providing health insurance for employees: They claim the added expense will put them out of business.

OR

Many small business employers have strong objections to the government mandate of providing health insurance for employees: they claim the added expense will put them out of business.

When a sentence appears in parentheses within another sentence, the sentence in parentheses should not begin with a capital letter, as in this example:

Some parents have gone so far as to have their children regularly tested for drugs (for example, Jeff's parents take him to a drug treatment clinic for testing every Friday) in order to keep them out of drug court.

How do I use capital letters for significant words in the titles of creative or scholarly works?

Conventions related to capitalization of titles depend on the discipline. The Modern Language Association (MLA) style calls for capitalizing every word in a title, except for articles, conjunctions, and short prepositions (unless one is the first word of a title), as in the following examples:

- *The Two Gentlemen of Verona*
- *The Complete Works of William Shakespeare*
- "Ode to the West Wind"
- "Active Learning with Online Context-Based Modules"

- "Interdisciplinary Problem-Based Learning: Linking Environmental Policy and Environmental Science"

In contrast, the American Psychological Association (APA) style calls for capitalizing only the first word of the title and subtitle and any proper nouns, as in these examples:

- *The two gentlemen of Verona*
- *The complete works of William Shakespeare*
- "Ode to the west wind"
- "Active learning with online context-based modules"
- "Interdisciplinary problem-based learning: Linking environmental policy and environmental science"

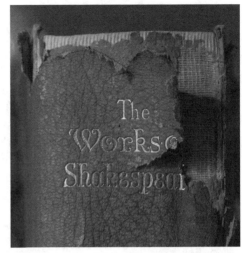

Depending on whether you're using Modern Language Association style or AP style, you might or might not capitalize words in a book title.

How do I use capital letters for names, titles, and proper adjectives?

When referring directly to someone by name or title, you need to capitalize the first word. However, if the title is not being used as a proper noun, it is not capitalized. This rule holds true both for professional titles (such as *doctor* or *professor*) and for family relationships (such as *sister* or *uncle*). Unless the word is part of the person's name, do not use a capital letter. Here are some examples:

My physician, Dr. Janice Brown, is married to Dr. Paul Earnest, Jr. He is also a doctor who specializes in family medicine.

My advisor, Professor Thomas, has an aunt who is also a professor. My Aunt Mary wanted to be a professor, but she never completed graduate school.

How do I use capital letters to indicate race and ethnicity or languages?

You should use a capital letter when referring to a language, or a religious, national, or ethnic name. Here are some examples:

Hinduism	Christianity
Hispanic	Spanish
Ramadan	Easter
Jewish	Buddha
Polynesian	

How do I use capital letters for directions, places, geographic features?

You should use a capital letter for a place name or geographic feature (*Detroit*, the *Missouri River*). If you are referring to a compass point (*northwest, southeast*), however, do not use a capital letter, unless you are incorporating the direction as part of the proper name of the location. Here are some examples:

> North Dakota is a state bordering Minnesota in the Midwest.

> She lives to the northwest of us on Elm Street.

> Lake Erie is one of the Great Lakes.

How do I use capital letters for events, seasons, times, or eras?

You should capitalize the names of historic events (*World War I, the Dark Ages, the Boston Tea Party*).

It is not necessary to capitalize the seasons of the year (*last winter, fall semester*).

You should capitalize the names of days, months, holidays, and eras (*Friday, May Day, Christmas, the Neolithic Era*).

Use capital letters when referring to nationalities, ethnicities, languages, and religions. For example, These people are "Hispanic Christians" not "hispanic christians."

How do I use capitalization for organizations, companies, or products?

You should capitalize the names of organizations, companies, and products. For internal capitalization, follow the convention of the company or organization, as in these examples:

the United Nations

Microsoft Corporation

Maricopa Community College

Boeing 737

iPhone 4s

QuarkXPress

MS-DOS

Internet

How do I use capitalization on the Internet?

Since some website addresses and email addresses are case sensitive, it is a good idea to type them exactly as they have been transmitted to you. Here are a few examples of the many ways in which Internet-related addresses appear:

www.info.com/UtahComputerServices

www.dell.com/CompanyComputers

www.sltrib.com

CHult@hotmail.com

USING ITALICS AND UNDERLINING CORRECTLY

In published texts, italic type and underlining are used interchangeably, but italic type is generally preferred to underlining.

How do I use italics for URLs and email addresses?

When you are writing a paper or an essay, the convention is to use italics to indicate an Internet address or an email address:

> You can find out more about your tax refund by contacting the Internal Revenue Service at *www.irs.gov.* If you wish to report a complaint to the IRS securities regulator, send an email to *phishing@irs.gov.*

How do I use italics for foreign words and phrases?

When you are writing in English, try to avoid using foreign words or phrases. If you do use a foreign word, however, the convention is to indicate its presence through italics:

> The French word for good day is *bonjour.*

> The Latin name for the American moose is *Alces americanus.*

> Many foreign words have become commonplace in English usage. Such words should not be italicized:

spaghetti

sauerkraut

yoga

curriculum

coffee

99

How do I use italics for titles of creative works?

Any creative work that stands alone as a complete project should be italicized when you are referring to it in your writing:

- *The Midnight Ride of Paul Revere*
- *The Shawshank Redemption*
- *The New York Times*
- *Economist*
- *The Fault in Our Stars*

How do I use italics for reference to words, letters, or numbers?

When you write about a word, letter, or number, you should italicize it to set it apart from the rest of the sentence:

Many people do not know how to spell *Mississippi*. It actually has 4 *s*'s.

My sister told me that her phone number has four *6*'s in it.

Don't forget to capitalize the *P* in *iPhone*.

How do I use italics for words being emphasized?

Occasionally, you will wish to emphasize a word or phrase by italicizing it in your writing. Using italics in this manner, however, should be done sparingly:

A voter in Woodstock says she abandoned Mr. King because of his *nasty* campaign ads.

USING ABBREVIATIONS CORRECTLY

What are abbreviations?

Abbreviations are shortened versions of words. Abbreviations are typically informal and should be used in formal writing very infrequently.

How do I use abbreviations correctly for titles, ranks, degrees?

You may wish to use a title, rank, or degree either before or after a person's name:

> Dr. Michael Ballard OR Michael Ballard, PhD

> Prof. Jeannette Thompson OR Jeannette Thompson, Prof.

> Gen. Colin L. Powell OR Colin L. Powell, Gen.

> If you are using a title and a surname only, spell out the title:

> General Powell

> Professor Thompson

> Senator Reid

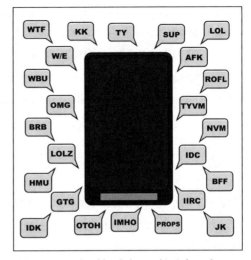

Abbreviations should only be used in informal writing, such as when texting on a phone, not in formal writing, such as a college essay or business correspondence.

How do I use Latin abbreviations correctly?

Some Latin abbreviations have become accepted in formal writing, particularly in academia. You should surround the abbreviations with commas when inserting them into a sentence. Here are two you might wish to use: e.g. (*exempli gratia*, meaning "for example") and i.e. (*id est*, meaning "that is").

> Many famous people have worn hats made in Peru, e.g., Teddy Roosevelt.

> Latin America's ties with China are more recent, i.e., the Chinese have courted trade with Latin America vigorously in recent years.

How do I abbreviate numerical dates and times?

When writing out dates and times, the abbreviations B.C. (before Christ) or B.C.E. (before the common era) are accepted; others include A.D. (*anno Domini*, or "year of our Lord," and C.E. ("common era"):

> The text dated from 124 B.C.

OR

> The text dated from 124 B.C.E.

> The music was written in A.D. 564.

OR

> The music was written in 564 C.E.

Another commonly used abbreviation indicates whether a particular time is A.M. (*ante meridiem*) or P.M. (*post meridiem*):

We usually have breakfast at 7 A.M. and dinner at 8 P.M.

In formal writing, you should not abbreviate the names of days, months, or holidays:

In December, we celebrate both Christmas and Hanukkah.

USING NUMBERS CORRECTLY

How do I write numbers for numerical dates and times?

Numbers can be used in formal writing to indicate a numerical reference to times, dates, or figures:

10:00 P.M.
65 A.D.
March 18, 2014
from 1920–1930
$25 million
65 mph
3.275%
1030 East 25th St.
PO Box 8543
Route 89
pages 14–18

When should I write out numbers?

You should write out numbers that can be expressed in one or two words or that begin a sentence:

Fifteen of the students were invited to the play, but one-third of them decided not to attend.

USING ELLIPSES CORRECTLY

What is an ellipsis?

An ellipsis (plural: ellipses) is a series of three spaced periods, typically used to indicate an omission from a quotation. If the end of the quotation is a period, follow the end punctuation with a space and then three spaced periods:

American workers have had no news this good for years.... Unemployment has sunk to 6.1%, the lowest rate in almost six years.

How do I show a pause in a sentence?

Occasionally, a writer might wish to use an ellipsis to indicate a dramatic pause in a sentence:

I began wondering if I had been overly optimistic … but then I remembered that optimism is a positive trait.

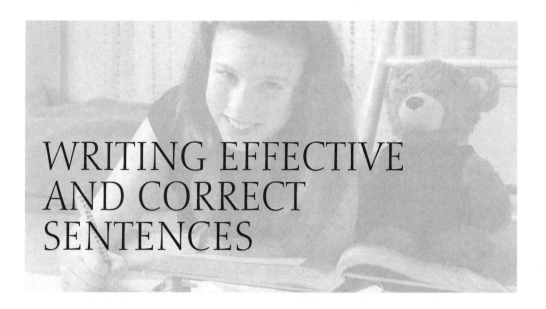

WRITING EFFECTIVE AND CORRECT SENTENCES

MAKING YOUR SENTENCES READABLE

How long should my sentences be?

In an age of tweets, text messages, and *Facebook* posts, English sentences seem to be decreasing in length. Sentences in English can vary from one word (*Help!*) to forty or more words. To keep your sentences both readable and meaningful, however, you will want to stay in the fifteen- to twenty-word range most of the time. Longer sentences can make it hard for a reader to follow your train of thought, and shorter sentences may seem too simplistic. The following sentence is 49 words long:

> By far the most influential factor in the rise of Standard English was the importance of London as the capital of England, and it is altogether likely that the language of the city would have become the prevailing dialect without the help of any of the factors previously discussed. [long sentence]

The sentence would be easier to read if it were divided into two sentences as follows:

> By far the most influential factor in the rise of Standard English was the importance of London as the capital of England. Indeed, it is altogether likely that the language of the city would have become the prevailing dialect without the help of any of the factors previously discussed. [revised into two sentences]

How do I keep my sentences parallel in form?

We often link ideas in sentences using coordinating conjunctions such as *and, but, or,* and *nor*. When linking ideas, take care to keep the forms of the linked parts the same, as in the following examples:

> Marta enjoys *swimming* and *running*. [both verbs]

105

He fell for our prank *hook, line*, and *sinker*. [all nouns]

The military protects us *on the sea, on the land*, and *in the air*. [all prepositional phrases]

Sometimes a sentence can go awry if the parallel items are not kept parallel in form, as in the following example:

A competent lawyer will assess a client's general problems and goals for resolving the case will be presented to the client. [faulty parallel structure]

A competent lawyer will assess a client's general problems and present goals for resolving the case to the client. [revised with parallel form]

Why do some writers get into trouble with clauses and antecedents?

Using modifiers (word, phrases, or clauses) to qualify or add information can make your writing richer and more interesting. Sometimes writers get into trouble, however, when they do not keep descriptive phrases and clauses close to their antecedents. Here, from a social services application, is a sentence with misplaced modifiers:

In accordance with your instruction, I have given birth to twins in the enclosed envelope. [faulty; misplaced modifiers]

You should also avoid dangling modifiers, that is, modifiers that do not have a clear referent. Here are two examples:

Running down the hall, the infant began to cry for his mother. [faulty; the infant is not running down the hall]

Running down the hall, the infant's mother reacted swiftly to his cry. [revised]

How do I keep my sentences from being choppy?

Writing becomes choppy when a writer chooses several short sentences over a single more complex sentence. A longer sentence tends to not only be less choppy, it also tends to better show the relationships between the various ideas by using both coordination and subordination. Here is an example:

The exchange student was from Korea. She lived with an American family. They were her host family. She went to school and studied hard. She improved her English language skills.

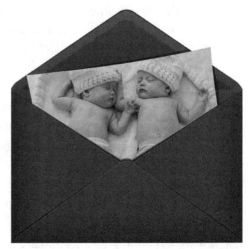

Saying "I have given birth to twins in the enclosed evelope" is an example of a grammatical error implying that the babies are actually in the envelope.

106

She went home to Korea. Her English conversational ability was very good. [faulty; 7 choppy short sentences]

The Korean exchange student lived with an American host family in order to go to school and improve her English language skills. When she returned home to Korea, her conversational ability in English was very good. [revised and combined into 2 sentences]

How can I eliminate repetition and redundancy?

Repetition may be used to keep the train of thought firmly in the mind of the reader. If you include too much repetition, however, it can become annoying. Check your sentences to be sure you have not said the same thing more than once, either through repetition (saying the same thing using the same words) or redundancy (saying the same thing using different words). Here are some examples:

Time seems to go quickly in time. [repetitive]

Our experiences are often most meaningful the first time we have our experiences. [repetitive]

You should repeat again the training that you did last week. [redundant; *repeat* already includes the meaning of *again*]

The new innovation will change the way we function at work. [redundant; an *innovation* is always *new*]

What are some ways to eliminate wordy phrases?

Several phrases in common usage are unnecessarily long or redundant (also called "wordy"). Whenever possible, replace such long or redundant phrases with their more succinct versions. Here are some examples. (*See also* Appendix G.)

Wordy Phrase	Succinct Substitute
a bigger degree of	more
a decreased number of	fewer
a lesser degree of	less
a lot of	many
absolutely essential	essential
advance notice	notice
advance reservations	reservations
all across	across
all of a sudden	suddenly
as a matter of fact	in fact
as a way to	to
at a later date	later
at the conclusion of	after
at the present time	presently
at this point in time	now

Wordy Phrase	Succinct Substitute
due to the fact that	because
eliminate altogether	eliminate
equally as good	equal
every single one	each one, all
fall down	fall
few and far between	rare
few in number	few
filled to capacity	filled
final outcome	final
first priority	priority
first and foremost	first
fly through the air	fly
for the purpose of	for
foreign imports	imports
free gift	gift
frozen ice	ice
future plans	plans
gain entry into	enter
gather together	gather
general consensus	consensus
give an indication of	indicate
give consideration to	consider
grave crisis	crisis
grow in size	grow
hand in hand	together
has the ability to	can
has an effect on	influences
hear the sound of	hear
heat up	heat
I myself	I
in a way that is clear	clearly
in all likelihood	probably
in close proximity	near
in connection with	about
in excess of	more than
in light of the fact that	because
in the event that	if
in reference to	about/regarding
in today's society	today
in spite of	despite
in spite of the fact that	although
in the area of	around
in the final analysis	finally
in the vicinity of	near
in this day and age	now
inadvertent error	error

Wordy Phrase	Succinct Substitute
inner feelings	feelings
is a reflection of	reflects
is going to	will
is helpful in understanding	clarifies
is in conflict with	conflicts
is in contrast to	contrasts with
is of significant importance	is important
is well aware that	understands
it seems as though	seems
it could happen that	could/may/might
it is rarely the case that	it rarely happens
join together	join
joint collaboration	collaboration
last but not least	finally
until such time as	until

How can I avoid a noun-heavy style?

Some writers try to make their writing sound more important by using more nouns than verbs in their sentences. Such a noun-heavy style is hard to read and can sound pretentious. This style of writing also tends to use forms of the verb *to be* excessively. You can check your writing for a noun-heavy style by searching for *am, are, is, was,* and *were.* This style also results in strings of prepositional phrases, as in the following example:

Once you are practicing walking mindfully as a formal exercise and you are experienced in what is involved, you will find that you are easily able to practice in a more informal mindfulness of walking in many different circumstances. [noun-heavy style]

Once you practice mindful walking as a formal exercise and you have some experience in it, you can easily practice a more informal mindfulness in many different circumstances. [revised]

What are some ways to improve the variety of sentences in prose?

You can improve the variety of your sentences in the following ways:

1. Vary the sentence structure

Use the different types of sentences (*simple, compound, complex,* or *compound-complex*) to vary sentence structure and therefore make your writing more interesting. Here is a paragraph with several different types of sentence structures:

The battle over control of the world's oceans has increased over the past few decades due to the discovery of vast mineral and fossil resources located under the sea. In 1958, the United Nations held the first Conference on the Law of the Sea. This conference established territorial seas, measuring 12 nautical miles

(12.24 kilometers) from the shore of coastal nations that are under the full control of that country. (The United Sates, along with such countries as North Korea, Chad, Liberia, and Iran, have refused to sign the treaty.) Additionally, countries have mineral, fuel, and fishing rights in an Exclusive Economic Zone (EEZ) that spans 200 nautical miles (370.6 kilometers) from shore. Problems arise when two countries' zones overlap. Median lines between countries have been drawn in most cases, but there are still many areas of disagreement.

—Tucci and Rosenberg

2. Vary the sentence lengths

Another way to improve sentence variety is to vary the lengths of sentences. Changing sentence lengths from time to time will add interest to your writing, as in the following paragraph:

The Kashmir goats, which make the fine wool known as cashmere, do come from the Kashmir region in India (a disputed area not controlled by any one nation). This region, which is located in northern India bordering on Pakistan, is plagued by violence and unrest. In 1947 the British decided to split the colony of India into two separate countries—one Hindu (India) and one Islamic (Pakistan). The state of Jammu-Kashmir has a mixed population of Hindus and Muslims, which has led to conflict within the region. India and Pakistan have waged three wars over this region, and sporadic violence continues today.

—Tucci and Rosenberg

How can I keep my sentences active?

The most lively writing uses primarily the active voice, in which the sentence's actor occupies the subject slot. Choose active voice for most of your sentences. Here are some examples of active sentences:

In 43 C.E., the Emperor Claudius decided to undertake the actual conquest of the British Isles. [the focus is on the action of the Emperor]

The Romanization of the province inevitably followed the military conquest. [the focus is on the Romanization]

When is it appropriate to use passive voice?

In passive sentences, unlike in active sentences, the subject slot is occupied by whatever is being acted upon. Passive sentences are appropriate when the focus is on that which is being acted upon rather than on the actor, as in the following examples:

The actual conquest of the British Isles was undertaken by the Emperor Claudius in 43 C.E. [the focus has shifted to the conquest]

The military conquest was inevitably followed by the Romanization of the province. [the focus has shifted to the military conquest]

In general, it is better to write sentences in the active voice. Passive voice sentences add words, change the order in which the subjects acts upon the object, and can make a sentence more difficult to understand.

You may also wish to eliminate the actor (found in the *by* phrase) of the sentence if it is not relevant:

The actual conquest of the British Isles was undertaken in 43 C.E. [eliminates the *by the Emperor Claudius* phrase]

What is an expletive?

An empty word such as *there* or *it* occupying the subject slot in a sentence is called an *expletive*. Check to see if many of your sentences begin with *there* or *it*. If so, revise those sentences to place the real subject into the subject slot, as in the following sentences:

There are many things that I can do with my new smart phone. [expletive]

My smart phone allows me to do many things. [revised]

It is imperative that all employees remain at their desks during the morning business hours. [expletive]

All employees must remain at their desks during the morning business hours. [revised]

How do I connect sentences with coordinate conjunctions?

When two parts of a sentence are coordinate in meaning, you should place them into the same grammatical form, linked by a coordinating word:

Captain James Cook discovered the Hawaiian Islands in 1778. His supporter was John Montagu, the Fourth Earl of Sandwich, so he named them the Sandwich Islands.

How do I connect sentences with semicolons?

Two independent clauses (sentences) that are closely related in meaning may be joined together using a semicolon rather than beginning a new sentence, as in the following:

Arkansas is the only state with a diamond mine; located in southwestern Arkansas, the mine is now a state park, named the Crater of Diamonds State Park.

No, it's not about cuss words; an "expletive" actually refers to an empty word such as *there* or *it* that occupies the subject slot in a sentence without adding much meaning.

How do I connect sentences with subordinate conjunctions?

You may wish to indicate that one clause is subordinate in meaning to another in a sentence. This subordinate relationship is signaled by using a subordinate conjunction:

Although Minnesota is known for its "10,000 lakes," Wisconsin is actually the state with the most lakes.

What are some ways to avoid sentence fragments, comma splices, and run-on sentences?

Sentences that are punctuated incorrectly can result in difficult-to-read constructions. The most common sentence-level grammatical problems are sentence fragments, comma splices, and run-on sentences.

1. Sentence Fragments

A *sentence fragment* is a grammatically incomplete sentence. To be complete, a sentence must have both a grammatical subject and a complete predicate. It cannot stand alone as a subordinate clause. (which makes it a subordinate clause that must be attached to an independent clause). Here are some examples:

The man with the blue coat. [fragment; lacks a predicate]

The man with the blue coat was loitering outside the grocery story. [revised; added a predicate]

Flies like a bird. [fragment; lacks a subject]

The new Air Force jet flies like a bird. [revised; added a subject]

Although we liked the painting. [fragment; begins with a subordinating conjunction]

Although we liked the painting, we decided it was too expensive. [revised; added an independent clause]

2. Comma Splices

When two independent clauses are joined with a comma, the resulting sentence contains the grammatical error we call a *comma splice* (the comma is splicing together two sentences that should be punctuated independently). Here are some examples:

The fastest skis are performance skis, these skis are custom-built to fly down the mountain. [comma splice; two independent clauses joined by a comma]

The fastest skis are performance skis. These skis are custom-built to fly down the mountain. [revised; separated into two sentences]

A starling once built a nest on our roof, we put up a grate to keep it from nesting there again this year. [comma splice; two independent clauses joined by a comma]

A starling once built a nest on our roof, so we put up a grate to keep it from nesting there again this year. [revised; used a coordinating conjunction]

Smart phones seem to be coming down in price, therefore more people are buying them. [comma splice; two independent clauses joined by a conjunctive adverb]

Smart phones seem to be coming down in price; therefore more people are buying them. [revised; added a semicolon between the two independent clauses]

3. Run-on Sentences

A run-on sentence is the result of fusing two independent clauses together. It is similar to the comma splice described above, except the comma is left out. Here are some examples:

Laptops have better keyboards than tablet computers they are less portable. [run-on]

Laptops have better keyboards than tablet computers, but they are less portable. [revised; coordinating conjunction]

Some problems facing communities are the result of poverty in the past communities have done little to get to the root causes. [run-on]

Some problems facing communities are the result of poverty; in the past, communities have done little to get to the root causes. [revised; semicolon divides the two independent clauses]

How do I make sure my subjects and verbs agree in number?

Each subject must agree in number with its verb; that is, if the subject is plural, the verb must also be plural, but if the subject is singular, the verb must also be singular. This is called subject–verb agreement. Although some ESL speakers may have trouble with subject-verb agreement, most native speakers have no trouble, unless they are unsure of whether or not the subject is plural. Here are some examples:

"English and math *is* my favorite subjects" would certainly be an example of a mistake in subject–verb agreement.

He rides his bike to work every morning. [singular subject and verb]

They ride their bikes to work every morning. [plural subject and verb]

When using compound subjects joined by *and*, typically the meaning of the subject will be plural and thus the verb should also be plural, as in the following:

English and math were my most difficult subjects in college. [plural subject and verb]

How does agreement work with indefinite pronouns?

When subjects are indefinite pronouns, such as *anybody, everyone, nothing, each, every, everyone, someone,* they are most often grammatically singular and thus take a singular verb:

Nothing is new under the sun. [singular subject and verb]

Someone needs to answer the phone. [singular subject and verb]

Each and every candidate is a winner. [singular subject and verb]

The indefinite pronouns *both* and *others* are plural and therefore require a plural verb:

Both of the twins were very lively and intelligent. [plural subject and verb]

Some like their oatmeal hot. Others like it cold. [plural subjects and verbs]

The indefinite pronouns *some, all, any, more*, and *none* can be used with either a singular or a plural verb, depending on the meaning of the sentence. Here are some examples:

Some of their attention was focused on their classmates rather than the teacher. [singular subject (*attention*) and singular verb]

Some of the students had a hard time paying attention. [plural subject (*students*) and plural verb]

114

How does agreement work with collective nouns?

Another potential area of confusion comes when the subject is a collective noun, such as *faculty, committee,* or *team*. Although these nouns can be used to refer to a group, they typically take a singular verb:

The faculty is disgruntled about the recent pay raise policy. [singular subject and verb]

The committee were never able to see eye to eye on anything. [singular subject and verb]

The committee members were never able to see eye to eye on anything. [plural subject (*committee members*) and plural verb]

How does agreement work with a disjunctive subject?

Sometimes a subject will be composed of two nouns or pronouns that are joined by *either/or, neither/nor,* creating a disjunctive subject. The verb in a sentence with a disjunctive subject should agree in number with the second part of the subject, as in the following sentences:

Either my brother or my parents are travelling next weekend. [plural subject in the second part (*parents*) and therefore a plural verb]

Neither my parents nor my brother is going to the wedding. [singular subject in the second part (*brother*) and therefore a singular verb]

How does agreement work with a plural noun used collectively?

When a noun subject is plural in form but singular or collective in sense, use the singular. Such words as *economics, athletics, politics*, or *news* may look plural because they end in an -*s*, but in actuality, they are collective and thus need the singular verb, as in these examples:

The news is often hard to read because it is so upsetting. [singular subject and verb]

Athletics is the route to a scholarship for some students. [singular subject and verb]

How does agreement work with a linking verb?

Make sure when you use a linking verb (*is, are, was, were*) that the verb agrees in number with the subject, not the object complement, as in these examples:

Peter's main interest in the summer is girls. [singular subject and verb]

Girls are Peter's main interest in the summer. [plural subject and verb]

115

"Peter *is* interested in girls," *but* "Girls* are *Peter's main interest*" illustrates how a linking verb needs to be changed, depending on whether the subject is singular or plural.

How can I expand simple sentences to make them more interesting?

There are three primary ways to expand sentences: modifying with words, modifying with phrases, and modifying with clauses.

1. The first way to expand a simple sentence to make it more interesting is to modify with words. Nouns can be modified by adjectives, as in the following:

   The train went down the track. [simple sentence]

   The little black train with the yellow caboose went down the track. [expanded with adjective modifiers and a modifying prepositional phrase]

   Verbs, adverbs, and adjectives can be modified by adverbs, as in the following:

   Birds fly. [simple sentence]

   Colorful blue birds fly swiftly around my yard. [expanded with adjective and adverb modifiers]

2. Another way to add interest to sentences is by modifying with phrases. A phrase is a group of words consisting of a noun plus the words related to it or a verbal plus words related to it. Phrases can be used to expand simple sentences and add detail to subjects, verbs, objects, and complements. Here are some examples of adding prepositional phrases to expand sentences:

The icemaker doesn't work. [simple sentence]

The icemaker in the refrigerator doesn't work without the water hookup. [expanded with prepositional phrases]

Margaret was angry. [simple sentence]

After the fight, Margaret was angry beyond all rational explanation. [expanded with prepositional phrases]

Here are some examples of adding verbal phrases (infinitives and gerunds) to expand sentences:

The President was eager to enact the legislation.

He gave us the opportunity to contact our representatives.

We were anxious to help him achieve his agenda.

Chasing her children around all day makes Susan tired in the evening.

Her favorite way to relax is taking a long soak in the tub.

Her husband helps by putting the children to bed while she is soaking.

3. A third way to add interest to sentences is by modifying with clauses. A clause is a group of words that includes both a subject and a predicate. Clauses can be either

Instead of writing something boring such as "Birds fly," you can add adjectives and adverbs (apologies for the black-and-white photo above), as in: "Brightly hued ibis fly gracefully over Africa."

independent (standing alone as a sentence) or subordinate (needing to be attached to a main clause). Adding subordinate clauses to main clauses is a good way to expand sentences, thus adding both interest and variety. Here are some examples:

If you cannot find the information you want, use the search function.

The fire fighter who is the most prepared will be ready for all emergencies.

The office where I work the best is in my home.

We were never sure how the fire started.

SOME COMMON SENTENCE PROBLEMS WITH ADJECTIVES AND ADVERBS

How can I tell an adjective from an adverb?

An adjective is a word that is used to modify a noun. Oftentimes, an adjective will take the form of either the present or past participle of a verb (a *babbling* brook, a *roasted* chicken). Some other frequently used adjectives are *his/her* (his or her book), *this/that* (this or that sandwich), or *which* (which way?).

An adverb is a word that modifies a verb, adjective, another adverb, or a clause. Most of the time an adverb is used to answer one of the following questions: *who, what, when, why, where, how,* or *how much.* Following are some examples of adverbs:

Paul often goes to church on Sundays. [modifies the verb]

She made a very bad decision. [modifies the adjective]

The cake was turned almost upside down. [modifies the adverb]

Happily, I was able to find my way to the hotel. [modifies the clause]

How do I avoid adjective and adverb confusion?

Some adjectives and adverbs are frequently confused. The pairs of words *good/well* and *bad/badly* are often misused. You need to remember that *good* and *bad* are adjectives, whereas *well* and *badly* are adverbs. Following are some examples:

Pedro speaks English well for a recent immigrant. [adverb *well* modifies the verb *speaks*]

He uses good pronunciation. [adjective *good* modifies noun *pronunciation*]

I feel very bad about my grades. [adjective *bad* modifies the noun *I*]

I studied badly all semester. [adverb *badly* modifies verb *studied*]

What are the comparative and superlative forms of adjectives and adverbs?

Both adjectives and adverbs are useful for making comparisons. Comparisons typically come in three forms: positive, comparative, and superlative. The comparatives and superlatives are formed by adding *-er* or *-est* to the adverb or adjective.

Regular Adjective Forms

Positive	Comparative	Superlative
hard	harder	hardest
pretty	prettier	prettiest
poor	poorer	poorest
late	later	latest

Following are some examples:

Peter felt that working in the library was *hard* and working in the restaurant even *harder*, but working on the farm was the *hardest* of all of them.

To become a beauty queen it is not enough to simply be *pretty*; you must be the *prettiest* girl in town.

What are the comparative and superlative forms for irregular adverbs and adjectives?

Some adverbs and adjectives form comparatives and superlatives in an irregular fashion, as in the following. These irregular forms will simply need to be memorized:

Irregular Adjective Forms

Positive	Comparative	Superlative
well	better	best
much	more	most
little	less	least
bad	worse	worst

Following are some examples:

He spoke French very *well*, but he spoke Spanish even *better*.

In the Yucatan the trinkets cost very *little* and the food costs even *less*.

What are the comparative and superlative forms for three-syllable adjectives?

When an adjective is more than two syllables long, it is combined with the words *more* or *most* to make the comparative and superlative forms.

She was judged to be the *prettiest* [superlative] girl in school, so she was chosen homecoming queen.

Three-Syllable Adjective Forms

Positive	Comparative	Superlative
beautiful	more beautiful	most beautiful
courageous	more courageous	most courageous
outstanding	more outstanding	most outstanding
colorful	more colorful	most colorful

Following are some examples:

Fall leaves in New England are *more colorful* than those found in the Midwest.

The New England states have the *most outstanding* displays of fall color found anywhere in the country.

It is incorrect to use both the -*er*/-*est* endings and *more/most* with the same adjective:

She was the most prettiest girl I ever saw. [faulty]

How do I make accurate comparisons using adjective forms?

To make comparisions accurately, remember these tips:

1. When you are comparing two items, use the comparative form; when you are comparing three or more items, use the superlative form:

   Of the two dresses, I like the pink one *better*.

   Of the three pairs of shoes, I like the gold ones the *best*.

2. When you are comparing count nouns (such as books, toys, or flowers), use the adjectives *few, fewer,* and *fewest*; however, when you are comparing non-count nouns (such as democracy, water, or progress), use *little, less*, and *least*:

   There were *fewer* flowers in the meadows than we anticipated.

   There was also *less* water flowing in the stream.

3. Your comparisons should be complete, including both parts of a comparison:

   The food is much better at the Chinese restaurant. [faulty; better than what?]

   The food is much better at the Chinese restaurant than it is at the Mexican restaurant down the street. [revised]

4. Some adjectives cannot be used in comparisons because their meaning expresses an absolute condition. For

When choosing from among more than two items use the superlative: "Of the dozen dresses on the rack, she liked the floral print the *best*.

example, it is impossible to be more or less pregnant (either you are pregnant or you are not). Following are some absolute adjectives that do not take comparative forms: *dead, final, unique, incomparable, pregnant.*

SOME COMMON SENTENCE PROBLEMS WITH PREPOSITIONS

How do I use the prepositional pair *different from* and *different than* correctly?

The prepositional pairs *different from* and *different than* are not interchangeable. When making comparisons between two persons or things, use *different from*:

My ideas about throwing an effective party are *different from* hers.

When the object of the preposition is an entire clause, use *different than*:

Her experiences while travelling abroad turned out to be *different than* she had expected them to be.

How do I use the prepositional pair *between/among* correctly?

Another confusing prepositional pair is *between/among*. When comparing two things, use *between*. When comparing more than two things, use *among:*

The feud was *between* the Hatfields and the McCoys.

The fighting *among* the women family members was often as nasty as the fighting among the men.

May I end a sentence with a preposition?

Ending a sentence with a preposition is grammatically correct in English. According to a popular anecdote, Winston Churchill rejected the rule against ending a sentence with a preposition by saying: "This is the sort of English up with which I will not put." Be aware that if you do end a sentence with a preposition, however, it may make your writing sound too informal:

Where is the library *at*?

SOME COMMON SENTENCE PROBLEMS WITH PRONOUNS

How do I make a pronoun agree with its antecedent?

Remember to match, in both number and gender, the pronoun to the antecedent. That is, if the antecedent is masculine and singular, the pronoun used to refer back to that antecedent must also be masculine and singular, as in the following example:

Robert was always very generous with his money.

Sometimes writers become confused about agreement when using the following indefinite pronouns: *some, anyone, somebody, no one, everything, each*. Most indefinite pronouns are singular and therefore the pronoun should also be singular:

Some of the cake had lost its frosting.

Everything was in its place.

Somebody needs to pick up his or her clothes.

Each of the men had taken along his camping gear.

A few indefinite pronouns (*some, all, more*) can also be used in a plural sense and thus the pronoun must be plural:

Some of the teachers had lost their enthusiasm.

All of the students had improved their behavior over the course of the year.

More of the flowers were losing their petals.

A collective noun (*team, class, jury*) can be either singular or plural, depending on its meaning in a sentence:

The team worked together to achieve their victory.

The team agreed on a logo for its T-shirts.

How do I punctuate possessive pronouns?

Writers are sometimes confused about how to punctuate the possessive pronouns (*his, her, hers, its*, etc). The rule to remember is that possessive pronouns never use an apostrophe because they are already possessive in form:

The dog loved it's bone. [faulty; *it's* is the contraction for *it is*]

The dog loved its bone. [correct]

How do I make sure to use non-sexist pronouns?

In the past, the male pronouns *he, him,* and *his* were used in generic statements to refer to both sexes. In today's world, however, it is considered sexist to always refer to males. Here are three ways to revise your sentences to avoid sexism.

If you write, "The dog loves *it's* bone," expanding the contraction will reveal your mistake: "The dog loves *it is* bone."

122

A common error among English speakers is using *their* with a singular subject: "Each athlete should bring their [should be "his or her"] own equipment."

1. Make both the pronoun and its antecedent plural:

A student is expected to bring his books to class. [sexist]

Students are expected to bring their books to class. [revised; plural]

2. Reword the entire sentence to get rid of the sexist language:

A parent should always listen to his children. [sexist]

It is important for parents to be good listeners. [reworded sentence]

3. Use an occasional disjunctive pronoun such as *his or her*:

Each athlete should bring along their own equipment. [faulty]

Each athlete should bring along his or her own equipment. [revised]

How do I make sure a pronoun refers to a specific noun antecedent?

To avoid ambiguity, strive to be clear in relating a pronoun back to its noun antecedent. Here are some examples:

Mark is a cardiologist and *his* father is a psychiatrist.

The doctor was always eager to meet *her* new patients.

The committee was unsure of the work *it* was supposed to accomplish at the meeting.

Just one of the cheerleaders knew all of her routines by memory. [the pronoun *her* refers to *one* and not *cheerleaders* and therefore is singular]

Neither Margaret nor Betty knew what she was supposed to fix for dinner. [unclear referent]

Neither Margaret nor Betty knew what Margaret was supposed to fix for dinner. [revised]

They say that text messaging is ruining our writing style. [vague]

Some experts say that text messaging is ruining our writing style. [revised]

How do I avoid the vague use of the pronouns *this, that, which*, and *it*?

Sometimes a writer uses one of the pronouns above to refer broadly to an entire statement. In such a case, the sentence should be revised to indicate a clear antecedent, as in the following example:

According to scientific experts, global climate change is causing the ocean temperatures to rise. This is leading to catastrophic weather events around the world. [vague use of *this*]

According to scientific experts, global climate change is causing the ocean temperatures to rise. This ocean temperature increase is leading to catastrophic weather events around the world. [revised]

How do I avoid the vague use of *you*?

You should avoid using the pronoun *you* in formal writing, unless you wish to specifically refer to the reader (as I have done in this sentence). Here is an example:

You never can tell how much money something is going to cost until you look at the price tag. [vague]

Shoppers cannot tell how much money something is going to cost until they look at the price tag. [revised]

What is pronoun case and why does it matter?

The term *case* refers to the way in which a pronoun functions in a sentence. The pronoun can function as a subject of a clause (the *subjective case*) or as an object of a clause (the *objective case*). It is important to learn the pronoun case because there is often confusion as to when to use one or the other.

The subjective case is required for all pronouns that are being used as a subject, including compound subjects, as in the following examples:

We have been saving for our trip for months now. [subjective case]

How can I be consistent with *that* and *which*?

Writers are often confused about whether to use *that* or *which* in a sentence. The relative pronoun *that* is used only when you wish to restrict the meaning of a clause to help identify the noun it is modifying:

First prize in the competition went to the red, white, and blue sailboat that came all the way from Boston. [restricts the meaning to the one from Boston; there may have been other red, white, and blue sailboats in the competition]

First prize in the competition went to the red, white, and blue sailboat, which came all the way from Boston. [nonrestrictive; adds more information but is not essential to the meaning]

To be safe, you may want to use *that* for restrictive (essential) clauses and *which* for nonrestrictive (non-essential) clauses, although this is not a hard-and-fast grammatical rule. *Which* is more versatile and can actually be used for either type of clause. It is important, however, that you be consistent in your use of *that* and *which* within a particular text.

Who will be the first off the ship—he or I? [compound subject of the clause]

She and Maria are going to the swimming pool this afternoon. [subjective case]

It appears that only Al and I passed the exam. [compound subject of the clause]

The objective case is required for all pronouns that are being used as an object, including indirect objects, object complements, objects of prepositions, and compound objects, as in the following examples:

Would you please give the blanket to her? [direct object]

The captain invited Paul and her to sit at the head table. [objective case]

How do I test for pronoun case with compound constructions?

The case of the pronoun will always depend on its function in the sentence. Sometimes you may be unsure about which case to use in a sentence with a compound construction. One way to tell whether or not to use the subjective or objective case is to use the pronoun alone. Here are some examples:

The coach gave Pedro and [me/I] a private session. [compound construction]

The coach gave [me] a private session. [use the pronoun alone]

The coach gave Pedro and me a private session. [correct pronoun case]

Pedro and [me/I] greatly appreciated the extra help. [compound construction]

125

I greatly appreciated the extra help. [use pronoun alone]

Pedro and I greatly appreciated the extra help. [correct pronoun case]

[We/us] Europeans tend to be cautious of outsiders. [compound construction]

[We] tend to be cautious of outsiders. [use the pronoun alone]

We Europeans tend to be cautious of outsiders. [correct pronoun case]

Sometimes people from other countries are upset by [we/us] Europeans. [compound construction]

"My uncle and *I* have fun gardening" is correct, instead of "My uncle and *me* … " or "Me and my uncle…."

Sometimes people from other countries are upset by us. [use pronoun alone]

Sometimes people from other countries are upset by us Europeans. [correct pronoun case]

What are the various cases for pronouns?

	Subjective	Objective	Possessive
1st person singular	I	me	my, mine
2nd person singular	you	you	your, yours
3rd person singular	he, she, it	him, her, it	his, her, hers, its
1st person plural	we	us	our, ours
2nd person plural	you	you	your, yours
3rd person plural	they	them	their, theirs
Relative & interrogative	who, whoever	whom, whomever	whose

How are relative or interrogative pronouns used in clauses?

Writers are frequently confused about how to correctly use the relative and interrogative pronouns (*who, whoever, whom, whomever, whose*). When these pronouns are used in questions they are called *interrogative pronouns*. When they are used in clauses they are called *relative pronouns*. As with other types of pronouns, the form used is based on how the pronoun functions in its clause. That is, if it functions as a subject, use the subjective case; if it functions as an object, use the objective case.

Who is going to the party tonight? [subjective case]

With whom are you going to the party tonight? [objective case]

She would like to thank the one who was responsible for her pay raise. [subjective case]

She would like to thank the one from whom she received a pay raise. [objective case]

How do I choose the correct *Wh-* form?

When you are writing, you need to decide whether the *wh-* word is functioning as a subject or an object in the clause in which it appears. Following are two ways you can test for the correct form:

1. Isolate the *wh-* word and transpose the clause in which the pronoun occurs:

[Who/Whom] are you going to invite to your party?

You are going to invite him to the party. [transpose the clause; objective case]

Whom are you going to invite to the party? [objective case is correct]

2. Substitute different pronouns for the *wh-* word to see which one sounds best. Then, select the pronoun with the corresponding case:

She would like to support the organization volunteers from [who/whom] she received the help.

She would like to support them. [substitute a pronoun]

She would like to support the volunteers from whom she received the help. [objective case is correct]

How do I use possessive pronouns correctly?

Possessive pronouns are used to show ownership. There are two types of possessive pronouns, *attributive* and *nominal*. Note that these possessive pronouns never take an apostrophe.

The *attributive* possessive pronouns (*my, your, her, his, its, our, their*) attribute ownership to a noun:

- *my* bike
- *your* life
- *her* hair
- *his* money
- *its* food
- *our* home
- *their* program

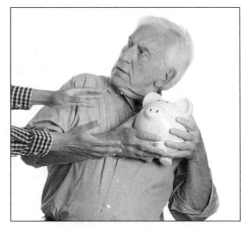

"Grandpa insisted that it was *his* piggy bank not *yours.*" In this example, *his* is an attributive possessive pronoun and *yours* is a nominal possessive pronoun.

The *nominal* possessive pronouns (*mine, yours, hers, his, its, ours, theirs*) are used with a linking verb (form of *to be*) to name something:

- The bike is *mine*.
- The good life is *yours*.
- The golden hair is *hers*.
- The money is *his*.
- The bone is *its* food.
- That home is *ours*.
- The new program is *theirs*.

How do I use possessive pronouns with gerunds?

Gerunds are verb phrases that are acting as nouns in a sentence. Because they function as nouns, they require an attributive possessive pronoun:

[His/Him] helping out around the yard was of great benefit to his grandfather.

His helping out around the yard was of great benefit to his grandfather. [attributive possessive pronoun]

How do I use pronouns in comparisons?

When comparing items using pronouns, you need to choose the pronoun based on how it functions in the sentence (subject or object). In order to decide, be sure to complete the comparison and then select the correct pronoun.

She has more money than him. [faulty]
She has more money than he has. [revised; completed comparison]
Peter likes running more than me. [faulty; he likes running more than he likes me]
Peter likes running more than I [like running]. [correct; he likes running more than I do]
She has as many problems as me. [faulty]
She has as many problems as I [have problems]. [correct; she has as many problems as I do]

SOME COMMON SENTENCE PROBLEMS WITH VERBS

What are phrasal verbs?

Phrasal verbs consist of a verbal (a verb form) and its related words. Phrases are used to add details to your sentences. The three types of verbals are infinitives, gerunds, and participles. Here are some examples of phrasal verbs:

We wanted to trim the bushes. [infinitive phrase]

Lifting weights all afternoon made Joan tired. [gerund phrase]

Having decided to move to Phoenix, Peter began looking for apartments. [participial phrase]

How do I sequence verb tenses?

When you are writing extended texts, you need to be sure that you do not randomly change verb tenses. The sequence of tenses should be kept consistent throughout. That is, if you begin a text using present tense, do not suddenly shift to past tense. You will want to provide your reader with a consistent time framework. Here are some examples:

Casey wants to go to the movies, but Carlos does not. [tenses consistent in compound sentence]

Before you drive the car, fasten your seat belt and adjust the rear-view mirror. [tenses consistent in complex sentence]

Cathy expects me to get good grades in school. [tenses consistent with infinitive phrase]

Running away from the road, the tiger obviously sensed danger. [tenses consistent with participial phrase]

What is the literary present?

When writing about a work of literature, it is acceptable to use the present tense, also called the literary present, even though the action being reported happened in the past. Here are a couple of examples:

In the novel *East of Eden*, Adam Trask learns about his wife's true character gradually. [describing events that happened in a work of literature]

Steinbeck uses Cathy and Adam Trask to illustrate his point about the pure evil that exists in human nature. [discussing what an author has done in a literary work]

What is a boring "to be" verb?

When writers overuse the *to be* verb, they end up with boring writing. The verb should carry the action of a sentence; therefore it is important to use active verbs, rather than empty forms of *to be*.

We were at the front door of Central High School and we were at the threshold of the place where angry segregationist mobs were not letting us go in. [faulty; empty *to be* verbs]

We stepped up to the front door of Central High School and crossed the threshold into that place where angry segregationist mobs had forbidden us to go.

[revised; active verbs]

USING WORDS EFFECTIVELY AND CORRECTLY

USING A DICTIONARY AND A THESAURUS

What types of dictionaries are there?

Dictionaries come in print and electronic formats. Some people prefer to use traditional printed dictionaries, whether in a desk size or a handy pocket size. Others prefer to use any of the numerous electronic dictionaries available on the Internet or packaged with a word processing program. Any dictionary will provide you with a great deal of information about each word.

When should I use a dictionary?

You should use a dictionary whenever you wish to learn something more about a word. Types of information listed for each word include the following:

definition
spelling
word division
pronunciation
parts of speech
word endings
word senses
etymology (word origin)
related words
synonyms
common usage

131

How do I know the correct spelling of a word?

A typical dictionary entry will begin with the word, correctly spelled and divided into syllables. If there is more than one correct way to spell a word, the alternate spelling will also be listed. The preferred spelling will be listed first. Here is an example of a word with an alternate spelling:

> 1. Neigh-bor—a person who lives (or is located) near another

> Synonyms: neighbour

Of course, many people use online dictionaries now, but there are still a lot of fans of the old printed versions.

How does the dictionary help me to know where to divide a word?

The dictionary will show the word's syllables, which will indicate to you how the word should be divided at the end of a line, as in this example:

> au·to·graph *n.*

How do I know the way to pronounce a word?

Many dictionaries will indicate pronunciation phonetically, as in this example:

> au·to·graph (ô' te-graf)

Some online dictionaries will include an audio file that pronounces the word for you.

How do I know the parts of speech for a word?

The dictionary will indicate the possible parts of speech for a word and may also use it in a sentence so you can get a sense of the word's usage. In the following example *n.* = noun, *tr.v.* = transitive verb, *adj.* = adjective, *adv.* = adverb:

> au·to·graph (ô' te-graf)

> *n.*

> 1. A person's own signature or handwriting.

> 2. A manuscript in the author's handwriting.

> *tr.v.* au·to·graphed, au·to·graph·ing, au·to·graphs

> 1. To write one's name or signature on or in; sign.

> 2. To write in one's own handwriting.

adj.

Written in the writer's own handwriting: *an autograph letter.*

[Late Latin *autographum*, from neuter of Latin *autographus, written with one's own hand*, from Greek *autographos* : auto-, *auto-* + graphein, *to write*; see - graph.]

auto·graphic, auto·graphi·cal *adj.*

auto·graphi·cal·ly *adv.*

How do I know the etymology or origin of a word?

A good dictionary will also give you the origin of the word, as in the above example for *autograph*. Note that the word has both Latin and Greek roots:

[Late Latin *autographum*, from neuter of Latin *autographus, written with one's own hand*, from Greek *autographos* : auto-, *auto-* + graphein, *to write*; see - graph.]

When should I use a thesaurus?

A thesaurus is a listing of words with their possible synonyms (words with the same meaning) and antonyms (words with opposite meanings). Using a thesaurus will help you to find the exact word you are looking for. A thesaurus may also help you avoid repetition by suggesting other words that will add variety to your writing. Most computer word processing programs now include a built-in thesaurus. You can simply highlight a word and open the thesaurus to see what suggestions come up. Here is what I found by highlighting the word *puzzle*: use a thesaurus whenever you're having a tough time finding just the right word, or if you want to find a novel way to say something.

puzzle (*n.*)

Meanings:

mystery (*n.*)

mystify (*v.*)

Use a thesaurus whenever you're having a tough time finding just the right word, or if you want to find a novel way to say something.

133

Synonyms:
mystery
enigma
riddle
conundrum
poser
problem
dilemma
brainteaser
Antonym:
explanation

DENOTATION AND CONNOTATION

What is the difference between denotation and connotation?

The basic dictionary meaning of a word is its *denotation*. The subtle nuances of meaning for a word are its *connotations*. For example, the words *walk* and *stroll* have similar meanings (denotations), but their connotations differ: stroll has the connotation of a slow, more leisurely walk. The word *hike* also means *walk,* but again the connotation differs: to hike implies a vigorous walk, perhaps in nature, whereas a walk is more straightforward and ordinary.

How do I choose the right denotation for a word?

When thinking about the right word to choose in a given context, make sure that you understand the dictionary meaning first. You might need to look the word up in a dictionary to make certain that you understand the meaning correctly. In the example below, the writer wished to say that his family was very important to him. For his intended meaning, the correct word is *essential* and not *superfluous*.

My family is *superfluous* to my happiness. [superfluous = not required, or surplus]

My family is *essential* to my happiness. [essential = required, not surplus]

How do I choose the right connotation for a word?

When trying out new words in your writing, it is not only important to understand the dictionary meaning, it may be critical to consider the connotation of the word. Sometimes a word has a pejorative sense to it and may not be the best choice in a particular context. For example, the words *convoluted* and *complicated* are listed in the dictionary as synonyms of each other, but they have different connotations—*convoluted* typically has a more negative connotation than *complicated*. In the following sentence, the writer wished to say that finding happiness can be a complex process; she did not wish to imply that it was tortuous. The second of the two sentences below more accurately reflects the connotation she had in mind:

The road to happiness is often *convoluted*. [convoluted = tortuous or very twisted]

The road to happiness is often *complicated*. [complicated = complex or intricate]

How do I add specific details to my general statements?

When you write, you will use a mixture of general statements interspersed with specific details. By adding specific details, you enrich the meaning of your sentences. Notice the difference in meaning in the following sentences when we add specific details:

Just after the fire alarm, the firefighters went to the barn.

Right after hearing the fire alarm, the firefighters rushed to the burning barn.

When they heard the fire alarm, the firefighters immediately jumped to their feet, slid down the pole, grabbed their gear, and rushed to their fire engines to speed along country roads towards the burning barn.

What are concrete and abstract nouns?

Concrete nouns, such as *dog, table, lettuce,* refer to objects that are tangible. Abstract nouns, such as *freedom, love, anger,* refer to concepts that are intangible. Writers should use a mix of concrete and abstract nouns. Sometimes concrete nouns can help to describe otherwise abstract concepts, as in the following examples:

My love is like a red, red rose that's newly sprung in June.

Freedom is a state of mind. All across this country, Americans are celebrating the freedoms they enjoy by being citizens of this great nation.

Cynicism, mistrust, and anger towards others are the toxic core of many workaholics.

"Patriots wave flags in appreciation of their freedom." Here, *patriots* and *flags* are concrete nouns, while *freedom* is an abstract noun that expresses a concept, not a physical object.

LEVELS OF FORMALITY

How do I find the right level of formality?

In addition to denotation and connotation, words vary in their level of formality or informality. When you are writing for school or work, you will typically use formal language, as I have used in this book. When you are writing to friends via email or text messages, on the other hand, it is perfectly appropriate to use informal language. The most important thing to remember is to use vocabulary that is appropriate to the context. Another term for the level of formality is the *register* in which you are writing. Be consistent in using the same register throughout a piece of writing without sudden shifts from formal to informal.

What are some examples of levels of formality?

Below are some examples of informal and formal words that mean the same thing.

Informal Register	Formal Register
funny	humorous
tapped out	penurious
careful	painstaking
honest	approachable
do over	retry
use up	expend
grab	seize
broke	insolvent, bankrupt
take stock	contemplate

What are some examples of formal words?

You will typically use formal vocabulary when writing for school or work. Many of the formal, academic words come from Latin and Greek roots. These types of words are often tested on standardized tests such as the ACT and SAT. Here are some examples:

acupuncture

analgesic

amateur

botany

bromide

critical

ebullient

egocentric

fidelity

gestation

hedonism

idiosyncrasy
incubation
juxtaposition
kinetic
latitude
memorial
narrative
octagon
pathology
polymer
quartile
reptile
rheostat
saccharin
stalactite
tapestry
tachometer
ungulate
vacuum
velocity
xerography
xylem

What are some examples of informal words?

You will use informal vocabulary when writing in ordinary contexts, typically outside of school or work settings. Informal words are often words that are derived from the Germanic as opposed to the Latin or Greek roots, for example *laugh, buy, throw, keep*. Germanic words tend to be shorter than Latin and Greek words. They are also often used with prepositions to make what we call *idiomatic expressions*, such as, *take stock, do over, buy up, go faster*. Here are a few more examples of informal, idiomatic expressions in English:

pull my leg
drop a line
keep an eye out
spilled the beans
feeling blue
rocket science
break a leg

137

get to the bottom of

take apart

When is it acceptable to use contractions?

Contractions are shortened forms of words, created by the omission of letters. Contractions should only be used with the informal register, and not in academic or workplace writing. Following are some examples of contractions:

- not = -n't [I don't know the answer and I won't know until I get her letter.]
- let us = let's [Let's make a deal.]
- I am = I'm [I'm the one you want.]
- I will = I'll [I'll be coming home on Monday.]
- I would = I'd [I'd sooner not eat dinner tonight.]
- did = 'd [Where'd he go with the money?]
- it is = it's [It's not over 'til the fat lady sings.]
- is not = isn't [Isn't she the one you need?]
- she is = she's [She's standing over on the sidelines.]
- they will = they'll [They'll be happy to see her.]
- we will = we'll [We'll be happy, too.]

When should I avoid jargon, slang, or dialect?

There are many different varieties of English in addition to the Standard Edited English that is used throughout this book. Other varieties of English are not wrong or even ungrammatical; they are just different. Some examples of specialized versions of English include *jargon, slang*, and *dialect*.

Jargon is any specialized, technical language that is known by a particular group of insiders. Use jargon only when writing specifically to an insider group and avoid jargon in other contexts. Some examples of jargon include words used by computer specialists (*cache, serial port, binary, memory, CPU*), or by sports enthusiasts (*roughing, touchdown, choker, offense, and defense*).

Slang is a novel form of speech specific to groups, such as teenagers or music aficionados, or subcultures, such as steampunk, bodybuilding, and gaming. Slang comes and goes quickly and is not appropriate to use in an academic or workplace writing situation. As with jargon, slang is meant to be exclusive and understood only by insiders. Here are some examples of hip-hop slang: *hyphy, holla, bounce, challax, ginormous, scraper, perkin, faded, bootsie, stunnas.*

A *dialect* is a version of English used by a specific regional or ethnic group. A dialect is characterized by unique pronunciations and even some grammatical patterns that differ from standard English. For example, in some ethnic dialects, you might hear a sentence such as "He be tryin' hard." Within the dialect, speakers would understand this sentence to be grammatical. Dialect, however, is not appropriate in formal writing situations, so speakers of a dialect need to learn formal, written English in addition to their own native dialect.

When should I avoid clichés?

A cliché is a figure of speech that has become worn out and overused. You should avoid clichés in formal writing. Some examples include the following:

- beating around the bush
- dark and stormy night
- lesser of two evils
- lock, stock, and barrel
- once upon a time
- good old days
- as easy as pie
- new normal
- monkey see, monkey do
- thinking outside the box
- two wrongs don't make a right
- what she said
- it was a slam dunk
- step up to the plate
- keep your nose clean
- go for the gusto

Clichés such as "think outside the box" are tired, worn-out phrases that should be avoided in good writing. We've heard them all before; think of a fresh way to express your ideas.

How should I use figurative language?

Figurative language uses words in colorful, creative ways to enhance the meaning of a sentence. The two most common figures of speech are *similes* and *metaphors*. In both cases, the familiar is used in a comparison to explain the unfamiliar. Figurative language should be used very infrequently and only to achieve a particular effect. Here are some examples:

Similes [comparison: explicit using *like* or *as*]

> The *mist* was like a gauzy *fabric*. [The mist is compared to fabric.]

> *She* is sweeter than *candy*. [The woman is compared to candy.]

> *He* is like a refiner's *fire*. [The man is compared to fire.]

Peter is as angry as a *bear*. [Peter is compared to a bear.]

Metaphors [comparison: does not use explicit markers]

The neighbors agreed to a *ceasefire* regarding the disputed fence. [The dispute is compared to a war.]

Every day is an uphill *battle*. [Daily life is compared to a battle.]

His company had a *sister* factory in China. [The factories are compared to relatives.]

Necessity is the *mother* of invention. [Necessity is compared to a relative.]

He knew he would be *toast* when he got home. [His situation is compared to toast.]

It was a *recipe* for disaster. [The situation is compared to cooking.]

LANGUAGE AND IDENTITY

What is correctness in language?

Even though there is a version of English that is privileged in places like American institutes of higher education, termed *Standard Edited English*, that does not mean there is only one correct way to communicate with others. The correctness of language is relative. That is, it depends on the context. The most competent speakers and writers know how to adapt their vocabulary and style to suit the context. Linguists call this ability to adjust from one style to another *code shifting*. In some situations, using jargon, slang, or dialect may be the correct choice, because doing so is necessary to communicate with the target audience and to establish a common bond. You might think about correctness in language the same way you think about correctness in dress. When deciding what to wear for a particular occasion, you consider the context. You would probably not choose shorts and sandals for a formal wedding reception. In the same way, you would not choose slang or jargon for a formal writing project.

What is a persona?

Language is closely related to a speaker or writer's identity. The choices you make with language tell your listeners and readers a great deal about you and your relationship to your subject and your audience. We sometimes call the stance a writer adopts his or her *persona*. When you are thinking about word choices, you also need to think about the context in which you are writing and the persona you wish to portray to your target audience. You will want to choose the vocabulary and the writing style that will most appeal to those with whom you are communicating.

What is race and ethnic bias in language?

Race and ethnic bias is similar to gender bias in that it reinforces cultural stereotypes. You want to take care not to make sweeping ethnic generalizations or use ethnic jokes in your speech or writing. Terms such as *welfare mother, illegal alien, inner-city resident*, though seemingly innocent on the surface, can hide ethnic stereotypes that are harmful or demeaning to a particular group.

What is gender bias in language?

Sometimes word choices can reinforce stereotypes that are unconsciously held within a society. For example, if I were to call someone a *woman doctor*, the implication is that doctors are typically men and so I need to distinguish this particular doctor as female. Similarly, if I call someone a *male nurse*, I am implying that the word *nurse* typically implies a woman. Take care that when you are writing you are not unconsciously promoting gender bias. For the same reason, you should vary your pronouns and not always use the generic pronoun *he*. Here are a few more examples of gender-biased words:

gender-biased	gender-neutral
businessman	business person
mankind	humankind
salesman	salesperson
workmen	workers
stewardess	flight attendant
policeman	police officer
foreman	supervisor

What other types of language can discriminate?

Any group that is different from the norm can face language bias. For example, age-related stereotypes and jokes can demean older members of our society. The adjective *old-timer* is one example of a term that denigrates age. Other groups, such as members of particular religions or those with physical disabilities, are also sometimes the victims of language discrimination or bias. It is important to find out which terms the people in the group prefer (*differently abled* or *person with a disability* instead of *disabled* or *handicapped*, for example) and use those terms.

ACADEMIC WRITING

What is academic writing?

Academic writing is school and college writing. In many classes, students demonstrate how well they understand what is being taught through writing: essays, term papers, research reports, lab reports, and written exams. Through both reading and writing, students learn to think critically, to solve problems, and to make decisions. The ability to write, to communicate clearly and effectively, is one of the most important skills students learn in school.

How important to success in school is writing?

Writing well is a skill that can make all the difference to a student's success. Much of the communication that occurs in school is written. Although students also participate in class by talking with, and listening to, instructors and classmates, they almost certainly show what they know about a subject through writing. The process of writing also helps students to clarify their thinking about a topic. When students write, they begin to understand their own opinions and beliefs better, and at the same time they realize the extent of (and gaps in) their own knowledge base. This is sometimes called "writing to learn." Writing is also used in schools to test students' knowledge. Students are frequently asked to write on standardized tests to gauge their understanding of a subject. Many students are faced with taking college entrance exams, such as the ACT and the SAT. These tests also include writing exams, so a student's writing ability is important to making the move from high school into college.

How does a person become an expert writer?

Learning to write is a lifelong task—just as doctors and lawyers "practice" medicine and law throughout their careers, professionals of all kinds "practice" writing and continue to develop as writers throughout their lifetimes, not only in school but well beyond,

What is the writing process?

Writing is not a neat or orderly process; it is often very messy. For most, writing proceeds in fits and starts, with repeated cycles of drafting, researching for information, rereading what has been written, revising and editing, and then writing new material and starting over. Writers may write in "chunks," piecing these chunks together into a final paper by cutting and pasting files. Writers may multitask while they are writing, moving easily between researching online, texting friends, writing an outline, and downloading songs to a smart phone. No matter the technology employed, however, writing always consists of some configuration of these major parts: planning, gathering information, formulating arguments, drafting, structuring sentences and paragraphs, and finally revising, editing, and proofreading to make sure the writing is both correct and effective.

into their work and personal lives. Students sometimes find themselves confused about the reading and writing assignments in their various classes. If students approach their assignments thoughtfully, however, they will soon learn the differences and similarities among them. For example, why is the personal writing style, liberally scattered with "I" and "me," used for a high school English essay not appropriate for a college political science paper? Through guided practice with a variety of types of writing, students can become lifelong writing practitioners.

Does technology make a difference to our writing?

The rise of electronic communication has dramatically altered both school and work. The tools available to writers are almost limitless: email, text messages, wikis, online work groups, *Twitter, Linked-in*, blogs, and more. The fact is that we now spend much less time communicating orally—face to face or on the phone—than we did before electronic communications. Because so much of our communication is now written rather than oral, skilled writers are more valuable than ever. Even though the tools may change, however, the principles of writing do not. It is always important to understand the audience to whom you are writing and to select the most effective words and sentences to reach that audience. Writing, regardless of the technology employed, needs to be clear, direct, error-free, logical, and to-the-point in order to communicate its message.

What do academic writers do?

First and foremost, academic writers ask questions. They are curious about the world around them and how it works. In the process of searching for answers, these writers observe carefully and consider what others have had to say about the topics and issues being considered. They should be open to seeing things in a new light. Most of all, academic writers should understand the value of complexity and not seek easy answers to

Good academic writers have inquisitive, open minds, do their research, and keep in mind that ninety-nine percent of the job is perspiration, and only one percent inspiration.

their questions, as most issues can be approached from varying points of view, all with a certain amount of validity. Intelligent writers do not jump to hasty conclusions. As students ask questions, observe, and examine alternatives, they need to read what others have written on their topics. In essence, students need to join an ongoing conversation in order to first understand an issue and then contribute their own ideas about that issue. No one person has all the answers. Rather, knowledge is formed collectively. Writing is always an ongoing process; it does not happen spontaneously. Thomas Edison said that "genius is one percent inspiration and ninety-nine percent perspiration." By the same token, writing well is one percent inspiration and ninety-nine percent perspiration.

WRITING IN DIFFERENT DISCIPLINES

What are disciplines?

Every college catalog lists distinct subjects of study, such as chemistry or business or journalism. The subject fields in college typically share ways of building knowledge and ways of communicating their understanding of the world. We call such knowledge clusters *disciplines*. There is the discipline of chemistry and the discipline of accounting, for example. Often disciplines correspond to subjects for majors and degrees: perhaps a

Bachelor of Science in Biology degree or a Master of Arts in Music degree. Related disciplines are commonly clustered together into departments, schools, and colleges. There may be a department of English that includes such related disciplines as literary studies, technical writing, and folklore. A college of science would likely include such related disciplines as math, chemistry, biology, and physics, and a college of humanities and arts would include such disciplines as history, music, fine arts, foreign languages, and theatre. All college students do a great deal of writing in a variety of disciplines.

What is disciplinary discourse?

Within the disciplines, there are customary ways of sharing knowledge through communication, sometimes called *disciplinary discourse*. In the first few years of college, students learn about communicating in many disciplines. For example, regardless of the major, if students are required to take a general education course in American History, they need to learn not only the facts about that history (its subject matter), but also the questions that historians typically ask and how they use historical texts to answer those questions and communicate their understanding to a particular audience through written texts. Once students decide on a major, they will become apprentices in a discipline, learning not only the subject matter and its vocabulary, but also learning to understand and engage in the larger communication goals of the particular discipline. Each discipline will employ specific formats in which to organize its writing. The lab report, for example, is a specific format used in scientific writing.

What are some distinguishing features within disciplinary writing?

The use of visuals is especially important in fields within the sciences and social sciences. Often data are presented in the form of visuals—tables, graphs, and charts. Readers of disciplinary discourse expect to find certain organizational patterns, certain types of connections between ideas, and a logical sequence.

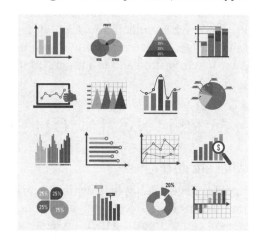

Another distinguishing feature of disciplinary discourse is style—that is, the customary sentence patterns chosen by writers in that discipline. Features of style that can differ by discipline include *tone* (How objective is the writing? How formal is the tone?), *rhetorical stance* (Do the writers try to achieve distance from their audience? Or do they try to identify with their audience?), and *sentence style* (How long are the sentences and paragraphs in this discipline? Are the verbs active or passive? Are headings and subheadings used?)

In disciplinary writing, authors often use charts, tables, and graphs to help illustrate their data.

146

All disciplines use what is called *documentation* to show readers what source information was used and how to find those sources, but there are differences in the formatting conventions across disciplines.

What is a discourse community?

Discourse communities are groups of people who are engaged in the common task of producing meaning or knowledge within that group. Those who use similar formats, language structures, research methodology, and terminology to communicate with each other about a particular subject matter are said to belong to a *discourse community*. Most people belong to a number of discourse communities: for example, one at their job, one among their close personal friends, one on *Facebook*, and one in their major field of study. The members of a discourse community share common assumptions about what to expect from the writing of others in that community, and about the kinds of knowledge and knowledge-making that will occur within the community. People within a discourse community often use vocabulary words that are specific to the discipline of that community, so those joining must learn its vocabulary. Sometimes the vocabulary is specialized: in the discipline of biology, for instance, many of the terms are based on Latin root words. Other times the vocabulary is jargon that is specific to the field—words and phrases that make up a specialized or technical language of a trade or profession. For example, the language used when writing about business information systems might be considered technical jargon.

What is writing in the humanities?

Disciplines in the humanities include classical and modern languages and literature, history, and philosophy. Humanists deal in significance, insight, imagination, and the meaning of human experience. They write to express their understanding of some aspect of the world. In general, humanists inquire into consciousness, values, ideas, and ideals as they seek to describe how experience shapes understanding of the human condition. Written texts in the humanities fall into three broad categories: 1. creative writing (such as fiction, poetry, memoir, etc.); 2. interpretive and analytical writing (such as literary, film, and art criticism); and 3. theoretical writing (such as historical, philosophical, and social theories of literature and art). Much of the writing that occurs in college art and literature courses is interpretive. Instructors generally expect students to make a claim about a literary or art work and then support that claim through reasoned arguments and evidence from the work itself. The goal of interpretive writing is to shed light on an aspect of the work that the reader might not otherwise see.

What is writing in the natural sciences?

Scientists formulate and test theories about the natural and physical world, and their findings are used to solve problems in such fields as medicine, industry, and agriculture. Typically, the natural sciences are classified into two categories: pure and applied. The pure sciences include life sciences (such as biology and botany), physical sciences (such

What is the scientific method?

To solve problems in a systematic way, scientists use the scientific method, and writing plays a critical role in each step of the process.

1. Express the problem.
2. Gather information needed to solve the problem.
3. Formulate a hypothesis.
4. Design and conduct controlled experiments to test the hypothesis.
5. Analyze the experiments to see if they support the hypothesis.
6. Restate the hypothesis as a conclusion that explains how the experimental data supported, refuted, or modified the initial hypothesis.

as mathematics, physics, and chemistry), and earth sciences (such as geology and geography). The applied sciences include medical sciences (such as forensics, pathology, surgery, and ophthalmology), engineering (such as mechanical, environmental, aerospace, civil, and electrical), and computer science. Most scientific writing takes the form of research reports, which are based on primary research conducted by scientists. The motivation for much primary research in the natural sciences is an event or experience that challenges existing ideas and promotes inquiry. In general, the aim is to improve the congruency between theories and concepts about the world and actual experiences or experimental results.

What is writing in the social sciences?

The social sciences—psychology, anthropology, political science, sociology, and education—focus on the systematic study of human behavior and human societies. They are comparatively young disciplines; most came into their own in the early twentieth century. In part to establish their academic credibility, they adopted many of the methods used in the natural sciences. Many social scientists use the scientific method to study people and their behaviors: they develop hypotheses and then design and conduct controlled experiments to test those hypotheses. As with the sciences, writing plays a role at every stage of social scientific experimentation. Writing often begins with the careful recording of field or observation notes. From these notes, the social scientist formulates a hypothesis, and then he or she seeks to test that hypothesis through further systematic experiments or observations. Notes from these experiments are then analyzed and compared to the hypothesis. Finally, the social scientist writes a conclusion explaining how the experimental and observational data supported, refuted, or modified the initial hypothesis. The entire process is recounted in a research report. The research report may be summarized and evaluated by other social scientists in a review of literature.

ACADEMIC RESEARCH

What is academic research?

Broadly defined, all research is systematic inquiry designed to further our knowledge and understanding of a subject. By this definition, much of the work done in college is research. Students and professors seek to discover information about people, objects, and nature; to revise their findings in light of new information that comes to light; and to interpret experience and communicate that interpretation to others through writing. Researchers in the disciplines have customary ways in which they formulate questions and test hypotheses. Anyone who is learning about a specific discipline will also be learning how to argue a case and present evidence in that discipline. Evidence can vary from quantitative (e.g., using statistical and numerical data) to qualitative (e.g., using observations and interviews). Data can be presented in the form of visuals such as tables, graphs, and charts, or it can be described in case studies, narratives, or stories. Information can be gathered either through primary sources (firsthand data collection) or through secondary sources (reading and reporting on the work of others).

What is the difference between primary and secondary research?

Academic writers use two main types of sources: primary and secondary. Primary sources are those that have been generated by the researcher or author him or herself—that is, the data and reports that come from laboratory experiments, field work, survey research, creative writing, letters or journals, and so on. Secondary sources are those that are written about the primary sources, often in the form of a review of the research or a report in the sciences and a critique, analysis, or interpretation in the humanities. In college, students will most likely use both primary and secondary sources.

What is the difference between popular and scholarly sources?

Sources can be roughly divided into two kinds, those in the popular press and those in the academic press. The popular press includes newspapers, magazines, newsletters, and other popular venues such as on-

"Primary research" means that the academic writer is discussing information based on discoveries from original research.

line journals, blogs, wikis, or Internet news sites. The academic press includes articles written by experts in a discipline, such as psychology or sociology or biology. So, while searching for sources about depression, for example, a student might find an article in a popular press magazine that publishes on psychological topics, like *Psychology Today,* but might also find an academic journal that publishes articles about psychological topics, like the *American Journal of Psychological Research*. It is important to recognize the difference between articles in these two types of sources. The former will be written for lay readers in a popular style and will boil down and perhaps simplify research for that audience. The latter will be written for other experts in the field and will be peer-reviewed by other scholars to ensure its accuracy and reliability. The peer review process is one in which each article is carefully reviewed by other experts and evaluated by them before it is accepted for publication in the academic journal.

Typically in college, students should rely most heavily on the scholarly sources that are produced by academic presses specializing in work written by scholars, work that has been rigorously peer-reviewed. Articles in the popular press, such as those found in newspapers or *Wikipedia*, may be helpful for background information and for framing the relevant questions and issues. It is the scholarly articles found in academic journals, however, that will help make a writer's own arguments the most convincing.

How do I conduct an interview?

An interview is one type of primary research that is accessible to most students. The advantages of the interview include flexibility (the questioner can interact with the respondent), speed of response (the questioner immediately knows the responses), and nonverbal behavior (the questioner can gather nonverbal as well as verbal responses). Because interviews take time, however, fewer responses can be gathered. Another disadvantage is that the character of the interviewer can influence the outcome of the interview. Here are the steps for an effective interview:

1. Articulate a general goal for the interview and make initial contact with the subject.

2. Confirm the appointment the day before.

3. Be prompt, have your questions ready, and stick with the time allotted for the interview.

4. Ask your questions exactly as you wrote them down.

5. Politely probe any unclear or incomplete answers.

6. Review your notes immediately following the interview.

7. Follow up with a thank-you note to your subject.

How do I conduct an observation?

The general goal of observation is to describe and perhaps evaluate customary behaviors. Observation is best suited to the collection of nonverbal data. The observer watches people behave in customary ways in a particular environment or setting and takes notes. You might observe where people stand in an elevator, for example, or how they cross a street at an unmarked crosswalk. Through observation, you accumulate *field notes*, which are used to analyze trends and discern customary behaviors. The disadvantages of observation include lack of control over the environment, lack of quantifiable data, and small sample size. Also, whenever an observer enters the environment to observe people, the participants' behaviors may cease to be natural. For example, if you stand in an elevator taking notes about people's behavior, eventually they will notice you, and they may no longer behave the way they ordinarily would. As you think about your research project, consider whether observational data would enhance your report. Be sure to gather enough background information prior to the observation itself to ensure its usefulness to your research project. Here are the steps for an effective observation:

1. Articulate a general goal for the observation.

2. Gather background information.

3. Plan your observation carefully so as not to influence the behaviors of those you are observing.

4. Take accurate notes during your observation and accumulate them in a research notebook.

5. Analyze your observation notes for trends or patterns

How do I conduct a survey?

Ideally, an entire population would be studied to gain insights into its society. Polling an entire population is seldom feasible, however, so surveys are used to sample small segments of the population

For a survey to be effective, numerous people need to be polled, and one way to do that efficiently is through telephone surveys.

151

selected at random. The most frequently used sampling technique is random-digit dialing of the telephone. Another common kind of survey is the questionnaire, a form that asks for responses to a set of questions. Designing questions is a science that has been developed over many years, and researchers have refined sampling techniques to be extremely accurate. Although the details are beyond the scope of this book, here are a couple of basic principles: write questions that are clear and understandable; write them in such a way that the responses will be easy to tabulate. Researchers generally agree that closed questions, which require checking a box or answering "yes" or "no," yield more usable data, but open-ended questions, which require a short written response, can provide valuable insights (though they are harder to interpret). Think through your research topic to see whether a questionnaire might yield useful data.

How do I find source information on a topic?

Much of the work done in college involves using both the library and the Internet to locate relevant secondary sources in academic journals on a particular academic subject. Professors will expect students to be able to find numerous articles in the library or on library databases to help them read broadly on some topic of interest or relevance to the class. Professors will also expect students to make good use of the Internet as they search for sources additional to those found in the library databases. In order to formulate good starting questions and to conceive and write cogent arguments, students first need to read what other experts in the discipline are saying about a subject. Always begin by conducting some preliminary background research.

The most reliable way of conducting a search on any academic subject is through a college library's database services. Academic libraries provide their patrons with access to numerous indexes that list sources, as well as to full-text sources on academic subjects. The advantage of searching through a library's databases is eliminating a lot of the extraneous "noise" that occurs from a *Google*-type search. If you simply type keywords into *Google or another search engine*, you will get commercial sites, advertising sites, popular press, personal blogs, and so on. A *Google Scholar* search is better than a gen-

---

What types of library databases are there?

Each library organizes its databases differently, so students need to take the time to become acquainted with the system used on their campus. Reference librarians and any online help system provided at the library's website can get a student started. For example, at Utah State University, the library's opening search screen (Electronic Resources and Databases) provides a full range of information that can be found via the library's Web portal—everything from full-text collections to searches by academic subject, specialized database searches, and encyclopedias and dictionaries.

eral *Google* search, but it will lead you only indirectly to the full-text databases to which your library subscribes.

How do I use online library databases to find information?

First, find a broadly based, all-around database from the library's main Web page. Many librarians suggest starting with *Academic Search Premier, CQ Researcher*, or *EBSCO-host* databases. Next, compile a list of keywords on the subject you are researching. Any background reading you have already done is a good source for compiling a list of keywords. Using the advanced search feature of the database, you can combine keywords and refine your search until the desired types of articles are being located. It may take some time to come up with the best keywords, so be willing to experiment. As you search the databases, look for articles that are relevant to your topic and that may provide answers to your starting questions. Generally, the databases will list the titles of the articles retrieved by your search as well as provide you with a brief abstract summarizing the content of each article. They will also list keywords, which you should write down in a research notebook. By previewing the list generated by the database, you can sort through to see which ones might be relevant to your topic and questions. By clicking on the links to either the PDF or the HTML full-text version, you can read the articles themselves. Once you have located an article that is relevant to your search, you have the options of downloading, printing, or saving it for future reference.

How do I keep track of sources found via a database?

It is very important to keep track of all the sources you locate through a particular database. If you ever need to find the article again, you will need to know where it was located. As you browse the titles, you can add them to a computer file or folder in which you store all the relevant information from this particular search. Once items are in the folder, you can save to a thumb drive or other storage device, print, email, or archive at the database those items you wish to retain for future reference.

How do I search the Internet to find information?

The Internet is now an important research tool in all fields of study. A biologist observed that he can locate information crucial to his research in minutes via the Internet, when it used to take days or even weeks of searching through print sources. But remember, it is better to begin with the library's databases, to be sure that you are reading from reputable sources.

One of the primary benefits of the Internet is that it connects computer users to information on computer networks around the world. People use the Internet for a variety of purposes, such as communicating with each other, playing games, sharing information, and selling products. The Internet also has many educational uses. An Internet search can locate a great deal of information published by educational institu-

153

The Internet has become an indispensible research tool for writers, but there is a learning curve on how to use it properly, including how to find the best, most reliable resources online.

tions, libraries and service organizations, commercial and corporate providers, the public press, and the government.

As you begin searching the Internet, however, you need to realize that this process is not an exact science. Searching the Internet is time-consuming, convoluted, and often frustrating for students, as the process can result in numerous dead ends and false starts. Sometimes you will find far too many sources and sometimes none at all. I recommend persistence and attention to using search tools wisely. The only way to see if your search is yielding the results you are after is to browse through the listing of sites found by the search tool. Most search tools provide a brief description of the site, so you can quickly ascertain whether or not the search is finding relevant sources. If it is not, try again with new search terms or keywords, subject areas, or limiters (such as Boolean operators *and, or, but*). Make use of the search tool's help screen if you are not achieving the results you desire, or, better yet, ask an academic librarian for help.

How do I respect copyright?

The amazing growth of the Internet has spawned numerous debates about censorship and freedom of information. At issue is the amount of control that governments should be able to exercise with regard to information found on the Internet. Because information that you access electronically is in the form of pixels and not print, everything from the Internet that you see on your screen is a copy of a file located on someone else's computer. Electronic sharing of information via the Internet is predicated on the copying of files—including files of digitized music, art, graphics, or films—from one computer to another.

> ## How do I keep track of my Internet search?
>
> **B**oth *Firefox* and *Explorer* help you keep track of important websites and to retrace the steps of your Internet search. The GO feature keeps a running list of the websites you have visited during your current Internet session. It will disappear when you close down the browser.
>
> If you have found a page that you want to visit frequently, add this site's address to your list of favorites. You can add a page to your favorites by visiting that page and then choosing ADD TO FAVORITES from the bookmark menu or button. You can also arrange your favorite sites into folders.
>
> To retrace your steps after an Internet search, use the HISTORY feature of your browser (found as a button on the toolbar in *Explorer*). This is useful if you visited a site recently but can no longer recall its address or how you found it.

This ability to copy the work of others has led some people to ask legislators to place restrictions on copying, or "borrowing," information from the Internet.

Current legal interpretation of copyright law indicates that anything (such as text, graphics, or music) placed on the Internet by an individual or group is presumed to be copyrighted by its authors. The ease with which information can be copied and distributed via the Internet, however, makes it nearly impossible to enforce such a rigid interpretation of copyright law. The debate over rights is likely to continue, as commercial authors and publishers seek to receive just compensation for their work, and Internet boosters try to preserve the free flow of online information.

How do I use materials ethically on my own websites?

Students need to behave ethically and responsibly when using Web materials and when publishing their own work on the Web. In any piece of writing, including Web pages, be certain to cite all sources, including Internet sources, in such a way that readers can find the sources themselves. When writing your own Web pages, be sure to download only images or texts that are considered "freeware"—that is, that are offered by the site to users free of charge. If you are not certain, you should email the author or site sponsor for permission to either download the material or link to it from your own page.

What is plagiarism and how do I avoid it?

It is never acceptable to copy and paste source information from the Internet, or from anywhere else, into your own writing and present it as though you wrote it. To do so is to commit the academic offense called plagiarism. This is considered a serious offense in academia and may result in a failing grade not only for the paper, but also for the course. You must always paraphrase, or on rare occasions, quote, information and provide in-text

155

source documentation as well as a listing in your bibliography. If you wish to quote a portion of another's work in your own research paper, you may do so, but sparingly. Short quotations are acceptable with appropriate documentation. Long quotations (more than a few lines) are a distraction and can interrupt the flow of your argument. Writing that is pieced together from quotations is called "patch writing" and is very difficult to read. It is better to paraphrase information into your own words and then provide a source citation, linking the paraphrase to your works-cited or bibliography page.

One of the hazards of the digital age is that it is easier than ever to copy not only text files but also photographs, audio, and video. Ethical researchers must respect copyright and fair use laws.

What is fair use on a Web page?

If you wish to use a portion of another's work on a Web page you have created for academic purposes, the rule of thumb is that duplicating ten percent or less of the work constitutes fair use. To use more than this from a source, you must secure permission. Be sure to include the statement "Reprinted by permission" when you have secured permission. Of course, you should include appropriate citation information about the original source, for both material for which you have obtained permission and material that falls under fair use guidelines.

How do I locate information on specific sites, such as the Library of Congress website?

There are many government-sponsored websites with useful information that is widely available and free. For example, students may wish to use the Library of Congress online catalog: http://catalog.loc.gov/. This site lists e-resources and online catalogs that provide free databases, ejournals, and ebooks accessible at the Library of Congress.

How do I evaluate the information I find?

Once you have located relevant sources, you need to continue to build your subject matter knowledge base by reading those sources critically. One of your most important tasks as a writer in today's digital culture is to critically evaluate what you read. The tendency to believe everything you read, either in print or online, is a dangerous one. Some—though certainly not all—print sources undergo a process of peer review and evaluation before they are published. Peer-reviewed sources can generally be trusted to present information accurately. In contrast, the screening process for Internet materials is unpredictable. Many people who create websites or blogs have a sense of personal integrity, but others are less than forthright in the ways they use the medium to promote themselves or their viewpoints. Reading with a critical eye is always important, but it is particularly vital in dealing with Internet information.

How do I choose legitimate sources?

Because you will be relying on your sources to provide evidence and authority to support your thesis, you need to choose legitimate, credible sources. Your credibility or ethos as a writer may be at stake. Whether you are evaluating print or online material, choosing legitimate sources is a two-step process:

1. Decide whether or not the source is relevant and reliable enough to be worth reading.

2. Decide whether or not the source is worth using in your research paper.

For both print and online sources, you apply the same basic criteria for determining the source's legitimacy and applicability to your research project. Because Internet content is not regulated, however—anyone with a computer and online access can contribute—you will need to ask additional specialized questions to evaluate online research materials.

How do I decide if the print source is relevant?

Quickly scan the work to see whether or not the information it contains relates to your project. Ask yourself if the source addresses the topic you are researching. Sometimes a title will mislead you; checking subheadings in articles and tables of contents in books can help you see whether a source is actually about another topic entirely or only a narrow aspect of your topic. If a source is not relevant, move on.

How do I know if the book or journal's publisher is reliable?

Ask the following questions to help decide if the book or journal is reliable: Who is the sponsoring organization or publisher? Is the article in a popular magazine like *Vanity Fair* or a scholarly journal like the *Journal of Behavioral and Social Sciences*? If the publisher is an academic press or professional society, you can generally trust the source

---

How do I decide whether a print source is reliable?

The mere fact that something has been published does not guarantee its veracity or accuracy. For this reason, efficiently perusing print sources with an eye toward deciding whether they are legitimate and relevant to your topic is essential. You will need to evaluate the publisher or sponsor, the author, the work's timeliness, and cross references by asking critical questions about the source. In addition, you will need to evaluate the content's tone and language, looking for potential biases.

to be reliable for use in an academic paper. If it is a piece from the popular press, such as a newspaper or magazine, you would want to be careful about using the information as a source for a scholarly paper. For many college papers, the popular press—and particularly major newspapers like *The New York Times*, or news magazines like *Time* or *Newsweek*—can certainly be useful, particularly as background information, but be on the lookout for bias, in which a writer's, editor's, or publisher's personal opinion clouds the narrative and precludes objectivity. Generally you can rely on the information found in publications produced by academic entities. No information, however, regardless of its publisher or sponsoring agency, should be accepted without critical evaluation.

There are literally hundreds of periodicals published each year, but some are more scholarly and reliable than others. Take this into account when quoting from secondary sources.

What do I know about the author of the article or book?

Ask the following question to determine authorship: Who is the actual author of the material? Books and journals may include an "About the Author" section, or the author's affiliation may appear on the title page. If no biographical data are provided, you may want to seek additional information to confirm an author's credentials—either at the library, within the sponsoring publication, in a biographical reference text, or via an Internet search. The sponsoring organization or publisher may provide the author with some degree of credibility; we assume, for example, that writers for *The Wall Street Journal* or the *Chicago Tribune* have appropriate credentials.

How timely is the article or book?

Ask the following question to determine timeliness: When was the article or book published? In many fields, the timeliness of information is as important as the information itself. For example, if you are researching a medical topic, you want to be certain that your sources are current. With print sources, you need to be especially careful about when a piece was written. Months or even years may go by between when something is discovered and when it finally appears in print. In rapidly changing fields, access to current information is crucial.

What other works are cross-referenced in the article or book?

Ask the following questions to determine cross-referencing: Is the source you are looking at cited in other works on the subject? Is the author cited in other works? You can sometimes make decisions about a work's credibility by considering how—and how often—the work is cited by other sources. You may find that one author's name comes up repeatedly in references and discussions. That author is probably an expert on the topic; it would be worth your while to find material written by that person. Likewise, once you have identified a source as reliable, you can use the references to other sources included in it to locate additional research material.

How do I decide whether an Internet source is reliable?

The same general criteria are used to evaluate both websites and print sources. An additional challenge in evaluating electronic material is that some of the questions you will need to ask—such as who an author or sponsoring organization is and when the site was published or last updated—may be difficult to answer because the information is hard to find, intentionally hidden or vague, or, in the most extreme cases, just not there.

How do I find out about the site's publisher or sponsor?

Ask the following questions about the publisher: Who is the site's publisher or sponsor? How credible is that person or group? What is their agenda or purpose? Well-known academic organizations and trustworthy commercial sources (such as publishers of reputable online journals, magazines, or newspapers) are generally considered reliable. The viability as an academic research source of any sponsor that falls outside of this relatively finite group is questionable, however, and you will have to do additional work to confirm who the sponsor is and where the site originates. Certainly any site for which you cannot identify a sponsor should be discarded as a source for a research project. Even when you can confirm the existence of the sponsoring organization of a website, it can be hard to tell much about the group. One clue to the nature of the sponsoring organization is the URL itself. Internet conventions have been established to assign a standardized tag to Web addresses, called a domain type. Domain types tell you something about the nature of the sponsoring organization. Looking at the domain type of a website will help you to understand the purpose behind the page—whether educational

How do I decide if the Internet source is relevant?

Ask the following question to determine relevance: Do the title and subtitle of the online source suggest that it addresses your research topic and questions? Although titles and subtitles are a good initial indicator, remember that titles of online sources, like those of print sources, can be misnomers. An "About This Site" or "About This Organization" link is especially worth reading because it functions as a mission statement for the website's sponsoring organization, and it can also serve as a map for the site's contents.

(.edu) or commercial (.com), for example. These distinctions between domains are important, because they can give you indications about a website's reliability as a source.

How do I find out about the site's author?

Ask the following question to determine authorship: Is there an identifiable author, and is he or she credible as an expert on your topic? Many websites include either a biographical blurb about an author or an "About the Author" page. The sponsoring organization itself may also provide some level of author credibility. Keep in mind, however, that for Internet sources you may need to do additional research to clarify your evaluation of an author. If you have any doubt about an author's authority, trustworthiness, or possible biases on a given issue, you can and should use his or her name and whatever limited biographical information you obtain from the original source to investigate further—either via the library or by using an online search engine like *Google*.

Is the source an open-access, interactive forum, such as an online bulletin board, newsgroup, wiki, chat room, or blog? Assessing the reliability of authors in an interactive forum can be difficult. Those who enter into such forums are usually individuals who have an interest in, and an opinion about, the topic; occasionally you may find an expert on the topic with professional credentials, but usually you will find casual participants like yourself expressing subjective, and in many cases unsupported, viewpoints. Like the information you find on an open source encyclopedia such as *Wikipedia*, the opinions you encounter and share in these forums can be helpful for generating ideas and discovering interesting areas for further research, but they will not be much help as sources for a research paper. As a general rule, verify any information you find in such sources with at least one or two other reliable information sources.

What other sites are cross-referenced?

Ask the following questions about cross-referencing: Is there a Works Cited section or some other kind of references list? Are there footnotes or endnotes? Are there any hyperlinks within the text? Check out any referenced sources to confirm the site's credibility. On many commercial websites, hyperlinked phrases are embedded in the main text. Evaluating these references can reveal the level of scholarship and support the author has for his or her position, as well as the site or author's stances or biases; ideally, it can guide you to other related online information on your topic.

How useful and/or legitimate are the sites the source offers as links? What outside sources link to the site under consideration, and are they credible? In addition to fully evaluating a website's contents, look to see what other sources link to the site and what other sites it links to, as this can speak to a source's reliability. If the links seem to indicate biases or credibility issues, the source should probably be rejected for academic research purposes.

THE TERM OR RESEARCH PAPER

What is a term or research paper?

Academic papers or projects vary in scope, depending on the particular task or assignment. In some cases, students are asked to read and write about an issue using a single book or article for source information. In other cases, students are expected to conduct research, either primary research that includes experiments or secondary research that includes numerous sources of varying type, for an entire semester. The culmination of the research is a written paper, often called either a term paper or research paper. The process of writing a term paper does not differ markedly from the process of writing any other paper. The difference between a term paper and most essays is that you will be using information from a variety of sources, in addition to your own ideas, as support for your thesis in a term paper.

How do I decide what to write about?

The research process often begins with a question or a troubled feeling about something experienced, read, or observed. Research questions can also be found in the textbooks you are using for your classes. Alternately, the research process may

A solid research (or term) paper combines research from secondary sources with the student's own ideas and interpretations.

begin with a specific assignment from a professor. Your professor may set up the problem or question for you and may expect your writing to follow a conventional pattern based on the discipline. For example, if you are assigned to do a lab report, there will typically be a lab experiment to conduct in order to answer a specific question. The lab report itself will be written in a standardized format or genre. Once you determine which writing format is appropriate, you can make use of conventions of the discipline to help you generate your paper.

How can I paraphrase sources appropriately and avoid plagiarism?

As you take notes on sources, you will often record them in the form of paraphrases. The objective of paraphrasing is to present an author's ideas clearly and accurately, using your own words and phrases in place of the words and phrases of the author. This important academic skill deepens your understanding of the author's ideas. It also helps you to avoid plagiarism, which is the unauthorized or misleading use of the language and thoughts of another author.

What is the process used to write a term paper or research paper?

If you have never done a research project before, you may be overwhelmed at the thought of such a large and complex task. If you break the job down into smaller parts, however, it will seem much more manageable. Formulating a time frame in which to complete your research project will help. If your instructor has not given you deadlines, set your own dates for accomplishing specific tasks.

For a major project, allow at least three to four weeks for a focused search. As you begin to work in the library and on the Internet, you will see that searching and reading are time-consuming. Plan to spend one or two hours in the library and/or on the Internet

---

What are some guidelines for effective paraphrasing?

There are several ways to paraphrase text from another source, including:

1. Place the information in a new order.
2. Break the complex ideas into smaller units.
3. Use concrete, simple vocabulary in place of technical jargon.
4. Use synonyms for words in the source.
5. Accompany each important fact or idea in your notes with the source author and page number. Use that information to identify the paraphrase.
6. Incorporate the paraphrase smoothly into the grammar and style of your own writing by using a signal phrase.

each day for the first month of your research project. After that, you may find that you can spend less time. If your project involves primary research, allow one to two weeks for designing, conducting, and analyzing the primary research. Schedule at least one to two weeks for preliminary writing and drafting. If you are a slow writer, you will need more time.

To make sense of your subject and answer your starting questions, you will need to spend time studying and evaluating your sources, brainstorming, and prewriting. Eventually you should be able to express your understanding of the subject in a working thesis statement, which will control the shape and direction of the research paper and provide the readers with a sense of the paper's main idea or argument.

Finally, give yourself enough time to plan, organize, and write a first draft and then several revisions. You need time to outline and construct your argument, using source information to reinforce or substantiate your findings in a clearly documented way. Most students need one to two weeks to organize and write a rough draft and an additional week to revise, edit, and proofread. Many research projects take an entire college term to complete.

How can I pace myself when writing a term paper?

The following sample schedule suggests a paradigm one might use to research and write a term paper. Pacing oneself is a good way to avoid rushing one's work, which can result in mistakes and poor organization.

Week 1

Select a preliminary research topic.

Articulate starting questions.

Begin background research.

Schedule a time frame.

Begin to focus the topic.

Week 2

Build a working bibliography by using online library catalogs, databases, and the Internet.

Begin to locate library and Internet sources.

Week 3

Read, evaluate, and take notes on sources.

Print out or save to a file information from the Internet.

Write down complete bibliographical information and make note of URLs.

Week 4

Conduct any primary research.

Complete the reading, evaluation, and paraphrasing of sources.

Identify gaps in the research and find more sources if necessary.

Week 5

Begin preliminary writing by summarizing key information.

Brainstorm on the topic and direction for the paper's argument.

Write a few possible thesis statements.

Week 6

Write a working thesis statement.

Sketch an outline of the paper.

Find more sources as needed to support the thesis.

Week 7

Write a rough draft.

Keep careful track of sources through accurate citations, taking care to distinguish quotations and paraphrases.

Write a References or Works Cited list.

Week 8

Revise and edit the rough draft.

Spell-check and check sentence structure and usage for correctness.

Check documentation of sources and in-text citations.

Solicit peer review of the draft.

Revise according to any peer reviews or instructor comments.

How do I decide what my stance or main point is going to be?

Once your research is complete, you will want to write a thesis that states for readers the central idea that your paper will argue. It is not unusual for the working thesis statement to be revised during the actual writing process. Many research papers argue a position. Your instructor may require that your thesis (and thus your research paper) have an argumentative edge. If so, make sure that you have taken a stand that can be supported through arguments in the paper. If your research paper is informational rather than argumentative, your thesis should reflect the fact that you are reporting data rather than taking a stand on an issue. Neither type of research paper is inherently better; the two types are simply different. Your thesis statement should clearly tell readers what direction your paper will take. Readers should not be surprised at the end by a position that was not acknowledged up front in the paper's introduction.

What is a thesis statement and how do I write one?

A thesis statement concisely identifies the topic and main point of a piece of writing. Many writers like to formulate a working thesis statement early in the writing process. Your working thesis statement should ideally have two parts: the first part defines the specific focus to be covered in the paper, and the second part makes a strong point about the topic. An effective thesis also provides the reader with a blueprint for the direction the paper will take. In other words, the thesis not only states the writer's opinion on the topic but also indicates how the writer intends to support that opinion. When evaluating and revising your working thesis, ask yourself these questions: Does my thesis define a specific topic? Does it make a strong point about the topic? Does it provide a blueprint for the paper's development?

How do I plan a structure for my term paper?

In addition to constructing an effective thesis, you will need to revisit your rhetorical stance. Your purpose for writing the paper and your anticipated readers, plus the ways you want to appeal to them, will influence what you include and how you arrange the information in your paper. By

Deciding on a thesis for your paper can be difficult, but it might be easier if you allow your thesis to change as you discover facts through your research.

far, the most frequently used principle of organization in college writing is logic. With any logical organizational pattern, you are providing your reader with a familiar way of ordering experience, whether through the classic five-part method, specific patterned genres like proposals or lab reports, or some other logical pattern. Reviewing possible patterns at this point will help you construct an organizational plan.

How do I write an outline?

Once you have decided which organizational pattern best suits your working thesis, you may find it useful to construct an outline for your paper. You need not be overly concerned with formal outline structure at this point, unless your instructor stipulates a particular outline format. An outline should serve as a guide as you write—not a constraint that confines and limits your thinking. You may need to change your outline several times as you make new discoveries during drafting.

What is a formal outline?

A formal outline is typically structured in a conventional hierarchy, with numbered and lettered headings and subheadings. A formal outline can be either a topic outline, in which words or phrases are used, or a sentence outline, in which complete sentences are used.

Formal Outline Pattern

Thesis Statement

I. First main idea
   A. First subordinate idea
      1. First example or illustration
      2. Second example or illustration
         a. First supporting detail
         b. Second supporting detail
   B. Second subordinate idea
II. Second main idea
etc.

What is an informal outline?

Informal outlines are not structured as rigidly as formal ones. For example, in a formal outline, you are not allowed to have a number one subheading unless there is also a number two subheading. Informal outlines allow you to create any hierarchies you like, without paying close attention to issues of format.

Informal Outline Example

Thesis Statement

First main idea
Subordinate idea

First example
An illustration
Second main idea
Second example
etc.

How do I write a draft of my term paper?

There is no one right way to compose a first draft of your paper. As they develop their own writing-process knowledge, writers also develop procedures that work for them. One of the best ways to get started is to simply freewrite at your computer, jotting down in an uncensored fashion all of the thoughts that come to you. You might also want to transcribe into a computer file any notes you have taken while reading. Please be aware that composing a first draft is seldom a neat, orderly process. Composing may proceed in fits and starts, including periods of incubation and illumination alternating with periods of further preparation and verification.

How do I use the building-block method of drafting?

Many writers first compose a skeleton of the finished text and then expand it by adding new arguments, supporting examples and evidence, or illustrative details—the "building blocks" of a text. Some writers like to write their central paragraphs—the middle blocks of a text—first and add the introductory and concluding blocks later. You can decide which blocks will be easiest and write those blocks first, saving the more difficult parts for last. Once you have a preliminary draft, you can return to your text to amplify sections, one block at a time. To create blocks, you can use transcribed notes and outline documents. Use the headings in your outline to expand and build your text. CUT and PASTE text from your notes to place under the headings; then rewrite and amplify the text to create blocks. In this way, you avoid having to retype information from your notes as you compose.

How do I use the top-down method of drafting?

You may prefer to work from the beginning of your paper straight through to the end. You can use your working thesis statement and the corresponding organizational plan to compose in this way. Type or COPY and PASTE your working thesis statement into a new document. Your thesis statement can provide a blueprint for composing. With the thesis statement at the top of your screen, begin writing your draft, following the blueprint suggested by your thesis. Remember, your working thesis is just that—working. You can revise it at any time. Be flexible and open to new directions that may occur to you as you write.

How do I avoid writer's block?

Each writer develops his or her own writing rhythms. You need to discover what your rhythms are. If you find yourself "blocked" as a writer, set your work aside for a few hours or even a few days. If you cannot put the work aside for this long, at least get up and stretch; make yourself a cup of coffee or grab a bottle of juice before returning to your draft. Coming to it again fresh may give you renewed energy. If you find the writing is flowing well, try to keep at it—writing often takes on a life of its own and generates its own momentum. Finally, do not expect perfection from a first draft. Remember that writing is essentially rewriting: everything you write should undergo extensive revision in a continuous cycle of writing, revising, editing, and writing again.

Every writer's worst fear is getting "blocked." To get your creative juices flowing againg, try taking a break from your paper.

What are some questions I can ask myself to make sure my research paper is on track?

Focus

- Do I have a clearly stated thesis that controls the content?
- Do all the major points refer back to and support my thesis?
- Are all the examples and illustrations relevant to my point?

Coherence

- Are individual sentences and paragraphs held together by transitions?
- Are the transitions I have used the best available?
- Have I avoided overusing any transitions?

Organization

- Are the major points arranged in the most effective order?
- Are my strongest arguments placed near the end?
- Are the supporting points arranged to best advantage?
- Have I followed through with the organizational pattern I selected?

Development

- Is my thesis adequately supported?
- Are my major points backed up by specific details and examples?
- Is there at least one paragraph for each major point?

- Are my paragraphs developed proportionately?

Tone

- Is my tone appropriate to my rhetorical stance and consistent throughout?
- Do my language choices reflect my intended tone?
- Have I eliminated contractions and first-person pronouns if the piece is formal?

Format

- Does the "look" of my text help convey its meaning?
- Is the font I have used readable and appropriate to the topic?
- Are the headings descriptive and helpful in orienting the reader?
- Are the graphics appropriate and meaningful?

How do I edit and proofread the term paper draft?

During editing, you concentrate on refining words and sentences. The goal of editing is to make writing easier to read. Like a car buff putting the final finish on a classic automobile, an editor "finishes" a piece of writing—in general, refining what has been done and making it aesthetically pleasing as well as functional. In academia, paying close attention to editing is particularly important. Your credibility as a writer, your ethos, suffers when you are careless about editing. Your grade in a course may also suffer. Proofreading is the final phase in rewriting. At this stage of the process, academic writers look closely for distracting punctuation and mechanical errors that will interfere with the reader's understanding. By proofreading after revising and editing, you can concentrate on details related to manuscript preparation, such as typographical errors, missing words, and irregular spacing, as well as errors in punctuation or documentation that you may have missed in earlier stages.

How do I revise the term paper draft?

To be a skillful reviser, you must put yourself in the place of your reader. When you read your own work, however, you may have trouble seeing what you have actually written. Instead, you may see only what you *intended* to write. You need to shift roles from writer to reader when you review your writing.

If possible, allow at least a day between the time you finish a draft and the time you read it over to revise, edit, and proofread. You will be astonished at how much more clearly you can view your writing if you take a break from working on it. If you are facing a tight deadline, even several hours away from the work can be helpful. Try to schedule more than one session for revising. During revision, you concentrate on making the piece focused, organized, and well developed.

What critical editing and proofreading questions should I ask myself when reviewing my paper for errors?

Sentence Structure

- Are all of my sentences complete?
- Have I avoided both comma splices and run-on sentences?
- Do paired elements have parallel structures?

Wordiness

- Have I avoided using unnecessary words, such as *in order to* instead of simply *to*?
- Have I replaced two-word and three-word phrases, such as *new innovation* and *repeating recurrence,* where one word is sufficient?

Repetition

- Have I avoided excessive use of a single word?
- Have I avoided repetition of a single idea that is not the thesis?

Verb Usage

- Have I primarily used active rather than passive voice?
- Have I replaced overused, general verbs with more vivid, specific verbs where possible?

Proofreading

- Is my end punctuation correct?
- Is my internal punctuation correct?
- Have I used quotation marks appropriately?
- Have I used other punctuation marks appropriately?
- Is my spelling correct?
- Are my mechanics correct?

DOCUMENTATION

What is documentation?

Providing a documentation trail that leads back to the original sources is a feature that distinguishes scholarly or academic writing from writing found in the popular press. Scholars and researchers in all disciplines base their own work on the work that others have done in the past. The thread of knowledge can be traced from one scholar to another. In academic writing, providing readers with evidence of that thread of knowledge is essential, not only so that readers can trace the thread if they so desire, but also to let them know that the information is from reliable sources.

> ## What are the commonly used documentation styles in academia?
>
> **A** documentation style or format denotes the customary way in which the thread of knowledge within a research article is tracked. The documentation style or format used by a researcher will vary by discipline. The American Psychological Association (APA) style is commonly used in the social sciences. The Modern Language Association (MLA) style is commonly used in the humanities, particularly languages and literature. The Council of Science Editors (CSE) style is used in the sciences. *The Chicago Manual of Style* (CMS) is often used by writers in business, communications, journalism, and economics. Even though the formats will vary from style to style, the guiding principles are the same: 1. Show readers that you are using source information within the text itself by providing in-text citations or footnote numbers; 2. Provide readers with complete bibliographical information so that they can find the source should they wish to do so.

What is APA style?

The documentation style commonly employed in the social sciences was developed by the American Psychological Association (APA). Detailed documentation guidelines for APA style are included in the *Publication Manual of the American Psychological Association*, 6th ed. (Washington, DC: APA, 2010). Since the currency of information is critical in the social sciences, APA style for in-text citation identifies each source by the author's name and the date of publication, located in parentheses within the text. The date of publication is also emphasized in the References list, which appears at the end of a research paper. The References list in APA style is alphabetical by the primary author's last name.

APA in-text citation:

As Hacking (1995) points out, many recent publications discuss how memories are formed in patients with multiple personality disorders.

APA References listing for a book:

Hacking, I. (1995). *Rewriting the soul: Multiple personality and the sciences of memory.* Princeton, NJ: Princeton University Press.

What is MLA style?

The Modern Language Association (MLA) documentation style has been adopted by many scholars in the fields of language and literature (Joseph Gibaldi, *MLA Handbook for Writers of Research Papers*, 7th ed., New York: MLA, 2009). The MLA style consists of two parts: 1. In-text citations (in parentheses), which include the author's last name and the page number of the source information; 2. A list of works cited, arranged alphabetically by authors' last names, found at the end of the research paper.

MLA in-text citation:

According to Coogan, service learning is a way for students to affect social change in their communities (128).

MLA Works Cited listing for a journal article:

Coogan, David. "Service Learning and Social Change: The Case for Materialist Rhetoric." *College Composition and Communication* 57.4 (2006): 127–35. Print.

What is CSE style?

There is no one uniform system of citation within the sciences. Various disciplines tend to follow their own styles, typically developed by their professional societies. Many scientists, however, now use the guide created by the Council of Science Editors (CSE), as found in *Scientific Style and Format: The CSE Manual for Authors, Editors, and Publishers*, 8th ed. (Reston, VA: Council of Science Editors in cooperation with The Rockefeller University Press, 2014).

CSE in-text citation:

Much can be learned by studying the expression of wolves[3].

CSE References page entry for a journal article:

3. Schenkel R. Expression studies on wolves. Behavior. 2007;1: 81–129

What is Chicago Manual of Style (CMS) style?

Source citations in business, communications, journalism, and economics typically follow the guidelines outlined in *The Chicago Manual of Style*, 16th ed. (Chicago: The University of Chicago Press, 2010). This two-part system uses footnotes or endnotes and a bibliography to provide publication information about sources quoted, paraphrased, summarized, or otherwise referred to in the text of a paper. Footnotes appear at the bottom of the page; endnotes appear on a separate page at the end of the paper. The Bibliography, like the Works Cited list in the MLA documentation style, is an alphabetical listing by author of all works cited in the paper

CMS in-text citation:

In *A History of Reading*, Alberto Manguel asserts that "we, today's readers, have yet to learn what reading is."[1]

CMS footnote for a book:

1. Manguel, Alberto, *A History of Reading* (New York: Viking, 1996), 23.

What Latin abbreviations are commonly used in writing?

Below is a list of abbreviations you will often see used in English text.

Abbreviation	Full Text	Meaning
A.D.	*anno Domini*	in the year of the Lord

Abbreviation	Full Text	Meaning
B.C. or B.C.E.		"before Christ" or "Before Common Era"
c. or ca.	*circa*	around
C.E.	"Common Era"	(used frequently now in lieu of A.D.)
cf.	*confer*	bring together or compare
cp.	*compare*	compare
CV	*curriculum vitae*	course of life
e.g.	*exempli gratia*	for example
et al.	*et alii*	and others
etc.	*et cetera*	and the rest
ff.	*foliis*	and following
i.a.	*inter alia*	among other things
ibid.	*ibidem*	in the same place, book.
id.	*idem*	the same
i.e.	*id est*	that is
n.b.	*nota bene*	note well
op. cit.	*opere citato*	the work cited
Ph.D.	*Philosophiae Doctor*	Doctor of Philosophy
pro tem	*pro tempore*	for the time being
p.s.	*post scriptum*	after what has been written
re	*in re*	concerning
sic.	*sic erat scriptum*	thus it was written
viz.	*videlicet*	namely
vs.	*versus*	against

ESSAYS AND ESSAY EXAMS

How do I write in good essay form?

An essay is a short literary composition on a particular theme or subject, usually written in prose. Essays can be argumentative, analytic, speculative, or interpretive. One of the most common formats used in academic writing is the five-paragraph essay. The first paragraph serves as an introduction, the next three paragraphs develop the body of the essay, and the final paragraph is the conclusion. The thesis statement typically comes at the end of the introductory paragraph. Of course, there will be many variations of this format, depending on the topic, the purpose of the piece, and its intended audience, but the five-paragraph essay is a good place to begin.

What is an essay exam?

Many instructors judge students' success in a course by how well they are able to analyze and apply course material in a timed essay exam. Students are expected to learn the material well enough to be able to remember and write about it without access to notes or textbooks. They are given an essay prompt and then asked to write about it for a specified period of time. Key to success in an essay exam is not only the student's knowledge

Essay exams are quite challenging because they require students to not only know the material but also to communicate their answers in original, well-thought-out prose within a certain time limit.

of the subject being covered, but also his or her ability to assess what the question is asking and then to write a cogent response that is structurally and grammatically correct.

How do I prepare for an essay exam?

You can prepare by keeping up with course assignments and discussions on a daily basis throughout the term. You should attend class and read your textbooks carefully, looking for key ideas and arguments. Pay close attention to chapter summaries, subheadings, and key terminology. Write the key ideas and terms down in a notebook for later review. When your instructor lectures, do not write down everything; rather listen for and record main points and ideas that show relationships. Before the exam, review your notes, paying particular attention to your lists of key ideas and terms. Many students find that organizing a study group to discuss and review the course materials is helpful. Avoid the last-minute cram session, which seldom works. Instead, pace your studying over several days and try to get a good night's sleep so that you will be fresh for the exam itself.

How do I attend to the writing process when writing an answer to an exam question??

The first step in succeeding on an exam question is to analyze it carefully. The question itself will guide the organization of your response. An essay question will ask you to focus on a specific issue; address that issue rather than cataloging everything you learned from the course. If the exam contains more than one question, determine how much time you have to devote to each question so that you do not run out of time. You might want to prepare a brief outline of the points you want to cover in your answer. Begin your response with a thesis statement to capture the main thrust of your response. In subsequent paragraphs elaborate with examples and details. Try to cover the most important points first, leaving the less important ones for last. Remain focused as you draft your response. When you read over your essay, look for the flow of your argument. Perhaps insert transitional words or phrases that will help your instructor follow your argument. Add more examples if needed. Your instructor will not expect your writing to be perfect in a timed writing situation. He or she will, however, expect your exam response to be readable and clear. If possible, write your response in pencil so that you can easily erase and correct errors. Take a few minutes to proofread and also to check your penmanship. If your response is unreadable, your instructor cannot evaluate it fairly.

What should I do to write successful essay exam responses?

To write successful responses to essay questions:

1. Show an understanding of the question by including a thesis statement at the beginning of the response.
2. Organize the response so as to present ideas in a logical progression that supports the thesis.
3. Use the specific details, facts, or analyses called for in the question.
4. Show independent thoughts and insights in the response.
5. Conclude with a brief sentence that sums up the gist of the response.
6. Evaluate, revise, and edit the response as time allows.

WRITING IN SCIENCES AND TECHNOLOGY

What is science writing?

In the Western world, the sciences hold an authoritative position and are a dominant force in our lives. The sciences have been enormously successful at formulating and testing theories related to phenomena in the natural and physical world. These theories have been used to solve physical and biological problems in medicine, industry, and agriculture. Generally, the sciences have been divided into life sciences (such as biology and botany), physical sciences (such as physics and chemistry), and earth sciences (such as geology and geography). Scientific insights and methods have also been carried over to fields of applied science and technology, such as computer science and engineering. Science writing seeks to convey the results of scientific research. Scientific research, broadly defined, is systematic inquiry designed to further our knowledge and understanding of a subject. Scientists communicate to each other the information they discover and revise theories in light of new information that comes to their attention; scientists interpret their experience and communicate those interpretations to others through writing. This is how learning proceeds both for all of us as individuals and for human beings together as we search for knowledge and understanding of our world.

What is observation in the sciences?

The motivation or impetus for much scientific research is an observed event or experience that challenges our existing ideas and promotes inquiry. In the context of existing theories, such an event is incongruous and thus sparks in the researcher's mind a question or problem to be investigated. The researcher must be prepared to recognize the inconsistency and see its importance. Therefore, he or she must be familiar with current theories and concepts about the natural and physical world. In general, the aim of scientific writing is to improve the relationship between our ideas (theories and concepts about the world) and our actual experiences (observations of the world).

What is hypothesis testing in the sciences?

On the basis of a scientist's prior knowledge and preparation, he or she formulates a hypothesis to account for the observed phenomenon that presents a problem.

Arriving at a hypothesis takes effort on the part of the researcher. Brainstorming for possible hypotheses is an important component of research, because the researcher can creatively make conjectures based on prior experience. The researcher may have to test several possible hypotheses before deciding which one seems to account for the observed phenomenon. For example, Sir Alexander Fleming, an English biologist, hypothesized that the clear circle he observed around the bacteria he was studying had resulted from a contaminating microorganism in the culture. Fortunately for us, Fleming decided to study the phenomenon at length to discover the properties of this secretion on cultures of staphylococcus bacteria. As it turned out, the secretion was a variety of the fungus *Penicillium*, from which we now make the antibiotic penicillin. Fleming designed experiments that tested his hypothesis concerning the effects of *Penicillium* on bacteria and, eight months later, he wrote up and published his research findings, demonstrating through his scientific experiments that *Penicillium* was effective against bacteria.

What is the scientific method?

The following outline describes the systematic way scientists customarily proceed, often called the "scientific method." Using the scientific method, a researcher is able to integrate new data into existing theories about the natural and physical world.

1. The scientist formulates a question and develops a hypothesis that might shed light on the question posed.

2. On the basis of the hypothesis, the scientist predicts what should be observed under specified conditions and circumstances.

3. The scientist makes the necessary observations, generally using carefully designed, controlled experiments.

4. The scientist either accepts or rejects the hypothesis depending on whether or not the actual observations corresponded with the predicted observations.

What is critical scientific research?

Though much of the research conducted by scientists is an attempt to incorporate new data into existing theories, another type of scientific research, critical scientific research, attempts to challenge currently held beliefs and theories in an effort to im-

Part of the scientific method is testing hypotheses through experimentation and gathering of hard data.

prove them. Critical scientific research investigates the adequacy, or the sufficiency, of theories about the natural and physical world. In this context, the question asked is, How well do current theories actually explain the natural and physical world as we know and observe it? A particular field of science may operate for years under certain theoretical assumptions. For example, Newtonian physics, based on the theories of Isaac Newton, dominated the scientific world for some time, and thousands of scientists conducted regular experiments based on Newton's theories. When physicists encountered numerous phenomena that were incompatible with Newton's laws of physics, though, new theories became necessary. The physicist Albert Einstein challenged the agreed-upon Newtonian physics by presenting an alternative system that accounted for more of the observed data. Most physicists have now adopted Einstein's more comprehensive theories, or have gone on to develop and adopt new theories. This process of challenging and replacing scientific theories is one way scientific fields advance their knowledge and understanding of the natural or physical world. So scientific thought progresses both by regular scientific observation and experimentation, using widely accepted theories and beliefs, and by critical scientific research that challenges those widely held theories and suggests new theories.

What is replicability in the sciences?

Scientists who have created and tested a hypothesis must then report their findings to other scientists in writing, as Fleming did by publishing his experimental results in the British *Journal of Experimental Pathology*. The goals of publishing one's findings include having other scientists accept the hypothesis as correct, communicating knowledge, and/or stimulating further research and discussion. A report of the research must necessarily include a careful, accurate description of the problem, the hypothesis, and the method (experimental design) used to test the hypothesis, in addition to the researcher's experimental findings and conclusions. Other scientists then test the validity and reliability of the findings by attempting to repeat the experiment described by the researcher. A carefully designed and executed scientific experiment should be accurately described in writing so that other scientists using a similar experimental process can replicate it. The community of scientists as a whole then critiques the new research, deciding collectively whether or not it is good, sound research. To do this, other scientists will test the experiment's validity (Did it measure what the researcher said it would measure?), its reliability (Can it be repeated or replicated with similar results by other scientists?), and its importance (How does this experiment fit into a larger theoretical framework and what does it mean for our currently held assumptions and beliefs?). The forums of science, the professional organizations and journals, universities, scientific societies, and research laboratories combine to resolve scientific issues to the benefit of all scientists. The best research in the world will be of no consequence if the scientist is unable to clearly communicate his or her results to other scientists through writing.

What is paraphrasing?

Paraphrasing may be defined as restating or rewording a passage from a text, giving the same meaning in another form. Writers paraphrase from sources in order to present the source ideas without plagiarizing. Of course, always give proper attribution to the source, whether quoting or paraphrasing. The objective of paraphrasing is to present an author's ideas in your own words. When paraphrasing fails, it may be because the reader misunderstood the passage, the reader insisted on reading his or her own ideas into the passage, or the reader partially understood but chose to guess at the meaning rather than fully understanding it. To paraphrase accurately, you must first read closely and understand completely what you are reading. Here are five suggestions that will help you as you paraphrase:

1. Place the information found in the source in a new order.
2. Break the complex ideas into smaller units of meaning.
3. Use concrete, direct vocabulary in place of technical jargon found in the original source.
4. Vary the sentence patterns.
5. Use synonyms for the words in the source.
6. Give proper attribution to the source's author with a citation.

What are some examples of paraphrasing?

The examples below show acceptable and unacceptable paraphrasing:

Original Passage

During the last two years of my medical course and the period which I spent in the hospitals as house physician, I found time, by means of serious encroachment on my night's rest, to bring to completion a work on the history of scientific research into the thought world of St. Paul, to revise and enlarge *The Quest of the Historical Jesus* for the second edition, and together with Widor to prepare an edition of Bach's preludes and fugues for the organ, giving with each piece directions for its rendering. (Albert Schweitzer, *Out of My Life and Thought*. New York: Mentor, 1963, p. 94.)

A Poor Paraphrase

Schweitzer said that during the last two years of his medical course and the period he spent in the hospitals as house physician he found time, by encroaching on his night's rest, to bring to completion several works.

[Note: This paraphrase uses too many words and phrases directly from the original without putting them in quotation marks and thus is considered plagiarism. Furthermore, many of the ideas of the author have been left out, making the paraphrase incomplete. Finally, the student has neglected to acknowledge the source through a parenthetical citation.]

A Good Paraphrase

Albert Schweitzer observed that by staying up late at night, first as a medical student and then as a house physician, he was able to finish several major works, including a historical book on the intellectual world of St. Paul, a revised and expanded second edition of *The Quest of the Historical Jesus,* and a new edition of Bach's organ preludes and fugues complete with interpretive notes, written collaboratively with Widor (Schweitzer 94).

[Note: This paraphrase is complete and appropriate; it does not use the author's own words, except in one instance, which is acknowledged by quotation marks. The student has included a parenthetical citation that indicates to the reader the paraphrase was taken from page 94 of the work by Schweitzer. The reader can find complete information on the work by turning to the bibliography at the end of the student's paper.]

How do I write from scientific sources?

Reading actively and taking accurate and careful notes in the form of paraphrases and summaries are the first important techniques for working with scientific sources. Your reading notes will form the basis for all your subsequent writing about that particular source. There are three important approaches to source books and articles that result in three different kinds of writing. These are (1) summarizing the main points of the source book or article in condensed form, (2) synthesizing the information found in two or more related sources, and (3) critiquing the information found in one or more sources. When summarizing, the writer takes an entirely objective approach to the subject and the source. The writer of summaries is obliged to accurately record the author's meaning. In contrast, when synthesizing, you will approach your material with an eye to finding the relationships among sources. Your purpose will be to discern those relationships and

What should I include in an article critique?

When writing a critique of an article, include the following:

1. An introduction of the subject you wish to address and the source article you wish to critique: be sure to include a complete citation for the source.

2. A statement of your judgment about the issue in the form of a thesis: in that thesis statement, give your own opinion, which will be supported in the critique itself.

3. The body of the critique: first, briefly summarize the source itself; then review the issues at hand and explain the background facts and assumptions your readers must understand to share your judgment. Use the bulk of your critique (about two-thirds) to review the author's position in light of your judgment and evaluation.

4. Your conclusion: a reminder to the reader of your main points and the reasons you made them.

present them coherently and persuasively to your potential readers. Again, the process begins with the active reading of the sources. In the third kind of writing from sources, critiquing, the writer takes a critical or evaluative approach to a particular source. When writing critiques, you argue a point that seems important to you according to your own evaluation of the issues and ideas you have encountered in your sources. Your purpose for writing summaries will be different from your purpose for writing syntheses or critiques. Although the source or subject may remain the same, your approach to that source or subject can change, depending on your purpose. Using different approaches to the same sources will help you to understand those sources better.

How do I write a lab report?

In the sciences, the method by which an experimenter solves a problem is as important as the result the experimenter achieves. Guided by the scientific method, researchers investigate the laws of the physical universe by asking and answering questions through empirical research. A researcher must describe in great detail both the method used in the experiment and the results achieved. A report of the experimental findings will be based on the laboratory notes taken during the experiment. All researchers must keep written records of their work. In the natural sciences, such records generally take the form of a laboratory notebook. The researcher uses the notebook to keep a complete, well-organized record of every experiment and each experimental variable (phenomena not constant in the experiment). The researcher must record information in a clear, easy-to-understand format so that he or she (and coworkers) will have easy access to it when it is time to draw conclusions from the experiment.

Scientific experiments in college will typically be connected with a laboratory. For example, many courses in the physical sciences, such as chemistry or physics, are accompanied by laboratory sections for practical lab experimentation. Laboratory courses still involve writing. It is important to realize that the scientific method employed by laboratory researchers necessitates the careful, organized, and complete presentation of methods and results through written reports. (*See* Appendix J for an example of a lab report.)

How do I write a research report or a field report?

In research reports, scientists describe in detail research that they have conducted

A good lab report must contain accurate and precise details on both the experimental methods used and the empirical results of the experiment. Keeping thorough written records as you work is essential.

themselves in order to share their findings with the scientific world in general and thus advance knowledge in their field. Because it is important that scientists be able to replicate each other's research, a customary format for organizing research reports has developed that can be easily recognized by all scientists. In some scientific disciplines, empirical or experimental work is supplemented by field observations that occur outside the laboratory. For example, a biologist interested in moose behaviors might visit Yellowstone National Park and observe juvenile moose and their parents to determine whether maternal or paternal examples are imitated in feeding behaviors. The parts generally found in the research report are *Title, Abstract or Summary, Introduction, Materials and Methods, Results, Discussion and Conclusions, Literature or Works Cited*. These parts correspond generally to the scientific method:

1. The scientist formulates a question and develops a hypothesis that might possibly answer the question posed. [The hypothesis is typically posed in the research report *Introduction*.]

2. On the basis of the hypothesis, the scientist predicts what should be observed under specified conditions and circumstances. [The prediction of expectations is typically posed in the research report *Introduction*.]

3. The scientist makes the necessary observations, generally using carefully designed, controlled experiments. [The detailed description of the experiment is included in the *Materials and Methods* section of the research report.]

4. The scientist either accepts or rejects the hypothesis depending on whether or not the actual observations corresponded with the predicted observations. [The scientist's decision to accept or reject the hypothesis is generally included in the *Results* section of the research report. This section is typically followed by a *Discussion and Conclusion* section that interprets results for the readers.]

When writing a research report, you will not necessarily write it in the order that it finally appears. In fact, you may find it easiest to write the *Materials and Methods* section first, since it is here that you will describe in detail the experiment itself. The *Discussion and Conclusions* section is probably best written near the end, after you know

How do I write an engineering research report?

Although reports in technology and engineering have much in common with reports in the sciences, there are also some differences. In addition to the report of research, these other types of reports may be used in technology and engineering: problem analyses reports, recommendations reports, equipment evaluation reports, progress/periodic reports, and laboratory reports. The format of each report will vary depending upon its purpose and audience. Most, however, follow what is called the ABC format: Abstract, Body, Conclusion.

exactly what you want to say in your *Results* section. Other parts, like the *Abstract* and the *Works Cited*, can be incorporated near the end of your drafting process. Any primary data may be included in one or more appendixes, included immediately after the works cited list.

How do I write a scientific review paper?

In the scientific review, sometimes called a literature review, a writer analyzes for readers the present state of knowledge in an ongoing field of research as it has been reported in books and journals. The scientific review, therefore, interprets, organizes, and presents complex information to make it easily accessible to the reader. In the scientific review paper, a writer will argue a particular position with support from the literature and review the topic through paraphrase and summary as objectively as possible, without introducing any new primary data. Several library research principles and skills are important. These include:

1. A familiarity with library research tools, including databases, bibliographies, and indexes used in science and technology

2. The ability to understand and evaluate information and data from a variety of sources

3. The ability to paraphrase and summarize information and data in your own words

4. The ability to synthesize the gathered information and data into an organized presentation

5. The ability to employ the formal conventions of scientific review papers

How do I make my writing active?

Many science writers slow down their readers by using complex nouns in their sentences instead of the more active verbs that those nouns come from. For example, *decision* is the noun form (nominalization) of the verb *to decide*, and *invasion* is the noun form of *to invade*. Somehow writers have gotten the erroneous impression that the use of nominalizations makes their writing sound more important or official. Changing your verbs into nouns robs them of their power and motion, thus slowing the reader's progress. Wherever possible, change nominalizations to action verbs, as in the following examples:

The range land habitat of the kestrel *had the appearance of* being arid. [nominalization]

The range land habitat of the kestrel *appeared* arid. [revised with verb]

Another way that writing is slowed is through the use of the passive rather than the active voice. Although passive voice has a legitimate function, it is often overworked in science writing. To keep the pace of your writing moving along and to provide your readers with often essential information, try to use the active voice wherever possible. For example:

The question of seasonal variation in fiber composition in the pectoralis muscle *needs to be examined*. [passive verb]

We need to examine whether or not fiber composition varies by season. [revised to be active]

How can I avoid commonly misused words in science writing?

The following words are frequently misused in science writing:

It is correct to say "The kestrel population declined *because of* bad weather and a scarcity of food"; *because of* modifies the verb *declined*.

- *Due to*: Correctly used following a subject to attribute something to that subject, it acts as an adjective to modify a noun. Do not use *due to* when you mean *because of*, which modifies a verb to act like an adverb:

The kestrel's decreased weight is *due to* its lack of food during winter. [correct]

Due to bad weather, the kestrel population declined. [faulty]

Because of bad weather, the kestrel population declined. [revised; correct]

- *Compared to*: Correctly used to indicate an analogy between items that are essentially not alike:

He *compared* the small brown bats *to* a hibernating bear. [correct]

Compared to humans, bats have a very slow heart rate. [correct]

- *Compared with*: Correctly used when referring to the similarities and differences between things of the same type:

When *compared with* eagles, kestrels are more efficient fat-burners. [correct]

The teacher *compared* the paper written by Sally *with* the paper written by Mark. [correct]

- *Data, Criteria, Phenomena*: These words are all plural and generally take a plural verb.

The *data suggest* that birds of prey have excellent eyesight. [plural]

Several *criteria are used* to analyze the data. [plural]

We know that *the phenomena are* not unique. [plural]

In some fields, however, *data* is used in the singular as well. Check with your field's style manual for its suggested guidance on the issue.

The *datum* suggests that further research is needed. [singular]

The *data suggests* that further research is needed. [singular]

- *Amount/Number: Amount* refers to mass or quantity. Follow *amount* with the preposition *of* and a singular noun (*amount of ammonia*). *Number* refers to things that can be counted and is followed by the preposition *of* and a plural noun (*number of mice*).

- *Cite/Site: Cite* is a verb meaning to quote or use material from another source. The noun form of cite is *citation. Site* is a noun referring to a location.

  It is appropriate to *cite* your sources using a *citation*.

  The *site* of the field study is in Egypt's Valley of the Kings.

- *e.g., for example (Latin = exempli gratia)*: Scientists sometimes use the abbreviation *e.g.* prior to an example.

  Birds of prey, *e.g.,* hawks and falcons, have excellent vision.

- *Former/Latter: Former* means the first mentioned of two items; *latter* means the second mentioned of two. When you are referring to more than two items, use *last*.

  Mark and Hans are both scientists; the *former* is a physicist and the *latter* is a biologist. They are the *last* in their family to graduate college.

- *i.e., that is (Latin = id est)*: Scientists use *i.e.* as shorthand for *that is*.

  The study was conducted ethically, *i.e*, it conforms to guidelines for human subjects.

- *Media/Medium: Media* is the plural from of *medium*.

  The *media* are responsible for disseminating scientific information to the public. The *medium* of choice today is the Internet.

- *Utilize/Use: Utilize* is a verb meaning to put to use or make practical use of something. *Use* is a verb meaning to deploy something. Do not substitute utilize for use.

  Plants *utilize* sunlight for photosynthesis. The scientists *used* many tropical plants in their experiments.

(Please refer to the commonly misused words in social science writing, since there is considerable overlap. See also Appendix H for a listing of other commonly misused word pairs.)

How do I use punctuation correctly in science writing?

Following are some specific examples of punctuation problems encountered in science writing, but for detailed information on correct punctuation in general, please refer to the "Using Punctuation Correctly" chapter.

Commas are used in the following situations:

1. To separate a sentence's long introductory material from the rest of the sentence

2. To set off interrupting material from the rest of the sentence

Gary and Melinda checked on the crop's progress. The *former*, holding a clipboard, is a horticulturist, and the *latter*, checking out the leaves, is a botanical engineer.

3. To separate items in a series

4. To separate independent clauses joined by a conjunction (and, but, or, for, nor, yet)

Semicolons are used in the following three cases:

1. To join two independent clauses

2. To connect two independent clauses joined with a conjunctive adverb (however, nevertheless, moreover, furthermore)

3. As a super-comma in a series already containing commas:

The patients were given low-fat diets of complex carbohydrates; lean meats, fish, and poultry; fat-free dairy products.

Capitalization is used for:

1. The scientific names of Phylum, Class, or Family:

Most fish species are included in the group *Teleostei.*

2. The complete common name of a species:

Only three species, the *Ash-throated Flycatcher, Scrub Jay,* and *Plain Titmouse,* consistently provide high counts in the sampling period.

Italics (or underline) are used for:

1. Use italics for the scientific name of a genus, species, subspecies, or variety:

Herring sperm (*Clupea pallasii*) are inactive in sea water.

2. Use italics to indicate foreign words and phrases: *ad nauseum, in vitro, et alium*.

3. Use italics to indicate a word or phrase you wish to emphasize.

The depth at which a subject is placed into the chamber *can* alter your results.

Abbreviations:

1. Typically in science writing, terms of measurement in the text are abbreviated if they are preceded by a number. The same symbol is used for either singular or plural and no period is used:

1 hr (one hour)

12 hr (twelve hours)

3 l (3 litres); m = meter, min = minute, s = second, wk = week, yr = year, mo = month, da or d = day

2. Do not abbreviate the name of a unit of measure that follows a spelled-out number, as at the start of a sentence:

Ten litres were required for proper dosing.

3. A genus name can be shortened to the first letter of the genus if the name has been presented earlier in the paper:

We surveyed adult Nile crocodiles (*Crocodylus niloticus*) and two crocodiles from southern Mexico (*C. acutus* and *C. moreletii*).

Parentheses:

1. Use parentheses to indicate the scientific name when the common name of a species is mentioned for the first time.

2. Use parentheses to refer to information in a table or figure in the text: (see Figure 1) or (Table 2).

3. Use parentheses to enclose a comment or explanation that is structurally independent of the rest of the sentence:

Roby (1989) also used total body electrical conductivity (TOBEC) on the birds in his study.

4. Use parentheses to label enumerations within a paragraph: (1) (2)

5. Use parentheses for internal citations:

Fat content varies with age, sex, species, and nutrition (Sturkie, 1996).

Brackets:

Use brackets to enclose information within parentheses:

Migratory birds use fat as their main energy source (twice as much as carbohydrates [Schmidt-Nielsen, 1990]).

Numbers:

1. A decimal number of less than one should be written with a zero (0) preceding the decimal point:

   Twenty-five birds had a narrow range of weight and their value was much lower, 0.676.

2. Spell out a number that occurs at the beginning of a sentence:

   Fifteen of the birds were weighed with the feathers removed.

3. Numbers that modify an adjective should be written as a whole number and separated from the adjective with a hyphen:

   The weight of the male kestrels was monitored for a five-year period.

4. Numerical values of sample size are customarily identified by the letter n (or N):

   The variation in values was influenced by the position of the subject within the chamber (n=15).

5. Day of the month typically precedes the month. No commas are used:

   We monitored the male birds at site A from 10 July 2004 to 10 January 2005.

6. In most situations, use words for numbers one through nine and numerals for larger numbers. Treat ordinal numbers as you would cardinal numbers: *third, fourth, 33rd, 54th.*

Sometimes it is better to use a direct quotation than to paraphrase. In such instances, make sure you quote accurately, cite your source, and, if any of the text has been deleted or altered, use ellipses or brackets to indicate the changes.

How do I use direct quotations in science writing?

Most of the time you will use summaries and paraphrases to incorporate source material into your writing. Occasionally you will want to directly quote an author who has said something in a particularly succinct or memorable way. To incorporate direct quotations smoothly, observe the following principles. For guidelines specifically suited to your discipline, consult the style manual of your discipline.

1. Always follow a quotation with a citation, either a footnote or a parenthetical citation. Typically, you will want to introduce the quotation with a signal phrase to alert your reader that a quotation will follow:

   According to Barnes-Svarney and Svarney, "It is thought that the *Barosaurus*, or "heavy lizard," had the longest neck of any known dinosaur."[4]

2. Introduce quotations using a verb tense that is consistent with the tense of the quotation:

   The authors stated, "There is some disagreement as to the smallest dinosaur fossil yet found."[4]

3. Change a capital letter to a lower-case (or vice versa) within the quotation if necessary:

   All of the theropods "shared many adaptations specific to the catching, killing, eating, and digesting of meat."[4]

4. Use brackets for explanations or interpretations not in the original quotation:

   "If the impact had occurred perpendicular to Earth [straight down], most of the energy would have been directed into the planet's interior."[4]

5. Use an ellipsis (three spaced dots) to indicate that material has been omitted from the quotation. If an ellipsis occurs at the end of the sentence, place the period before the three spaced dots:

   "The material forced into the upper atmosphere … would have cooled the climate … effectively killing the remaining dinosaurs."[4]

6. Punctuate a direct quotation as the original was punctuated, but change the end punctuation to fit the context of your own sentence. For example, a quotation that ends with a period may require a comma when integrated into your own sentence.

7. Use a colon instead of a comma to introduce the quotation if the introductory material or signal phrase prior to the quotation is long.

8. When your quotations are four lines in length or less, surround them with quotation marks and incorporate them into your text. When your quotations are longer than four lines, set them off from the rest of the text by indenting five spaces from both right and left margins or ten spaces from the left margin only. You do not need quotation marks with block quotations.

How do I use graphics or visuals in science writing?

Sometimes you will find that you need to illustrate your work using graphics or visuals. Types of graphics include tables (usually showing quantitative data), figures (charts, graphs, or technical drawings), or illustrations (including photographs). You first need to determine whether or not your readers would benefit from the inclusion of a graphic. Sometimes repeating information in graphic form will help readers to remember it. The following principles may help you decide:

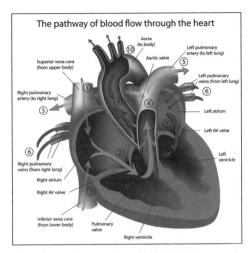

When discussing complex subjects it is often a good idea to use an illustration so that readers can better visualize what is being discussed.

1. Use a graphic when words alone cannot describe a concept or object adequately.

2. Use a graphic to summarize an important point.

3. Use a graphic when it can help to conveniently display complex information.

You also should determine what you want the graphic to accomplish and where it would best be included in your paper. When aligning your graphic, remember that the graphic should be easy to read and displayed with ample white space so that it stands out from the text background. You should refer at least once to each graphic, either directly or parenthetically, in the text itself. Ideally, the graphic should be placed on the same page in which it is mentioned and labeled with both a title and a source.

How do I label figures and tables correctly in science writing?

If you are using figures or tables in your science writing, you will need to decide on a standard numbering and labeling system. When your document has a variety of photographs, charts, illustrations, or tables, you should label them with captions that identify them all as *figures*. If they are all of one type, perhaps they are all tables, you can label them as such, e.g., (see Table 1, Table 2). Typically, prior to the graphic, you will introduce it in the text with a parenthetical phrase, e.g., (see Figure 12.1). Below the graphic itself, you will type a caption, e.g., *Figure 12.1: Rocket Velocity*. Captions should be consistent in style throughout the document. Consistency includes wording, level of detail, typography (font style and size), and layout. Your word processing software may assist you in generating automated captions. Captions are typically placed directly beneath the images they identify.

If your document requires only a few graphics or if they always appear within the text that discusses them, you may decide to include a descriptive caption beneath each image but choose not to use formal, numbered figure labels.

What are the typical parts included in scientific papers?

Title

Generally, title pages contain three kinds of identifying information: the title of the paper, the author identification, and course or company identification (including date). If you do not need a separate title page, put your name, date, and any other identifying information on the upper right-hand corner of the first page. Center the title on the first page three or four lines below the identifying information or, if you use a separate title page, one inch from the top of the page. The title should not be underlined, surrounded by quotation marks, or typed in capital letters. Leave three or four lines between your title and the beginning of the text. For longer documents, you may wish to type an outline or Table of Contents immediately after your title.

Numbering

Number each page starting with the first page of text after the title page, which would be numbered page 2. [Note: some styles omit the page number from page 1.] Place the numbers in the upper right-hand corners or centered at the bottom of the pages. Your word processing program will allow you to automatically number your pages and to suppress numbering on any pages where they are not needed. For example, numbering is generally not needed on the endnotes page or the references page. Rather, they can be identified with the appropriate heading centered one inch from the top of the page and followed by three or four blank lines. Some styles recommend headers along with the page numbers (for example, Hult p. 2).

Indentation

Use uniform indentation for all paragraphs (five spaces is standard). Indent long quotations (more than four lines long) five spaces from both right and left margins or ten spaces from the left margin only. Leave two spaces between each sentence and after a colon or semicolon. Divide words at the end of lines according to standard rules. Use your dictionary if you are unsure of where to divide a word.

The Abstract

An abstract is a very short summary of a paper, usually one-tenth to one-twentieth the length of the whole. The purpose of an abstract is to condense the paper into a few, succinct lines. The reader must be able to understand the essence of the paper from reading just the abstract, without actually reading the paper. Your abstract should cover the purpose of your paper as well as the major topics you discuss. To write an abstract, you will need to compress information into a few compact sentences. Even though the information in your abstract will necessarily be densely packed, it should still be readable and understandable.

The Endnotes Page

If your paper will have endnotes, type them on a separate page immediately after the text of your paper (and before the references page). Center the title, "Notes" or "Endnotes," one inch from the top of the page, and type it in capital and lower-case letters (not all capitals). Do not use quotation marks or underlining. Leave three or four blank lines between the title and the first line of your notes. Type the notes in consecutive order based on their appearance in the text. Indent the first line of the note five spaces from the left margin, type the superscript number, and leave a space before beginning the note. For any run-over lines of each note, return to the left margin.

The References Page

Center the title "References," or "Works Cited," and type it one inch from the top of the page in capital and lower-case letters (not all capitals). Do not use quotation marks or underlining. Leave three or four blank lines between the title and the first line of your references. The references themselves should be typed, double spaced, and listed in alphabetical order by the author's last name (or the title, if the author is not known). [Note: In the citation-sequence system, references are listed consecutively as they appear in the text.] The references page follows the last page of the body of your paper, or the endnotes page (if included), and need not be numbered. For the format of each citation on your references page, please refer to the style manual for your discipline. Many in the sciences use the CSE style manual (*Scientific Style and Format: The CSE Manual for Authors, Editors, and Publishers*, 8th ed., Reston, VA: Council of Science Editors in co-operation with The Rockefeller University Press, 2014).

The Annotated References List

In some cases it is helpful to provide your readers with more information about the sources you used in your research than is typically given in a references list. An annotated references list serves this purpose. To construct one, you would first compile all of your references, alphabetize them, and format them according to the documentation style for your discipline. Then, following each bibliographical entry, you would state in a sentence or two the gist of the source you had read and its relevance to your paper. An

---

What is the correct documentation format to use in science writing?

There is no uniform system of citation in the sciences and technology, but all disciplines follow either a journal style or a style guide (e.g., styles developed by the American Chemical Society and the American Medical Society). Many scientists use the guide created by the Council of Science Editors (*Scientific Style and Format: The CSE Manual for Authors, Editors, and Publishers*, 8th ed. Reston, VA: Council of Science Editors in cooperation with The Rockefeller University Press, 2014).

The sciences use in-text (internal) citation and list the references at the end of the text. How recently the source was published is important, so the year of publication is stressed in the citation. Entire journal articles rather than specific pages may be cited, and direct quotations are seldom used.

annotated references list can help your readers to decide which of your sources they would like to read themselves. It should not be difficult for you to annotate (that is, provide brief glosses) for sources that you have used to write your paper.

The Appendix

Material that may not be appropriate to the body of your paper may be included in an appendix. You may use the appendix for collations of raw data, descriptions of primary research instruments, detailed instructions, and so on. The appendix is located after the bibliography or references page and is clearly labeled. If you use more than one appendix, label them Appendix A, Appendix B, and so on. When referring to the appendix in the paper itself, do so in parentheses, e.g. (See Appendix B).

What is the Council of Science Editors (CSE) style for in-text citations?

The CSE style manual offers three alternative formats for in-text citations, each of which is linked to an end-of-paper references list:

1. The citation-sequence style, in which numbers are used within the text, assigned based on when the source was first cited. The numbers refer to end references.

2. The name-year style, in which in-text references consist of the last name of the author(s) and the year of publication, listed in parentheses.

3. The citation-name style, in which an alphabetical references list is created and numbered, and the number for each source is used within the text as a superscript, no matter where the in-text reference appears. This is the style used by the CSE manual. The models below use the citation-name style for in-text citation:

Temperature plays a role in the rate of gastric juice secretion[3].

Recent studies [3, 4, 8–10] show that antibodies may also bind to microbes and prevent their attachment to epithelial surfaces.

What is the CSE style for the references list?

The references list, found at the end of your scientific paper, contains all the sources actually used in the paper. The title of this page is "References," "Works Cited," or "Literature Cited." The purpose of the references list is to help readers find the materials you used in writing your paper. Therefore, you must give complete, accurate information. The following principles are generally accepted for the references list in the sciences and technology:

1. On the references or work-cited page, references are arranged in alphabetical order and may be numbered. (Note: The citation-sequence style proceeds consecutively, that is, in the order in which the sources appear in the text.)

2. Authors are listed by surnames and initials.

3. Generally the first word only of a title is capitalized, the title of an article is not enclosed in quotation marks, and the title of a book is not underlined.

4. Names of journals are often abbreviated.

5. The volume and page number system often resembles that found in the indexes (for example, 19: 330–360). Sometimes the volume number is in boldface type.

6. The year of publication appears either immediately after the author's name or at the close of an entry, depending upon the particular journal's publication style.

Book in CSE Style

Golub, E. S. 1987. Immunology: A synthesis. Boston: Sinaur Associates.

Article in CSE Style

Milleen, J. K. 1986. Verifying security. ACM Computing Surveys 16:350–354.

or

Milleen, J. K. Verifying security. ACM Computing Surveys 16:350–354; 1986.

See also Appendix K.

WRITING IN SOCIAL SCIENCES

What is social science writing?

Social sciences, such as psychology, anthropology, political science, sociology, economics, and education, have as their overall goal the systematic study of human behavior and human societies. The social sciences developed much later than the natural and physical sciences, and so are comparatively young disciplines. Because social sciences followed the enormously successful and influential natural and physical sciences, they understandably adopted much of the scientific method—its goals, procedures, and standards. The field of sociology, for example, has been called the science of social organization; psychology has been called the science of the mind. Many social scientists today study people using the scientific method: they develop hypotheses and design and conduct controlled experiments to test those hypotheses. Social science writing seeks to convey the results achieved through research conducted by social scientists.

What is observation in the social sciences?

A great number of the experiments created by social scientists are designed to observe human behavior. Since the goal of any science is the systematic, objective study of phenomena, the social sciences have to study those aspects of humans that are observable. The only objectively observable part of humanity is behavior. We cannot observe human emotions or consciousness directly, but we can observe the behavior that results from feelings and thoughts in human consciousness. The social sciences, consequently, have focused heavily on behavior and thus have been called the behavioral sciences.

What is the importance of understanding human consciousness?

Many people, both within and outside the social sciences, have felt that the objectification of observable human behavior produces a false picture of human beings. The real "inside" of a person may be missed when only the behavior manifested on the "outside" is observed. **197**

Human beings are conscious beings; we have thoughts, feelings, and intuitions that are private and never seen by others. Some in the social sciences argue that because we cannot observe consciousness directly, it is not a proper subject for scientific study at all. Others take the position that it is not only appropriate to study human consciousness, but essential, because consciousness is what makes us uniquely human. Modern social scientists have developed methods of exploring human consciousness that are admittedly subjective, but nevertheless reveal important information about how people think and feel. Such methods include case studies of individuals, clinical evaluation, psychoanalysis, and hypnosis.

What is hypothesis testing in the social sciences?

Hypothesis testing is the process of positing an answer to a question (a hypothesis) and then systematically testing its validity. For example, in one of his last books, *Civilization and Its Discontents*, the famous psychologist Sigmund Freud expressed his views on the broad question of the human being's place in the world. Freud posed the question,

"Why is it hard for humankind to be happy in civilization?" Through his years of preparation and study, Freud was able to posit the hypothesis that unhappiness is due to the inevitable conflict between the demands of instincts (aggression and ego gratification) and the restrictions of civilized society:

> If civilization imposes such great sacrifices not only on man's sexuality but on his aggressivity, we can understand better why it is hard for him to be happy in that civilization. In fact, primitive man was better off in knowing no restrictions of instinct. To counterbalance this, his prospects of enjoying this happiness for any length of time were very slender. Civilized man has exchanged a portion of his possibilities of happiness for a portion of security.

(Sigmund Freud, *Civilization and Its Discontents*, edited and translated by James Strachey, New York: W. W Norton, 1961.)

Famous psychologist Sigmund Freud tested his hypothesis about human unhappiness with numerous psychological case studies.

Freud's sociological theories have been as influential as his psychological theories. Verification of this particular hypothesis—that instinct and society conflict—was achieved through Freud's extensive citation of examples taken from psychological case studies and from primitive and modern societies (including the Soviet Union and the United States). Through these examples, Freud showed that human instincts are often in conflict with society's constraints.

What is the difference between objectivity and subjectivity in social sciences?

In the sciences, researchers attempt to remove their own particular preferences, desires, and hopes from the experimental process as much as possible. Scientific researchers are looking for "objective" truth. What about the social sciences? Can the researchers in this field be objective in their search for knowledge and understanding? Many would charge that subjectivity and values are inescapable and necessary parts of social science research. The social scientist studies people, social systems, and social conventions. As a person, the researcher is necessarily a part of the system being studied. Perhaps this is not altogether a bad thing. A social scientist's own beliefs, attitudes, and values can contribute to his or her understanding of what is being observed. Some- **199**

How important is it to understand human interaction?

Social scientists also study the interaction among people in societies. A social scientist attempting to discover social rules and conventions is somewhat analogous to a natural scientist attempting to discover laws of nature. The social rules and conventions adopted by a particular society are important for an understanding of human behavior within the society. For example, a Polynesian native accustomed to using shells as money would have a rude awakening in an American marketplace where, by convention, slips of paper are used to trade for goods and services. The slip of paper we accept as a dollar bill has meaning for us only within our particular set of social conventions. Much of the work done in social sciences attempts to describe and define the social laws, rules, and conventions by which people operate within societies.

times a social scientist can, to a certain degree, detach himself or herself from a situation and function as a relatively impartial observer. In the end, the question of objectivity and subjectivity in the social sciences is not easily resolved, because it is not always possible to know exactly what subjective influences are affecting "objective" research. The issue of subjectivity versus objectivity is the cause of much ferment and continual debate within the social science fields as these young disciplines seek to define for themselves an appropriate method, whether it is modeled after the scientific method or something quite different.

How do I use sources effectively in social science papers?

The most successful social science research papers incorporate information from several sources into the flow of the paper. The least successful papers tend to rely too heavily on just one source for support of the main argument. Instead of coming up with their own thesis and argument, writers of poor research papers cobble together the opinions of three or four authors, one right after the other, without interpreting their meaning or relationship. This type of writing is termed "patch writing" and is to be avoided. Instead, you will want to use the source information found in your research in support of your own argument. It is a good idea to take notes from each source that are both substantive and interpretive. That is, record in your notes both what the source author is saying (summary) and what you think about it (critique). When you incorporate support information from sources into your own research paper, you need to place in quotation marks any word, phrase, or sentence that you copied directly from a source. Similarly, you must acknowledge paraphrases and summary restatements of ideas taken from a source, even though you have cast them in your own words. Essentially, any material that comes from an independent source, whether in print, Internet, audio, or video format, needs to be acknowledged.

How do I analyze a source article?

As you read a source article, ask yourself the following questions:

1. What is said, by whom, and to whom?

2. How significant are the author's main points and how well are the points made?

3. What assumptions does the author make that underlie his or her arguments?

4. What issues has the author overlooked or what evidence has he or she failed to consider?

5. Are the author's conclusions valid?

6. How well is the source written (clarity, organization, language)?

7. What stylistic or rhetorical features affect the source's content?

What is primary research in the social sciences?

The social sciences have incorporated many of the research techniques of the natural and physical sciences and have developed some research methods of their own, as well. The primary aim of the social sciences is to study human beings and their interaction with society and the environment. Social scientists seek to help us understand the events that happen around us and to communicate that understanding to others. Systematic inquiry is essential in the social sciences.

Because researchers must communicate the social knowledge they acquire through their research, they need a clear written form for transmitting their insights. As in the natural and physical sciences, researchers in the social sciences employ a version of the scientific method. The following steps are generally followed in the researching of a social science question:

How do I critique a source article?

Critiquing begins with active reading and careful notetaking from a source article. You must identify the author's main ideas and points before you can evaluate and critique them. Once you understand the source and the issues it addresses, you are in a position to appraise it critically. To think critically about a source, look behind the arguments themselves to the basis for those arguments. What reasons does the author give for holding a certain belief? In addition, try to discern what assumptions the author is making about the subject. Do you share those assumptions? Are they valid? It is your job to evaluate fairly but with discerning judgment because this evaluation will be the core of your critique. Formulate a thesis that states your evaluation. Do not feel that your evaluation must necessarily be negative; it is possible to make a positive critique, a negative critique, or a critique that cites both positive and negative aspects of the source.

1. Choosing the research problem and stating the hypothesis

2. Formulating the research design and method

3. Gathering the data

4. Analyzing the data

5. Interpreting the results of the data analysis in order to test the validity of the hypothesis

What are two main social science research designs?

The research designs most commonly used by social science researchers are experiments, surveys and questionnaires, interviews and case studies, and observations. Each has advantages and disadvantages that should be considered when designing a research project.

Experiments

The social science experiment is a highly controlled method of determining a direct link between two variables, for example, between high temperature and riots. The researcher must have control over the research environment so that no external variables can affect the outcome, but this is especially difficult in social science experiments. A re-

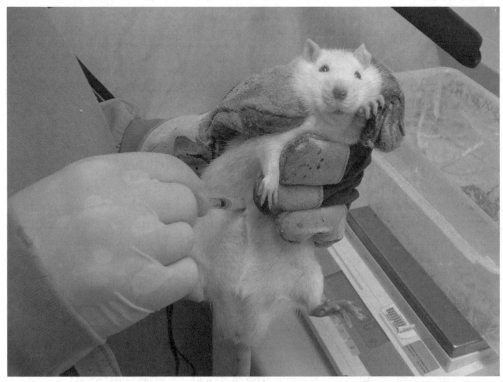

Rats are used quite a lot in experiments because, interestingly, they are similar in some ways to humans. In one experiment, scientists studied rats to see if overpopulation pressures resulted in riots.

searcher who is interested in the causes of riots should not attempt to create a riot in the laboratory for study, but he or she can study laboratory animals and posit hypotheses about human behavior based on the experimental results. For example, to test the hypothesis that crowding can cause riots, some researchers studied populations of rats and varied the population density to test their hypothesis. They found that for the rat populations, crowding did indeed cause antisocial behavior. From this result, the researchers hypothesized that a similar phenomenon may exist for people; that is, overcrowded cities may contribute to antisocial behavior. Though experimental research is the best means of definitively establishing causal links (variable A causes variable B; overcrowded living conditions cause antisocial behavior), experiments may be limited in applicability. In the case of the above experiment, people may or may not behave as rats do.

Surveys and Questionnaires

Ideally, we would study an entire population to gain insights into its society; finding out how all Americans intend to vote in an upcoming election would accurately predict the outcome. Polling an entire population is seldom feasible, however, so pollsters sample small segments of the entire population at random. The most frequently used sampling is random-digit-dialing over the telephone. Researchers have refined sampling techniques to the point at which polls can be quite accurate. Thus, CBS News can announce the outcome of a presidential election hours before the returns are in for much of the country. One particular kind of survey is the questionnaire, a form that asks for responses to a set of questions. Large numbers of people can be polled for their opinions by means of questionnaires over the telephone, through the mail, or in person. The advent of computers has radically changed the survey business: it is now possible to survey large populations, input and code their responses into a computer database, and obtain immediate analyses of the data. As with most other research in both the natural sciences and social sciences, the first, and perhaps most important, step in survey research is the articulation of a hypothesis. Developing the hypothesis provides the key ingredient to structure all subsequent parts of the project: the questionnaire, the sample, the coding, the tabulation forms, and the final report itself.

A questionnaire is not given simply to gather random facts; rather, it is a problem-solving enterprise. The researcher poses a hypothesis in an attempt to shed light on a particular research problem. The questionnaire works to either support or counter the hypothesis. For example, in a study of the relationship between the elderly and the police, the researchers presumably would try to solve a problem: that

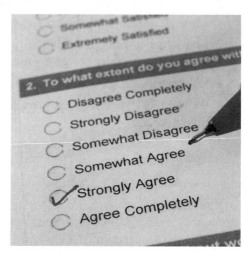

Questionnaires are a useful way to conduct surveys of large samples of people.

203

the elderly do not see the police in a positive light and therefore hesitate to call on them in an emergency situation. The researcher, then, might hypothesize that the real problem lies in the elderly population's erroneous perceptions of the police. A questionnaire could be designed to elicit their perceptions and to try to understand the origins of their distrust. In fact, when a study like this was conducted in a major metropolitan area, researchers discovered that an elderly person's level of distrust of the police was in direct proportion to the number of hours of TV viewed—in particular, TV crime shows.

Student-Designed Questionnaire

The accompanying questionnaire was designed by a student to discover the attitude of foreign students toward Utah State University and the education they were receiving. The student researcher hypothesized, based on his own experiences as a foreign student, that responses would be generally very favorable. During several visits to the library, the student researcher polled 60 foreign students, representing a variety of nationalities. He found that, in general, foreign students were satisfied with university administrative policies but less satisfied with interpersonal relationships between them and their teachers and classmates.

QUESTIONNAIRE

1. What is your nationality?

2. How long have you been a student at USU?

3. What is your native language?

4. Do you feel classes at USU are designed with consideration of the needs of foreign students? yes no

5. Do you feel your instructors are unbiased toward you and your nationality during class? yes no

6. Do you feel you have received an undeserved grade from an instructor because of a bias against foreign students? yes no

7. Do you feel any language difficulties (limited vocabulary, accent, etc.) cause communication barriers between you and your instructors? yes no

8. Do you feel accepted as an equal by your American classmates? yes no

9. Do you feel USU's administrative policies regarding foreign students are fair and unbiased? yes no

10. Do you feel USU provides an equal opportunity for a sound education for its foreign students? yes no

Interviews and Case Studies

Interview studies are one particular type of survey. Their advantages over the questionnaire include flexibility (the questioner can interact with the respondent), response rate (the questioner immediately knows the respondent's answer), and nonverbal behavior (the questioner can gather nonverbal clues as well as verbal). Interviews have other advantages as well, but the disadvantages are also great. Primarily, the time and

When framing questions for an interview, make sure you don't pose questions that can easily be answered by "yes" or "no," or else that might be the only response you get.

expense of interviews make them difficult to conduct. Consequently, fewer responses can be gathered. In addition, the interview is actually a complex interaction between individuals and thus can hinge on the characteristics of the individuals involved. If a respondent is put off by the interviewer, for example, his or her interview answers may be affected. Nevertheless, interviewing is an important research method in the social sciences that can result in rich, high-quality data.

Some considerations when designing interviews:

1. Be certain that the questions are written down and asked exactly as worded.

2. Be certain that you probe any unclear or incomplete answer.

3. Be certain that inadequate or brief answers are not probed in a biasing (directive) way.

Interview with a Pediatrician

The accompanying interview was conducted by a student who was interested in the relationship between emotions and the onset of asthma attacks in asthmatic children. Prior to the interview, she obtained the subject's permission to tape-record for later data analysis.

Interview with Dr. John W. Carlisle, September 10, 1988

(Pediatrician with extensive experience treating asthmatic children)

1. Do emotions cause asthma? Dr. Carlisle feels that the misconception "emotions cause asthma" is easily explained by the fact that stressful emotional situations frequently trigger asthma attacks. People who may have already been prone to asthma may experience their first attack in an emotionally stressful situation. In actuality, asthma is a physical disease that can be irritated by emotional stress or trauma.

2. What emotional or psychological effects on your asthmatic patients have you observed? Dr. Carlisle targeted several detrimental effects of asthma on children's emotional and psychological well-being. Older children (8–12 years) feel "defective" in some way because they are suddenly different from their peers (they often have to take medicine or other precautions to prevent an attack). Older children may rebel against parents who expect them to take on the extra responsibility for controlling their own disease. Younger children tend to regress, become very frightened, and cling to parents because they are not yet capable of understanding their disease.

3. What suggestions do you have for treating the emotional aspects of asthma? In Dr. Carlisle's opinion, the best emotional support parents can give childhood asthmatics is to make sure they understand the disease and what is happening to them. At the same time, try to reinforce the fact that there will always be someone there to help them if they need help. This can alleviate a great deal of the anxiety that can aggravate their condition.

Observations

Observation is best suited to the collection of nonverbal data. In this method, the observer takes notes on people behaving in customary ways in a particular environment or setting. In this way, the researcher accumulates "field notes," which are used to analyze trends and discern customary behaviors. The disadvantages of observation include lack of control over the environment, lack of quantifiable data, and small sample size. Also, whenever an observer enters the environment to observe people, the participants' behavior may no longer be natural. The goal of social research based on observation and description is a general one: to describe and perhaps evaluate a culture or subculture in as much detail as possible. An example of this type of observational research is sociologist Margaret Mead's book *Coming of Age in Samoa*. In this book, Mead describes the complex culture of the Samoan Islands, paying particular attention to customs surrounding the transition from adolescence to adulthood.

How do I interpret social science data?

Analyzing the Data

Researchers analyze their data quantitatively (using numbers) to discern relationship to their hypotheses. Depending on the research method used, the researcher will rely to a greater or lesser degree on statistical analyses of the data. Often, researchers will code their data to make it suitable for computer processing. Computers can quickly and accurately process data and correlate variables. As an example of data analysis, students in a political science class were asked to analyze the crime statistics data in a table from the FBI Uniform Crime Reports. First, the students were asked to compare the data for two states, in this case Alaska and Arizona, to see whether the differences were statistically significant. Then they were asked to explain or interpret their results.

Interpreting the Results

The relationship among variables suggested by the hypothesis is tested at this stage in the research, often through statistical measures. In the social sciences, a hypothesis can never be proved or disproved "beyond the shadow of a doubt." Researchers can statistically calculate the probability of error for the hypothesis, however, and thus can strongly suggest the truth or validity of the hypothesis. In other words, a social scientist may be able to either reject or fail to reject a hypothesis based on a careful marshalling of the evidence. For example, in comparing the crime reports for Alaska and Arizona, the students noticed that the rates per 100,000 population differed in potentially interesting ways: Arizona exceeded Alaska in total property crimes per 100,000 residents (burglary, larceny-theft, motor vehicle theft: Arizona = 6,576, Alaska = 4,922). Alaska, on the other hand, topped Arizona in forcible rapes (Arizona = 41, Alaska =65). The students needed first to find out whether these perceived differences were significant, using statistical tests. If so, they then could interpret their results by positing plausible explanations (hypotheses) to further explore and test. The students, for example, hypoth-

In the social sciences, one can never show a result can be proven with 100% certainty. Therefore, statistics are used to illustrate trends and probabilities.

esized that the high number of rapes in Alaska could be related to the scarcity of women. To test this hypothesis, the students could perhaps compare Alaska and Arizona to other states with similar demographics.

How can I avoid commonly misused words in social science writing?

Following are some words and phrases that may be misused in social science writing.

- *Accept/except: Accept* means to receive whereas *except* means with the exclusion of:

  The psychologists will *accept* their award on Tuesday. Everyone *except* Dr. Wang will attend the ceremony.

- *Affect/effect/impact: Affect* is a verb meaning to influence. Effect is a noun meaning what has resulted from some influence. You should avoid using the noun *impact* as a verb in place of the verb *affect*:

  The sociologists were worried about how they might *affect* the outcome of the project. The *effect* of the researcher on his or her subject is a known risk.

  How can I *impact* the outcome of this project? [faulty]

  How can I *affect* the outcome of this project? [revised; correct]

- *Awhile/a while: Awhile* is an adverb modifying a verb and meaning for a short time. *A while* is a noun phrase meaning a period of time:

  The subjects intended to stay *awhile*. After traveling all night, they rested *a while*.

- Because/since: *Both terms indicate a relationship.* Because *indicates a strong causal relationship;* since *is used to indicate a time relationship.*

  Our experiment will be successful *because* we chose our subjects carefully.

  They have been included in the study *since* the summer.

- *Bi-/semi-:* Both are prefixes that indicate time intervals. *Bi-* indicates two of something or an event that happens twice; *semi-* indicates half or partial.

  The sociological society meets *bi-annually*. Attendance is *semi-automatic*.

- *Index/indexes/indices: Index* is the singular form, whereas *indexes* is the plural. The term *indices* is used to refer to measurable quantities.

  The researcher prepared an *index* to accompany his book. Additional *indexes* to vocabulary terms were included. The publisher used several *indices* to gauge the book's influence.

- *Over/under*: Do not use *over* or *under* to replace *more than* or *less than* when describing quantities.

  We found *over* 60% deviation from the norm. [faulty]

  We found *more than* 60% deviation from the norm. [revised; correct]

- *Parameter*: Has a specialized meaning in statistics; do not use loosely for *variable, quantity, quality, determinant,* or *feature.*

  The study had several *parameters*. [faulty]

  The study had several *variables*. [revised; correct]

- *Percent/percentage: Percent* may be a noun, adjective or adverb; *percentage* is a noun meaning part of the whole as expressed in hundredths. When percent is used with a number, it is indicated with the % symbol rather than with the word.

  They made a *percentage* error in their calculations. [faulty]

  They made a *percent* error in their calculations. [revised; correct]

  The *percentage* of red blood cells in the patient had risen after treatment. [correct]

  Thirty *percent* of the participants tested positive. [correct]

  There was a .05 *percent* standard deviation. [faulty]

  There was a *.05%* standard deviation. [revised; correct]

- *Significant/significance*: In social science papers, confine the use of this term to statistical judgment; do not use loosely for *important, notable,* or *distinctive.*

  The results of the study were statistically *significant.*

Please refer to the commonly misused words in science writing, since there is considerable overlap. See also Appendix H for a listing of other commonly misused word pairs.

How do I avoid punctuation errors in social science writing?

Chapter 6 contains detailed information on correct punctuation. Listed here are some specific examples of punctuation problems encountered in social science writing.

Commas:

1. Use a comma to separate long introductory material in a sentence from the rest of the sentence:

   Because of increased risk of suicide, adolescents are provided with several early interventions.

2. Use commas to set off interrupting material from the rest of the sentence:

   These interventions, and the relationships thereby formed with therapists, can lead to a reduction in suicide attempts.

3. Use commas to separate items in a series:

   Risk behavior measures may predict the risks for dropping out of school, experimenting with drugs, and attempting suicide.

4. Use a comma to separate independent clauses joined by a conjunction (*and, but, or, for, nor, yet*). DO NOT use a comma to separate two independent clauses without a conjunction because this results in a comma splice:

This risk is most apparent in adolescents, it is also apparent to some degree in young adults. [faulty; comma splice]

This risk is most apparent in adolescents, but it is also apparent to some degree in young adults. [revised; correct]

Semicolons:

Semicolons are used in the following three cases:

1. To join two independent clauses:

This risk is most apparent in adolescents; it is also apparent to some degree in young adults.

2. To connect two independent clauses joined with a conjunctive adverb (*however, nevertheless, moreover, furthermore*):

The benefits of high density lipoproteins is well documented; however, some have questioned the effects of very low levels of cholesterol.

3. As a "super-comma" in a series already containing commas:

The subjects were given low-fat diets of complex carbohydrates; lean meats, fish, and poultry; and fat-free dairy products.

Colons:

The main use for the colon is to introduce items in a series:

Their diet consisted of the following items: lean meats, fish, poultry, and grains.

The colon may also be used to introduce a direct quotation:

In the Framingham study, the following is stated: "A relationship between cholesterol levels and prognosis in men and women does exist."

Italics (or underline):

Use italics to indicate foreign words and phrases: *ad nauseum, et cetera.* Use italics to indicate a word or phrase you wish to emphasize:

The length of time in which a subject is exposed to stimuli *can* alter your results.

Abbreviations:

Typically in social science writing, terms of measurement in the text are abbreviated if they are preceded by a number. The same symbol is used for either singular or plural and no period is used:

1 hr (one hour)

12 hr (twelve hours)

3 l (3 litres); m = meter, min = minute, s = second, wk = week,

yr = year, mo = month, d or da = day

Do not abbreviate the name of a unit of measure that follows a spelled-out number, as at the start of a sentence:

Ten litres were required for proper testing.

Parentheses:

1. Use parentheses to refer to information in a table or figure in the text: (see Figure 1) or (Table 2).

2. Use parentheses to enclose a comment or explanation that is structurally independent of the rest of the sentence:

Roby (1989) also used total body immersion on the subjects in his study.

3. Use parentheses to label enumerations within a paragraph: (1) (2)

4. Use parentheses for internal citations:

Fat content varies with age, sex, and nutrition (Sturkie, 1986).

Brackets:

Use brackets to enclose information within parentheses:

Hostility in the group toward one student was palpable (twice as many criticisms [Schmidt-Nielsen, 1990]).

Numbers:

1. A decimal number of less than one should be written with a zero (0) preceding the decimal point:

Thirty subjects had a narrow range of weight and their probability was lower, 0.676.

2. Spell out a number that occurs at the beginning of a sentence:

Fifteen of the subjects were weighed with their clothing still on.

3. Numbers that modify an adjective should be written as a whole number and separated from the adjective with a hyphen:

The weight of the anorexic girls was monitored for a 5-year period.

4. Numerical values are customarily identified by the letter n:

The variation in values was influenced by the position of the subject within the chamber (n=15).

5. The day of the month typically precedes the month. No commas are used:

We monitored the girls from 15 May 2014 to 15 December 2014.

6. In most situations use words for numbers one through nine and numerals for larger numbers. Treat ordinal numbers as you would cardinal numbers: *third, fourth, 33rd, 54th.*

Many times, interview questions may be paraphrased or summarized, but if you are quoting someone famous (such as the late Timothy Leary [left] and Aldous Huxley's widow, Laura Huxley), direct quotations make for stronger writing.

How do I use direct quotations in social science writing?

Much of the time you will summarize or paraphrase a primary source, but direct quotes are used when something particularly memorable has been said and you wish to record it, or, too, if you are quoting a well-known person. To incorporate direct quotations smoothly, observe the following principles. It would be wise to consult the style manual of your discipline for any style variations.

1. Always follow a quotation with a citation, either a footnote or a parenthetical citation. Typically, you will want to introduce the quotation with a signal phrase to alert your reader that a quotation will follow:

   According to Peterson, "Anorexia and bulimia are more common among teenage girls than teenage boys" (Peterson, 2014, p. 73).

2. Introduce quotations using a verb tense that is consistent with the tense of the quotation:

   A woman of twenty admitted, "I really could not see how thin I was" (Peterson, 2014, p. 75).

3. Change a capital letter to a lower-case (or vice versa) within the quotation if necessary:

   "She pours her time and attention into her children, whining at them to "eat more, drink more, sleep more" (Peterson, 2014, p. 75).

4. Use brackets for explanations or interpretations not in the original quotation:

"Evidence reveals that boys are higher on conduct disorder [behavior directed toward the environment] than girls" (Peterson, 2014, p. 80).

5. Use ellipses (three spaced dots) to indicate that material has been omitted from the quotation:

"Fifteen to twenty percent of anorexia victims die of direct starvation or related illnesses … [which] their weak, immune-less bodies cannot combat" (Peterson, 2014, p. 80).

If an ellipsis occurs at the end of the sentence, place the period before the three spaced dots.

6. Punctuate a direct quotation as the original was punctuated, but change the end punctuation to fit the context of your own sentence. For example, a quotation that ends with a period may require a comma when integrated into your own sentence.

7. Use a colon instead of a comma to introduce the quotation if the introductory material or signal phrase prior to the quotation is long.

8. When your quotations are four lines in length or less, surround them with quotation marks and incorporate them into your text. When your quotations are longer than four lines, set them off from the rest of the text by indenting five spaces from both right and left margins or ten spaces from the left margin only. You do not need quotation marks with block quotations.

How do I use graphics or visuals in social science writing?

Sometimes you will find that you need to illustrate your work using graphics or visuals. Types of graphics include tables (usually showing quantitative data), figures (charts, graphs, or technical drawings) or illustrations (including photographs). You first need to determine whether or not your readers would benefit from the inclusion of a graphic. Sometimes repeating information in graphic form will help readers to remember it. The following principles may help you decide:

1. Use a graphic when words alone cannot describe a concept or object adequately.

2. Use a graphic to summarize an important point.

3. Use a graphic when it can help to conveniently display complex information.

You also should determine what you want the graphic to accomplish and where it would best be included in your paper. When aligning your graphic, remember that it should be easy to read and displayed with ample white space so that it stands out from the text background. You should refer at least once to each graphic, either directly or parenthetically, in the text itself. The graphic ideally should be placed on the same page in which it is mentioned and labeled with both a title and a source.

How do I label figures and tables correctly in social science writing?

If you are using figures or tables in your social science writing, you will need to decide on a standard numbering and labeling system. When your document has a variety of photographs, charts, illustrations, or tables, you should label them with captions that identify them all as *figures*. If they are all of one type, perhaps they are all tables, you can label them as such, e.g., (see Table 1, Table 2). Typically, prior to the graphic, you will introduce it in the text with a parenthetical phrase, e.g., (see Figure 9.1). Below the graphic itself, you will type a caption, e.g., *Figure 9.1: Bulimia Frequency by State*. Captions should be consistent in style throughout the document. Consistency includes wording, level of detail, typography (font style and size), and layout. Your word processing software may assist you in generating automated captions. Captions are typically placed directly beneath the images they identify.

If your document requires only a few graphics or if they always appear within the text that discusses them, you may decide to include a descriptive caption beneath each image but choose not to use formal, numbered figure labels.

What are the typical parts included in social science papers?

The parts of a social science paper are very similar to the parts of a science paper. They are typically as follows:

Title

Generally, title pages contain three kinds of identifying information: the title of the paper, the author identification, and course or company identification (including date). If you do not need a separate title page, put your name, date, and any other identifying information on the upper right-hand corner of the first page. Center the title on the first page three or four lines below the identifying information or, if you use a separate title page, one inch from the top of the page. The title should not be underlined, surrounded by quotation marks, or typed in capital letters. Leave three or four lines between your title and the beginning of the text. For longer documents, you may wish to type an outline or Table of Contents immediately after your title.

Numbering

Number each page starting with the first page of text after the title page, which would be numbered page 2. [Note: some styles omit the page number from page 1.] Place the numbers in the upper right-hand corners or centered at the bottom of the pages. Your word processing program will allow you to automatically number your pages and to suppress numbering on any pages where they are not needed. For example, you typically do not need to number the endnotes page or the references page. Rather, identify them with the appropriate heading centered one inch from the top of the page and followed by three or four blank lines. Some styles recommend headers along with the page numbers (for example, Hult p. 2).

Indentation

Use uniform indentation for all paragraphs (five spaces is standard). Indent long quotations (more than four lines long) five spaces from both right and left margins or ten spaces from the left margin only. Leave two spaces between each sentence and after a colon or semicolon. Divide words at the end of lines according to standard rules. Use your dictionary if you are unsure of where to divide a word.

The Abstract

An abstract is a very short summary of a paper, usually one-tenth to one-twentieth the length of the whole. The purpose of an abstract is to condense the paper into a few, succinct lines. The reader must be able to understand the essence of the paper from reading just the abstract, without actually reading the paper. Your abstract should cover the purpose of your paper as well as the major topics you discuss. To write an abstract, you will need to compress information into a few compact sentences. Even though the information in your abstract will necessarily be densely packed, it should still be readable and understandable.

The Endnotes Page

If your paper will have endnotes, type them on a separate page immediately after the text of your paper (and before the references page). Center the title, "Notes" or "Endnotes," one inch from the top of the page, and type it in capital and lower-case letters (not all capitals). Do not use quotation marks or underlining. Leave three or four blank lines between the title and the first line of your notes. Type the notes in consecutive order based on their appearance in the text. Indent the first line of the note five spaces from the left margin, type the superscript number, and leave a space before beginning the note. For any run-over lines of each note, return to the left margin.

The References Page

Center the title "References," or "Works Cited," and type it one inch from the top of the page in capital and lower-case letters (not all capitals). Do not use quotation marks or underlining. Leave three or four blank lines between the title and the first line of your references. The

In the example above, the abstract is indicated by the box around it. Abstracts are summaries of the content of a paper.

references themselves should be typed, double spaced, and listed in alphabetical order by the author's last name (or the title, if the author is not known). The references page follows the last page of the body of your paper, or the endnotes page (if included), and need not be numbered. For the format of each citation on your references page, please refer to the style manual for your discipline. Most of the social sciences use the APA style manual (*Publication Manual of the American Psychological Association*, 6th ed., Washington, DC: APA, 2010).

The Annotated References List

In some cases it is helpful to provide your readers with more information about the sources you used in your research than is typically given in a references list. An annotated references list serves this purpose. To construct one, you would first compile all of your references, alphabetize them, and format them according to the documentation style for your discipline. Then, following each bibliographical entry, you would state in a sentence or two the gist of the source you had read and its relevance to your paper. An annotated references list can help your readers to decide which of your sources they would like to read themselves. It should not be difficult for you to annotate (that is, provide brief glosses) for sources that you have used to write your paper.

The Appendix

Material that may not be appropriate to the body of your paper may be included in an appendix. You may use the appendix for collations of raw data, descriptions of primary research instruments, detailed instructions, and so on. The appendix is located after the bibliography or references page and is clearly labeled. If you use more than one appendix, label them Appendix A, Appendix B, and so on. When referring to the appendix in the paper itself, do so in parentheses, e.g. (See Appendix B).

What is the APA style for in-text citations?

Following are some general principles for incorporating source material into your social science papers.

1. If the author's name is used to introduce the source in a signal phrase, provide the year of publication in parentheses just after the name:

What is the correct documentation format to use in social science writing?

Most of the social sciences use the APA style manual (*Publication Manual of the American Psychological Association*, 6th ed., Washington, DC: APA, 2010). The social sciences use in-text (internal) citation and a list of references at the end of the text. How recently the source was published is important, so the year of publication is stressed in the citation.

Hacking (1995) covers much that is on public record about multiple personality disorder.

2. If the author's name is not used to introduce the source, provide the author's last name and the year of publication in parentheses at an appropriate place. Include a comma between the author's name and the date of publication:

In antiquity and through the Middle Ages, memory was a valued skill (Hacking, 1995).

3. When quoting directly in the author's words, provide a page number:

There may be a causal explanation for multiple personality disorder, because "multiplicity is strongly associated with early and repeated child abuse, especially sexual abuse" (Hacking, 1995, p. 73).

What is the APA style for the references list?

The references list, found at the end of your social science paper, contains all the sources actually used in the paper. The title of this page is "References," "Works Cited," or "Literature Cited." The purpose of the references list is to help readers find the materials you used in writing your paper. Therefore, you must give complete, accurate information. The following principles are generally accepted for the references list in the social sciences:

1. On the references or works-cited page, references are arranged in alphabetical order by the author's last or surname.

2. Authors are listed by surnames and initials.

3. Generally the first word only of a title (and subtitle, if any) is capitalized; the title of an article is not enclosed in quotation marks, but the title of a book is italicized.

4. Names of journals have first letters capitalized and are in italics.

5. The journal's volume and page number are formatted as follows: *15*(2)

6. The year of publication appears in parentheses immediately after the author's name.

7. Entries are formatted with second and subsequent lines indented.

BOOK in APA Style

Bolick, C. (1988). *Changing course. Civil rights at the crossroads.* New Brunswick, NJ: Transaction Books.

ARTICLE in APA Style

Popenoe, D. (1993). American family decline, 1960–1990: A review and appraisal. *Journal of Marriage and Family, 55*(3), 527–555.

WRITING IN THE ARTS AND HUMANITIES

What is writing like in the arts and humanities?

The humanities, such as classical and modern languages and literature, history, and philosophy, have as an overall goal the exploration and explanation of the human experience. Some would include the fine arts (music, art, dance, and drama) in the humanities, but others view the arts as a separate category. In most disciplines in the humanities, written texts are extremely important, particularly in history, philosophy, and literature. Historians attempt a systematic documentation and analysis of past events related to a particular people, country, or period. Philosophers endeavor to examine coherent, logical systems of human ideas. Literary authors and artists attempt to communicate to others their own human experiences and their own understanding of the world. The humanities involve inquiry into consciousness, values, ideas, and ideals, as they seek to describe how experience shapes our understanding of the world.

How important are texts in the arts and humanities?

Most of the work done by humanists is done in writing. Written texts in the humanities are generally of three types: (1) creative writing (literature, poetry, and drama); (2) interpretive writing (literary and art criticism); and (3) theoretical writing (historical and social theories of literature and art). Creative writing produces numerous literary texts that provide us with an aesthetic experience and capture new insights into humanity. Creative writing is comparable to other creative, artistic endeavors in that it often has this twofold objective: the aesthetically pleasing (or emotionally moving) and the imaginative reenactment of human experience. We ask a work of art to move us and to mean something to us, to show us a way of looking at ourselves and the world that we may not otherwise have seen.

219

What is literary and art criticism?

As we receive creative art and literature as an audience, interpretive questions arise, such as: What sort of work is it? How are we to respond to it? Much of the writing connected with the humanities is interpretive critique, since the audience tries to understand both the meaning and significance of a particular creative work. Often, an interpretive critic will attempt to disclose the particular intention of the artist: the novelist's attitude toward the heroine, for example, or the intended aesthetic effect of a dance. Interpretive critics will research their claims by using the evidence found in the work itself to support the hypothesis—that is, the critic's particular "reading" of the text or work of art. Critical researchers necessarily use their own interpretations of a work of art or literature in critiquing it. But those subjective interpretations are based on experience and reflective thought, and they are expressed in well-chosen language. Criticism in the humanities is not just a string of personal opinions. The critical researcher builds a solid argument to substantiate his or her interpretation or theory. Such an argument is based on research involving a close reading of the text itself (in literary criticism) or a close analysis of the work of art (in art criticism). The argument will also take into account social and historical factors that bear upon the interpretation of the literary text or work of art.

What is philosophical research?

The philosophy researcher investigates the truths and principles of being, knowledge, and human conduct. Alfred North Whitehead, in his book *Process and Reality* (New York: Free Press, 1929), describes the process of research in speculative philosophy:

Art critics have a difficult job because their interpretations of art and its merits must be a blend of scholarly knowledge and personal assessment. (Pictured here is Turkish art critic, professor, and scholar Hasan Bülent Kahraman.)

The true method of discovery is like the flight of an aeroplane. It starts from the ground of particular observation; it makes a flight into the thin air of imaginative generalization; and it again lands for renewed observation rendered acute by rational interpretation.

Here Whitehead is describing the general process of inquiry by which all research proceeds. As he says, the success of any imaginative speculation is the verification of it through extended application. He sees the work of philosophical research as an attempt to frame a coherent, logical system of the general ideas of humanity. In Whitehead's work, he presents a scheme that can be used to interpret or frame the "cosmology." He shows how his philosophical scheme can be used for "the interpretation of the ideas" and problems that form the "complex texture of civilized thought." Thus, the philosophical laws are verified in their application to actual philosophical problems encountered in human experience.

What is historical research?

Historical researchers proceed in much the same fashion as philosophy researchers, except that historical researchers investigate events as well as ideas. A historian researches the events that have occurred in a person's life or at a particular time. Historians also use the data gathered by social scientists—the surveys and statistical counts conducted by so-

An historical researcher investigates not only ideas but also events. The discovery and examination of historical artifacts also greatly aids such research.

ciologists, economists, or political scientists. Once historians are ready to share, they present their understanding of the past, often in a story or narrative form intended to help the reader imagine past events through descriptions and interpretations of what those events might have been like for the participants. In this way the study of history bridges the gap between the social sciences and humanities such as literature and the arts.

What is acceptable evidence in the humanities?

In the humanities, there is no absolute proof that leads unerringly to a particular interpretation or theory. Rather, the humanist will make a claim and argue for that claim. What is demanded in the humanities is not proof, but sensitivity and perceptiveness. The way of knowing required in the humanities can be cultivated by hard work and study. The evidence that is acceptable in literary and art criticism or interpretation comes from the interpreter's sensibility, from the work of art or literature itself, and from the context. Some interpretations and theories may seem more insightful than others because they cast the work in a new light or integrate it into a wholeness we had not originally perceived. The claim or hypothesis made by a theorist is accepted as valid if it fits the work and helps the audience understand it. Critical and theoretical research can expand our consciousness, deepening and broadening our sensitivity to experiences. We could say, as did William James, that the performance of a piece of violin music is "the scraping of the hair of a horse over the intestines of a cat." Though the description is true enough, it is certainly not an adequate description of violin music; in fact, the remark leaves out just about everything that is really important in the performance of a violin piece.

A valid interpretation illuminates a work in a way that makes it more meaningful to us. The evidence that is acceptable in historical and philosophical research is that which is based either on verifiable facts or adequate interpretations that fit known human experience. Humanistic researchers insist on the role of the researcher's insight and imagination in elucidating experience and in describing and predicting what human beings are and how they think and act. Acceptable evidence in all the humanities is evidence that supports those imaginative and insightful descriptions and interpretations.

How do I use sources to support my own arguments?

When writing a term paper in the arts and humanities, you will want to use information from source books and articles in support of your own ideas, arguments, and interpretations. Remember, you must acknowledge any original information, ideas, and illustrations that you find in another author's work, whether it is in print or on the Internet. You should use a number of authors to provide supporting evidence for your paper in order to achieve credibility with your readers. First, preview each source, paying attention to key words and phrases and trying to get the general idea of the work's purpose and structure. Then, read the source carefully, stopping to take notes. As you read, keep in mind the main question your research is asking and the main point you are trying to make. Decide how the source information you are reading relates to your own interpretation or argument and also how each source's ideas relates to other sources. If

What is a good example of historical research?

One example of a historical researcher at work is Frank Maloy Anderson (*Mystery of "A Public Man": A Historical Detective Story*, Minneapolis: U of Minnesota Press, 1948). Anderson was confronted with the problem of who wrote the important "The Diary of a Public Man," a document of questioned authorship that first appeared in 1879 in the *North American Review*. Many historical, little-known facts about Abraham Lincoln were revealed in the diary. Anderson spent nearly thirty-five years trying to identify the document's author, using every historical clue he could find. He searched congressional records, hotel registries, business documents, and newspaper subscriptions. Out of this extensive search, he posited two hypotheses: (1) the diary was a fiction, or (2) it was a combination of fiction and truth. Anderson decided on the second hypothesis, because he could find nothing that was provably false in the document. He arrived at a probable author in Sam Ward, but could never prove this beyond all doubt. Nevertheless, Anderson's historical case is a good one, based as it is on intuitive speculation combined with factual evidence.

you read each source with a clear focus, you will be able to use source information in support of your own arguments.

How do I write an interpretive essay in the humanities?

Research in the humanities often begins with a primary text of particular interest to the researcher. The researcher must read the text very carefully as preparation, noting any significant events, themes, characters, and so on. After finishing the close reading, much as researchers in the social sciences do, the humanities researcher posits a hypothesis—that is, a plausible interpretation of the work and its significance. Then the researcher collects evidence from the text itself and perhaps from other, related sources: works written by the same author, sources used by the author, and historical works on events occurring during the period when the work was written. These related sources are used to help verify or refute the initial hypothesis. Ultimately, the humanities researcher seeks to explain and interpret a primary text in such a way that its richness of meaning is increased for its readers.

How do I conduct a life-history interview?

The methods of humanities research may at times approximate the methods in social science research even more closely than the above description suggests. Historical research, for example, may include surveys and interviews of participants in a significant historical event, and very often historical research relies on the statistics gathered by social scientists.

One example of a humanities researcher is Studs Terkel (1912–2008), author of the book *Hard Times: An Oral History of the Great Depression* (New York: Pantheon: 1970), which chronicles life during the 1930s. Terkel's primary sources for his work were people who had lived through the Depression. He interviewed people from various walks of life and parts of the country, inquiring into their own life histories. The interviews were taped and transcribed. From the transcripts, Terkel wrote his version of the life history of each individual, bringing his own interpretations and explanations to

Pulitzer Prize-winning author, historian, and broadcaster Studs Terkel was famous for his oral histories of everyday Americans.

the interview data. Terkel presented these explanations to readers in story form; the pieces describe and recreate events in each informant's life and together give a composite picture of life during the Depression.

Below is an example of an interview by Studs Terkel.

Emma Tiller (transcribed tape)

by Studs Terkel (used by permission of the author)

… a white in the south is like they is i guess in most other places they will not give and help especially the ones who is turned out to be tramps and hoboes uh they come to their door for food they will drive them away white tramps they will drive them away but if a negro come they will feed him they always go and get something another and give him something to eat and they'll even give them a little do you smoke or do you you dip snuff or uh or any do you use anything like that yes ma'am yes ma'am well they would uh give him a quarter or uh fifty cents you know and give him a little sack of food and a bar of soap or something like that well uh but they own color they wouldn't do that for them then the negro woman would uh uh say you know well we've got some cold food in there we'll give you she said oh no i don't give them nothing he'll be back tomorrow you know so so they won't dispose it [Terkel: Oh, you mean the Negro woman who works] yes [for the white] yes [mistress] yes [the white —] she would take food and put it in a bag and sometimes wrap it in newspaper and ah we would hurry out and sometimes we'd have to run down the alley because he'd be gone down the alley and holler at him hey mister and he would stop you know and say come here and he'd come back and said look you come back by after while and i'll put some food out there in a bag and i'll put it down side the can so that you don't see it if we could see soap we'd swipe a bar of soap and face rag or something or you know and stick it in there for them negroes always would feed these tramps even sometimes we would see them on the railroad track picking up stuff and we would tell them you know come to our house and give them the address and tell him to come back that we would give him a old shirt or a pair of pants or some old shoes and some food we always would give them food many times i have gone in in my house and taken my husband's old shoes and his coat and some of them he he needed them hisself but i didn't feel he needed them as bad as that man needed them because that man to me was in a worser shape than he was in regardless of whether it was negro or white i would give them to him.

"Emma Tiller" (pages 60–61)

From *Hard Times: An Oral History of the Great Depression*, by Studs Terkel, Copyright © 1970 Studs Terkel. Reprinted by permission of Pantheon Books, a division of Random House, Inc.

When tramps and hoboes would come to their door for food, the southern white people would drive them away. But if a Negro come, they will feed him. They'll even give them money. They'll ask them: Do you smoke do you dip snuff? Yes, ma'am, yes, ma'am. They was always nice in a nasty way to Negroes. But their own color, they wouldn't do that for 'em. They would hire Negroes for these type jobs where they wouldn't hire whites. They wouldn't hire a white woman to do housework, because they were afraid she'd take her husband.

When the Negro woman would say, Miz So-and-So, we got some cold food in the kitchen left from lunch. Why don't you give it to 'im?' she'll say, "Oh, no, don't give 'im nothin'. He'll be back tomorrow with a gang of 'em. He ought to get a job and work."

The Negro woman who worked for the white woman would take food and wrap it in newspapers. Sometimes we would hurry down the alley and holler at 'im: 'Hey, mister, come here!' And we'd say, 'Come back by after a while and I'll put some food in a bag, and I'll set it down aside the garbage can so they won't see it.' Then he'd get food, and we'd swipe a bar of soap and a face razor or some-thin', stick it in there for 'im. Negroes would always feed these tramps.

Sometimes we would see them on the railroad tracks pickin' up stuff, and we would tell 'em: 'Come to our house.' They would come by and we would give 'em an old shirt or a pair of pants or some old shoes. We would always give 'em food.

Many times I have gone in my house and taken my husband's old shoes some of 'em he needed hisself, but that other man was in worser shape than he was. Regardless of whether it was Negro or white, we would give to 'em.

How do I write a humanities report or research paper?

Some of the writing you will be expected to do in the humanities is report writing, in which you report on the current consensus within the field on a particular topic or issue. In report writing, you research only in the sense of finding out what others have said on a topic. Usually, reports are written on noncontroversial subjects in which the writer can discover the facts easily and present them without the need to interpret their significance. Such a report is also sometimes called a "review of the literature."

In contrast, a research paper does more than report the facts or widely held beliefs on a particular topic. A research paper is necessarily more evaluative than a report because it interprets the available evidence. Often, a research paper will be written about a subject or topic that has sparked controversy in the field. An issue is considered controversial when scholars in the field do not agree on interpretations, or when the range of known facts is great enough to allow differing opinions.

There is room for differences of opinion in the humanities, provided those opinions are supported by, and consistent with, the known facts on the subject. The researcher will arrive at a thesis through lengthy preparation and investigation. Then the researcher will verify that thesis by constructing a persuasive argument woven from and supported by the known facts. Such a thesis will be a reasonable answer to the question, an answer that fits the known facts and helps to explain them.

See Appendix K for an example of a humanities research paper.

How do I avoid punctuation errors in humanities writing?

If you are looking for more detailed information on punctuation in general, please refer to Chapter 6. Following are some specific examples of punctuation problems encountered in humanities writing.

Commas:

1. Use a comma to separate long introductory material in a sentence from the rest of the sentence:

   To put this another way, Capote can be seen as guilty of aestheticism.

2. Use commas to set off interrupting material from the rest of the sentence:

What is the literary present?

In writing interpretively about literature, the commonly accepted practice is to use the present tense, also called the *literary present*, when describing events that happened in the work. For example, in the following sentence, the present tense is used: "In Steinbeck's book *East of Eden*, Adam Trask *learns* about his wife's true character slowly." Similarly, use the present tense when discussing what an author has done in a specific literary work: "Steinbeck *uses* Cathy and Adam Trask to *illustrate* his point about the pure evil that *exists* in human nature."

At the same time, it can be argued that in his silences Capote allows himself to identify, and allows us to identify, with Perry.

3. Use commas to separate items in a series:

Mailer carefully records every burst of laughter, applause, titter, and mood shift.

4. Use a comma to separate independent clauses joined by a conjunction (*and, but, or, for, nor, yet*). Do not use a comma to separate two independent clauses without a conjunction because this results in a comma splice:

It carries for her the suggestion of danger, it implies that we will see her vision of imminent catastrophe. [faulty; comma splice]

"To put this another way, Capote can be seen as guilty of aestheticism" is an example of using a comma to separate a long introductory clause (Capote pictured).

It carries for her the suggestion of danger, and it implies that we will see her vision of imminent catastrophe. [revised; correct]

Semicolons:

Semicolons are used in the following three cases:

1. To join two independent clauses:

Closely related is the rhetoric of particularity; it is also the rhetoric of gaps.

2. To connect two independent clauses joined with a conjunctive adverb (*however, nevertheless, moreover, furthermore*):

There are similar gaps following Didion's interpretative statements; however, Didion does not elaborate.

3. As a "super-comma" in a series already containing commas:

Her sense of spontaneity is reflected in her use of parentheses; repeated predicates, multiple conjunctions, and cumulative modifications; and appositives used to unpack generalizations.

Colons:

The main use for the colon is to introduce items in a series:

I write for the following reasons: to find out what I'm thinking, what I'm looking at, what I see, and what it means.

The colon may also be used to introduce a direct quotation:

Wolfe describes himself arriving in New York in the early sixties: "I couldn't believe the scene I saw spread out before me. New York was pandemonium with a big grin on."

Italics (or underline):

1. Use italics to indicate foreign words and phrases: *ad hominum, et cetera*

2. Use italics to indicate a word or phrase you wish to emphasize:

Capote continually puts us in the position of reading externals, even more in the *apparently* trivial scenes.

Parentheses:

1. Use parentheses to refer to information in a table or figure in the text: (see Figure 1) or (Table 2).

2. Use parentheses to enclose a comment or explanation that is structurally independent of the rest of the sentence:

Jim distinguished himself (unlike several other officers) by attending the trial.

3. Use parentheses to label enumerations within a paragraph: (1) (2)

4. Use parentheses for internal citations:

Once Brown had referred to their similarities (Reichard 548), Jim was reminded of his own guilt.

Brackets:

Use brackets to enclose information within parentheses:

Hostility toward Jim was palpable (He was surrounded by the screaming crowds [Reichard 548]).

Numbers:

1. Spell out a number that occurs at the beginning of a sentence:

Three of the authors used narrative as a version of nonfiction.

2. Numbers that modify an adjective should be written as a whole number and separated from the adjective with a hyphen:

Critics explained that the writer was essentially a hermit for a five-year period.

3. In most situations, use words for numbers one through nine and numerals for larger numbers. Treat ordinal numbers as you would cardinal numbers: *third, fourth, 33rd, 54th.*

How do I use direct quotations in humanities writing?

Most of the time you will use summaries and paraphrases to incorporate source material into your writing. Occasionally you will want to directly quote an author who has

Don't forget to use the modern technology at your disposal when conducting interviews. In today's world, there is no need to travel to do a live interview; you can use tools such as Skype and record the interview and transcribe it later.

said something in a particularly succinct or memorable way. To incorporate direct quotations smoothly, observe the following principles. It would be wise to consult the style manual of your discipline for any style variations.

1. Always follow a quotation with a citation, either a footnote or a parenthetical citation. Typically, you will want to introduce the quotation with a signal phrase to alert your reader that a quotation will follow:

   According to Anderson, "Rather than be guilty of betraying unmanly exhilaration or fear, the pilots learned to describe their experiences indirectly through various 'codes' and ironically understated stories" (Anderson 15.)

2. Introduce quotations using a verb tense that is consistent with the tense of the quotation:

   The pilot exclaimed, "We've obviously got a man in the cockpit who doesn't have a nerve in his body!" (Anderson 15).

3. Change a capital letter to a lower-case (or vice versa) within the quotation if necessary:

   The true pilot always understates danger, drawling about the "little ol' red light up here on the control panel" (Anderson 15).

229

4. Use brackets for explanations or interpretations not in the original quotation:

"The confessions, though they answered questions of how and why, failed to satisfy his [Dewey's] sense of meaningful design" (Anderson 63).

5. Use ellipses (three spaced dots) to indicate that material has been omitted from the quotation:

Dick and Perry are "predisposed to severe lapses in ego-control which make possible the open expression of primitive violence, born out of previous … traumatic experiences" (Anderson 63).

If an ellipsis occurs at the end of the sentence, place the period before the three spaced dots.

6. Punctuate a direct quotation as the original was punctuated, but change the end punctuation to fit the context of your own sentence. For example, a quotation that ends with a period may require a comma when integrated into your own sentence.

7. Use a colon instead of a comma to introduce the quotation if the introductory material or signal phrase prior to the quotation is long.

8. When your quotations are four lines in length or less, surround them with quotation marks and incorporate them into your text. When your quotations are longer than four lines, set them off from the rest of the text by indenting five spaces from the left margin. You do not need quotation marks with block quotations.

What are the typical parts included in humanities papers?

Standard essay format is used for most humanities papers. Formal research papers may have additional components, as outlined below.

Title

Ask your instructor whether you need a title page. If the answer is yes, find out what information should appear there. Generally, title pages contain three kinds of identifying information: the title of the paper, author identification, and course identification (including date). If you do not need a separate title page, put your name, date, assignment name, and any other identifying information on the upper left-hand corner of the first page. Center the title on the first page two lines below the identifying information or, if you use a separate title page, one inch from the top of the page. The title should not be underlined, surrounded by quotation marks, or typed in capital letters. Leave two or three lines between your title and the beginning of the text. Some instructors will require you to type an outline or Table of Contents immediately after your title. Check to see if your instructors would like such an outline included.

Numbering

Number each page starting with the first page of text after the title page, which would be numbered page 2. [Note: some styles omit the page number from page 1.] Place the numbers in the upper right-hand corners or centered at the bottom of the pages. Your word processing program will allow you to automatically number your pages and to suppress numbering on any pages where they are not needed. For example, you typically do not need to number the endnotes page or the references page. Rather, identify them with the appropriate heading centered one inch from the top of the page and followed by three or four blank lines. Some styles recommend headers along with the page numbers (for example, Hult, p. 2). Check the help function on your word processing program for help in generating such automatic headers.

Indentation

Use uniform indentation for all paragraphs (five spaces is standard). Indent long quotes (more than four lines long) ten spaces from the left margin only. Indent the second and subsequent lines of the reference-list entries five spaces. Leave two spaces between each sentence and after a colon or semicolon. Divide words at the end of lines according to standard rules. Use your dictionary if you are unsure of where to divide a word.

The Endnotes Page

If your paper will have endnotes, type them on a separate page immediately after the text of your paper (and before the references page). Center the title, "Notes" or "Endnotes," one inch from the top of the page, and type it in capital and lower-case letters (not all capitals). Do not use quotation marks or underlining. Leave two or three blank lines between the title and the first line of your notes. Type the notes in consecutive order based on their appearance in the text. Indent the first line of the note five spaces from the left margin, type the superscript number, and leave a space before beginning the note. For any run-over lines of each note, return to the left margin.

The References Page

Center the title "References," or "Works Cited," or "Bibliography" and type it one inch from the top of the page in capital and lower-case letters (not all capitals). Do not use quotation marks or underlining. Leave two or three blank lines between the title and the first line of your references. The references themselves should be typed, double spaced, and listed in alphabetical order by the author's last name (or the title, if the author is not known). The references page follows the last page of the body of your paper, or the endnotes page (if included), and need not be numbered.

It is vital that you accurately cite your sources in your paper so that your readers can consult these works later, if desired, to both confirm what you have written and study the subject further on their own. Of course, citing sources also protects you against charges of plagiarism.

Most of the humanities use the MLA style manual (Joseph Gibaldi, *MLA Handbook for Writers of Research Papers*, 7th ed., New York: MLA, 2009). The MLA style uses in-text parenthetical citations and a bibliography at the end of the paper. Since it is often important in the humanities to locate an exact quotation, MLA style includes both the author's name and the page number on which the information can be found in the parenthetical citation.

The Annotated References List

In some cases it is helpful to provide your readers with more information about the sources you used in your research than is typically given in a references list. An annotated references list serves this purpose. To construct one, you would first compile all of your references, alphabetize them, and format them according to the documentation style for your discipline. Then, following each bibliographical entry, you would state in a sentence or two the gist of the source you had read and its relevance to your paper. An annotated references list can help your readers to decide which of your sources they would like to read themselves. It should not be difficult for you to annotate (that is, provide brief glosses) for sources that you have used to write your paper.

What is MLA style for in-text citations?

When you rely on information from sources to support your arguments in the humanities, your readers will want to know who wrote each source and where it can be located. MLA documentation therefore requires that you provide that information—the author's last name and the page number where your source information can be found—in the body of your paper in the form of an in-text citation (also called a parenthetical reference). The in-text citations are linked to the Bibliography or Works Cited page.

Following are some general principles for incorporating source material into your humanities papers:

1. If the author's name is used to introduce the source in a signal phrase, provide the page number in parentheses at the end of the sentence:

Mullins makes an interesting point that Billy Bonney "was no better and no worse than many others of that area and era" (6).

2. If the author's name is not used to introduce the source, provide the author's last name and the page number in parentheses at an appropriate place. Do not include a comma between the author's name and the page number:

Legends relate tales of Billy killing his first man when he was twelve (Tuska 4).

What is MLA style for the works cited or bibliography?

You need to provide your readers with a complete and accurate alphabetical list of all the sources used in your paper so that they can readily find these sources if they wish to do so. This list, usually called Works Cited, should appear at the very end of your paper. If you include works that were useful to you in your research but not directly cited in your paper, the list should be called Bibliography. A bibliography that includes brief summaries of the works is called an Annotated Bibliography. The following principles are generally accepted for the works cited list in the humanities:

1. On the references or works cited page, references are arranged in alphabetical order by the author's last or surname.

2. If a work lists more than one author, the first author is listed by surname, followed by a comma and then first name. Subsequent authors are listed in the order they are given on the book's title page. Reverse the name of the first author only, putting the last name first; separate the authors' names with commas:

   Fiorina, Morris P., Samuel J. Abrams, and Jeremy C. Pope. *Culture War? The Myth of a Polarized America.* New York: Longman, 2005. Print.

3. Important words of the title are capitalized, the title of an article is enclosed in quotation marks, and the title of a book is italicized.

4. Names of journals have important words capitalized and are in italics.

5. The journal's volume and issue number are formatted as follows: 57.4

6. The year of publication appears after the publication information.

7. The medium of publication, whether in print or on the Web, is indicated in the citation.

8. The inclusive page numbers for articles follow the publication information.

9. Entries are formatted with second and subsequent lines indented.

BOOK in MLA Style

   Diamond, Jared. *Collapse: How Societies Choose to Fail or Succeed.* New York: Penguin, 2005. Print.

ARTICLE in MLA Style

   Cooper, Marilyn. "Bringing Forth Worlds." *Computers and Composition* 22.1 (2005): 31–38. Print.

ONLINE ARTICLE in MLA Style

   Cohn, Dorrit. "'First Shock of Complete Perception': The Opening Episode of *The Golden Bowl*, Volume 2." *Henry James Review* 22.1 (2001): 1-9. *Project Muse Journals.* 2003. Johns Hopkins UP. Web. 24 Apr. 2003.

BUSINESS WRITING

What is business writing?

Business writing is writing done on the job in a workplace setting. It is practical writing done typically to identify and solve a problem. Most business writing is aimed at an audience of multiple readers whose interests and needs may not be exactly the same. Some readers will only read parts of the writing or will skim it for main ideas, while others will read all of the writing to understand the details. Workplace writing is often done in collaboration with others. Business writing needs to be clear, concise, and easy-to-follow, with a predictable structure and correct grammar.

How do I write business emails?

A great deal of business writing will take the form of emails. It is important to be professional with work emails, as opposed to the informal way in which many people use email in their personal lives. Use the subject line of the email to quickly orient the reader to the content of the email. Address the email as you would a letter, using a conventional salutation, such as Dear Ms. Miller, followed by a colon. In the body of the email, begin by providing any background information that is necessary to understanding your message. You may need to reference previous correspondence on the subject. Then, quickly come to your purpose and focus on the main point of the email. It is better to keep each email focused on just one topic. Use simple sentences and short paragraphs to explain the point of your email, but be sure they are complete, grammatical sentences as if you were writing a professional letter. Keep verbs active and address your readers directly with personal pronouns. Keep your message as short as possible to get your point across. Reread it several times to correct for any errors or misstatements. You may want to set the email aside in your draft folder and come back to it with a fresh eye before sending it. Remember, once it is sent, it is difficult to get it back. It is also good to remember that, unlike written letters, emails are never strictly confidential. Take care that you do not say anything in an email that you would not want to become public knowledge at some point.

How do I write business letters?

Business letters are typically addressed to a specific person, but they may be circulated more widely than the addressee, so take care to say what you mean and not to reveal confidential information. If the letter is confidential, you should mark it as such on the outside of the envelope. Business letters are written for many different purposes: to inquire about something, to request something, to announce something, to sell something, to reply to someone, and so on. Most business letters are straightforward and "business-like" in tone. They should be professional but may also be friendly and not overly formal. You need to consider your purpose for writing the letter, what you hope to accomplish, when deciding on the tone. You also need to consider to whom you are writing: is the person likely to be favorably disposed to what you are writing, or is the person likely to be skeptical or unfavorable? Will the person need considerable persuasion, or is he or she likely to go along with what you are suggesting without questioning it? You can use a direct approach if the response is likely to be favorable. You will need to provide much more background and pay attention to persuasive arguments if the response is likely to be unfavorable. Try to word your letter to accentuate the positive—people typically respond better to positive letters than negative ones. This will not always be possible, of course. You want to be truthful and fair, even if it may push someone out of his or her comfort zone.

Although emails and even instant messaging and texting are becoming more in vogue with business professionals, hard-copy letters are still seen as more professional in formal business correspondence.

What is the typical format for business letters?

The traditional hard-copy business letter is still in use today, although it is fast being replaced by the email version. Whether a letter is printed on paper or sent as an email, it is important to have a clear purpose, provide enough background information, use correct grammar and spelling, and employ a professional tone. The format for a business letter begins with a return address (your own address) and date. These are followed by the recipient's address and the salutation. Typically a business letter will use the block paragraph format. It will conclude with a closing (e.g., Sincerely Yours) and signature.

3535 Highland Drive
Ft. Worth, TX 78494
caroline.lopez@gmail.com
Tel. (555) 453-3282

February 1, 2015

Rev. Jeffrey Silver
First Methodist Church
1450 Wilson Court
Ft. Worth, TX 78494

Dear Rev. Silver:

I am a board member for the non-profit group Loaves and Fishes in Fort Worth. We serve free meals to community members who may not otherwise have access to a nutritious meal. The meals are served in the local food pantry every Saturday from 11 a.m. to 1 p.m.

Our board has been meeting weekly in the public library for planning sessions. Since the library is scheduled for remodeling in the next several months, beginning in March of this year, we are looking for a small meeting room that we could use during the course of the remodel.

Would First Methodist have a room that we could use? We understand that you have classrooms and a study that may be suitable for small groups. Our meetings are on Tuesday evenings and last 2-3 hours, from 7-10 p.m. We typically have 6-8 board members present for each meeting.

Please let me know if one of your rooms might be available for us to use and, if so, what process we need to go through to get access to the building in the evening.

Thank you for your kind attention to this matter.

Sincerely,

Caroline Lopez
Board Member, Loaves and Fishes

An example of a formal business letter.

How do I write application letters?

When you are looking for a job, you will need to write application letters. The ability to write a good letter is key to a successful job search. The application letter, or cover letter as it is sometimes called, is a way in which you persuade an employer to consider your application for an open position. Your application letter is the way to make a good first impression on a potential employer. You need to be sure the letter is direct, positive, and free from any errors or misrepresentations. It is your way of "selling" yourself

3535 Highland Drive
Ft. Worth, TX 78494
caroline.lopez@gmail.com
Tel. (555) 453-3282

May 15, 2014

Mr. Pedro Fernandez
Director of Marketing
Essurance Company
646 South Elm St.
Ft. Worth, TX 78494

Dear Mr. Fernandez:

I am writing to apply for the internship in your marketing program that was advertised at the University of Dallas, where I am a graduating senior. I was impressed with your company's emphasis on market research, product placement, and sales. I would very much like to have the opportunity to intern with your organization to learn more about the marketing field.

Marketing and Public Relations have been my major at UD, and I will receive my diploma for a Bachelor of Sciences degree in Business Administration at the end of May. In college, I have maintained a 3.5 GPA and a place on the Dean's List. My course work has prepared me to be a strong communicator, as well as to understand the field of marketing. I have also had direct experience in merchandising with my job at the local Macy's department store in Fort Worth. In this position, I have had experience with retailing and market research, as well as handling customer complaints. My supervisors have praised me for my ability to work with difficult customers and to satisfactorily resolve their concerns.

Attached please find my résumé. I am available to interview at your convenience and am available to begin work after graduation on May 31. I look forward to hearing from you.

Sincerely,

Caroline Lopez

enclosure

An example of an application letter.

and your qualifications for the job. Keep the letter brief, one page if possible. Begin by stating the position you are applying for. Follow that with your qualifications for the position, being specific about why you are a good fit for the job. You may want to ask for an interview and let the employer know when you are available. Be sure to use correct business letter format and address the letter specifically to the hiring authority. You will usually accompany the application letter with a résumé or curriculum vitae (CV). The application letter highlights the accomplishments on the résumé that are relevant to the specific job you are applying for. A frequent mistake of job seekers is to use the same letter for all of the jobs they are applying for. If you do this, the potential employer will see immediately that you have not taken the time or trouble to research the specific position and tailor the letter to speak to the company's needs. Your letter should specifically emphasize how your skills would be of use to the company.

How do I write a résumé?

A résumé is a concise summary of someone's skills, experience, accomplishments, and personal strengths. It is more complete than the letter of application since it outlines comprehensively the person's background and abilities. It should still be concise and to the point, typically not more than one or two pages in length. A résumé should be tailored to each position you are applying for in order to emphasize the skills most relevant to the position. A typical résumé will include the following items:

1. Name and contact information

2. The position desired or career objective

3. Educational background

4. Experience or employment background

5. Related experiences or activities

6. (optional) References upon request

If you think your employment experience is more relevant than your educational achievements, you may wish to reverse those two categories. In any one category, the entries are typically listed in reverse chronological order (that is, with the most recent item first).

Should I include personal data in a résumé?

In some countries, it is expected that you will include personal data on your résumé, such as your age, marital status, religious affiliation, or other personal information. In the United States, however, it is illegal to consider such information in hiring, so it should not be included for any jobs in the United States. The only personal information should be your contact information.

How do I format a traditional résumé?

If you are preparing a traditional hard-copy résumé, you will want to pay attention to formatting it in such a way that it is not only readable but also pleasing to the eye. Use suitable margins and fonts; use headings and subheadings; use verb phrases rather than complete sentences; use active verbs. Print the résumé on either white or cream-colored paper. Avoid printing in color as it is harder to photocopy.

How do I format a scannable résumé?

Many companies today use computers to quickly scan large numbers of résumés into a database. This allows the company to do a keyword search to select only those applicants who fit a particular profile. If you are applying to a technologically oriented company, you should format your résumé to take advantage of this technology. When submitting a scannable résumé, you will want to pay attention to formatting it so that it is easily scanned. Since keywords

Résumés may be submitted in several ways these days: by traditional post, in an email, or directly to a company website to which you are applying. Carefully read which options are preferred by the potential employer before submitting your qualifications.

Caroline Lopez
3535 Highland Drive
Ft. Worth, TX 78494
caroline.lopez@gmail.com
Tel. (555) 453-3282

KEYWORDS: Marketing/management trainee, retail sales, Web site designer, marketing and public relations major, management experience, business administration degree, marketing planner, customer complaint department, product testing, merchandising

OBJECTIVE: Marketing/management internship

EDUCATION: Bachelor of Science, Business Administration, University of Dallas, May, 2014 (3.5 gpa; Dean's List). Completed 24 credits in communication.

BUSINESS EXPERIENCE: Retail sales, Macy's, Fort Worth, since September 2013. Sales associate, Web site designer, marketing planner, complaint resolution. Management of weekend operations from floor sales. Website design includes operational complaint-resolution system.

Waitress, Del Rio Restaurant. Fort Worth, TX, May 2012-September 2013. Responsible for three to four tables. Selected "Employee of the Month" for August 2013.

OTHER EXPERIENCE: President, University of Dallas Hispanic Student Caucus, September 2013 to present. Representative to the regional Student Association meeting held in Houston, January, 2014. Tutor at Worth Literacy Project through the Fort Worth Public Library. Volunteer for Big Brother, Big Sister organization in Fort Worth for three summers.

AWARDS: Dean's list four consecutive years while a student at UD. Scholarship recipient for College of Business Young Entrepreneur Scholarship, Junior and Senior years.

REFERENCES: Available on request from the University of Dallas Career Center: UMC 4850, University of Dallas, Dallas, TX 78491. Tel. (555) 453-1600.

An example of a scannable résumé.

will be an important way in which the company will sort résumés, it is a good idea to begin the résumé with the keywords that describe your experience and skills. Some possible keywords might be: marketing major, retail sales, website designer, management experience, marketing planner, product testing, merchandising, etc. Use a traditional font and a minimum of symbols that may be difficult for scanners to recognize.

What is a curriculum vitae (CV)?

In the education arena, a curriculum vitae is more common than a résumé. The two documents are similar in intent, but the CV is more comprehensive and overviews a person's life accomplishments, particularly those that are relevant to academia or research.

A CV is a living document that grows as a person completes projects and teaching responsibilities. It is not unusual for a CV to be several pages in length. A typical CV will include the following information:

1. Name and contact information

2. Areas of academic interest

3. Education

4. Grants, honors, awards

5. Publications and presentations

6. Employment and experience

7. Scholarly and professional memberships

8. References

How do I write memos and e-memos?

The memo (short for memorandum) has become a standard form for business writing. Memos, whether printed or electronic, are typically short and to the point. They are usually addressed to just one person or a small group of people, generally within a department or business rather than being written to people outside the organization. The purposes for writing a memo are varied: to make a recommendation or request, to inform someone about something, to summarize a meeting or discussion. Most word processing programs include memo templates that you can use, and many companies have their own set memo format. Memos usually have the following four parts:

1. Header (To: From: Date: Subject:)

2. Introduction (two or three sentences of background or contextual information)

3. Body (a few succinct sentences or paragraphs)

4. Conclusion (summary in a sentence or two)

What is a report?

Reports are written to describe the outcome or results of an activity or experiment. For example, if a researcher conducts a chemical experiment, he or she may be asked to write a report of that experiment, detailing both the processes used and the results. Similarly, students are often asked to do field or library research on a topic and then subsequently to write a report detailing their findings. When an employee embarks on a business trip, he or she is typically asked to file a trip report upon returning, explaining what customers were visited, what results were obtained, and so on. There are many types of reports, each with its own special format and conventions. Engineers may write feasibility reports, biologists may write environmental impact reports, and so on. Short reports may have an audience of one or two people, whereas long reports may be widely circulated or even published, both inside and outside of the organization in which they were written.

To: MSU BioBank Project Directors and Staff

From: External Advisory Board

Date: December 10, 2014

Subject: Summary of Visit

The External Advisory Board visited Montgomery State University on November 27-28 to learn more about the MSU BioBank Project, to meet project directors, staff and faculty, and to participate in the project launch.

The project launch meetings and luncheon were well attended, and the grantees at the reception Thursday night were highly enthusiastic. The faculty and staff participating in the project are excited, energized, and ready to make the BioBank a reality at MSU.

As the External Advisory Board, we are privileged to be able to have a front-row seat to the exciting new changes happening at MSU. We are enthusiastic about your project and look forward to working with you in the upcoming semester.

An example of a memo.

How do I write a report?

Although specifics of format may vary by discipline or organization, in general reports have the same four parts found in a memo: header, introduction, body, and conclusion. Reports tend to be much longer than memos, however, and may have multiple audiences, including audiences external to the organization. Because many readers, particularly executives, are too busy to read the entire report, the structure typically helps

243

readers to skim by using advance organizers, headings, bulleted lists, and the like. It would be a good idea to find out what format is typically used in your organization before submitting a report. Here are some ideas to get you started:

1. Header (provides basic information about who it is for, who wrote it, when it was written, and what it is about)

2. Introduction (orients the readers to the topic of the report and to its purpose and claim)

3. Body (lays out the reasoning, arguments, and evidence in support of the claim)

4. Conclusion (summarizes the main points and provides recommendations)

What are some optional parts of reports?

Some reports, particularly lengthy reports, include additional information and sections to help busy readers become oriented to the reports' content. These optional parts of reports may include a title page, an abstract or an executive summary, a table of contents (for long reports), graphs and charts or other attachments, and a cover letter:

1. Title Page (a separate page that expands on the information typically found in a header: person or group addressed, names of recipients, names of writers, date, subject, and reference to funding sources)

2. Abstract or Executive Summary (a concise synopsis of the report, typically about 100–150 words long)

3. Table of Contents (an outline of the contents to help readers select the parts important for them to read; sections of the report are often numbered or outlined)

4. Attachments (graphs, charts, drawings, references, etc, that not every reader needs to read)

5. Cover Letter (an introductory letter addressed to specific readers to orient them to the report)

How do I write presentations?

Many people use presentation software, such as *PowerPoint*, in business settings. Presentation software has several advantages for writers, including templates that can be used to create slides and put together effective presentations. The advantages of *PowerPoint* presentations include their ability to project information in color; to include animation, video, and audio; and to be uploaded to websites for viewing in the future. In general, when writing presentations, keep in mind that each slide should be neatly and correctly formatted, easy to read from a distance, simple and uncluttered. Whenever possible, include visual imagery on each slide, not just words. A frequent mistake is cluttered slides. Simpler is better. Here are a few tips for writing effective presentations:

1. *Use slides to support, but not substitute for, your message.* Your audience is there to hear you talk, not to hear you read from slides. It is a good idea to first prepare your talk and then create slides that will support it.

Summary Report on iPhone Advertising
BJ Myers
February 12, 2015

Apple's popular product—the iPhone—combines three of the most widely used mobile devices in the world: a revolutionary mobile phone, a widescreen iPod with touch controls, and a breakthrough Internet communications device. Even with these features, however, the product cannot sell itself. Apple's new ad for the iPhone highlights its design; sells the product's look, features, label, and purpose; and lets viewers walk away with a clear mental image of their next purchase.

A first look at the ad shows a very straightforward approach: the product is clearly in view, held in a solitary hand against a black background. The text is simple and lists a number of the product's features. Links on the page lead to more detailed information, as well as demonstrations of various tasks. The iPhone is portrayed as being slick, lightweight, and full of capability.

The main focus of the advertisement is the appearance of the product. The iPhone's display consists of a grid of colored panels that serve as a menu for the phone's functions. The advertisement includes several of the icons present on the iPhone's display, highlighting its primary features. The picture is sharp and clear, suggesting a similar image quality in the iPhone.

After the viewer has initially looked over the product, he or she may be inclined to read the descriptive text next to the image, but the side-by-side placement continually draws the viewer's eyes back to the product. This ensures that the viewer will leave the advertisement with a clear picture of the sharp, bright screen and the sleek, simple user interface. The close-up view of the device allows the viewer to see its display in detail, even down to the text labels on the main menu. The viewer can see how self-explanatory the interface is, and knows that he or she could learn to use it quickly. The icons are clearer and more concise than the text menus found on most cell phones, and the features they will use the most are on the main menu, right at their fingertips.

Overall, Apple has done has an excellent job with this ad. It has been created to convey the iPhone's design by emulating the product's own look, feel, and format.

An example of a business report.

2. *Keep the slides visually straightforward and not overly fancy.* Special effects can easily be overdone and become distracting rather than supportive of your talk.

3. *Look for ways to use visuals to support your ideas.* Too many words on slides make them impossible to read or follow. Use bullet points and shorthand. Fill in verbally with your talk, rather than attempting to include all of your talk on each slide.

4. *Try to keep your talk active.* Sometimes a presentation can become mind-numbing to your audience. Look for ways to make it interactive, to provide time for ques-

tions and answers or listener comments, so that your audience does not become overly passive.

How do I write a white paper?

The "white paper," originally used to describe a government policy, has become a standard form of communication in the business world. White papers are used to describe a particular problem and propose a specific solution to that problem. White papers typically include the following:

1. Begin the white paper with a general title, e.g., "White Paper on Network Slowdown."

2. State the main problem your paper is addressing in one or two direct sentences (e.g., sales are decreasing, network speed is too slow, customers are complaining).

3. Include any necessary background information, taking care to consider your audience's need for detail. You do not want your white paper to be either too simple or too complex for your readers.

4. Write the body of the white paper, which will typically range from 1–5 pages. Begin the body by elaborating on the problem you identified in the introduction. Follow with the solutions you are proposing, including any step-by-step implementation that will be needed.

5. Close with a summary that reviews the problem, your suggested solution, and the anticipated results.

What is a proposal?

Many fields and disciplines use proposals to put forward or recommend something for consideration, discussion, or adoption. The purpose of all proposals is persuasion—persuading someone to take a recommended action, to adopt a specific point of view, to solve a problem in a particular way, to fund or approve a project. Proposals may be informal or formal. In undergraduate courses, proposals tend to be one-page informational descriptions of some course project the student hopes to do. In business and academia, proposals more often seek funding—sometimes millions of dollars—and are therefore much more formal and much longer. The following items are usually found in proposals:

1. Abstract (concisely states the purpose of the research, the problem being addressed, and the methodology)

2. A problem statement (a description of some problem that the proposal seeks to address)

3. Proposal body (The proposal writer will detail the ways in which he or she proposes to solve the problem using well-reasoned arguments.)

4. Schedule (The writer outlines specific dates for project "deliverables.")

5. Budget (The writer outlines costs associated with the project.)

U.R.C.O. Grant Proposal, Spring 2015
Stephanie Croasdell, Student, Department of Biology
Tim Gilbertson, Professor, Department of Biology

Cognitive Responses of Laboratory Rats in Relation to their Dietary Fat Preferences

Introduction

Thanks to previous work done by the Gilbertson lab on sensory cues for dietary fat and their relationship with dietary fat preference, it has been found that laboratory rats who exhibit a high fat preference and become obese on a high-fat diet are less responsive than those that tend to avoid fat and stay lean. Continuing studies are exploring the "underlying genetic differences between obesity-prone and -resistant animals in order to more clearly understand the role that nutrient chemoreception may play in the control of food (e.g. fat) intake."

Hypothesis

A relationship occurs between fat intake and the speed of cognitive responses. The more obese the animal, the longer it takes them to perform a basic operant test.

Procedure

One group of rats will be used as the control group, given a normal diet in the attempt to maintain a healthy weight. Another group will be placed on a high-fat diet of their pre-determined preference, allowing each rat to reach a state of obesity. Each test group of rats will then be placed within an operant chamber and required to perform basic operant condition tasks. The reinforcement contingencies will be based on each rat's individual diet. Observation of the frequency and reliability of responses will be made and compiled for any possible correlation.

Timeline

February, 2015: Order rats, establish diet
March, 2015: Operant Conditioning of rats
April, 2015: Complete conditioning, compile results
May, 2015: Submit results to Vice President for Research Office
Fall, 2015: Present research

Conclusion

It is a well-known fact that American society</sq>s obesity rates are increasing at a very fast rate, and although there has been an incredible amount of research done on the topic, there is still a great deal of mystery concerning why our bodies respond to fats the way they do, engendering the negative consequences that occur. This is why this type of research and that similar to it is so important. I have always been fascinated by the

An example of an effective proposal.

6. Conclusion (The writer sums up the request for help and summarizes the proposal's main points.)

7. Other possible items, such as references and attachments

How do I write a proposal?

To write an effective proposal, you will first want to carefully read the RFP (Request for Proposal). Prepare yourself to write the proposal by identifying a problem that needs solving. Determine what you need in the way of background information, guidance, or financial support. Next, define the problem you want to address and sketch out a solution. Have good reasons for your solution. Consider both your audience and your purpose. Who will be reading your proposal? What are you trying to accomplish? Read widely about the subject and gather good information. Make yourself aware of arguments, both pro and con, about your proposed solution and its alternatives. Write out a rough outline of your proposal, including the key elements of proposals listed in the section above. Be sure that your proposal exactly follows the directions found in the RFP as to length, format, sections to be included, etc. Revise your draft for coherence, accuracy, completeness, and flow. It would also be a good idea to have another reader check your proposal before submission.

INVITATIONS AND ANNOUNCEMENTS

How do I write correct print invitations?

An invitation is an important part of an event or social function because it helps to set the overall tone of the event. It will also help you to determine the number of guests who will attend. Following are some things to think about as you craft a formal invitation. (*See also* Appendix J.)

1. At the top of the invitation, place the organization's or host's logo or a graphic or photo of your choice that captures the spirit of the event.

2. List the host's full name on the invitation, but leave off the honorific (such as Dr., Mr., Mrs.) unless it is an official event being given by an official, e.g., Provost Marcus Allen.

3. Write the invitation itself. The most formal wording is "We request your presence." Less formal is "We cordially invite you to attend."

4. Next provide all of the specific information about your event. Try to be succinct but descriptive: an award ceremony, a banquet, an engagement ceremony, a wedding reception.

5. State the purpose of the event, e.g., an engagement ceremony in honor of....

6. Provide the date of the event. The most formal way to do so is to write the date out completely in words, e.g., Saturday, the fourteenth of March. Writing it numerically, e.g., Saturday, 14 March 2015, is less formal. Be sure to always include the day of the week in addition to the date.

7. Provide the time of the event, including words such as "in the morning" or "in the evening" if this needs clarification, e.g., Saturday, the fourteenth of March, at 7:30 in the evening. Using A.M. and P.M., e.g., Saturday, March 14, 2015, at 7:30 P.M., is a less formal way of indicating the time of day.

8. Provide the specific location of the event along with a street address and directions, if necessary, e.g., 120 Center Street, Moab, Utah; one block east of the city library.

9. Provide any special instructions if necessary. For example, you might want to include a map, in which case you would state, "directions enclosed." If you want to discourage gifts, you would state, "no gifts, please."

10. Include your RSVP information. RSVP is an abbreviation for the French phrase *Répondez s'il vous plaît* which in English means "Please respond." It is especially important to get an RSVP when your event has specific seating or food requirements and you need a very close count of expected guests. Be sure to specify to whom and how a response should be made, along with a phone number or email address.

11. Provide a response card as needed. If you are including a response card, you should state on the main invitation, "Response card enclosed." It is also wise to give a date by which responses need to reach you, typically two weeks prior to the event. The response card should be stamped and addressed to you. The response card may also ask for meal preferences or other information that will help you plan. Print the response card in the same style as the invitation.

12. There are many online sites that will help you to craft your print invitations. Check out a few online templates to see what they are like before deciding on which one to use.

13. Be sure to proofread your invitation several times before printing it. Check grammar and spelling very carefully. Do a test printing and proofread it on paper as well as online. Sometimes we miss things when reading on a screen. Perhaps have another person proofread it as well. It is very expensive to reprint something. It is also very embarrassing to send out a printed invitation in which something is misspelled.

How do I write correct announcements?

As with invitations, the first task for writing an announcement is to decide to whom you are writing. Determining your audience will help you to determine the level of formality to use. Next you need to determine the purpose for which you are writing. This can vary from announcing a job-related party or retreat to announcing the birth of a new baby.

Formal invitations, such as to a wedding, require full and complete information, including day, time, specific place, reason for the event, specific instructions (if needed), people's full names, and so on.

Your tone will vary dramatically depending upon both your audience and your purpose, so consider them carefully before you write. Once you have determined what and to whom you need to communicate, you can write the body of your announcement. Be careful to use correct grammar in any announcement you write. People are justifiably annoyed when they receive announcements with misspellings and typos. Take care to proofread any announcements carefully; even better, have someone else proofread the announcement as well before you send it out. Check the advice in the grammar section of this book if you have any questions about spelling, grammar, or usage. Free sample announcements on the Internet may provide you with guidance as well. (*See also* Appendix J.)

What is a PSA and how do I write one?

The abbreviation PSA is short for Public Service Announcement. A PSA is written and produced for publication in a newspaper or newsletter or for broadcast on a radio or television station. Generally PSAs are sent as ready-to-air audio or video tapes, although some radio stations prefer a written script that their announcers can read live on the air. Many service organizations and non-profits find that PSAs are an economical way to get information out to their target audience. PSAs are most effective at encouraging an audience to do something, or to refrain from doing something. For example, a PSA may encourage the audience to call a phone number or visit a website to obtain more information, or a PSA may encourage the audience to have their pets spayed or neutered. Here are some tips for writing an effective PSA:

1. Target your audience. This will help you decide what media outlets to use and what content will be most effective in the PSA.

2. Survey the media outlets in your area to determine which ones might be available to you. Find out their rules and regulations surrounding the PSAs that they run.

3. Because your PSA will be only 30 seconds or less, use simple and vivid language. Take your time writing the PSA so that you make every word count.

4. Think of "hooks" in your writing that will grab attention. A catchy phrase or a startling statistic may be a good hook.

5. Typically the PSA should request a specific action of the audience, such as calling a number or visiting a website for more information.

6. Be sure the PSA is focused on one salient point. Resist the temptation to cover everything in one PSA.

7. Check and double-check your facts to be certain that everything is correct in your announcement.

8. Consider brainstorming with others in your organization and in your target audience for ideas.

9. Check online for other ideas and tips about writing effective PSAs.

LEARNING ENGLISH AS A SECOND LANGUAGE

What is ESL?

Students study English as a Second Language (ESL) for a variety of purposes. Some may wish to learn the language well enough to be integrated into a society that uses English as its medium of communication. Others may wish to learn English for instrumental reasons—traveling to an English-speaking country, for example, or communicating with English speakers who are visiting their country. In each case, however, the learner wishes to achieve a certain communicative competence in the target language. There is no one sure way to learn another language. Each learner will need to explore his or her own learning style and adapt to the situation or context. To learn another language means to learn all four skills of communication: speaking, listening, reading, and writing. Linguists have uncovered several common problem areas for ESL learners, which are discussed in this chapter.

ESL PROBLEMS WITH VERBS

What are phrasal verbs?

A *phrasal verb* is a verb that is made up of the verb plus one or two particles, either prepositions or adverbs, e.g., *burn up, get by without*. Phrasal verbs can be difficult for ESL learners because they often mean something other than what you would expect from the words composing the phrase. For example, if someone says, "I *ran up* a debt at Nordstrom," it has nothing to do with actual running. Rather it means that the person incurred debt over time. To further complicate the issue, phrasal verbs can be either transitive or intransitive; that is, they may or may not have a direct object. To master the English language, learners must learn hundreds of such phrasal verbs. Books and websites listing phrasal verbs can be helpful for ESL students. Following are some examples:

The reporter *dug up* some dirt on the congressman. [transitive phrasal verb meaning *to find* with direct object *dirt*]

The students wished their teacher would *speak up*. [intransitive phrasal verb meaning *talk more loudly*]

Martin always tried *to show up* his brother. [transitive phrasal verb meaning *to do better than*]

Martin always tried *to show* his brother *up*. [some transitive phrasal verbs may be split]

John wanted *to go over* the paper with his tutor. [transitive phrasal verb meaning *to look closely at*]

Teaching English as a Second Language takes special skills because the educator needs to understand that his or her students can have very different understandings of syntax and grammar.

John wanted *to go* the paper *over* with his tutor. [faulty; this phrasal verb may not be split]

What are verb complements?

Verb complements are gerunds, e.g., *running*, and infinitives, e.g., *to run*. The problem for ESL learners is that some verbs take certain complements while others do not. There is no particular reason for the differences, so the verbs simply need to be memorized. Following are some examples:

- Paul *dislikes running*. [gerund complement]
- Paul *dislikes to run*. [faulty; English speakers would not use this sentence]
- Paul *likes to run*. [infinitive complement]
- Paul *does not like running*. [gerund complement]
- Paul *wants to swim*. [infinitive complement]
- Paul *wants swimming*. [faulty; English speakers would not use this sentence]

Which verbs take gerund (-*ing*) verb complements?

The following verbs take gerund (-*ing*) verb complements, but not infinitive verb complements. For example:

He *advised leaving* the show early. [correct]

He *advised to leave* the show early [faulty]

acknowledge

254   admit

advise

anticipate

appreciate

avoid

cannot (can't) help

complete

consider

consist of

delay

deny

depend on

detest

discuss

dislike

dream about

enjoy

escape

evade

finish

forgive

give up

have trouble

imagine

insist on

involve

keep

mention

mind

miss

object to

plan on

postpone

practice

put off

quit

recall

recommend

regret

report

resent

resist

result in

resume

risk

succeed in

suggest

talk about

tolerate

understand

Which verbs take infinitive (*to*) verb complements?

The following verbs take infinitive (*to*) verb complements, but not gerund verb complements. For example:

He *decided to go* to bed. [correct]

He *decided going* to bed. [faulty]

afford

agree

appear

arrange

ask

attempt

care

claim

consent

decide

demand

expect

fail

get

happen

hesitate

hope

intend

learn

manage

mean

need

offer

plan

prepare

pretend

promise

refuse

seem

struggle

tend

threaten

wait

want

wish

yearn

Which verbs take either (*-ing*) or (*to*) verb complements?

The following verbs take either gerund (*-ing*) verb complements or infinitive (*to*) verb complements. For example:

He *continued practicing* his English. [correct]

He *continued to practice* his English. [correct]

begin

cannot (can't) stand

continue

dread

forget

hate

like

love

remember

stop

try

With three of the verbs (*forget, remember, stop*), the meaning of the sentence changes depending on whether the complement is the gerund or the infinitive form. For example:

Peter *forgot to buy* some milk at the store. [i.e., He did not buy the milk.]

Peter *forgot buying* milk at the store. [i.e.,He did buy the milk, but then forgot he had done so.]

We must *remember to save* our receipt. [i.e., We need to remember to save it.]

We must *remember saving* our receipt. [i.e., We saved it and we need to remember that fact.]

He *stopped trying* because he didn't get any positive feedback. [i.e., He quit trying.]

He *stopped to try* on some new shoes. [i.e., He physically stopped somewhere to try on the shoes.]

What are verbs of state?

Verbs of state are verbs that do not indicate events or actions. Rather, they indicate a condition or state of something. Verbs of state can present problems for ESL learners because they cannot be used in the progressive tense (indicated by a form of the verb *be* plus a verb ending with *-ing*). For example:

The baseball game *was consisting* of nine innings. [faulty; use of progressive tense]

The baseball game *consisted* of nine innings. [correct]

The following verbs of state may not be used in the progressive tense:

appear

believe

belong

consist of

constitute

contain

correspond

differ from

exist

involve

know

mean

need

possess

represent

result in

seem

suppose

understand

want

What are modal auxiliary verbs?

The *modal auxiliary* verbs include *can, could, may, might, must, will, would,* and *should.* The modal auxiliary verbs can cause problems for ESL learners because they have several different shades of meaning for English speakers. Each modal auxiliary has at least two different meanings. The first meaning often relates to social niceties, e.g., *May* I have more potatoes? The second meaning often relates to logical possibility, e.g., It *may be* colder this winter than last winter. Any verb immediately following the modal auxiliary must be in the verb's base or simple form, not in the infinitive or gerund form. For example:

Oftentimes, fathers *can teach* their children many important life lessons. [correct]

Oftentimes, fathers *can teaching* their children many important life lessons. [faulty; use of gerund]

Oftentimes, fathers *can to teach* their children many important life lessons. [faulty; use of infinitive]

Another feature of modal auxiliary verbs is that they may only be used one at a time. For example:

If I work hard, I *might could* get a promotion. [faulty]

If I work hard, I *might* get a promotion. [correct]

If I work hard, I *might be able to* get a promotion. [correct]

ESL PROBLEMS WITH NOUNS

What is the difference between a count and a noncount noun?

ESL learners often have problems with understanding the difference in English between count and noncount nouns.

259

ESL students may have quite a problem understanding the difference between count and noncount nouns in English.

Count nouns refer to things that have a distinct physical or mental form and therefore can be counted. Some examples are *plate, fork, car, truck, orange, professor, idea.* All of the items in this list can be numbered and made plural: *four plates, two forks, several cars, two trucks, five oranges, ten professors, many ideas.* Following are some examples of count nouns:

They set the table with *four plates* but only *two forks.*

Several cars plus *two trucks* were for sale.

The *ten professors* shared the *five oranges.*

We have *many ideas* about how to improve our city.

Noncount nouns refer to items that do not have a distinct physical or mental form as a whole. Some examples are *water, air, electricity, power, rice, courage,* and *fortitude.* As their name implies, noncount nouns cannot be counted. They also cannot be made plural. An English speaker would not say "There are *two airs* in that tire." [faulty] Instead, in English, noncount nouns are quantified by using expressions such as *a lot of, many, some, much.* For example:

There is *much more water* in that tub than you need.

You need *a lot of air* to blow up a balloon.

The recipe calls for *one cup of rice* and *two cups of water.*

260 The hikers showed *much fortitude* by climbing up the side of the mountain.

Can a noun be both a count noun and a noncount noun?

A few words in English can be used as either count or noncount nouns: *wine, cloth, thought, beauty, hair, reading*. Whether or not the word is being used in a general or a specific sense will determine whether or not it is countable. Following are some examples:

I enjoy *reading* poetry, but I did not enjoy *the reading* given by the poet last night. [The first is a general noncount noun and the second is a specific count noun.]

All of the wine made by that winery is excellent. I always like *a wine* with a rich bouquet. [The first is a general noncount noun and the second is a specific count noun.]

Although *beauty* is in the eye of the beholder, everyone who sees her would say she is *a beauty*. [The first is a general noncount noun and the second is a specific count noun.]

ESL PROBLEMS WITH ARTICLES

What are articles?

Articles are determiners that come before a noun. The English articles are *the, a*, and *an*. English speakers and writers use articles to help determine information about the noun being introduced. Does the noun refer to something specific? Does it refer to something in general? When someone is referring to something specific that he or she assumes is known by the reader or listener, the article *the* is selected. When someone is referring to something in general, the article *a/an* is selected. For example:

Take *the books* on the table along with you when you leave. [referring to specific books]

Take *a book* from the shelf along with you when you leave. [referring to any of the books on the shelf]

Articles may also be used for emphasizing something's uniqueness. For example:

Bumgarner is arguably *the best pitcher* in the World Series.

An hour after boarding, our plane was still on *the ground*.

Articles may also be used when a noun is followed by a phrase or clause that restricts its identify or if you refer to the same thing again. For example:

The boy with the red jacket is a student of mine.

The theory of evolution was posited by Darwin.

We bought *milk* at the store today. Please put *the milk* in the refrigerator.

How do I use an article with a proper noun?

Proper nouns are names of persons, locations, holidays, companies, and organizations. Proper nouns are capitalized in English. What can be confusing is that, even though they identify a specific thing, most proper nouns do not take articles. Whether or not to use an article with a particular proper noun is something that most ESL learners need to memorize. For example:

J. S. Bach [not, *the* J. S. Bach]

Microsoft [not, *the* Microsoft]

You might, however, want to use the article for special emphasis. For example:

He played music by *the one and only J. S. Bach*.

The Microsoft that we know and love continues to be a business leader.

There are many proper nouns that do take the definite article. For example:

The United States of America

The Vietnam War

The Fourth of July

The University of Maryland

The Vatican

The Capitol

Other proper nouns do not. For example:

Vatican City

Oak Street

Burger King

Capitol Hill

How do I use articles with nonspecific references?

When not referring to a specific thing, use *a* or *an*. Notice that *an* is used when the noun begins with a vowel sound, e.g., *a* plate, *an* apple, *an* airplane, *a* plane. When a nonspecific noun is made plural, the determiner is not used. For example:

An apple a day keeps the doctor away. [singular]

Apples are good for your health. [plural]

Furthermore, if the nonspecific noun is not countable, the determiner is not used. For example:

Water is a precious commodity. [noncount noun]

A waterfall was tumbling over the cliff. [count noun]

Waterfalls often appear in the spring. [plural count noun]

What are the other determiners?

There are three other kinds of determiners in addition to articles: *quantifiers, demonstratives,* and *possessive adjectives*. Each kind will be used to begin a noun phrase. Note, however, that you may not use more than one determiner with any one noun phrase.

Quantifiers are used to indicate some amount of a noun. Some quantifiers can only be used with count nouns, e.g., *many, several, few, a few, a couple of*, and *each*. Other quantifiers are only used with noncount nouns, e.g., *much, not much, little, a little*. Still others may be used with either count or noncount nouns, e.g., *some, no, enough, any, a lot of*. Following are some examples of quantifiers:

We picked *many pinecones* off the driveway. [quantifier plus count noun]

We had only *a few apples* on the tree this year. [quantifier plus count noun]

They don't have *much patience* with children. [quantifier plus noncount noun]

Try *a little tenderness*. [quantifier plus noncount noun]

Some tolerance is to be desired. [quantifier plus noncount noun]

Some apples were all we could spare. [quantifier plus count noun]

Demonstratives are used to specify the person or thing being referred to. *This* and *these* indicate something nearby or just mentioned, whereas *that* and *those* indicate something more distant. Following are some examples of demonstratives:

This laptop computer will be easy to carry in your backpack. [specific item nearby]

That bird is going to build a nest in your tree. [specific item at a distance]

Possessive adjectives are used to indicate ownership of something. Possessive adjectives resemble possessive pronouns (*mine, yours, theirs*, etc.) but their function in a sentence is to initiate a noun phrase rather than substitute for a noun phrase. For example:

Our food is on the table. [possessive adjective]

The food on the table is *ours*. [possessive pronoun]

ESL PROBLEMS WITH WORD ORDER

Is word order flexible in English?

No. English word order is relatively fixed. This fact can give ESL learners problems if their own language is more flexible about word order. Changing the order of words in English sentences can actually change meaning. For example:

The *arm chair* was damaged. [i.e., The "arm chair" is a piece of furniture.]

The *chair arm* was damaged. [i.e., One part of the chair, the arm, was damaged.]

He had completed all his homework. [declarative sentence]

Had he completed all his homework? [interrogative sentence]

When you change word order, can structure change?

Yes. Sometimes a change in the order of content words (words such as nouns, most verbs, adjectives, and adverbs—words that refer to some object, action, or characteristic) is accompanied by other structural changes. For example:

In some languages, such as German, subjects and objects can be indicated by words such as articles, and therefore word order is not as essential as it is in English.

I gave Susan a book. [simple statement of fact]

I gave a book *to* Susan. [simple statement of fact]

The teacher asked the student a question. [simple statement of fact]

The teacher asked a question *of* the student. [simple statement of fact]

I had owned a speedboat at one time. [simple statement of fact]

If I had owned a speedboat, I would have invited you to water ski. [conditional clause signaled by *if*]

Had I owned a speedboat, I would have invited you to water ski. [conditional clause signaled by reversing word order]

ESL STUDENTS AND VOCABULARY PROBLEMS

What is one of the biggest challenges for ESL students?

Vocabulary is a challenge for ESL students. They must learn thousands of vocabulary words in order to be able to express their thoughts completely. There are three areas of vocabulary with which ESL learners particularly struggle: *cognates, collocations,* and *idioms.*

What are cognates?

Cognates are words that look or sound similar in different languages, perhaps because they share a common Latin or Greek root word. If an ESL learner's native language is closely related to English, using cognates can help him or her learn new words. When cognates are similar, it is easy for speakers to learn them. For example, *abbreviation* (English) and *abreviacion* (Spanish) are easily recognized as the same word. In most cases, you can trust a cognate to have a similar meaning, if not exactly the same meaning. You can easily find long lists of Spanish/English cognates on the Web.

What is a "false friend"?

When a cognate looks like it should have the same meaning, but it does not, we call it a "false friend." You cannot just assume that words that look alike always will have the same meaning. For example, the English *jubilation* means "great happiness" whereas the Spanish *jubilation* means retirement pension. You can find comprehensive lists of false friends on the Web. Here are some examples of false cognates between English and Spanish:

Word	Spanish Meaning	English Meaning
actual	at present	real
apologia/apology	eulogy	request for forgiveness
bizarro/bizarre	valiant	weird
bonanza	fair weather	a treasure
colorado	the color red	the U.S. state of Colorado
conductor	driver	a driver of a public conveyance, an orchestra leader, a material that can carry an electric current
coraje/courage	anger	bravery
desgracia/disgrace	misfortune	dishonor
disgusto/disgust	trouble	repugnance
eventual	possible	final or last
falacia/fallacy	deceit	false reasoning
informal	unreliable	casual
lunatico/lunatic	temperamental	insane
mayor	larger	government official
once	eleven	one time
papa	potato	father
particular	private	specific
real	royal	genuine
sensible	sensitive	reasonable
voluble	moody	talkative

What is a collocation?

Collocations are words that commonly occur together in a sentence. One example is the word *advice*, which commonly occurs with the verbs *give, get*, and *receive* and with the adjectives *good, bad*, and *sound*. The ESL learner should strive to memorize such collocations. The best way to learn them is by paying attention to the phrases that English speakers use around you. By doing so, you can get a feeling for which words typically are used together in English. There are also lists of collocations on the Web and in books about learning English. Following are some examples:

The counselor always *gave sound advice* to her clients.

The client felt that his lawyer had *given him bad advice*.

The lawyer *presented* me some *nice advice*. [faulty collocation; wrong verb and adjective for *advice*]

During the matinee's intermission, the movie-goers went outside to *spread* their legs. [faulty collocation]

During the matinee's intermission, the movie-goers went outside to *stretch* their legs. [revised]

Some students tend to make *wide statements* about things they know little about. [faulty collocation]

Some students tend to make *broad statements* about things they know little about. [revised]

The rapid *upsweep in the stock market* elated many traders. [faulty collocation]

The rapid *rise in the stock market* elated many traders. [revised]

What is an idiom?

An idiom is a special type of collocation, or collection of words that typically are used together. An idiom may not necessarily be made up of the sum of its parts. For example, if you know the words *bucket* and *list*, you still may not know what a *bucket list* refers to. The phrase *bucket list* is used to denote a listing of the things a person would like to do before he or she dies. It comes from another idiom, *kick the bucket*, which means to die. As with other collocations, the best way to learn idioms is to listen to native speakers of English. There are also websites and books that list English idioms. Many idioms are slang or folk dialect and therefore should not be used in formal English. Other idioms are largely accepted. Following are some examples:

We felt the candidate only *paid lip service* to balancing the budget.

In English "papa" means father, but in Spanish it means "potato"; this is an example of "false friend" words.

Voting for her is *out of the question*. She is *too clever by half*.

By and large, young people favored the other candidate.

He was not one *to beat around the bush*.

I wish my friend wouldn't *talk a mile a minute*.

You *hit the nail on the head* this time.

I felt that he had *cut me off at the knees* with that remark.

We went over the area *with a fine-tooth comb*.

That *flies in the face of* everything I believe.

She did it out of *the goodness of her heart*.

That remark really *hits below the belt*.

Don't *lose your head* over that girl.

I wouldn't hesitate *to put your oar in*.

ENGLISH IN THE ELECTRONIC AGE

ELECTRONIC COMMUNICATION

How is grammar affected by new media?

In this world of multiple electronic communication options, you need to pay close attention to both the audience with whom you are communicating and your purpose for writing. In every act of communication, a rhetorical triangle is in operation: your audience, your persona, and your chosen arguments all interact with your topic. Depending on the aim of your writing, some electronic tools may be better suited than others. For example, it is probably not appropriate to text-message your professor or your boss because of the informality of the medium, whereas it may be perfectly acceptable to send an email message, provided you use an appropriate tone—that is, do not start out your email, "Yo, Boss." Just as it is not appropriate to talk to your teachers, supervisors, or bosses the same way you talk to your friends or family, it is not appropriate to *write* to them the same way. You will want to use the grammar of formal, edited English when communicating in school and work settings, regardless of the medium.

How formal should I be when using electronic communications?

Levels of formality vary widely among electronic communications. For example, instant messages and text messages are very informal and chatty in tone. On the other hand, email can be formal or informal, depending on the rhetorical stance you wish to adopt. The rhetorical stance is based on your audience, as well as your persona (how you wish to come across). If you are a student who is writing to a professor to clarify an assignment, you will want to address him or her formally, make the request politely, and present yourself as an engaged and diligent student. Do not ask a professor "what you missed" when you were not in class! That is the number one complaint professors have

How effective is multitasking?

Although the ability to multitask is a good skill to develop, it can get us into trouble. Sometimes we try to do too much at once, and our communications become sloppy as a result. For example, even though it might seem efficient, it may not be a good idea to email your boss with a question while taking notes in a meeting, text-messaging with a friend, or surfing the Internet. When your mind is on more than one task, you are likely to do none of them very well. When in doubt, focus on one thing at a time—particularly if the person you are communicating with is important to you or the communication situation is a formal one. If you inadvertently make a mistake in etiquette or hit the SEND button too soon, the written record of your error in judgment may come back to haunt you.

about student emails. Similarly, if you are an employee writing an email to a supervisor, you will want to write in a business-like manner with an appropriately formal tone.

What is the line between public and private conversations?

Electronic communication often blurs the line between what is a private and what is a public conversation. Sometimes we act as though everything we say online is private, between ourselves and our immediate correspondent. You should remember, however, that email, text messages, *Facebook* posts, and chat-room conversations are in a sense "public," because they can be archived on someone's computer or cell phone, forwarded to others, and even subpoenaed in a court of law. Take particular care not to write anything from a shared computer that you do not want made public—because it just might end up that way. Of even more concern are postings to personal Web pages, blogs, *Facebook*, and so on, where people often put forth a great deal of personal information, sometimes to their own detriment. Again, use good judgment about what you put out on the Internet, because unscrupulous individuals can distort the information and use it for their own purposes. Do not forget that what may at first glance seem like a private communication may in fact become extremely public.

How do I use email communications effectively?

In the academic and business worlds, email is now the standard for communicating information. While individual professors may have particular preferences with respect to email use in their classes and companies may have specific protocols, here are general email tips:

1. When writing emails, type a very specific subject on the subject line to alert your recipient to the message's topic. Rather than sending a message that is long and complex and covers several topics, it may be better to send a second message with a different subject line to keep your ideas focused.

2. On the "CC" or "BCC" line, include addresses of additional recipients who may be interested in the content of your message. Use your email client's BCC (Blind Carbon Copy) feature to preserve the privacy of recipients. Put one recipient in the To field (that can be your own email address to keep other addresses *really* private) and put all other addresses in a BCC field. That way everyone gets the message but no one can see the other recipients' addresses.

3. Think carefully about whom you want to copy; many people receive hundreds of emails daily and would prefer not to be copied on messages unless they have expressed a specific interest or need to know.

4. Most email programs will allow you to attach a document, picture, or other file to your email message. Be sure that the document you attach is in a format that can be opened by your recipient. Think carefully, too, about the content of your attachment. As discussed earlier in this chapter, you need to be sure that the content of your message and all attachments suit the occasion and the recipients.

5. Always sign your message so that recipients know how to respond. Most email programs allow you to create and store a signature file that you can insert at the end of emails, and many automatically insert this file if instructed to do so.

6. Your email program will probably offer multiple options for text format, including font style and size, HTML coding, and so on. When selecting your format, think primarily in terms of readability. Using a dark background, for example, or very small type can make messages difficult to read.

7. Your email program will allow you to reply to the sender or to everyone on the recipient list. When responding to an email, you can use the REPLY TO or REPLY TO ALL option, depending on whether you want to reply only to the sender or to everyone who received the original email. Make sure you consciously decide which to use, rather than always clicking REPLY TO ALL. One of the major annoyances cited by those who use email frequently is being included in mindless replies to groups of recipients rather than to individuals.

8. Check to be certain that the subject line reflects the content of your reply. If you have changed the subject of your message midstream, be sure to change the subject line as well. If your message is in response to a long trail of emails, you may want to revise the subject heading to more clearly reflect the actual content of your message. You will also want to clean up the content of the message trail to include only relevant information. If you include the original message, you may wish to incorporate your response directly into the text of the previous message, but be careful to delineate your text from the original text in some fashion. You can set your text apart using a colored font, CAPS, italics, or bold, depending on the capability of your email program. Be careful to delete any information in the previous stream that is irrelevant or sensitive.

9. You may wish to forward messages to additional recipients. If you decide to forward a message, check carefully to see whether personal communications within

the current message need to be deleted first. Be particularly careful about forwarding long email trails without reading every message. If you have any doubt about the appropriateness of forwarding a message, secure the original sender's permission before doing so.

10. Be conscious of exposing all the recipients' email addresses to others. Use the BCC option to hide email addresses and clean up the body of the message to make sure everyone's email addresses are not included. If you are going to pass along something you think is worthwhile, you should take the time to clean up both the TO/BCC list *and* the body of the email. Of course, there are situations in which it is best not to forward a message, for example, any chain letter, that list of top ten jokes, the political satire you pulled off the Web, and the link to the latest *YouTube* video. Hard as it may be to hear, most people who receive these things are too polite to tell you to cut it out.

11. Be judicious about sending numerous messages to the same recipient. Emails should be brief, but most recipients would prefer a slightly longer, coherent message to a series of quick thoughts. Try to gather your thoughts first and craft one email that covers the topic thoroughly, rather than sending a number of short emails as ideas occur to you.

12. Most email programs allow you to store multiple addresses in a distribution group under one heading, such as "work group." If you routinely send messages to the same group of people—your coworkers or classmates, for example—consider creating a group for those addresses so you can send to the group rather than to individuals.

What is netiquette?

The term netiquette has sprung up recently. It refers to etiquette on the Net. Internet users have developed a set of conventions to keep the medium friendly and courteous. Here are a few cautions to keep in mind:

Flaming

Using angry or abusive language in an electronic setting is considered harassment and is completely inappropriate in email, text, or Internet messages. If you are flamed, do not reply in kind. Either ignore the message or respond calmly.

Spamming

Sending numerous messages, such as chain letters or advertisements, randomly to a large number of recipients is both irritating and bothersome because it needlessly clutters up everyone's electronic mailbox.

Dating

It is not appropriate to use work or school email addresses to ask someone for a date. It is also inappropriate to write personal emails to classmates or coworkers whom you do not know outside of class or work. These email addresses should be used only for activities related to class or work.

Here are more tips on netiquette:

1. Always type a subject heading for your email that describes the message's content accurately and specifically.

2. Use an appropriate salutation. For informal messages, you can use just a name; for business or academic messages, use a standard salutation (Dear Ms. Smith, Dear Dr. Kennedy).

3. Keep messages brief and to the point.

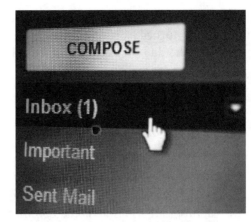

Remember, when composing email many of the subtleties of conversation that can be understood when talking in person or on the phone can be lost or misinterpreted. Choose your words carefully.

4. End messages with your name and address or affiliation so that the recipient is clear about who is sending the message and can respond to it.

5. Forward messages only if you have a compelling reason to do so. People who send you emails are communicating with you, not some undetermined audience.

6. Do not quote from an email message unless the writer has given you explicit permission to do so.

7. Avoid using all capital letters. This is the electronic equivalent of SHOUTING.

8. Reread your message before sending it. If there is any chance that the message could be misinterpreted, take time to revise it.

Should I use email or text message shorthand?

Because email and text messaging is conversational, users have evolved a kind of shorthand based on diacritics: acronyms, asterisks, emoticons, and other characters or punctuation used to add emphasis or other flavoring to messages. This habit has become most widespread in text messages, where space is limited. You may be familiar with the following acronyms:

Shorthand	Definition
BTW	by the way
FWIW	for what it's worth
FYI	for your information
IMHO	in my humble opinion
LOL	laugh out loud
TIA	thanks in advance
TTYL	talk to you later

Emoticons are those combinations of standard keyboard characters that look like faces when turned sideways. Although these abbreviations are fine in informal messaging, they should never be used in formal communications or academic or professional writing.

:) smile

;-) wink

:-o surprise or shock

: (frown

Here are some suggestions about using diacritics judiciously:

1. Always be conscious of your audience when using emoticons. Emoticons are never appropriate in professional communications, such as a memo, a report, a formal paper, or an email to a professor or supervisor. Include them only when the situation is appropriately informal.

Typing in emoticons is slowly being replaced by simple email plugins that allow you to select sophisticated-looking graphics like these.

2. When writing to your friends, creativity is the rule, but take care not to overuse diacritics, or the content of your message may become lost.

3. If your system does not allow underlining or italics, putting an asterisk before and after a word or phrase is the most common way to indicate emphasis or contrast:

That exam was *way* too hard, if you ask me!

4. Some people use UPPERCASE LETTERING for emphasis, but take care because this can seem like SHOUTING.

5. Use emoticons only in extremely informal writing situations.

What are mailing lists, bulletin boards, newsgroups, and blogs?

Mailing lists, which are special-interest email lists, distribute messages simultaneously to their many participants or subscribers. Thousands—perhaps millions—of such lists exist to facilitate a myriad of activities: scholarly discussions, committee meetings, fan club talk, even class discussions and research projects. One subscriber hosts the list, providing the host server and the necessary software. (The most common software program is called *listserv*.) Many lists allow anyone who wishes to join to do so; other lists are selective about their participants and limit the number who can join. In either case, you must subscribe to the list in order to participate or access its archives.

Like mailing lists, *bulletin boards* provide a forum for discussion. Instead of sending email messages to subscribers, however, bulletin boards post messages electronically for anyone to access and read. There is no need to subscribe in order to read bulletin board messages.

A *newsgroup* is a type of bulletin board consisting of a collection of messages tied to a specific topic. *Usenet* has the most extensive array of public newsgroups. *Google Groups* has archived *Usenet* discussions going back for many years and has largely taken over the function of *Usenet*. *Twitter* is another way to gain specialized information quickly by following an individual or group.

By far the fastest growing use of the Internet is *Weblogs, or blogs*—customized online journals. Blogs can be completely personal (an hourly recount of one individual's life) or organized around a topic like politics or sports. College courses sometimes have blogs for posting and sharing student work. Individual students may use blogs for a similar purpose—that is, as a collection site for notes, ideas, and work in progress.

How do I use text messaging appropriately?

Most cell phones now permit users to exchange text messages as well as voice messages. Although text messages can move back and forth in real time at the rate of conversation, they can also be saved, accessed, and responded to later, as time permits. With text-messaging between cell phones, the rhetoric is difficult to control. Because of the constraints of the electronic medium itself, text messages are often full of shorthand, abbreviations, and truncated sentence structures. Thus, text messaging is rarely an appropriate way to communi-

What is file-sharing space on the Internet?

With a file-sharing space, such as *Dropbox* or *Google Drive*, you can post a document to the Web for others to download and read. File sharing works particularly well for reviewing and commenting on one another's files. Once the document has been commented on, it is then uploaded once again to the file-sharing space so that the original author can read the comments. Many offices and classrooms make use of file-sharing space for collaborative writing and work groups.

cate with professors or supervisors. You should reserve text messaging for very brief and informal messages to family and friends. The shorthand language used to write text messages is never appropriate in formal writing situations, such as at school or at work.

How do I write online email invitations?

Inviting people to events, meals, or meetings is a very common practice in business settings. These invitations are often made online, through email, or through a corporate website. You will want to think carefully about the audience to whom you are writing; the level of formality of the invitation will depend upon whom you are inviting: colleagues, customers, or clients. If you want them to say "yes" you should make the event sound important, interesting, and exciting. The invitation should be formatted in an attractive way, perhaps including the company logo. No matter the level of formality, though, do not forget to proofread, proofread, proofread. In your email, be sure to include the following:

1. What you are inviting them to
2. Why they are invited
3. When and where the event will take place, plus directions if needed
4. A request for confirmation about attendance
5. An offer to answer any questions about the event

How do I use *evite* or other online invitation websites?

If your recipients are likely to be on the Internet, as most are these days, you may wish to use one of the free online invitation sites available on the Web. On the *evite* website, for example, you select your invitation design, add your guests' email addresses, and the site sends out the invitation via email for you. You choose whatever features you want to include in your invitation and your guests reply online so you can automatically track the head count. You also have options of adding polls for your guests to answer (such as what food or music everyone likes), letting the guests select what to bring (great for potlucks), and allowing guests to invite others as well.

Further Reading

Baugh, Albert C., and Thomas Cable. *A History of the English Language*. Englewood Cliffs, NJ: Prentice-Hall, 1978.

Elliott, Rebecca. *Painless Grammar*. New York: Barrons, 2006.

Fromkin, Victoria, and Robert Rodman. *An Introduction to Language*. New York: Holt, 1874.

Hoffman, Richard L., and L. M. Myers. *The Roots of Modern English*, 2nd ed. Boston: Little, Brown, 1979.

Hubbell, Robert D. *A Handbook of English Grammar and Language Sampling*. Englewood Cliffs, NJ: Prentice-Hall, 1988.

Hult, Christine A. *Researching and Writing in the Humanities and Arts*. Boston: Allyn & Bacon, 1996.

———. *Researching and Writing in the Sciences and Technology*. Boston: Allyn & Bacon, 1996.

———. *Researching and Writing in the Social Sciences*. Boston: Allyn & Bacon, 1996.

Hult, Christine A., and Thomas N. Huckin. *The New Century Handbook*, 5th ed. New York: Longman, 2011.

Kaplan, Jeffrey P. *English Grammar: Principles and Facts*. Englewood Cliffs, NJ: Prentice-Hall, 1989.

Kolln, Martha. *Rhetorical Grammar: Grammatical Choices, Rhetorical Effects*. New York: Macmillan, 1991.

———. *Understanding English Grammar*, 2nd ed. New York: Macmillan, 1986.

Quirk, Randolph, and Sidney Greenbaum. *A Concise Grammar of Contemporary English*. New York: Harcourt, 1973.

Sedley, Dorothy. *Anatomy of English*. New York: St. Martin's, 1990.

Truss, Lynne. *Eats, Shoots & Leaves: The Zero Tolerance Approach to Punctuation*. New York: Gotham, 2003.

Useful Websites

Daily Writing Tips: www.dailywritingtips.com

English Club: www.englishclub.com

English Language Smart Words: www.smart-words.org

The English Page: www.englishpage.com

Good Reads: http://www.goodreads.com/

Oxford Dictionaries: www.oxforddictionaries.com

Write Express: http://www.writeexpress.com

Appendix A:
Irregular Verb Chart

An *irregular verb* is a verb whose past tense and past participle are not formed in the regular manner, which adds *-d* or *-ed*. Instead, irregular verbs have some variation from the base form, e.g., *run/ran/run*; *know/knew/known*. Irregular verbs simply have to be memorized. Below is a comprehensive listing.

Base Form	Past Tense	Past Participle
A		
arise	arose	arisen
awake	awakened/awoke	awakened/awoken
B		
backslide	backslid	backslidden/backslid
be	was/were	been
bear	bore	born/borne
beat	beat	beaten
become	became	become
begin	began	begun
bend	bent	bent
bet	bet	bet
bid (say farewell)	bid/bade	bidden
bid (offer an amount)	bid	bid
bind	bound	bound
bite	bit	bitten
bleed	bled	bled
blow	blew	blown
break	broke	broken
breed	bred	bred
bring	brought	brought
broadcast	broadcast	broadcast
browbeat	browbeat	browbeat
build	built	built
burn	burned/burnt	burned/burnt
burst	burst	burst
buy	bought	bought

C

can	could	(been able)
cast	cast	cast
catch	caught	caught
choose	chose	chosen
cling	clung	clung
clothe	clothed/clad	clothed/clad
come	came	come
cost	cost	cost
creep	crept	crept
crossbreed	crossbred	crossbred
cut	cut	cut

D

daydream	daydreamed/daydreamt	daydreamed/daydreamt
deal	dealt	dealt
dig	dug	dug
disprove	disproved	disproved/disproven
dive (jump in head-first)	dived/dove	dived
dive (scuba diving)	dived/dove	dived
do	did	done
draw	drew	drawn
dream	dreamed/dreamt	dreamed/dreamt
drink	drank	drunk
drive	drove	driven
dwell	dwelt	dwelt

E

eat	ate	eaten

F

fall	fell	fallen
feed	fed	fed
feel	felt	felt
fight	fought	fought
find	found	found
fit	fitted/fit	fitted/fit
flee	fled	fled
fling	flung	flung
fly	flew	flown
forbid	forbade	forbidden
forecast	forecast	forecast
forego	forewent	forgone
foresee	foresaw	foreseen
foretell	foretold	foretold
forget	forgot	forgotten
forgive	forgave	forgiven

forsake	forsook	forsaken
freeze	froze	frozen
frostbite	frostbit	frostbitten

G

get	got	gotten/got
give	gave	given
go	went	gone
grind	ground	ground
grow	grew	grown

H

hand-feed	hand-fed	hand-fed
handwrite	handwrote	handwritten
hang	hung	hung
have	had	had
hear	heard	heard
hew	hewed	hewed/hewn
hide	hid	hidden
hit	hit	hit
hold	held	held
hurt	hurt	hurt

I

inbreed	inbred	inbred
inlay	inlaid	inlaid
input	inputted/input	inputted/input
interbreed	interbred	interbred
interweave	interweaved/interwove	interweaved/interwoven

J

jerry-build	jerry-built	jerry-built

K

keep	kept	kept
kneel	knelt	knelt
knit	knitted/knit	knitted/knit
know	knew	known

L

lay	laid	laid
lead	led	led
lean	leaned/leant	leaned/leant
leap	leaped/leapt	leaped/leapt
learn	learned/learnt	learned/learnt
leave	left	left
lend	lent	lent
let	let	let

283

lie (in bed)	lay	lain
lie (not tell the truth)	lied	lied
light	lighted/lit	lighted/lit
lip-read	lip-read	lip-read
lose	lost	lost

M

make	made	made
may	might	—
mean	meant	meant
meet	met	met
miscast	miscast	miscast
misdeal	misdealt	misdealt
misdo	misdid	misdone
mishear	misheard	misheard
mislay	mislaid	mislaid
mislead	misled	misled
mislearn	mislearned/mislearnt	mislearned/mislearnt
misspeak	misspoke	misspoken
misspell	misspelled/misspelt	misspelled/misspelt
misspend	misspent	misspent
mistake	mistook	mistaken
misteach	mistaught	mistaught
misunderstand	misunderstood	misunderstood
miswrite	miswrote	miswritten
mow	mowed	mowed/mown
must	had to	—

O

offset	offset	offset
outbid	outbid	outbid
outbreed	outbred	outbred
outdo	outdid	outdone
outdraw	outdrew	outdrawn
outdrink	outdrank	outdrunk
outfight	outfought	outfought
outfly	outflew	outflown
outgrow	outgrew	outgrown
outleap	outleaped/outleapt	outleaped/outleapt
outride	outrode	outrun
outsell	outsold	outsold
outshine	outshined/outshone	outshined/outshone
outshoot	outshot	outshot
outsing	outsang	ousung
outspeak	outspoke	outspoken
outspend	outspent	outspent
overbid	overbid	overbid
overbuild	overbuilt	overbuilt

overbuy	overbought	overbought
overcome	overcame	overcome
overdo	overdid	overdone
overdraw	overdrew	overdrawn
overeat	overate	overeaten
overfeed	overfed	overfed
overhang	overhung	overhung
overhear	overheard	overheard
overlay	overlaid	overlaid
overpay	overpaid	overpaid
override	overrode	overridden
overrun	overran	overrun
oversee	oversaw	overseen
oversleep	overslept	overslept
overspeak	overspoke	overspoken
overspend	overspent	overspent
overtake	overtook	overtaken
overthrow	overthrew	overthrown
overwrite	overwrote	overwritten

P

partake	partook	partaken
pay	paid	paid
plead	pleaded/pled	pleaded/pled
prebuild	prebuilt	prebuilt
predo	predone	predone
premake	premade	premade
prepay	prepaid	prepaid
presell	presold	presold
preset	preset	preset
preshrink	preshrank	preshrunk
proofread	proofread	proofread
prove	proved	proven/proved
put	put	put

R

read	read (pronounced "red")	read (pronounced "red")
reawake	reawoke	reawaken
rebid	rebid	rebid
rebind	rebound	rebound
rebroadcast	rebroadcasted/rebroadcast	rebroadcasted/rebroadcast
rebuild	rebuilt	rebuilt
recast	recast	recast
recut	recut	recut
redeal	redealt	redealt
redo	redid	redone
redraw	redrew	redrawn
regrind	reground	reground

regrow	regrew	regrown
rehang	rehung	rehung
rehear	reheard	reheard
reknit	reknitted/reknit	reknitted/reknit
relearn	relearned/relearnt	relearned/relearnt
relight	relighted/relit	relighted/relit
remake	remade	remade
repay	repaid	repaid
reread	reread	reread
rerun	reran	rerun
resell	resold	resold
resend	resent	resent
reset	reset	reset
resew	resewed	resewed/resewn
retake	retook	retaken
reteach	retaught	retaught
retell	retold	retold
rethink	rethought	rethought
rewake	rewaked/rewoke	rewaked/rewoken
rewear	rewore	reworn
reweave	reweaved/rewove	reweaved/rewoven
rewind	rewound	rewound
rewrite	rewrote	rewritten
rid	rid	rid
ride	rode	ridden
ring	rang	rung
rise	rose	risen
roughcast	roughcast	roughcast
run	ran	run

S

saw	sawed	sawed/sawn
say	said	said
see	saw	seen
seek	sought	sought
sell	sold	sold
send	sent	sent
set	set	set
sew	sewed	sewed/sewn
shake	shook	shaken
shave	shaved	shaved/shaven
shear	sheared	sheared/shorn
shed	shed	shed
shine	shined/shone	shined/shone
shoot	shot	shot
show	showed	shown, showed
shrink	shrank	shrunk
shut	shut	shut

sight-read	sight-read	sight-read
sing	sang	sung
sink	sank	sunk
sit	sat	sat
slay	slayed/slew	slayed/slain
sleep	slept	slept
slide	slid	slid
sling	slung	slung
slink	slinked/slunk	slinked/slunk
slit	slit	slit
smell	smelled/smelt	smelled/smelt
sneak	sneaked/snuck	sneaked/snuck
sow	sowed	sowed/sown
speak	spoke	spoken
speed	speeded/sped	speeded/sped
spell	spelled/spelt	spelled/spelt
spend	spent	spent
spill	spilled/spilt	spilled/spilt
spin	spun	spun
spit	spat	spat
split	split	split
spoil	spoiled/spoilt	spoiled/spoilt
spread	spread	spread
stand	stood	stood
steal	stole	stolen
stick	stuck	stuck
sting	stung	stung
stink	stank	stunk
stride	strode	stridden
strike	struck	struck
string	strung	strung
strive	strived/strove	strived/striven
sunburn	sunburned/sunburnt	sunburned/sunburnt
swear	swore	sworn
sweat	sweated/sweat	sweated/sweat
sweep	swept	swept
swell	swelled	swelled/swollen
swim	swam	swum
swing	swung	swung

T

take	took	taken
teach	taught	taught
tear	tore	torn
tell	told	told
think	thought	thought
throw	threw	thrown
thrust	thrust	thrust

287

tread	trod	trodden/trod
typewrite	typewrote	typewritten

U

unbend	unbent	unbent
unclothe	unclothed/unclad	unclothed/unclad
underbid	underbid	underbid
undercut	undercut	undercut
underfeed	underfed	underfed
undergo	underwent	undergone
underlie	underlay	underlain
underspend	underspent	underspent
understand	understood	understood
undertake	undertook	undertaken
underwrite	underwrote	underwritten
undo	undid	undone
unfreeze	unfroze	unfrozen
unwind	unwound	unwound
uphold	upheld	upheld
upset	upset	upset

W

wake	woke	woken
waylay	waylaid	waylaid
wear	wore	worn
weave	weaved/wove	weaved/woven
wed	wedded/wed	wedded/wed
weep	wept	wept
wet	wetted/wet	wetted/wet
will	would	———
win	won	won
wind	wound	wound
withdraw	withdrew	withdrawn
withhold	withheld	withheld
withstand	withstood	withstood
wring	wrung	wrung
write	wrote	written

Appendix B: Idiomatic Expressions

An *idiomatic expression* is a phrase whose meaning cannot be predicted by the meaning of the individual words. It is the phrase that carries the meaning. Idioms should not be used in formal writing situations.

A

Acid test: Something proves the effectiveness of something else.

Actions speak louder than words: People's intentions can be judged better by what they do than what they say.

Add insult to injury: Someone is making an unfavorable situation worse.

Arm and a leg: An item is very expensive.

At the drop of a hat: Something is done without any hesitation.

B

Back to the drawing board: An attempt has failed and it's time to start all over.

Ball is in your court: You must make the next decision or step.

Barking up the wrong tree: Someone is looking for something in the wrong place or accusing the wrong person.

Be glad to see the back of: You are happy when a person leaves.

Beat around the bush: Someone avoids the main topic.

Best of both worlds: This refers to having all the advantages.

Best thing since sliced bread: Something is a good invention or innovation.

Bite off more than you can chew: You take on a task that is way too big.

Blessing in disguise: Something good that isn't recognized at first.

Break a leg: An expression you would use to wish someone good luck.

Burn the midnight oil: Someone is working late into the night.

C

Can't judge a book by its cover: You should not judge something primarily on appearance.

Caught between a rock and a hard place: You find it difficult to choose between two alternatives.

Changing your tune: You change your mind about something.

Chase your tail: You spend a lot of time on something that achieves little result.

Chip on your shoulder: You are holding a grudge against someone.

Costs an arm and a leg: Something is very expensive.

Cross that bridge when you come to it: You should deal with a problem when, and if, it becomes necessary.

Cry over spilt milk: You complain about something that has happened and cannot be changed.

Curiosity killed the cat: Being inquisitive can lead you into an unpleasant situation.

Cut corners: Something is done poorly to save money.

Cut the mustard: Something comes up to expectations.

D

Deliver the goods: You do what is expected or what you promised.

Devil's Advocate: You present a counter argument.

Don't count your chickens before the eggs have hatched: You shouldn't make plans for something that might not happen.

Don't give up the day job: You are not very good at something and could not do it professionally.

Don't put all your eggs in one basket: You shouldn't put all your resources in one possibility.

Drastic times call for drastic measures: When you are extremely desperate you need to take drastic actions.

E

Elvis has left the building: The show has come to an end. Something is all over.

Every cloud has a silver lining: You should be optimistic since even difficult times may lead to better days.

Explore all avenues: You should try out all possibilities to get a desired result.

F

Far cry from: Something is very different from something else.

Feel a bit under the weather: You are feeling slightly ill.

Fine-tooth comb: You examine something carefully so as not to miss any details.

G

Get the show on the road: You put your plan or idea into action.

Get your ducks in a row: You get things well organized.

Give the benefit of the doubt: You believe someone's statement, without seeking proof.

H

Heard it through the grapevine: You heard rumors about something or someone.

High as a kite: Someone is drunk or on drugs.

Hit the nail on the head: Someone does or says something exactly right.

Hit the sack / sheets / hay: You go to bed.

Hot potato: This is a current issue, usually controversial, that many people are talking about.

I

In the heat of the moment: You are overwhelmed by what is happening in the moment.

In the spotlight: You are the center of attention.

It takes two to tango: Actions or communications need more than one person.

J

Jump on the bandwagon: You join a popular trend or activity.

Jump the gun: You do something early or ahead of its scheduled time.

K

Keep something at bay: You intend to keep something away.

Keep your fingers on the pulse: You are constantly aware of the most recent developments.

Kill two birds with one stone: You try to accomplish two different things at the same time.

L

Last straw: Something is the final problem or event in a series of problems or events.

Let sleeping dogs lie: You should not disturb a situation as it is, since that may result in complications.

Let the cat out of the bag: You share information that was previously concealed or that should have been kept hidden.

M

Make a long story short: You come directly to the point, leaving out explanatory details.

Method to my madness: You assert that, despite your approach seeming random, there actually is structure to it.

Miss the boat: You express that someone missed his or her chance.

N

Not a spark of decency: Someone has no manners at all.

Not let the grass grow under your feet: You don't delay in getting something done.

Not playing with a full deck: Someone lacks intelligence.

O

Off one's rocker: Someone is crazy, demented, out of their mind, or in a confused or befuddled state.

On the ball: Someone understands the situation well.

Once in a blue moon: Something happens very rarely.

Out of the blue: Something unexpected happens.

P

Pay the piper: You need to face the consequences of your actions.

Penny for your thoughts: You are asking someone what they are thinking.

Picture paints a thousand words: A visual presentation is far more descriptive than words.

Piece of cake: A job, task, or other activity is simple.

Pull wool over other people's eyes: Someone tries to deceive someone else into thinking well of them.

R

Raining cats and dogs: It's raining in large amounts.

Rub someone the wrong way: You annoy or bother someone.

S

See eye to eye: You wish to say that two (or more people) agree on something.

Separate the sheep from the goats: You examine a group of people to determine their suitability for some task.

Shape up or ship out: You are warning someone that they need to improve or they will be fired.

Sick as a dog: You are very ill.

Sit on the fence: Someone does not want to choose or make a decision.

Speak of the devil: The person you have just been talking about arrives.

Steal someone's thunder: Someone takes the credit for something someone else did.

T

Take with a grain of salt: You do not take what someone says too seriously.

Taste of your own medicine: Something happens to you, or is done to you, that you have done to someone else.

To hear something straight from the horse's mouth: You hear something from an authoritative source.

W

Whole nine yards: Everything. All of it.

Wouldn't be caught dead: You would never like to do something like that.

Y

Your guess is as good as mine: You have no idea or do not know the answer to a question.

Appendix C: Homophones

Homophones are words that sound alike, but have different meanings. Below are some examples of homophones. [For a listing of frequently misused homophones, see Appendix E.]

A

acts/ax
ad/add
ads/adds/adz
aid/aide
ail/ale
air/heir/err
aisle/isle/I'll
all/awl
all ready/already
all together/altogether
allowed/aloud
alter/altar
ant/aunt
arc/ark
assent/ascent
assistance/assistants
ate/eight
aural/oral
away/aweigh
axel/axle
aye/eye/I

B

bail/bale
bait/bate

baize/bays
bald/bawled
ball/bawl
band/banned
bard/barred
bare/bear
baron/barren
base/bass
bases/basis
bazaar/bizarre
be/bee
beach/beech
beau/bow
been/bin
beet/beat
bell/belle
berry/bury
berth/birth
billed/build
bite/byte
blew/blue
bloc/block
boar/bore
board/bored
boarder/border
bode/bowed

293

bold/bowled
bolder/boulder
boos/booze
born/borne
bough/bow
bouillon/bullion
boy/buoy
braid/brayed
braise/braze
bread/bred
break/brake
brewed/brood
brews/bruise
bridle/bridal
broach/brooch
browse/brows
bur/burr
but/butt
buy/by/bye

C

cache/cash
callous/callus
cannon/canon
canvas/canvass
capital/capitol
carat/carrot/caret/karat
carol/carrel
cast/caste
cede/seed
ceiling/sealing
cell/sell
cellar/seller
censor/sensor
cent/scent/sent
cents/scents/sense
cereal/serial
cession/session
chance/chants
chased/chaste
cheap/cheep
chews/choose
chic/sheik

chilly/chili
choir/quire
choral/coral
chord/cord
chute/shoot
cite/sight/site
clause/claws
click/clique
climb/clime
close/clothes/cloze
coal/kohl
coarse/course
colonel/kernel
complacent/complaisant
complement/compliment
coo/coup
coop/coupe
cops/copse
core/corps
correspondence/correspondents
council/counsel
cousin/cozen
creak/creek
crews/cruise
cruel/crewel
cue/queue
currant/current
curser/cursor
cymbal/symbol

D

dam/damn
days/daze
dear/deer
defused/diffused
descent/dissent
desert (abandon)/dessert
deviser/divisor
dew/do/due
die/dye
disburse/disperse
discreet/discrete
doe/dough/do (musical note)

done/dun
douse/dowse
draft/draught
dual/duel

E

earn/urn
ewe/you/yew
eye/I

F

faint/feint
fair/fare
faun/fawn
faze/phase
feat/feet
ferrule/ferule
fie/phi
file/phial
find/fined
fir/fur
flair/flare
flea/flee
flew/flu/flue
flex/flecks
flocks/phlox
floe/flow
flour/flower
foaled/fold
for/four/fore
foreword/forward
fort/forte
forth/fourth
foul/fowl
franc/frank
freeze/frieze
friar/fryer
furs/furze

G

gait/gate
gays/gaze
gene/jean

gild/guild
gilt/guilt
giro/gyro
gnu/knew/new
gored/gourd
gorilla/guerilla
grate/great
grease/Greece
greave/grieve
groan/grown
guessed/guest

H

hail/hale
hair/hare
hall/haul
halve/have
hangar/hanger
hart/heart
hay/hey
heal/heel/he'll
hear/here
heard/herd
heed/he'd
heroin/heroine
hertz/hurts
hew/hue/Hugh
hi/high
higher/hire
him/hymn
hoard/horde
hoarse/horse
hole/whole
holey/holy/wholly
hoes/hose
hold/holed
hostel/hostile
hour/our

I

idle/idol
illicit/elicit
in/inn

insight/incite
instance/instants
intense/intents
its/it's

J

jam/jamb
jewel/joule

K

kernel/colonel
knap/nap
knave/nave
knead/kneed/need
knight/night
knit/nit
knock/nock
knot/not
know/no
knows/nose

L

laid/lade
lain/lane
lam/lamb
laps/lapse
lay/lei
lea/lee
leach/leech
lead/led
leak/leek
lean/lien
leased/least
lee/lea
lessen/lesson
levee/levy
liar/lyre
lichen/liken
licker/liquor
lie/lye
lieu/Lou
links/lynx
lo/low

load/lode
loan/lone
locks/lox
loot/lute

M

made/maid
mail/male
main/mane/Maine
maize/maze
mall/maul
manner/manor
mantel/mantle
marry/merry/Mary
marshal/martial
massed/mast
maybe/may be
me/mi
meat/meet/mete
medal/metal/mettle/meddle
might/mite
mince/mints
mind/mined
miner/minor
missed/mist
moan/mown
mode/mowed
moor/more
moose/mousse
morn/mourn
mote/moat
muscle/mussel
mustard/mustered

N

naval/navel
nay/neigh
none/nun

O

oar/or/ore
ode/owed
oh/owe

one/won
overdo/overdue
overseas/oversees

P

packed/pact
pail/pale
pain/pane
pair/pare/pear
palate/palette/pallet
passed/past
patience/patients
pause/paws
pea/pee
peace/piece
peak/peek/pique
peal/peel
pearl/purl
pedal/peddle/petal
peer/pier
per/purr
pi/pie
plain/plane
plait/plate
pleas/please
plum/plumb
pole/poll
pore/pour
pray/prey
presence/presents
prince/prints
principal/principle
profit/prophet

R

rack/wrack
rain/reign/rein
raise/rays/raze
rap/wrap
rapped/rapt/wrapped
read/red
read/reed
real/reel

reek/wreak
rest/wrest
retch/wretch
review/revue
right/rite/write
ring/wring
road/rode/rowed
roam/Rome
roe/row
role/roll
root/route
rose/rows
rote/wrote
rough/ruff
rung/wrung
rye/wry

S

sail/sale
sane/seine
satire/satyr
saver/savor
scene/seen
scull/skull
sea/see
seam/seem
sear/seer/sere
seas/sees/seize
serf/surf
sew/so/sow
shake/sheikh
shear/sheer
shoe/shoo
shone/shown
sic/sick
side/sighed
sighs/size
sink/sync
slay/sleigh
sleight/slight
slew/slue/slough
sloe/slow
soar/sore

297

soared/sword
sole/soul
some/sum
son/sun
staid/stayed
stair/stare
stake/steak
stationary/stationery
steal/steel
step/steppe
stile/style
story/storey
straight/strait
suite/sweet
surge/serge

T

tacks/tax
tail/tale
tare/tear
taught/taut
tea/tee
team/teem
tear/tier
teas/tease
tern/turn
their/there/they're
theirs/there's
threw/through
thrown/throne
thyme/time
tic/tick
tide/tied
to/too/two
toad/towed/toed
toe/tow
told/tolled
troop/troupe
trussed/trust

V

vain/vane/vein
vale/veil
vary/very
vial/vile
vice/vise

W

wade/weighed
wail/whale
waist/waste
wait/weight
waive/wave
want/wont
ware/wear/where
way/weigh/whey
ways/weighs
we/wee/whee
weak/week
weather/whether
we'd/weed
we'll/wheel/weal
wet/whet
we've/weave
which/witch
while/wile
whine/wine
whirl/whorl
whirled/world
whit/wit
white/wight
who's/whose
wig/whig
woe/whoa
wood/would

Y

yoke/yolk
yore/your/you're
you'll/Yule

Appendix D:
English Prepositions

A preposition (e.g., *in, on, for, of, by*) is a word that precedes a noun or pronoun and its modifiers to form a prepositional phrase. Here are some examples of prepositional phrases: *off* the top, *in* the middle, *across* the bow, *between* us, *for* awhile, *by* the way. Some prepositions are used in combinations with each other: *because of, in regard to, according to*, etc. Prepositions are also used in some phrasal verbs, such as *do over, put up with, burn down, burn up, turn off*, etc. As the English language evolves, new prepositional phrases are created. No list of prepositions can be totally comprehensive, but this list comes close.

A

à la

aboard

about

above

absent

according to

across

afore

after

against

ahead of

along

along with

alongside

amid/amidst

among/amongst

an

anti

apart from

apropos of

around

as (also an adverb and a conjunction)

as far as

as for

as long as

as of

as opposed to

as per

as regards

as soon as

as to

as well as

aside

aside from

astride

at

atop

away from

B

back to

bar

barring

because of

before

behind

below

beneath

beside

besides

between

beyond

but (also a conjunction)

but for

by

by means of

by virtue of

C

circa
close to
concerning
considering
contrary to
counting
cum

D

depending on
despite
down
due to
during

E

except
except for
excepting
excluding

F

far from
following
for (also a conjunction)
forward of
from
further to

G

given

I

in
in addition to
in between
in case of
in favor of
in front of

in lieu of
in spite of
in the face of
in view of
including
inside
instead of
into

L
left of
less
like

M
mid
midst
minus

N
near
near to
next
next to
notwithstanding

O
of
off
on
on account of
on behalf of
on board
on top of
onto
opposite
opposite from
opposite of
opposite to
other than

out
out of
outside
outside of
over
owning to

P

pace
past
pending
per
plus
preparatory to
prior to
pro
pursuant to

R

rather than
re
regarding
regardless of
respecting
right of
round

S

sans
save
save for
saving
since
subsequent to
such as

T

than
thanks to
that of

through
throughout
till (also a conjunction)
times
to
together with
touching
toward/towards

U
under
underneath
unlike
until
unto
up
up against
up to
up until
upon

V
versus
via
vis-à-vis

W
with
with reference to
with regard to
within
without
worth

Appendix E: Misused Homophones

Words that sound alike but are spelled differently are called homophones. Here is a list of commonly misused homophones.

Word	Part of Speech	Meaning
air	noun: atmosphere	The *air* up here is thin.
heir	noun: successor	She is *heir* to a fortune.
all ready	adjective: all prepared	I am *all ready* for today.
already	adverb: by this time	They have *already* left.
bare	adjective: naked	The bathers were *bare*.
bear	noun: large animal	The *bear* was friendly.
bored	verb: not interested	Larry is often *bored*.
board	noun: piece of wood	That *board* has come loose.
break	verb: smash	She tried not to *break* the dishes.
brake	noun: a slowing mechanism	He put on the *brakes*.
butt	noun: end	He crushed out the cigarette *butt*.
but	preposition: however	All *but* one came to the party.
cite	verb: to quote	I always *cite* the author's work.
site	noun: a place	We went to the building *site*.
complement	verb: to complete	The color *complements* the decor.
compliment	verb: to praise	He *complimented* me on the decor.
creek	noun: small stream	We crossed the *creek* three times.
creak	verb: make a squeak	The door opened with a *creak*.
die	verb: expire	We'll *die* trying.
dye	noun: coloring	They used natural *dye*.
discreet	adjective: tactful	She is always *discreet* with secrets.
discrete	adjective: distinct or separate	Each poem is a *discrete* chapter.
feet	noun: lowest part of leg	His *feet* were cold.
feat	noun: achievement	Climbing Everest is no mean *feat*.

305

Word	Part of Speech	Meaning
gorilla	noun: a large ape	*Gorillas* live in the jungle.
guerrilla	noun: rebel	The *guerillas* are fighting in Syria.
hare	noun: rabbit	The tortoise beat the *hare*.
hair	noun: tresses	His *hair* is dyed.
heard	verb: past tense of *hear*	We *heard* the gunfire.
herd	noun: group of animals	A *herd* of elk were grazing nearby.
hole	noun: gap or cavity	There is a large *hole* in the ground.
whole	adjective: complete	It takes up a *whole* block.
insure	verb: indemnify	You should *insure* your valuables.
ensure	verb: make sure	You should *ensure* their safety.
its	possessive pronoun	What is *its* title?
it's	contraction of *it is*	What if *it's* not any good?
loose	adjective: not tightly secured	My tooth is *loose*.
lose	verb: to fail to keep	I might *lose* my license.
meet	verb: to encounter	We agreed to meet later.
meat	noun: animal protein	Vegetarians don't eat meat.
one	adjective: single	Not one of them was happy.
won	verb: came in first place	He won first prize.
patients	noun: people under treatment	The *patients* are resting in bed.
patience	noun: steadfastness	The nurse's *patience* is unflagging.
peace	noun: opposite of war	We need *peace* in the world.
piece	noun: segment or part	They ate a *piece* of humble pie.
peak	noun: mountain	The *peak* was covered in snow.
peek	verb: to steal a look	Don't *peek* inside the package.
pique	verb: to interest	The woman *piqued* his interest.
plain	noun: flat piece of land	Buffalo lived on the *plain*.
	adjective: clear or evident	Their size makes them *plain* to see.
plane	noun: short for airplane	The *plane* will land in one hour.
pore	noun: tiny opening in skin	Her *pores* were clogged.
pour	verb: decant, or rain heavily	It's *pouring* outside.
presence	noun: opposite of absence	Your *presence* is requested.
presents	noun: gifts	Mary got *presents* on her birthday.
	verb: award something	May I *present* you with this prize.
principal	adjective: foremost	Our *principal* job is to keep order.
	noun: school leader	Jody is the *principal* of that school.
principle	noun: rule or standard	It's the *principle* of the thing.

Word	Part of Speech	Meaning
read	verb: interpret writing	She *reads* to her son nightly.
reed	noun: tall water plant	There are *reeds* along the bank.
site	noun: location	Their building *site* is well chosen.
sight	verb: act of seeing	It is in *sight* of the cathedral.
stationary	adjective: not moving	The bus is *stationary*.
stationery	noun: writing paper	Her *stationery* has a monogram.
sure	adjective: certain	I'm *sure* you'll be fine.
shore	noun: coast	The *shore* was eroded.
tail	noun: rear part of something	The airplane's *tail* was on fire.
tale	noun: story	Don't tell us any tall *tales*.
their	possessive form of *they*	*Their* house burned down.
there	adverb: in that place	Put the bike over *there*.
they're	contraction of *they are*	*They're* going cycling today.
threw	past tense of *throw*	He *threw* the snowball.
through	preposition	Walk *through* the door please.
thru	informal preposition	"Come right on *thru*."
time	noun: occasion or period	It's about *time*.
thyme	noun: herb	I season chicken with *thyme*.
to	preposition	They like *to* go swimming.
too	adverb: also	We like swimming *too*.
two	adjective and noun: *"2"*	They have *two* children.
tow	verb: pull	Can you give us a *tow*?
toe	noun: appendages on feet	My big *toe* is sore.
weak	noun: not strong	Today I feel very *weak*.
week	noun: seven-day period	Last *week* I felt stronger.
wield	verb: exert	The president *wields* power.
wheeled	verb: transport on wheels	The gardener *wheeled* the barrow.
weather	noun: climate	The *weather* here is damp.
whether	conjunction: either	He's coming *whether* you like it or not.
whole	adjective: entire	He ate the *whole* watermelon.
hole	noun: cavity or gap	Expenses have put us in a *hole*.
who's	contraction of *who is*	Guess *who's* coming to dinner.
whose	possessive form of *who*	*Whose* pony is that?
wine	noun: alcoholic beverage	She prefers red *wine*.
whine	verb: complain	Don't *whine* about your problems.
your	possessive form of *you*	*Your* uncle owns that pony.
you're	contraction for *you are*	*You're* the only one who rides.

Appendix F: Frequently Misspelled Words

Spelling in English is notoriously difficult. Here is a listing of some of the most commonly misspelled words.

A

a lot
acceptable
accidentally
accommodate
acquire
acquit
achieved
address
amateur
apparent
appropriate
argument
atheist
athlete
athletic

B

basically
believe
bellwether
beneficial

C

calendar
category

cemetery
changeable
collectible
column
committed
committee
conscience
conscientious
conscious
consensus

D

daiquiri
definitely
dependent
develops
discipline
drunkenness
dumbbell

E

embarrassment
environment
equipment
exaggerate
exceed

exhilarate
existence
experience

F
February
fiery
foreign

G
gauge
government
grateful
guarantee

H
harass
height
heroes
hierarchy
humorous

I
ignorance
immediate
independent
indispensable
inoculate
intelligence
its/it's

J
jewelry
judgment

K
kernel
knowledge

L
leisure

liaison
library
license
lose

M
maintenance
manageable
maneuver
medieval
memento
millennium
miniature
minuscule
mischievous
misspell

N
necessary
neighbor
noticeable

O
occasionally
occurred
occurrence

P
parallel
pastime
perseverance
personnel
playwright
possession
precede
principal/principle
privilege
pronunciation
publicly

Q

quantity

questionnaire

R

receipt

receive

recommend

reference

referred

relevant

restaurant

rhyme

rhythm

S

schedule

seize

separate

sergeant

success

supersede

T

their/they're/there

therefore

threshold

triathlon

truly

twelfth

tyranny

U

until

V

vacuum

W

weather

weird

without

Appendix G: Wordy Phrases

Several phrases in common usage are unnecessarily long or redundant (also called "wordy"). Whenever possible, replace such long or redundant phrases with their more succinct versions.

Wordy Phrase	Succinct Replacement
a bigger degree of	more
a decreased number of	fewer
a lesser degree of	less
a lot of	many
a number of	some/many
absolutely essential	essential
advance notice	notice
advance reservations	reservations
afford an opportunity	allow
all across	across
all of a sudden	suddenly
as a matter of fact	in fact
as a means of	to
as a way to	to
as prescribed by	under
at a later date	later
at the conclusion of	after
at the present time	presently
at this point in time	now
by means of	by, with
comply with	follow
due to the fact that	because
during the period of	for

eliminate altogether	eliminate
equally as good	equal
every single one	each one/all
fall down	fall
few and far between	rare
few in number	few
filled to capacity	filled
final outcome	final
first and foremost	first
first priority	priority
fly through the air	fly
for a period of	for
for the purpose of	for
foreign imports	imports
free gift	gift
frozen ice	ice
future plans	plans
gain entry into	enter
gather together	gather
general consensus	consensus
give an indication of	indicate
give consideration to	consider
grave crisis	crisis
grow in size	grow
hand in hand	together
has a requirement for	needs
has an effect on	influences
has the ability to	can
have an averse effect on	hurt
hear the sound of	hear
heat up	heat
I myself	I
in a way that is clear	clearly
in accordance with	by, following
in addition to	also
in all likelihood	probaby
in an effort to	to
in close proximity	near

in connection with	about
in excess of	more than
in lieu of	instead of
in light of the fact that	because
in order for	for
in order that	so
in order to	to
in reference to	about/regarding
in regard to	concerning/about
in relation to	about/with
in spite of	despite
in spite of the fact that	although
in the amount of	for/amounting to
in the area of	around
in the event that	if
in the final analysis	finally
in the near future	soon
in the process of	[omit use of this phrase entirely]
in the vicinity of	near
in this day and age	now
in today's society	today
in view of	because/since
inadvertent error	error
inner feelings	feelings
is a reflection of	reflects
is applicable to	applies to
is authorized to	can/may
is going to	will
is helpful in understanding	clarifies
is in conflict with	conflicts
is in consonance with	agrees with
is in contrast to	contrasts with
is of significant importance	is important
is responsible for	handles
is well aware that	understands
it could happen that	could/may/might
it is essential that	one must
it is incumbent upon one to	one should

it is rarely the case that	it rarely happens
it is requested that you	please
it seems as though	seems
join together	join
joint collaboration	collaboration
last but not least	finally
pertaining to	about
provides guidance to/for	guides
relative to	about
set forth in	in
similar to	like
successfully accomplish	complete
take action to	act
the month (or year) of	[omit use of this phrase entirely]
the use of	[omit use of this phrase entirely]
time period	time
under the provision of	under
until such time as	until
with reference to	about
with the exception of	except

Appendix H: Frequently Confused Word Pairs

Many words in English look or sound alike but have different meanings. Following is a listing of words that frequently cause trouble for writers.

Word Pair/Definitions

A

accept/except
   To *accept* means to receive; *except* means excluding. [Sara accepted everyone except Fred.]

adverse/averse
   Adverse means harmful; *averse* means strongly disliking. [She is averse to beans because of their adverse effect on her digestion.]

advice/advise
   Advice means guidance; *to advise* means to guide. [My advice to you is not to advise your students on their personal lives.]

affect/effect
   To affect means to influence; *the effect* means the result. [The effect of Joe's romantic overture has been negative. It is affecting Sue deeply.] *Effect* is occasionally used as a verb [We hope to effect a change in his behavior].

aisle/isle
   An *aisle* is a passageway between rows; an *isle* is an island. [The large building on the isle contains many aisles.]

all ready/already
   All ready means all prepared; *already* means by now. [We were all ready to go camping but our friends had already left town.]

all together/altogether
   All together means all in one place; *altogether* means on the whole. [*Altogether*, our family enjoys being *all together*.]

allusion/illusion
   An *allusion* is an indirect reference; an *illusion* is a false perception. [His allusion was to her illusion about UFOs.]

along/a long
   Along means moving or extending horizontally; *a long* refers to the length of something. [A long snake was slithering along the path.]

317

aloud/allowed

Aloud means out loud; *allowed* means permitted. [Speaking aloud was not allowed in church.]

altar/alter

Altar means a sacred table in a church; *alter* means to change something. [The parish committee decided not to alter the altar.]

amoral/immoral

Amoral means not concerned with right or wrong; *immoral* means not following accepted moral standards. [Some teenagers are amoral. Others behave in ways that are immoral.]

appraise/apprise

Appraise means to assess; *apprise* means to inform someone. [We asked the realtor to apprise us of how he would appraise the property.]

assent/ascent

Assent means agreement; *ascent* means climbing up. [The climbing team assented to the south-facing ascent.]

aural/oral

Aural means relating to hearing; *oral* means relating to speaking. [The oral speech was received aurally by the listeners.]

B

bad/badly

Bad (adjective) means awful; *badly (adverb)* means poorly. [Peter felt bad that he had played so badly.]

balmy/barmy

Balmy is pleasantly warm; *barmy* is crazy. [The endless balmy weather was enough to make a person barmy.]

bare/bear

Bare means naked; *bear* means to carry or put up with. [He could scarcely bear it that she was always bare.]

bated/baited

Bated means in suspense; *baited* means with bait attached. [With bated breath he baited the hook.]

bazaar/bizarre

Bazaar is a Middle Eastern market; *bizarre* means strange. [The bazaar had many bizarre items for sale.]

because of/due to

Use *because of* with a clause; use *due to* with a noun. [My unhappiness was because of the uncertainty of the situation. I feel much better due to your reassurances.]

berth/birth

A berth is a bunk in a ship or train; *birth* is the emergence of a baby. [His birth took place in the ship's berth.]

born/borne

Born is starting life; *borne* means carried. [She has borne his anger since the day he was born.]

bough/bow

A *bough* is a tree branch; *to bow* is to bend at the waist. [The tree bough looked like it was taking a bow.]

brake/break

A *brake* is a device to stop a car; *to break* is to separate into pieces. [He hit the brakes to keep from breaking the toy on the driveway.]

broach/brooch

To broach is to raise a subject for discussion; *a brooch* is a piece of jewelry. [She broached the subject of getting a new brooch.]

C

canvas/canvass

Canvas is strong cloth; *to canvass* is to seek votes. [The volunteers waited under a canvas tarp before canvassing the neighborhood.]

careen/career/carom

To careen implies motion that is tilted or side-to-side, as in swaying; to career indicates forward motion that is headlong at top speed; to carom signifies a hit and rebound type of motion, as with billiard balls. [The fishing boat careened helplessly over the waves. The police car careered across the intersection in a frantic chase. The hockey puck caromed off the boards and into the net.]

censure/censor

Censure means to criticize strongly; *to censor* is to prevent a film from showing. [The film had received wide censure, so the authorities decided to censor it.]

cereal/serial

Cereal is a breakfast food; *a serial* is something happening in series. [That brand of cereal was featured on the serial sitcom.]

chord/cord

A *chord* is a group of musical notes; *a cord* is a length of string. [The chord was pleasing. The bells were tied together with a cord.]

cite/site

To cite means to quote; a *site* means a place. [The professor cited Shakespeare's play *Othello*. The site of the drama was Venice.]

climactic; climatic

Climactic means forming a climax; *climatic* relates to climate. [A climactic event this century is global climatic change.]

coarse/course

Coarse means rough; *course* means a direction or a subject. [When teaching that course, the professor wore clothing of coarse fabric.]

complacent/complaisant

Complacent means smug; *complaisant* means willing to please. [While one waitress was complacent about her service, the other was complaisant with her customers.]

complement/compliment

To complement means to make something complete; *to compliment* is to express approval. [Margaret complimented Susan on the way the flowers complemented the table setting.]

council/counsel

A *council* is a group of managers; *to counsel* is to advise. [The council was willing to counsel us on the best action to take.]

conscience/conscious

Conscience (noun) means knowing right from wrong; *conscious (adjective)* means intentional. [She made a conscious decision to follow her conscience.]

criterion/criteria

The criterion is singular; *the criteria* is plural. [The criteria he used to make a judgment excluded the most important criterion.]

cue/queue

A *cue* is a signal; *a queue* is a line of people. [The ticket officer gave a cue to the people in the queue to start moving forward.]

currant/current

A *currant* is a dried grape; *a current* is a flow of water or air. [The currant jam was delicious. We felt a current of air moving in the kitchen.]

D

defuse/diffuse

To defuse is to make a situation less tense; *diffuse* is spread over a large area. [The troops were diffused in the region in order to defuse the situation.]

desert/dessert

A *desert* is a waterless area; *a dessert* is a sweet following a meal. [Honey is the only dessert found in the desert.]

different from/different than

Different from is used when comparing two things; *different than* is used when the comparison is a full clause. [My clothes are different from Mary's. Her taste is clothes is quite different than her mother would like it to be.]

discreet/discrete

Discreet means tactful; *discrete* means distinct. [I am always discreet about my love life; I have a discrete category for gossips.]

disinterested/uninterested

Disinterested means impartial; *uninterested* means not interested. [The judge served as a disinterested arbiter. The jury was largely uninterested in the testimony.]

dual/duel

Dual means having two parts; *a duel* is a fight between two people. [The swords served a dual purpose in the duel.]

E

elicit/illicit

To elicit (verb) means to bring forth; *illicit (adjective)* means illegal. [She wished to elicit from George whether or not he was having an illicit affair.]

emigrate/immigrate

To emigrate means to move permanently from one country to another; *to immigrate* means to move to another country. [Josef emigrated from Germany; America was the country to which he immigrated.]

320

eminent/immanent/imminent

Eminent means distinguished; *immanent* means embodied in; *imminent* means about to happen. [The imminent departure of the eminent ambassador was causing distress to his family; his spirit was immanent throughout his country.]

ensure/insure

Ensure means to make certain; *insure* means to protect property. [Her agent will ensure that she is adequately insured.]

envelop/envelope

To envelop is to surround; *an* envelope is a paper container for a letter. [He wished to envelop her with his love when she opened the envelope.]

exercise/exorcise

To exercise is to do physical activity; *to exorcise* is to drive out evil spirits. [We exercise every morning. The priestess tried to exorcise the demon.]

F

farther/further

Farther refers to distance; *further* refers to time. [Pedro always kicks the ball farther; he will go further in his soccer career than his friends will.]

fawn/faun

A *fawn* is a young deer; a *faun* is a mythical being. [The doe protected her young fawn as the strange faun from Narnia approached them.]

fewer/less

Fewer is used with items that can be counted; *less* is used with items that cannot be counted. [He had fewer cups and less water than I did.]

flaunt/flout

To flaunt is to display ostentatiously; *to flout* is to disregard a rule. [He flouted the regulations by flaunting his sign.]

flounder/founder

Flounder means to move clumsily; *founder* means to fail. [He floundered about aimlessly in an attempt not to founder.]

forbear/forebear

To forbear means to refrain; *a forebear* is an ancestor. [His sister wanted him to forbear looking for their forebears.]

foreword/forward

A *foreword* is an introduction to a book; *forward* means onward. [The publisher wanted him to move forward with writing the foreword.]

freeze/frieze

To freeze is to turn to ice; *a frieze* is a wall decoration. [The frieze on the building will freeze in the winter.]

G

good/well

Good (adjective) means high quality; *well (adverb)* means in a good way. [He always used good grammar when writing; he also spoke well.]

321

grisly/grizzly

> *Grisly* means gruesome*; a grizzly* is a type of bear. [The result of the grizzly bear attack was grisly.]

H

heard/herd

> *Heard (verb)* is the past tense of the verb *to hear. Herd (noun)* is a group of animals. [They heard the noise made by the herd of elephants.]

hoard/horde

> A *hoard* is an excessive store of something *; a horde* is a large group of people. [That horde of people hoarded their belongings.]

hole/whole

> A *hole (noun)* is an opening or gap*; whole (adjective)* means entire. [For his whole life he had avoided holes in roads.]

I

imply/infer

> *To imply* means to suggest something indirectly; *to infer* means to draw a conclusion from something. [He implied that she was not to infer anything from his attentions.]

incredible/incredulous

> *Incredible* means beyond the believable; *incredulous* means disbelieving. [He was incredulous when he saw the incredible feats of strength exhibited at the circus.]

its/it's

> *Its (possessive pronoun)* form of the pronoun *it; it's (contraction)* contracted form of *it is.* [It's not important for you to polish its surface.]

L

lay/lie

> *To lay* means "to place something" and takes a direct object; *to lie* means "to recline" and does not take a direct object. [They went to lay some flowers near the site of the accident; afterwards they wanted to lie down for awhile to rest.] Note that *lay* is also the past tense of the verb *lie*. [I lay down last night to sleep.]

lead/led

> *Led (verb)* is the past tense of the verb *to lead. Lead (noun)* refers to a type of metal. [Paul led us to where the lead was located.]

lend/loan

> *To lend (verb)* means to give something temporarily; *to loan (verb)* also means to give something temporarily; a *loan (noun)* means a credit. [Lend me a hand and give me a loan.]

like/as

> *Like (preposition)* should be used with a noun phrase; *as (conjunction)* should be used before a clause. [She looked like her mother and not as I thought she would.]

loath/loathe

> *Loath* is reluctant*; to loathe* is to hate. [He was loath to loathe other people.]

lose/loose

> *To lose (verb)* means not able to keep something; *loose (adjective)* means not tight. [You will lose your purse if you leave it loose at your side.]

322

M

meter/metre

A *meter* is a measuring device or measurement; *a metre* is a rhythm in verse. [The fabric was one meter long. The metre for that poem is catchy.]

militate/mitigate

Militate is to be a powerful factor against something; *to mitigate* is to make something less severe. [The general militated against the idea in order to mitigate its negative effects.]

moral/morale

Moral refers to a lesson from a story; *morale* is a feeling of well- being. [The moral of the story was to improve your morale.]

O

okay/OK

Use *Okay* or *OK* only in information writing to indicate approval. In formal writing, choose words such as *acceptable, pleasing, approved* instead.

P

palate/palette

The *palate* is the roof of the mouth; *a palette* is a board for mixing artist's paints. [He always places his tongue on his palate when using the palette.]

patience/patients

Patience means endurance; *patients* are those undergoing medical treatment. [The patients showed patience while awaiting their doctors.]

pedal/peddle

A *pedal* is a foot-operated lever; *to peddle* is to sell goods. [The tinker's cart had a pedal. He used the cart to peddle his goods.]

personal/personnel

Personal (adjective) means private; *personnel (noun)* refers to those who are employed by an organization. [Personal leave time was requested by the company's personnel.]

plain/plane

Plain (noun) is a flat piece of land; *plain (adjective)* means simple or clear. *A plane (noun)* is an airplane; *to plane (verb)* is to shave off a piece of wood. [It is plain that the farmer needed to plane the log before setting it out on the plain.]

pole/poll

A *pole* is a long, slender piece of wood; *a poll* is a survey prior to an election. [The flag was raised on the flag pole. The workers took a poll to predict the outcome of the election.]

pour/pore

To pour is to cause to flow; *a pore* is an opening in the skin. [The nurse poured ointment on his pores.]

prescribe/proscribe

To prescribe is to authorize use of medicine; *to proscribe* is to officially forbid something. [The AMA proscribes doctors from prescribing that medication.]

presence/presents

Presence means something is here and not absent; *presents* are gifts. [The presence of the presents excited the children.]

principal/principle

   Principal (adjective) means the most important. *Principal (noun)* is the leader of a school; *principle (noun)* means rule or standard. [The principle of honesty was adhered to religiously by the principal of the high school. He felt that honesty was the principal virtue.]

R

raise/rise

   Raise (transitive verb) means to lift something; *rise (intransitive verb)* means to stand up. [Rise up from your chairs so we can raise a glass in celebration of their marriage.]

real/really

   Real (adjective) means very; *really (adverb)* means extremely. Both terms are informal and should be avoided in formal writing. [I'm real sure that you should really stay away from him.]

respectfully/respectively

   Respectfully means politely; *respectively* means correspondingly or in order. [I respectfully submit that you should call on each of us respectively.]

S

set/sit

   To set (transitive verb) means to put something down; *to sit (intransitive verb)* means to have a seat. [She set the tea on the table and then invited us to sit.]

shall/will

   Shall and *will* are both modal or helping verbs. Use shall in place of will if you want to be very formal. [Shall we dance?]

sight/site

   Sight is the ability to see; *a site* is a location. [His sight confirmed that it was a good building site.]

skeptic/septic

   A skeptic is a person who doubts; *septic* is infected with bacteria. [I am a skeptic about the use of herbs to treat septic infections.]

stationary/stationery

   Stationary (adjective) means standing still; *stationery (noun)* is a type of paper. [The car was stationary so that Mark could write clearly on his stationery.]

storey/story

   A storey is a level of a building; *a story* is a tale or account. [He was on the seventh storey when he told his story.]

T

than/then

   Than (conjunction) is used to introduce the second part of a comparison. *Then (adverb)* indicates a point in time. [José was busier than Maria at work last night. Then today she had more customers than he did.]

that/which

   That (relative pronoun) is used with restrictive clauses. *Which (relative pronoun)* can be used with either type of clause, but is primarily used for non-restrictive clauses. [The ice cream that we like is sold only on campus. The campus store, which carries the ice cream, is across the street from Old Main.]

324

their/there/they're

Their (possessive pronoun) indicates possession; *there (adverb)* indicates place; *they're (contraction)* means *they are*. [Their intention was not to go there, but now they're committed to doing so.]

threw/through/thru

Threw (verb) is the past tense of the verb *to throw*; *through (preposition)* indicates passing across something; *thru* is the informal version of through. [He threw the football through the goal posts.]

till/until/'til

Till and until both mean awaiting and either is acceptable in formal writing. *'Til* is informal.

titillate/titivate

To titillate is to arouse sexual interest; *to titivate* is to make something more attractive. [We dressed up to titivate not to titillate.]

tortuous/torturous

Tortuous means full of twists and turns; *torturous* means full of pain and suffering. [That tortuous road was torturous to drive.]

U

use/utilize

to use and *to utilize* both mean to make use of. In general, the verb *use* is less pretentious. *Utilize* can be used when you mean "make practical use" of something. [We will use all of the soap you bought and also utilize the dishwasher.]

W

weak/week

Weak means not strong; *week* is the period of seven days. [Sara felt weak for over a week after the triathlon.]

weather/whether

Weather (noun) refers to the temperature and climate; *whether (conjunction)* means either or if. [Whether you like it or not, this weather is here to stay.]

who/whom

Who (relative or interrogative pronoun) and *whom (relative or interrogative pronoun)* are the subjective and objective cases respectively. The grammatical structure of the sentence will determine when to use who (subjective case) or whom (objective case). [Who is going to the movies? With whom are you going?]

who's/whose

Who's (contraction) means *who is*; *whose* is the possessive form of *who*. [Who's going to the movies tonight? Whose car will you take?]

wreath/wreathe

A wreath is a ring-shaped flower arrangement; *to wreathe* is to surround or encircle. [The florist wreathed the wreath in ribbons.]

Y

your/you're

Your is the possessive form of *you. You're (contraction)* means *you are*. [You're going to regret your decision someday.]

325

Appendix I:
Famous Quotations on Writing and Grammar

FAMOUS QUOTATIONS ON WRITING

1. "I try to create sympathy for my characters, then turn the monsters loose." —Stephen King

2. "The road to hell is paved with works-in-progress." —Philip Roth

3. "Prose is architecture, not interior decoration." —Ernest Hemingway

4. "It's none of their business that you have to learn to write. Let them think you were born that way." —Ernest Hemingway

5. "There is nothing to writing. All you do is sit down at a typewriter and bleed." —Ernest Hemingway

6. "Most writers regard the truth as their most valuable possession, and therefore are most economical in its use." —Mark Twain

7. "To gain your own voice, you have to forget about having it heard." —Allen Ginsberg

8. "And as imagination bodies forth
The forms of things unknown, the poet's pen
Turns them to shapes and gives to airy nothing
A local habitation and a name."
—William Shakespeare (from *A Midsummer Night's Dream*)

9. "You have to write the book that wants to be written. And if the book will be too difficult for grown-ups, then you write it for children." —Madeleine L'Engle

10. "If you can tell stories, create characters, devise incidents, and have sincerity and passion, it doesn't matter a damn how you write." —Somerset Maugham

11. "To produce a mighty book, you must choose a mighty theme." —Herman Melville

12. "If there's a book that you want to read, but it hasn't been written yet, then you must write it." —Toni Morrison

13. "It is perfectly okay to write garbage—as long as you edit brilliantly." —C. J. Cherryh

14. "It took me fifteen years to discover I had no talent for writing, but I couldn't give it up because by that time I was too famous." —Robert Benchley

15. "Lock up your libraries if you like; but there is no gate, no lock, no bolt that you can set upon the freedom of my mind." —Virginia Woolf

16. "There is no greater agony than bearing an untold story inside you." —Maya Angelou

17. "Any man who keeps working is not a failure. He may not be a great writer, but if he applies the old-fashioned virtues of hard, constant labor, he'll eventually make some kind of career for himself as writer." —Ray Bradbury

18. "One day I will find the right words, and they will be simple." —Jack Kerouac

19. "A blank piece of paper is God's way of telling us how hard it is to be God." —Sidney Sheldon

20. "Not that the story need be long, but it will take a long while to make it short." —Henry David Thoreau

21. "You never have to change anything you got up in the middle of the night to write." —Saul Bellow

22. "If you have other things in your life—family, friends, good productive day work—these can interact with your writing and the sum will be all the richer." —David Brin

23. "The difference between the right word and the almost right word is the difference between lightning and a lightning bug." —Mark Twain

24. "My own experience is that once a story has been written, one has to cross out the beginning and the end. It is there that we authors do most of our lying." —Anton Chekhov

25. "No tears in the writer, no tears in the reader. No surprise in the writer, no surprise in the reader." —Robert Frost

26. "I have been successful probably because I have always realized that I knew nothing about writing and have merely tried to tell an interesting story entertainingly." —Edgar Rice Burroughs

27. "First, find out what your hero wants, then just follow him!" —Ray Bradbury

28. "Most of the basic material a writer works with is acquired before the age of fifteen." —Willa Cather

29. "I love deadlines. I like the whooshing sound they make as they fly by." —Douglas Adams

30. "You must stay drunk of writing so reality cannot destroy you." —Ray Bradbury

31. "Words are a lens to focus one's mind." —Ayn Rand

32. "Poetry creates the myth, the prose writer draws its portrait."—Jean-Paul Sartre

33. "The road to hell is paved with adverbs." —Stephen King

34. "A writer without interest or sympathy for the foibles of his fellow man is not conceivable as a writer." —Joseph Conrad

35. "Science fiction writers, I am sorry to say, really do not know anything." —Philip K. Dick

36. "The only thing I was fit for was to be a writer, and this notion rested solely on my suspicion that I would never be fit for real work, and that writing didn't require any." —Russell Baker

37. "Half my life is an act of revision." —John Irving

38. "Writing is a socially acceptable form of schizophrenia." —E. L. Doctorow

39. "Don't tell me the moon is shining; show me the glint of light on broken glass." —Anton Chekhov

40. "People on the outside think there's something magical about writing, that you go up in the attic at midnight and cast the bones and come down in the morning with a story, but it isn't like that. You sit in back of the typewriter and you work, and that's all there is to it." —Harlan Ellison

41. "People do not deserve to have good writing, they are so pleased with bad." —Ralph Waldo Emerson

42. "Start writing, no matter what. The water does not flow until the faucet is turned on." —Louis L'Amour

43. "I went for years not finishing anything. Because, of course, when you finish something you can be judged." —Erica Jong

44. "Don't try to figure out what other people want to hear from you; figure out what you have to say. It's the one and only thing you have to offer." —Barbara Kingsolver

45. "A word is dead
When it is said,
Some say.
I say it just begins
To live that day."
—Emily Dickinson

46. "Writing a novel is like driving a car at night. You can only see as far as your headlights, but you can make the whole trip that way." —E. L. Doctorow

47. "Get it down. Take chances. It may be bad, but it's the only way you can do anything really good." —William Faulkner

48. "I am irritated by my own writing. I am like a violinist whose ear is true, but whose fingers refuse to reproduce precisely the sound he hears within." —Gustave Flaubert

49. "There's no money in poetry, but then there's no poetry in money either." —Robert Graves

50. "It is the writer who might catch the imagination of young people, and plant a seed that will flower and come to fruition." —Isaac Asimov

51. "The work never matches the dream of perfection the artist has to start with." —William Faulkner

52. "Begin with an individual, and before you know it you have created a type; begin with a type, and you find you have created—nothing." —F. Scott Fitzgerald

53. "Writing is its own reward." —Henry Miller

54. "The unread story is not a story; it is little black marks on wood pulp. The reader, reading it, makes it live: a live thing, a story." —Ursula K. Le Guin

55. "Almost anyone can be an author; the business is to collect money and fame from this state of being." —A. A. Milne

56. "A wounded deer leaps the highest." —Emily Dickinson

57. "Only in men's imagination does every truth find an effective and undeniable existence. Imagination, not invention, is the supreme master of art as of life." —Joseph Conrad

58. "Literature is all, or mostly, about sex." —Anthony Burgess

59. "Writers are always selling somebody out." —Joan Didion

60. "Anecdotes don't make good stories. Generally I dig down underneath them so far that the story that finally comes out is not what people thought their anecdotes were about." —Alice Munro

61. "You learn by writing short stories. Keep writing short stories. The money's in novels, but writing short stories keeps your writing lean and pointed." —Larry Niven

62. "Everywhere I go I'm asked if I think the university stifles writers. My opinion is that they don't stifle enough of them." —Flannery O'Connor

63. "I can't write five words but that I change seven." —Dorothy Parker

64. "There's no such thing as writer's block. That was invented by people in California who couldn't write." —Terry Pratchett

65. "Writing is not necessarily something to be ashamed of, but do it in private and wash your hands afterwards." —Robert A. Heinlein

66. "The more closely the author thinks of why he wrote, the more he comes to regard his imagination as a kind of self-generating cement which glued his facts together, and his emotions as a kind of dark and obscure designer of those facts. Reluctantly, he comes to the conclusion that to account for his book is to account for his life." —Richard Wright

67. "No one can write decently who is distrustful of the reader's intelligence or whose attitude is patronizing." —E. B. White

68. "A poet can survive everything but a misprint." —Oscar Wilde

69. "Rejection slips, or form letters, however tactfully phrased, are lacerations of the soul, if not quite inventions of the devil—but there is no way around them." —Isaac Asimov

70. "Fiction is about stuff that's screwed up." —Nancy Kress

71. "In general … there's no point in writing hopeless novels. We all know we're going to die; what's important is the kind of men and women we are in the face of this." —Anne Lamott

72. "Great is the art of beginning, but greater is the art of ending." —Henry Wadsworth Longfellow

73. "Tell the readers a story! Because without a story, you are merely using words to prove you can string them together in logical sentences." —Anne McCaffrey

74. "If science fiction is the mythology of modern technology, then its myth is tragic." —Ursula K. Le Guin

75. "All the information you need can be given in dialogue." —Elmore Leonard

76. "Everybody walks past a thousand story ideas every day. The good writers are the ones who see five or six of them. Most people don't see any." —Orson Scott Card

77. "All the words I use in my stories can be found in the dictionary—it's just a matter of arranging them into the right sentences." —Somerset Maugham

78. "Exercise the writing muscle every day, even if it is only a letter, notes, a title list, a character sketch, a journal entry. Writers are like dancers, like athletes. Without that exercise, the muscles seize up." —Jane Yolen

79. "If you write one story, it may be bad; if you write a hundred, you have the odds in your favor." —Edgar Rice Burroughs

80. "Finishing a book is just like you took a child out in the back yard and shot it." — Truman Capote

FAMOUS QUOTATIONS ABOUT GRAMMAR

1. "Writing is an act of faith, not a trick of grammar." —E.B. White

2. "The past is always tense, the future perfect." —Zadie Smith

3. "My spelling is Wobbly. It's good spelling but it Wobbles, and the letters get in the wrong places." —A.A. Milne, *Winnie-the-Pooh*

4. "Your grammar is a reflection of your image. Good or bad, you have made an impression. And like all impressions, you are in total control." —Jeffrey Gitomer

5. "If you have any young friends who aspire to become writers, the second greatest favor you can do them is to present them with copies of *The Elements of Style*. The first greatest, of course, is to shoot them now, while they're happy." —Dorothy Parker, *The Collected Dorothy Parker*

6. "It is very useful, when one is young, to learn the difference between 'literally' and 'figuratively.' If something happens literally, it actually happens; if something happens figuratively, it feels like it is happening." —Lemony Snicket, *The Bad Beginning*

7. "If you are literally jumping for joy, for instance, it means you are leaping in the air because you are very happy. If you are figuratively jumping for joy, it means you are so happy that you could jump for joy, but are saving your energy for other matters." —Lemony Snicket, *The Bad Beginning*

8. "It is really important that focusing on things such as spelling, punctuation, grammar and handwriting doesn't inhibit the creative flow." —Michael Morpurgo

9. "I might not use capital letters. But I would definitely use an apostrophe … and probably a period. I'm a huge fan of punctuation." —Rainbow Rowell, *Eleanor & Park*

10. "Grammar is a piano I play by ear. All I know about grammar is its power." —Joan Didion

11. "His sentences didn't seem to have any verbs, which was par for a politician. All nouns, no action. " —Jennifer Crusie, *Charlie All Night*

12. "A synonym is a word you use when you can't spell the other one." —Baltasar Gracián

13. "What really alarms me about President Bush's 'War on Terrorism' is the grammar. How do you wage war on an abstract noun? How is 'Terrorism' going to surrender? It's well known, in philological circles, that it's very hard for abstract nouns to surrender." —Terry Jones

14. "Like everything metaphysical the harmony between thought and reality is to be found in the grammar of the language." —Ludwig Wittgenstein

15. "A man's grammar, like Caesar's wife, should not only be pure, but above suspicion of impurity." —Edgar Allan Poe

16. "Anarchy is as detestable in grammar as it is in society." —Maurice Druon

17. "Ladies, if you want to know the way to my heart … good spelling and good grammar, good punctuation, capitalize only where you are supposed to capitalize, it's done." —John Mayer

18. "Art, whatever form it takes, requires hard work, craftsmanship and creativity. As a writer, I know my grammar, cadence, the music of prose, and the art of the narrative." —F. Sionil José

19. "It's hard to take someone seriously when they leave you a note saying, 'Your ugly.' My ugly what? The idiot didn't even know the difference between your and you're." —Cara Lynn Shultz, *Spellcaster*

20. "The greater part of the world's troubles are due to questions of grammar." —Michel de Montaigne, *The Complete Essays*

21. "This is a bawdy tale. Herein you will find gratuitous shagging, murder, spanking, maiming, treason, and heretofore unexplored heights of vulgarity and profanity, as well as non-traditional grammar, split infinitives, and the odd wank." —Christopher Moore, *Fool*

22. "And all dared to brave unknown terrors, to do mighty deeds, to boldly split infinitives that no man had split before —and thus was the Empire forged." —Douglas Adams, *The Hitchhiker's Guide to the Galaxy*

23. "The rule is: don't use commas like a stupid person. I mean it." —Lynne Truss, *Eats, Shoots & Leaves: The Zero Tolerance Approach to Punctuation*

24. "Let schoolmasters puzzle their brain,

With grammar, and nonsense, and learning,

Good liquor, I stoutly maintain,

Gives genius a better discerning."

—Oliver Goldsmith

25. "Glenn used to say the reason you can't really imagine yourself being dead was that as soon as you say, 'I'll be dead,' you've said the word I, and so you're still alive inside the sentence. And that's how people got the idea of the immortality of the soul—it was a consequence of grammar." —Margaret Atwood, *The Year of the Flood*

26. "Grammar is the greatest joy in life, don't you find?" —Lemony Snicket, *The Wide Window*

27. "It's perfectly obvious that there is some genetic factor that distinguishes humans from other animals and that it is language-specific. The theory of that genetic component, whatever it turns out to be, is what is called universal grammar." —Noam Chomsky

28. "I demand that my books be judged with utmost severity, by knowledgeable people who know the rules of grammar and of logic, and who will seek beneath the footsteps of my commas the lice of my thought in the head of my style." —Louis Aragon

29. "Forming grammatically correct sentences is for the normal individual the prerequisite for any submission to social laws. No one is supposed to be ignorant of grammaticality; those who are belong in special institutions. The unity of language is fundamentally political." —Gilles Deleuze, *Thousand Plateaus: Capitalism and Schizophrenia*

30. "If you can spell 'Nietzsche' without Google, you deserve a cookie." —Lauren Leto

31. "'I have no idea what that is, but yawn, anyway, just on principle. Eat up.' 'Pancakes is brain food.'

'Apparently not grammar food.'

'Wow. You college girls are mean.'"

—Rachel Caine, *Bite Club*

32. "Ill-fitting grammar are like ill-fitting shoes. You can get used to it for a bit, but then one day your toes fall off and you can't walk to the bathroom." —Jasper Fforde, *One of Our Thursdays Is Missing*

33. "This is the type of arrant pedantry up with which I will not put." —Winston S. Churchill

34. "People who cannot distinguish between good and bad language, or who regard the distinction as unimportant, are unlikely to think carefully about anything else." —B. R. Myers

35. "I don't know the rules of grammar. If you're trying to persuade people to do something, or buy something, it seems to me you should use their language." —David Ogilvy

36. "What the semicolon's anxious supporters fret about is the tendency of contemporary writers to use a dash instead of a semicolon and thus precipitate the end of the world. Are they being alarmist?" —Lynne Truss, *Eats, Shoots & Leaves: The Zero Tolerance Approach to Punctuation*

37. "We got through all of Genesis and part of Exodus before I left. One of the main things I was taught from this was not to begin a sentence with And. I pointed out that most sentences in the Bible began with And, but I was told that English had changed since the time of King James. In that case, I argued, why make us read the Bible? But it was in vain. Robert Graves was very keen on the symbolism and mysticism in the Bible at that time." —Stephen Hawking, *Black Holes and Baby Universes*

38. "I love you. You are the object of my affection and the object of my sentence." —Mignon Fogarty, *Grammar Girl's Quick and Dirty Tips for Better Writing*

39. "I can kick the can down the road, and I can also kick other modal verbs." —Jarod Kintz, *At Even One Penny, This Book Would Be Overpriced. In Fact, Free Is Too Expensive, Because You'd Still Waste Time by Reading It.*

40. "Vowels were something else. He didn't like them and they didn't like him. There were only five of them, but they seemed to be everywhere. Why, you could go through twenty words without bumping into some of the shyer consonants, but it seemed as if you couldn't tiptoe past a syllable without waking up a vowel. Consonants, you know pretty much where you stood, but you could never trust a vowel." —Jerry Spinelli, *Maniac Magee*

Appendix J: Model Papers

ARGUMENT PAPER

Source: English course at Utah State University, 2008. Used by permission.

Angela Napper
Professor Hult
English 1010
13 October 2008

Cybercensorship

With more and more regulations being formed about what citizens are allowed to view on the Internet, concerns as to the constitutional rights of these citizens are being raised. At public libraries, at colleges and universities, and at businesses the debate rages as to how much privacy users should have and whether censorship of certain materials is needed to protect the public welfare. More and more it is becoming clear that citizens need to take a stand to protect their right to privacy and freedom of speech on public computers as these rights are guaranteed to them in the US Constitution, specifically the First, Fifth, and Fourteenth Amendments.

Recently, the Board of Supervisors in Chesterfield County, Virginia, passed a law to prohibit access to any material deemed by the community to be pornographic or obscene. This includes any information on sex education and any Web sites containing prohibited words. Consequently, a site containing a recipe for chicken breasts would be banned. The new policy seems to be popular with some local residents. They have even started a Liberty Watch group in which citizens make a point of monitoring what those around them are accessing on the Web. Anything they deem illegal by the new standards is reported to the local authorities (Oder and Rogers).

With this type of system in place, citizens' right to access information—as guaranteed in the freedom of speech and freedom of press clauses of the First Amendment and the equal protection clause of the Fourteenth Amendment—is greatly infringed upon. The morals and beliefs of those in power have been forced upon everyone. It is exactly this type of regulation that the Founders were trying to escape when they created the

United States, a country where everyone would be free to live their lives as they chose, assuming they were not hurting others. I fail to see how attempting to access a recipe for chicken is hurting anyone. For that matter, gaining information on sex education is not infringing on the well-being of the community. Rather, it is likely improving the overall well-being by preventing unwanted pregnancies and diseases. Educator David Thornburg points out, "Libraries in schools and communities should be the last places to use censorship of any kind. Once the door to censorship is opened, how do we ever get it closed again?"

The debate between freedom of speech and censorship is also raging at a number of universities. At Snow College in southern Utah, administrators added software that blocked student access to all information deemed nonacademic. They said the motivation behind their actions had nothing to do with moral censorship. Rather, they claimed that students playing games and viewing pornography were using up too much computing time and power. Students who needed to use campus computers for homework had to wait in long lines and deal with slower computers. With the new policy in effect, the rate of hits on blocked sites (versus approved sites) dropped from thirty-five percent to less than five percent per day. This reduction speeded up the computers for those who used them for academic purposes. Students complained that they were never asked about their opinion beforehand and were not told about the decision after it had gone into effect. When asked what they would do if the student body voted against the new policy, school officials said the policy would be removed (Madsen).

Similarly, Indiana University banned the downloading of MP3s on school computers because it was using up too much of the school's bandwidth. Opposition came from a group called Students Against University Censorship, who began circulating a petition around the nation with the goal of gaining popular support as well as legal representation in their fight against these censorship policies. Their aim was to gain public support so as to have more power in a court of law or in negotiations with officials who could strike down censorship at universities nationwide (Ferguson).

However, some universities are in favor of giving students free rein. The University of Nevada, Las Vegas, refuses to put limits on what students can access on school computers or in the dorms. Officials state that they respect the students' rights and they want to make them feel at home when they are living in the dorms, which means allowing them access to all sites. If anyone on campus is offended by what another student is viewing, the offending student is simply asked to relocate to a more private computer. This type of policy respects the rights of all involved. It does not infringe on the freedom of speech rights of the students, while at the same time students who feel uncomfortable by material being viewed around them are accommodated appropriately (Ferguson).

More and more the battleground is moving into the workplace. Employers are looking to monitor what their employees access during work hours so as to prevent them from wasting company time on personal entertainment. Currently, over two thousand companies have begun using *Cyber-Patrol*, software that filters out any Web sites the company does not want its employees to access. Microsystems Software, Inc., the company that designs this software for corporations, claims it is not censoring anything but only filtering. It allows managers to personally inspect Web sites that have been accessed by company employees. Since every Web site *Cyber-Patrol* blocks has been viewed by a person, there is not blanket censorship based on what words a site may contain. All sites are placed into one of three categories: CyberYes, CyberNo, and Sports/Entertainment. With this system, any company can choose whether it wants its employees to be able to access sports and entertainment sites during work hours. It can also restrict any sites that have been deemed pornographic or violent (Markels).

This type of restriction seems less in violation of citizens' rights because it is designed to be used only in the workplace. Most would agree employers have the right to monitor what their employees are doing during office hours because the employers own the machines and are paying the employees for their time. Similarly, it might be argued that public libraries and universities also own their computers and consequently should have the right to censor them. It must be kept in mind, however, that those computers were purchased using taxpayers' money, so in reality they belong to the public. *Cyber-Patrol* is also improved in its format in that each Web site is individually viewed. Web sites with recipes for chicken breasts would consequently not be banned.

These same issues of the public's right to privacy have become a point of controversy in the post-9/11 era. Under provisions of the USA-PATRIOT Act, various governmental agencies such as the FBI and the Department of Homeland Security have been monitoring private citizens' Web use and emails. By gaining access to the records of any Internet service provider, government officials can track all people who have hit on any given site, or all of the sites accessed by any given computer. The government claims that such actions are necessary to prevent further terrorist attacks in the United States. Opposition to such government surveillance is led by Jerry Berman, the executive director of the Center for Democracy and Technology in Washington. He and his supporters claim that the government is moving too fast, not stopping to consider the long-term effects that this monitoring could have. The government's response to this claim is that it must use all the tools it can if further attacks are to be prevented. I think this is a scare tactic on the part of the government. Although we may need new laws to stop future attacks by terrorists in the United States, it is also vital to ensure that citizens' rights are not crushed in the process. As one human rights researcher has said, "If allowed to be controlled by a government, instead of a tool for democracy, the Internet may be employed as a tool by which more modern dictatorships can monitor and control their citizens" (Hansen).

With the debate raging as to how much privacy Americans are entitled to when it comes to the Internet and what information they should be able to access, it is the citizens' job to take a stand and fight for their rights. It is only by doing so that the ideals of freedom of speech and right to privacy that the Founders so highly valued will be preserved. As Supreme Court Justice William O. Douglas once said, "The right to be let alone is indeed the beginning of all freedom."

Works Cited

Ferguson, Kevin. "Net Censorship Spreading on University Campuses." *Las Vegas Business Press* 28 Feb. 2000: 20. Print.

Hansen, Stephen A. "Policing the Internet: Cybercensorship and Its Potential Impact." Slide presentation and lecture. *AAAS Science and Human Rights Program*. American Association for the Advancement of Science, 1999. Web. 9 Oct. 2009.

Madsen, Grant. "Snow College Officials Defend Net Censorship: Blocking Pornography Was Not for Moral Reasons." *Salt Lake Tribune* 16 Jan. 1999: D3. Print.

Markels, Alex. "Screening the Net; Microsystems Cleans Up Web for Kids, Workers: Screening the Internet for Nudity, Profanity." *Salt Lake Tribune* 5 May 1997: B1. Print.

Oder, Norman, and Michael Rogers. "VA County Public Library to Filter All Access." *Library Journal* 126 (2001): 15. Print.

Puzzanghera, Jim. "Privacy Advocates Argue Anti-Terrorism Plans Harm Free Society." *San Jose Mercury News* 27 Sept. 2001: 17. Print.

Thornburg, David. "Children and Cybercensorship." *PBS TeacherLine*. Public Broadcasting Service, 22 Aug. 2002. Web. 6 Oct. 2009.

LITERARY INTERPRETIVE PAPER

Source: English course at Utah State University, 2013. Used by permission.

Things Are Not Always What They Seem

Both Daisy Miller (from Henry James' "Daisy Miller") and Edna Pontellier (from Kate Chopin's *The Awakening*), defy typical roles that defined men and women without the chastisement that previously accompanied socially unaccepted actions, and because of this, they ironically possess more freedom than their male counterparts. Since the women in these stories both physically appear to be what the men envision as symbols of true womanhood, they assume that the women still support the formerly existing social codes of conduct. While the women exert their own independence, the men remain trapped in a false reality of time-held social conventions which blinds them to the fact that they are being manipulated or undermined by women. Although the men are periodically troubled by these women's defiance of tradition, they believe socially acceptable behaviors to be completely impenetrable for women who attract men like themselves, and they dismiss the women's actions as simply a fleeting fancy or temporary flaw. The absence of physical indications that should accompany social deviance and the male envelopment in romantic notions regarding their assumed sweethearts both work together to produce a partial role reversal of time-honored positions.

Neither Winterbourne (the hopeful beau of Daisy Miller) nor Leonce Pontellier (Edna's husband) acknowledge the possibility that "devilish ideas about the eternal rights of women" could be present in the women they love (Chopin 684). Since Daisy and Edna are both put on pedestals of womanly perfection, the idea that they would desire anything other than the protection and guidance of a man seems highly improbable to Leonce and Winterbourne. Instead, the men blame uncontrollable forces for the women's deviations from perfect conduct. When Daisy ignores Winterbourne, he excuses her behavior as simply being "her habit, her manner" (James 472). Winterbourne does not believe that Daisy is harmful, but rather just a "pretty American flirt" (474) who "holds no mockery, no irony" (472). He believes, that "they all do these things—the young girls in America" (478), as if Daisy's behavior is a phase that she will grow out of. Likewise Mr. Pontellier simply believes that his wife is acting rashly, as if she too is just going through a temporary phase and will soon recover. When Leonce does feel compelled to reprimand his wife, his actions are always followed with "subsequent regret and ample atonement" as if he is really the one behaving inappropriately. Even other men tell him to ignore Edna's behavior and let her do as she pleases. Mainly, both men are simply perplexed by the situations they find themselves in, unable to pinpoint what they think would be a logical explanation for each woman's behavior. Winterbourne is "puzzled" by Daisy's excessive flirtations and ignorance of social propriety (483) and Mr. Pontellier seems to believe that Edna is just a little "unbalanced mentally" (Chopin 677) and seeks the help of a doctor, believing that something must "ail her" for her to act with such independence. Rather than figure out what is really going on, both men revert to the idea that women are "moody and whimsical," their behavior simply being a silly notion that will soon pass (685).

Since Daisy and Edna both physically meet the standard of being perfect women, the men assume that the women also live up to the remaining ideals of being pious, pure, submissive, and domestic. Winterbourne believes that Daisy "looked extremely innocent" and since she looks innocent, of course she must be (James 474). Winterbourne is always observing Daisy for any signs that she might not be as wonderful as he wishes her to be, but since Daisy never blushes or gives any other indication that she is behaving unfavorably, he ignores her sense of impropriety because her "programme seemed almost too enjoyable" (475). Winterbourne still assumes that "Daisy meant no harm" (494) even after she harasses him for not visiting her sooner and promptly turns the conversation to "the beautiful Giovanelli," which should partially confirm rumors of her supposedly scandalous behavior (489). Mr. Pontellier also cannot imagine that his wife could be anything less than he imagines her to be. Pontellier is always trying to find something physical to blame for his wife's odd behavior. When Edna refuses to look at new fixtures with him, as a good wife should, he convinces himself that Edna looks "pale and very quiet" (674). However, when Ponetellier confides in Dr. Mandelet about his concerns he seems perplexed because Edna "seems well" (683). Also, everyone else ignores Edna's attempts to undermine her husband, because she looks "handsome" and "ravishing" (680). Surely if there was something amiss with her character she would not look like a "beautiful sleek animal," her "speech warm and energetic" (687). If there were something wrong with her actions, it would show in her countenance.

Both women receive a great deal of attention from multiple males, which seems to indicate that their overwhelming charisma is not focused on Winterbourne and Pontellier, but is universal to the male species. Daisy brags to Winterbourne about how she has always had a "great deal of gentleman society" (James 474). Edna enjoys the fact that even though she is married she draws the attention of Alcee Arobin and that Robert "live[d] in her shadow" (Chopin 640). One of the reasons why Edna even married Leonce was because "his absolute devotion flattered her" (646). While the women enjoy the attention, they still withhold themselves from actually being involved. Daisy does not seem to be bothered by the idea of having two men accompany her simultaneously (James 491), displaying her non-partial attitude to either male since typically if a woman is interested, she desires to be alone with the man of her choice. While Edna does find momentary satisfaction in the attentions of her male admirers, she realizes that the fulfillment will "melt out of her existence" (722) and more than anything she desires solitude, breathing a "big, genuine sigh of relief" when "at last alone" (688).

Although both women seek male interest, they shun the idea of being defined by their associations with men. When Madame Ratignolle comments that the Pontelliers would be "more united" if they were to spend more time together, Edna's response is "Oh! Dear no!" (Chopin 686). Edna dislikes the idea of belonging to another person so much that even when Robert, the man she believes herself to be in love with, expresses his desire that Edna could be his wife, she replies heatedly, "Your wife!" (717). In general, Edna does not particularly care about marriage. Edna pursues other men, but does not want to be viewed as a possession and does not seem to think that she gains anything by being married (717). She believes that "a wedding is one of the most lamentable aspects on earth" (684). She refers to her marriage to Leonce Pontellier as "an accident" which she had foolishly hoped would usher her into a "world of reality, closing the portals forever behind her upon the realm of romance and dreams" (647). Daisy also avoids the idea that her attentions should be devoted to one man. She refuses to inform Winterbourne as to whether she is engaged to Giovanelli or not, first telling him that she is and then when he says he believes her, she changes her mind saying, "Well, then—I am not" (502). Even when everyone, including her own mother, believes she is engaged, she has little concern to see it made official, refusing to tie herself so wholly to one individual.

On the other hand, the men embrace marriage as a romantic tradition, imagining the women they marry to be perfect and submissive. They are so involved in the ideals of what women and love should be that they do not see reality. Winterbourne has just barely met Daisy, but he daydreams about "guiding [her] through the summer starlight" (James 48) and he "could have believed that he was going to elope with her" (483). Likewise, Mr. Pontellier "fell in love as men are in a habit of doing" (Chopin 647). Because his wife is "the sole object of his existence" (636), Edna's attitude does not concern him, but rather the way society will perceive their marriage. He has full faith in Edna's loyalty towards him, but seems more worried about society's views, reminding Edna that they have "to observe *les convenances*" or the social conventions. When Edna tells him of her intentions to move to another house he worries about what his acquaintances will think about his "financial integrity," the idea of scandal "never enter[ing] into his mind" (706). To remedy this, he puts a brief notice in the newspaper that announces that their residence was "undergoing sumptuous alterations." Since his name and his wife's name are now safe, Pontellier believes everything, especially his marriage relationship, has returned back to its proper state.

While the men are oblivious to Edna and Daisy's abnormal social behaviors, other women realize what is going on, either supporting or condemning. Mrs. Costello (Winterbourne's aunt) calls Daisy a "dreadful girl" (James 477) who is "hopelessly vulgar" (486) and even Daisy's mother disapproves of her daughter's behavior, saying she "doesn't like her gentleman friends" (480). The opinion women have of Edna is not nearly as strong, although they do realize her intentions. Madame Ratignolle warns Edna that Alcee Arobin's "attentions alone are considered enough to ruin a woman's name" (Chopin 708), and even Madame Reisz—who is a partial social outcast—asks Edna why she likes Robert when she "ought not to" (697).

Ironically, both stories end in death. Although Edna's is intentional and Daisy's is more a consequence of bad decisions, it seems indicative that the only way to truly escape the judgments and attempted control of men is to leave this existence. In some ways, Daisy's death is even more intriguing than Edna's suicide. After her funeral, Winterbourne questions Giovanelli about the events leading to her bout with Roman fever, and Giovanelli says, "If she had lived, I should have got nothing. She would never have married me, I am sure" (James 506). Although Giovanelli did not directly kill Daisy, he did not try to prevent her death because he finally realized that she would not conform to a man's ideas of the perfect woman.

Although female infidelity is not a new concept, neither Daisy nor Edna are met by scorn or discipline from male society. Men only seem to have a vague idea that there is something amiss, but believe that women are incapable of disobeying the natural gender roles that are supposed to be in place. Men still see everything from the viewpoint that women are emotional and weaker beings. Because of the male and female perspectives shown, these texts portray a partial role reversal where women are acting more independently and thinking more logically, whereas men are tied to social protocols and caught up in romantic ideas.

Works Cited

Chopin, Kate. *The Awakening. The Norton Anthology of American Literature* Vol. C. Ed. Nina Baym. New York: Norton, 2003. 633–723.

James, Henry. "Daisy Miller: A Study." *The Norton Anthology of American Literature.* Vol. C. Ed. Nina Baym. New York: Norton, 2003. 468–506.

LAB REPORT

Source: Materials Science Engineering course at Utah State University, 2007.
Used by permission.

Material Science Lab Report MAE 2160
TENSILE TESTING
Sara Driggs 22 February 2007

Abstract:

This experiment explores the three stages of a material, steel 1020, under a tensile load. The first of the three stages is the elastic stage where the material completely recovers from the load and related linearity. The second stage is the uniform elastic stage where the material is loaded beyond the yield strength and becomes an exponential. The third stage is after the ultimate yield strength and necking begins until final fracture. The specimen showed all three stages of tensile loading and was within 10% of other standard values of steel of different heat treatments.

Introduction:

In engineering practices it is of utmost importance to know the properties and limits of the materials used in any application. One method of finding those limits of materials is a tensile test. By performing the tensile test it allows engineers to find the yield strength, the ultimate tensile strength (UTS) or tensile strength, the percent elongation, and the percent reduction in area. Not only the allowable loads are found but other properties of the material can be inferred as well, such as the stiffness, resilience, and the toughness of the material.

The purpose of the experiment is to perform the tensile test on a piece of steel 1020 to obtain the yield strength, ultimate tensile strength, percent elongation, and percent reduction in area. Also the test is to explore the nature of necking in a specimen to compare true stress and true strain to engineering stress and engineering strain.

Tensile testing typically involves gradually increasing the load in tension until complete fracture. The specimen being tested usually is flat or round and of various sizes. It is important to note that there are standard specimens which must be used otherwise the test is *not* valid. Usually the specimen has a flush reduced section creating grips on each end to insert into the testing apparatus, thus giving it a "dog bone" shape. Also noted on the reduced section is the gauge length, used for measuring the elongation of the specimen. *The test will not be valid if the failure is not within the gauge length.* Lastly, the ratio of the gauge length to the gauge diameter, usually 4, must be the same in order to compare results from other specimens from other tests.

The behavior of materials under tensile loads has three stages. The first stage of tensile loads is the elastic stage, which is where the load is proportional to the elongation of the material, but when the load is removed the material recovers completely, up until the yield point or elastic limit. This is a linear relationship between the stress and the strain of the material, and the slope of that line is called the Young's Modulus "E" (See Figure 1). Hooke's law shows the stress-strain relationship in this linear stage.

The second stage of the material under tensile load is the uniform plastic elongation stage. This is where the material goes beyond the yield point, and Hooke's law is not valid. This, and the third stage, is where the plastic deformation is permanent. Though to accurately attain the elastic limit, sensitive measuring instrumentation must be used. Stage two ends when the material begins to "neck." This is where the deformation uniformly occurs through the entire gauge length. Here the specimen requires higher and higher stress levels because of strain hardening, which is shown by the exponential relationship:

K and n are constants; n is the strain hardening exponent which is always less than one and K depends on the material.

Stage three is known as the non-uniform plastic elongation stage or the post necking stage. This stage begins after the material begins to neck and is loaded beyond the ultimate yielding strength, where extreme plastic deformation occurs. It is also here in this stage where much of the elongation of the specimen takes place. Necking can happen anywhere along the specimen. For the test to be valid the necking *must* be inside the gauge length, because where the necking occurs the deformation is confined to that point. When the specimen experiences the final fracture this is the end of stage three, and the end of the tensile test and analysis can begin (See Figure 1).

Experimental Work:

Materials

- Riehle tensile tester, a hydraulic system powered by a hydraulic pump to induce tensile loads.

- The specimen, steel 1020.

Method of Procedure

1. Measure the diameter of the gauge section of the specimen using a Vernier.

2. Mark the gauge length, 50 mm centered on the reduced section by marking the specimen with a permanent marker then scratching the permanent marker indicating the ends of the 50 mm.

3. Zero the floating red needle on the gauge by turning the knob *counter clockwise.*

4. Turn on the hydraulic pump.

5. Load the specimen by adjusting the upper grips using the elevation lever.

6. Lower the grips until the specimen ends are seated in the grips; *it is important that at least 75% of the specimen ends are in the grips!* (See fig. 1)

7. Tighten the screw at the top of the upper grips and lower grips so that the specimen is firmly placed in the grips.

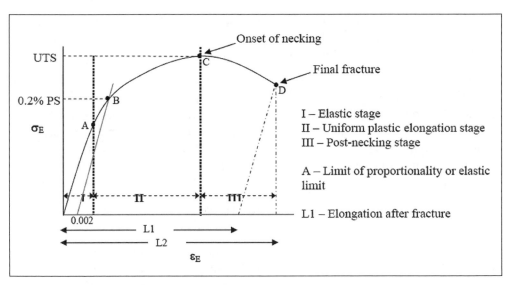

Figure 1: Typical Engineering Stress-Strain Diagram

8. Perform the test. Observing both the black and red needles, note when the black needle momentarily fluctuates (which it should be noted that not all materials show this kind of fluctuation). This is when the material begins to plastically deform.

9. After the fluctuation, the specimen then begins to neck. At this stage the black needle will be stationary for a few seconds, then the black needle drops off quickly. *Watch* the black needle and mark its location when you *hear* the fracture. This is the fracture load. The red needle marks the maximum load, which reading can be taken after the specimen has fractured.

10. Remove the ends of the specimen; turn off the Riehle Tester.

11. Record observations of the specimen surfaces.

12. Calculate the following data using the given equations:

Yield stress = <u>Yield load</u> UTS = <u>Max Load</u>

Original cross-sectional area Original cross-sectional area

% Elongation = Final gauge length—Original gauge length X 100

Original gauge length

%RA = Original cross-sectional area—Final cross sectional area X 100

Original cross-sectional area

Engineering fracture stress = <u>Fracture load</u>

Original cross-sectional area

True Fracture stress = <u>Fracture load</u>

Final cross sectional area

Original gauge diameter (mm) (Average of 3 measurements)	12.91
Original cross-sectional area (mm^2)	130.9
Final gauge diameter (at fracture locations) (mm)	8.96
Final cross-sectional area (mm^2)	63.05
Initial gauge length (mm)	50
Final gauge length (mm)	66.4
Yield load (N)	4626
Maximum load (N)	65390
Fracture load (N)	45370
Fracture location	Fracture within gauge length, just off center.

Figure 2: Experimental Data

Yield strength (MPa)	353.407
Tensile strength (MPa)	499.542
Engineering fracture strength (MPa)	346.600
True fracture strength (MPa)	719.553
% Elongation	32.8
% Reduction in area	51.8

Figure 3: Results

Results:

Observations

The fracture did occur within the gauge length. In the material necking and elongation had occurred, wherein the sheared stress stayed inside the necking, resulting in a shear lip. There was axial fracture and shear fracture resulting in a compound fracture. At the fracture site there were no other materials (inclusions) or anomalies. The surface looked dull and fibrous, and the two end pieces formed a cup and cone shape.

Discussion:

The results obtained were not inconsistent, and did reveal the yield strength, ultimate tensile strength. From the measurements the percent elongation and percent reduction area were able to be calculated. The limitations of the procedure are mostly in human error and the accuracy of the equipment used. Because the black needle had to be read very quickly at the instant of fracture, it is necessary to take the average of three values recorded by each person, and here the error could be greatest. Because the equipment is not super sensitive the yield strength could be inaccurate, because the needle had to fluctuate, and there human error could increase the inaccuracy. When the results are compared to other steel 1020 specimen's heat treated differently, the yield strength

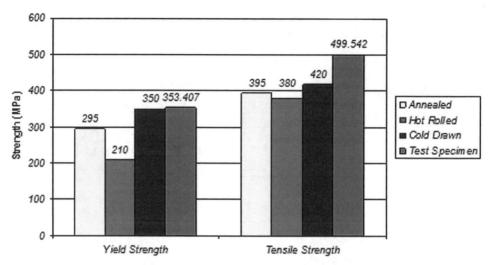

Figure 4: Comparison

and tensile strength is observed that the test specimen comes within 10% of the other values (See Figure 4).

Conclusion:

The specimen of steel 1020 clearly demonstrated a linear elastic region, ending at the yield point and into the uniform plastic deformation ending at the necking stage. The last stage of the non-uniform plastic deformation was clearly seen in the typical necking, forming the cup and cone shape, and to the final fracture within the gauge length. Mostly the calculated values of the stresses were within the 10% variation of the other heat-treated steel 1020 specimens.

ANTHROPOLOGY REPORT

(Source: Anthropology course at Utah State University, 2010. Used by permission.)

Our Ideal Textbook

In my conventional manner of reading a science textbook, I skim quickly over the history of who discovered what when, speed-read the flowery analogies and examples, and concentrate my study on important concepts and formulas. Reading Adovasio's book, The First Americans; In Pursuit of Archaeology's Greatest Mystery, is an entirely different experience. His language and style of presentation are casual, and the theories and models postulated in the book are treated as possibilities and not hard facts. These qualities of his work create the ideal textbook for the purpose of our class because they inspire participation, critical thinking, and internal debate.

"Who the hell are these people, where did they come from, and when did they get here?" Adovasio's swearwords and straightforward language help him to create a connection with his readers. Unlike the monotone and formal presentation style of most textbooks, his use of words hints at a tone of friendship as opposed to professorship. In the overture of the book he presents his own story, relaying how he both entered the controversial debates and achieved expertise on their history and supporting evidence. This personal addition to the book aids Adovasio in establishing rapport with readers not familiar with his work. Even still, his friendly tone often masks his biases and mockery of certain ideas and beliefs that perhaps should not find a place in an educational book. For example, his declaration of the Bible as a work of mostly poetry shows direct disrespect for the millions of people who still believe in it as a work of history. To me, such an overstepping of his casualty is distasteful and distracting from the focus of his work.

Adovasio's dynamic descriptions of the history of archaeology as a science in North America cause the recent past to seem as exciting and baffling as the mysteries the researchers were pursuing. Similar to various models presented of the first Americans, archaeology in North America has multiple persons attributed to be the founder. In addition, scientific study and interest in America's hidden history spread quickly throughout both the scientific and lay communities before decreasing to its intensity of modern times, not unlike the rapid spread of Clovis technology thousands of years previously. Recognizing how archaeology's origin in America mirrors, in some respects, the models it proposes led my studying to be intriguing and enjoyable.

As Adovasio delves into the late Pleistocene and early Holocene environment of the American continent, he not only presents the accepted data but also the models and theories that are based off that data. A prime example of this is his chapter on the mega-fauna that went extinct around the Pleistocene–Holocene boundary. First he presents the accepted extinction of the creatures: their fossilized remains suggest that they were here, but the lack of remains in Holocene deposits and their non-existence in the modern faunal landscape implies extinction around 11,000 years ago. Then he presents the postulates that they were killed off by the arrival of humans, or due to climate change as we entered the current interglacial. This manner of relaying the models and their evidence promotes critical thinking. As I contemplate the various models presented and analyze their support, the strength of the arguments leads me to believe almost all of them.

Overall, *The First Americans* is ideal for the purposes of our class. The presentation of postulated models compels investigation of the latest research and models they support. Adovasio's provocative manner, although overstepped at times, inspires controversy and debate. Furthermore, his friendly tone and dynamic descriptions make me feel as a companion to the archaeologists at the forefront of research today. Through reading this highly irregular science textbook, the arguments presented are not just scientist squabble to be read and discussed but also are raging in my head, enticing me to delve further into the debates and take my own stand.

BIOLOGY FIELD REPORT

(Source: Biology course at Utah State University, 2005. Used by permission.)

Independent Project: Differences in Morning and Evening Bird Abundance

By: Janene Shupe
Submitted To:
Dr. Kim Sullivan
Field Ornithology

INTRODUCTION

After I started birding, I began to hear various opinions about the best time of day to sight birds. Most people seem to be partial to observing birds in the morning, evening, or both. These differences made me wonder which opinion is correct. For my study, I decided to determine whether differences in bird abundance occur between morning and evening and if so, which times of day birds are most likely to be sighted.

To test my question, I needed to measure the abundance of birds in the morning and evening. To do this, I chose to conduct a line transect census without distance. This technique is performed by walking a preset line and recording each bird you see or hear (Sullivan, 1993). Abundance is measured by assuming that all species and individuals are equally noticeable from your study line (Johnston, 1985).

METHODS

The area I chose to study was the Canal Trail above Canyon Road in Logan, Utah. The trail borders a cement canal located on a slope with a southern aspect. Vegetation surrounding the canal and trail is comprised mostly of box elders, cottonwoods, birches and mountain shrubs, as well as several forbs and grasses. The slope above the trail is a sagebrush and bunch grass community with a few scattered junipers. Private property is located below the trail. This gives the area an assortment of habitats including pastureland, gardens, lawns, and a variety of native and introduced species. Some of the houses have feeders, adding to the diversity.

My transect line began at the trail's farthest west side at the metal gate. It ended approximately 300 yards past the easternmost bridge crossing the canal. To begin my study, I determined the approximate time of sunrise as 6:15 A.M. and the approximate time of sunset as 8:30 P.M. (U.S. Naval Observatory, 1977). I then determined that my transect would take 45 to 60 minutes to walk. From this information, I began my morning walks at about 15 minutes after sunrise and my evening walks at about an hour before sunset. Each time of day I walked with my back to the sun. On mornings I began on the west side and in evenings I started on the east side. In this way, I hoped to have similar lighting both times of day. I conducted my studies on five days within a nine-day period. I began on May 7 and ended on May 16. On each of the days I conducted my study, I recorded birds both in the morning and evening. I recorded every bird I saw or heard, including those that I could not identify.

RESULTS

After collecting my data, I totaled both the number of bird species and individual birds for each sheet within a set (a set being comprised of data from both times during the same day). With this information, I comprised a list of bird species, created line graphs, and performed statistical calculations. In all, I observed 33 species of birds, excluding unidentified birds (Appendix A). I chose,to exclude the unidentified birds from my species list since they are not very meaningful and many species may overlap. However, I did include these birds in my graphs and statistical tests.

The first graph represents differences in the number of bird species between each set (Appendix B). In every set, I observed more bird species in the morning than in the evening. The second graph represents differences in the numbers of individual birds observed (Appendix C). The majority of these sets also have more birds in the morning. However there was an exception on the fourth set. This difference may be explained by the weather. The morning of the fourth day was windy, but the evening was still.

To test the significance of the differences in my data, I chose to use a two-sample t-test. This test is used to determine whether the differences between the averages of two independent samples are significant (Freeman et al., 1991). Since my sample size is small, I chose to use the Student Curve to determine the significance of my findings.

First, I compared the difference between the number of individuals recorded in the morning and the evening (Appendix D). I calculated a p-value of five percent, which is statistically significant. Second, I compared the differences between the number of species recorded in the morning and evening (Appendix D). This also was statistically significant, with a p-value of five percent.

CONCLUSIONS

My results showed that birds were more abundant in the morning than in the evening. This might mean that birds are more abundant in the morning and that this is the best time to observe birds. However, I do not believe that this was proved by my experiment. Many factors could have varied my results. Also, my results may be true only for specific circumstances.

First, I believe it is important to consider bias. Bias may be caused by observers, birds, habitat, weather, or censusing methods (Sullivan, 1993). I tried to avoid as much bias as possible with my methods. However, I still see a lot of problems with my project. The main sources of bias in my experiment were due to my lack of identification skills and the human activity on my site.

I probably overlooked a lot of birds that I could not identify by song. Also, I had a lot of birds recorded that I could not identify by sight. Since my skills improved each time I walked my transect, I would have guessed that my species list would have increased each time. Still, I found more species in the morning than the evening. This may mean that the differences between morning and evening might have been larger.

Another consideration is the habitat I chose. Birds may have been more active in the morning due to human disturbance. The Canal Trail is used to access other trails leading to 400 North and Utah State University. It is also used by many people for recreation. Birds in this area may be more active in the morning to avoid the increase of people during the day and evening.

This project taught me a lot about censusing and censusing techniques. I was unaware of the amount of information you can find with census studies. Census studies can be used to generate species lists, estimate bird densities, discover abundance, and make numerous comparisons (Johnston, 1985). I also learned that there are many difficulties with conducting a census and that it takes a lot of time, effort, and experience to account for these. I also learned a lot about the many techniques that can be used to conduct a census. Some techniques are very difficult, such as the variable distance line transects that need skilled observers. Other techniques need special equipment such as mist nets and radio transmitters. However, many techniques are easy enough to be used by nearly any observer, such as the line transect used in this study.

This project taught me a lot about birding. By observing and recording birds, I rapidly improved my identification skills and began to associate birds with their songs. I also began to notice many things about their behavior, shape, and flight patterns. I also discovered that research studies seem to have endless results. I discovered new questions throughout my project. Related studies on bird preferences between morning and evening could focus on differences among species, seasons, weather, temperature, human *activity,* habitat, and numerous other factors.

REFERENCES

Freedman, David, 1991. Statistics: 2nd Edition. New York: W.W. Norton and Company.

Johnston, Richard F. (editor). 1985. Current ornithology, Volume 2. New York: Plenum.

Sullivan, Kim (lecture). 1993. Field ornithology, Fall Quarter.

United States Naval Observatory. 1977. Sunrise and sunset tables for key cities and weather stations of the U.S. Gale Research Company. Detroit, Michigan. No. 1296.

APPENDIX A: BIRD SPECIES LIST

1. Black-capped Chickadee
2. Mourning Dove
3. American Robin
4. Song Sparrow
5. Common Yellowthroat

6. Northern Flicker
7. Mallard
8. Empidonax (Flycatcher) spp.
9. House Finch
10. European Starling

11. Broad-tailed Hummingbird
12. Lazuli Bunting
13. Black-billed Magpie
14. Yellow Warbler
15. Black-headed Grosbeak
16. Western Tanager
17. Chipping Sparrow
18. Pine Siskin
19. Yellow-rumped Warbler
20. Brown-headed Cowbird
21. American Goldfinch
22. Ring-necked Pheasant

23. American Crow
24. Brewer's Blackbird
25. White-throated Swift
26. Northern Oriole
27. Tree Swallow
28. Cassin's Finch
29. White-crowned Sparrow
30. Wilson's Warbler
31. Rufous Hummingbird
32. MacGillavry's Warbler
33. White-breasted Nuthatch

APPENDIX B: COMPARISON OF NUMBER OF SPECIES

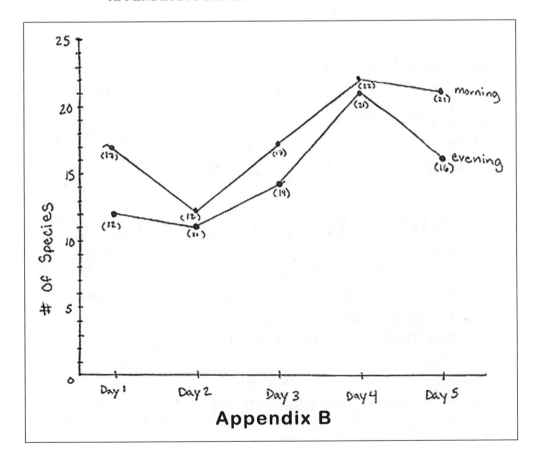

Appendix B

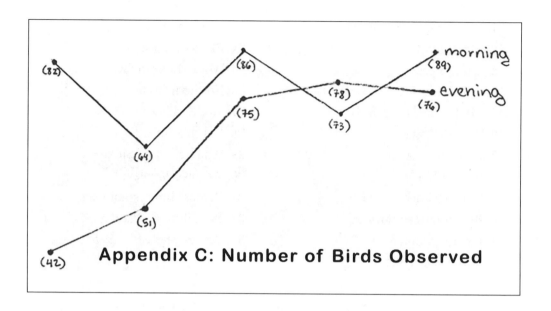

Appendix C: Number of Birds Observed

morning
evening

(82) (86) (89)
(78)
(75) (76)
(73)
(64)

(51)

(42)

APPENDIX D: DIFFERENCES AMONG INDIVIDUALS AND SPECIES

Differences among Individuals

Morning Average 79.8 S.D. 9.2 S.E.$_{sum}$ 20.6 S.E.$_{AVE}$ 4.1

Evening Average 63.4 S.D. 14.95 S.E.$_{sum}$ 33.4 S.E.$_{AVE}$ 6.7 S.E.$_{dif.}$ 7.9 T = 2.1 9 = 5%

Differences among Species

Morning Average 17.8 S.D. 3.5. S.E.$_{sum}$ 7.8 S.E.$_{AVE}$ = 1. 6

Evening Average 14.8 S.D. 3.5 S.E.$_{sum}$ 7.8 S.E.$_{AVE}$ 1. 6 S.E.$_{dif.}$ 2.3 T = 1.9 P < 5%

ENGINEERING DESIGN REPORT

(Source: Mechanical and Aerospace Engineering course at Utah State University, 2003. Used by permission.)

Preliminary Design of Thermal Coupling Switch to Use Aboard Spirit II

Professor J. C. Batty, Cryogenics Engineer
Marion D. Dart, Mechanical Engineering Student

FOREWORD

When the cryogenically cooled optical instruments of the Spatial Rocket-borne Interferometric Telescope (SPIRIT II) are in operation, it is desirable to couple them directly to the cryogen coolant to prevent them from warming past 25 K.

Currently, there is no coupling device in the design of SPIRIT II, and the optical instruments are allowed to warm continuously during the ten-minute flight. I was assigned by Dr. J. C. Batty to design a mechanical switch that will couple or decouple the instruments from the coolant upon demand.

SUMMARY

This paper reports the results of my preliminary design. This report presents the preliminary design of a thermal switch that will prevent the instruments aboard SPIRIT II from warming past 25 K during flight operation. When a coupling device closes the joint between the heat straps attached to the tank and the instruments, the heat entering the instrument chamber during flight is permitted to conduct directly to the cryogen tank. The size of the switch allows it to be added to the dewar system after SPIRIT II has been built. A simplified thermal analysis shows the only resistance to heat flow is the contact resistance in the joint. This resistance and mechanical efficiencies need to be determined in future testing. Based on the preliminary design, implementing the thermal switch on SPIRIT II is highly feasible.

1.0 INTRODUCTION

Optical instruments that operate in space frequently need to be cryogenically cooled. During times when the instruments are in operation, it may be desirable to couple the instruments directly to the cryogenic cooler. This is particularly advisable in the case of SPIRIT II because the instruments are cooled by the thermal conduction of heat from the instruments to the cryogen tank. The dewar system (the instruments and the cryogen tank) is made of 6061-T6 aluminum. This alloy's thermal characteristics are such that the thermal conductivity drops from 2000 w/(m*K) at 100 K to 20 w/(M*K) at 20 K (1). Because of the drop in thermal conductivity, the heat that enters the optical instrument chamber during operation has difficulty conducting to the cryogen tank before the instruments warm past 25 K.

When the instruments are allowed to warm past 25 K the risk of invalid data being collected is increased. This increase results from contaminants that collect on the walls of the dewar during cryogenic cool-down being released and interfering with operation of the sensors. The telescope and interferometer were designed to function at 20 K, and a change in operating temperature of more than 5 K can result in improper performance.

During flight 20 watts of heat flood the instrument chamber and must be removed quickly if the instruments are to stay within the required temperature range. A permanent coupling device would keep the instruments at 5 K, which is 10 K too cold for proper operation. The thermal switch described in this paper is designed to couple or decouple the optical instruments of SPIRIT II directly to the cryogen tank with high thermal conductivity heat straps. The thermal switch will allow the optics to stay within the desired operating temperatures before flight and remain cool when the 20 watts of heat enter the instrument chamber by conducting it directly to the liquid helium cryogen

353

tank. Aspects of the design covered in this report are: Constraints and Simplifications, Mechanical Components, Design Problems.

2.0 CONSTRAINTS AND SIMPLIFICATIONS IN DESIGN

SPIRIT II's structural design is complete, and no structural changes are to be made during implementation of the switch. SPIRIT II is to fly in July 1988, which allows three months for the design and implementation of the switch if it is to be used in the upcoming flight. This limitation in time calls for simplifications in the design. A simplified thermal analysis was utilized in the design of the switch.

2.1 STRUCTURAL CONSTRAINTS

Because no structural changes can be made to the dewar system, the thermal switch is designed so that it can be attached to the system after SPIRIT II has been built. The size of the switch is constrained so that it physically fits in the allowable space in the dewar system. Figure 1 shows the current design of the dewar system. An area of approximately 4 square inches is available on the main flange to attach the coupling device.

2.2 SIMPLIFIED THERMAL ANALYSIS

An approach to cooling the instruments that keeps with the same conduction theory used in the current dewar system is a thermal strap made of a high thermal conductivity metal, such as copper, fastened to the cryogen tank joined to another strap secured to the optical instruments. Where the thermal straps meet, a mechanical coupling device

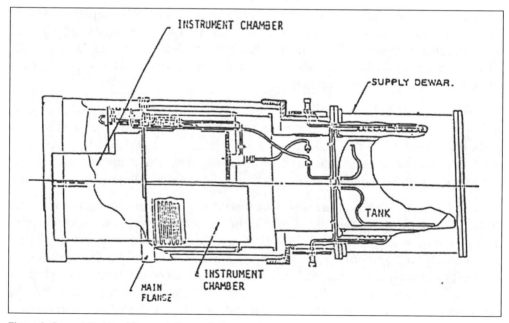

Figure 1. Current Design of Cryogenic Dewar System

mates the straps upon demand. The thermal analysis of the switch was simplified by using lumped parameters. The thermal strap fastened to the tank was lumped with the tank by assuming it was the same temperature as the tank, 4.2 K. The strap connected to the instruments was lumped with the optical instruments and assumed to be 20 K.

The assumptions of lumped parameters employ the fact that the straps are to be made of 99.99% pure copper. Copper with this purity has a thermal conductivity of 3000 w/(m*K) between 4 and 20 K (2). A thermal conductivity of this magnitude allows the resistances to thermal conduction in the heat straps to be neglected. With the impedance in the straps neglected, the only resistance in the conduction path is the contact resistance between the two straps when the coupling device closes the joint.

3.0 MECHANICAL DESIGN

The design of the switch consists of two parts: the design of the coupling device and the design and fastening technique of the heat straps.

3.1 COUPLING DEVICE

The coupling device is to ensure a junction between the straps connected to the tank and the ones connected to the instrument chamber. This joint must be closed with enough force to ensure minimized contact resistance between the straps. Because of the small area (4 square inches) allowed for attaching the coupling device, only a small motor can be used. A significant mechanical advantage is needed if the device is to perform as required. A commercially available motor was found that can supply 5 oz.-in. torque. This available torque is used to supply 50 lbs. force with the mechanism pictured in Figure 2. Appendices 1a. through 1c. describe the mechanism in more detail.

The motor pinion in Figure 2 drives the gear attached to the ball screw with an 18:1 gear ratio. When the ball screw turns, the ball nut moves linearly, causing the linkage connected to the nut to compress a spring. When the spring is compressed, 50 lbs. is applied to the ends of the heat straps in place on the device, forcing them into thermal contact. An indium gasket is between the adjoining straps to help ensure good thermal contact

3.2 HEAT STRAPS

The heat that floods the instrument chamber during operation will be conducted to the cryogen tank by means of

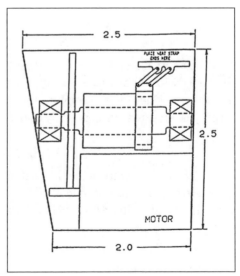

Figure 2. Coupling Device Mechanism Used in Switch

heat straps connected to the tank and the instruments. These straps are joined upon demand by the coupling device. The heat straps needed to be made of a high thermal conductivity metal so the heat can flow quickly to the cryogen tank without allowing the optical instruments to warm more than 5 K. A high-purity copper was chosen as the best metal because of its availability, malleability, and thermal conductivity.

3.2.1 HEAT STRAP DESIGN

The heat straps are designed to have as large a cross-sectional area as will fit in the available space. This will increase the validity of the lumped parameter heat transfer analysis by providing a large thermal mass. The straps fastened to the cryogen tank will have a cross section of 1.25 in. $\times$ 0.375 in. There will be two straps connected to the tank, each formed to run along either side of the telescope into place on the coupling device mounted on the main flange. The heat straps secured to the optical instruments will be flexible copper braids made of two hundred 20 AWG individual copper wires braided together. Two braids will be wrapped circumferencially around the instrument chamber, with an end of each braid run into place on the coupling device.

3.2.2 FASTENING TECHNIQUE

The heat straps connected to the tank are to be bolted securely to the tank, as described in Appendix 2. Between the copper straps and the helium tank, an indium gasket must be used. This gasket will reduce the contact resistance between the strap and the tank, making it negligible. The heat straps that are attached to the instrument chamber are made from. The braid will be wrapped around the chamber, and metal banding will secure the braid in place. It is important to attach the banding as tightly as possible and use an indium gasket between the chamber and the copper braid to minimize the contact resistance.

4.0 UNRESOLVED DESIGN ASPECTS

The short time allowed for this preliminary design has left parts of the design unfinished. Before the switch is built, thermal properties of materials used in the switch and the efficiency of the coupling mechanism at cryogenic temperatures must be determined. An extensive cost analysis will also need to be done.

4.1 REQUIRED TESTING

To ensure reliability of the thermal switch to maintain the optical instruments within the desired temperature range of 15 K to 25 K, tests that measure the contact resistance in the joint and evaluate the mechanical efficiencies of the coupling device should be run.

4.1.1 CONTACT RESISTANCE IN JOINT

The thermal contact resistance in the joint where the adjoining ends of the heat straps meet can only be determined by testing. Because this is the only resistance the heat flowing from the instrument to the tank sees, it is vital that the force in the coupling joint be great enough to overcome that resistance. Based on tests described in M. Baugh's lab book (3), 50 lbs. of force will overcome the contact resistance in the joint and allow 20 watts to flow to the tank. Proper tests can verify this assumption or determine the necessary force to overcome the contact resistance. Modifying the spring can produce more or less force.

4.1.2 MECHANICAL EFFICIENCIES

The efficiencies of the motor, ball screw and ball nut at cryogenic temperatures must also be determined. This can be done by testing the assembly at design conditions.

4.2 COST ANALYSIS

To date, no concern has been given to the cost of the switch. Many of the parts, however, are commercially available, which should reduce the initial cost. An extensive analysis should include testing costs and labor costs, along with the prices of individual components of the switch.

5.0 CONCLUSIONS

This report presents the preliminary design of a mechanical thermal switch. When the cryogenically cooled optical instruments of the SPIRIT II rocket are in flight operation, 20 watts of heat enter the instrument chamber. If this heat is not removed within seconds, the instruments will warm past 25 K. At temperatures above 25 K, the instruments are more likely to function improperly. A thermal switch that couples the instruments to the cryogen coolant will prevent the instruments from warming past the desired temperature. A preliminary design of the switch consists of the following:

1. Size constraints that allow the switch to be attached to the dewar system after SPIRIT II has been built

2. A cooling process that uses conduction heat transfer

3. Simplified thermal analysis using lumped parameter theory

4. Heat straps that are fastened to the instrument chamber and heat straps that are connected to the cryogen tank

5. A coupling device that joins the heat straps connected to the instrument chamber and tank to provide thermal conduction

6. Description of required tests to ensure switch reliability

    a) Contact resistance test

    b) Mechanical efficiency test

Based on the preliminary design, I feel that implementing a coupling switch on SPIRIT II is quite feasible.

WORKS CITED

(1) National Bureau of Standards. Handbook of materials for superconducting machinery: Mechanical, thermal, electrical, magnetic properties of structural materials. New York: Metals and Ceramics Information Center, Advanced Research Projects Agency and Cryogenics Division; 1977.

(2) Touloukian, J. Thermal physical properties of matter. New York: IFI/Plenum; 1970.

(3) Baugh, M. Senior design log book. Department of Mechanical Engineering, Utah State University, Logan, Utah; 2003.

APPENDIX 1A: LAYOUT OF MECHANISM

[Student also included additional appendices: 1b- Mechanism Mounts; 1c—Bracket and Linkage; 2—Cold Straps on Tank]

SCIENTIFIC REVIEW PAPER

(Source: Animal Biology course at Utah State University, 2000. Used by permission.)

Host Bacterial Interactions
Todd Quarnberg
Term Paper for Animal Biology

Outline

I. Introduction

II. Classification of disease-producing organisms

III. Transmission of microbes

IV. Multiplication and spread of bacteria

V. Spread of infection throughout the body

VI. Attachment of bacteria to epithelial surfaces

VII. External defense mechanisms

VIII. Inflammatory response

IX. Internal defense mechanisms

    A. Humoral immunity
    B. Cell-mediated immunity
    C. Phagocytosis

X. Summary

HOST-BACTERIAL INTERACTIONS

I. Introduction

The most important factor in the acquisition and eradication of human disease is the health and immunity of the host. In times past, the wrath of God was blamed for disease caused by living microorganisms. Sick people were either put to death or lived a life of ostracism and ridicule (Anderson 1988). Throughout my research on host-bacterial interactions, I have found that it is the level of host immunity that is the key issue in the acquisition of and recovery from infectious disease. Virulence factors of the microbes are of secondary importance. All pathogenic microbes are opportunists, but some require more severe and obvious host deficiencies to cause disease. When suppression of host defenses takes place, a particular microbe will enter this window of opportunity. Its presence at an opportune moment and the ability of the microbe to survive and multiply in the host are of vital importance in causing disease. Pathogenic microbes must also be able to resist host defense mechanisms for a period sufficient to reach the numbers required to produce disease.

II. Classification of Disease-Producing Organisms

There are three different classifications of disease-producing microorganisms. First are extracellular parasites, which produce infection by multiplying primarily outside phagocytic cells (blood cells that ingest and destroy foreign bacteria). Such parasites produce disease if they avoid the human defense mechanisms. Second are facultative intracellular parasites, which may be destroyed by phagocytic cells, but are resistant to intracellular killing by them. Last are the obligate intracellular parasites, which cannot multiply unless they are within cells (Youmans et al. 1986). All humans have microbes that normally live in or on our bodies; this population of organisms is called our normal flora, or indigenous microbiota. The normal flora are becoming a more frequent cause of human illness by taking advantage of deficiencies in host defenses. Decreases in host resistance can allow the normal flora to invade and establish disease. Knowledge of the different organisms present at various body sites may give a clue to the type of infection that might occur following injury at these sites. It also is clear that the normal flora are important in stimulating the immune system. For example, germ-free mice lack good immune systems because they lack stimulation of their immune systems; thus pathogens are free to spread throughout their bodies (Sommers 1986).

III. Transmission of Microbes

There are several different modes of transmission of disease and pathogens. Man is the major reservoir for human disease, and coughing, sneezing, touching, and intimate contact are ways the transmission of microbes can occur. In our time, overcrowding in day-care centers, hospitals, and so on also increases disease transmission. Disease in developed countries has been on the increase because of the overcrowded conditions (Youmans et al. 1986).

IV. Multiplication and Spread of Bacteria

Bacteria multiply by dividing into two daughter cells in a process known as binary fission. Their growth is exponential (1- -2- -4- -8- -16, etc.), with an average twenty- to thirty-minute doubling time. Scientists have demonstrated that animals infected with highly virulent bacteria will die or show signs of infection only when a certain bacterial population has been reached in the infected animal. It follows that the larger the infecting agent, the quicker death or signs of disease will occur. It also follows that a smaller infecting dose will usually result in a longer incubation period. It is possible to measure the number of bacteria necessary to produce disease in an experimental animal. Lethal dose 50 (LD 50) is the number or dose of bacteria that when injected into experimental animals will eventually cause 50% of the population to die. The LD 50 is useful in comparing relative virulence of bacterial strains and the relative susceptibility of experimental animals. Observation of natural human infections indicates that certain bacteria are more virulent than others and that humans vary in their susceptibility. People infected with the same strain of the same bacterium will either die from infection or recover.

Consider it a race between two opposing forces, the most important factor in eradicating a disease being the ability to mount a specific immune response in time, which may be anywhere from five to ten days. It is also possible for a person to develop an immune response before enough bacteria are present to actually cause disease. This is called an inapparent or subclinical infection (Youmans et al. 1986). When an infected host recovers from an infection caused by an extracellular parasite, usually all the bacteria are killed. In some infections caused by facultative intracellular parasites, some of the microbes may survive and become dormant. They can become active again when resistance has been lowered.

V. Spread of Infection Throughout the Body

Depending on the effectiveness of host defenses, an infection may remain localized or spread throughout the body. There are three ways infection may spread. First is direct extension to neighboring tissues. Second is direct entry into a blood vessel (hematogenous spread). And third is spread by the lymphatic system (lymphatic spread), with the latter as the most common method. Microbes can easily enter the blood from the lymphatics and spread infection throughout the body (Wyss 1971).

VI. Attachment of Bacteria to Epithelial Surfaces

Some bacteria are directly deposited inside human tissue by traumatic entry. Other bacteria must first attach to epithelial (protective) tissue to cause infection and disease. The respiratory tract is the most common route of invasion, and the bacteria use small hair-like projections (pilli) to attach to a specific binding site on host cells. Normal flora microbes may help to prevent colonization of respiratory tract surfaces by covering up specific attachment sites required by pathogenic microbes. Flora are also in competition with pathogens for nutrients. Some normal flora organisms even produce inhibitory products to kill pathogens and limit disease (Anderson 1988).

VII. External Defense Mechanisms

The body has several external defense mechanisms to limit disease and infection from entering the body. The skin represents a mechanical barrier to the entry of microbes. Infection through the skin takes place only when the skin has been damaged. The skin has normal flora that help maintain an acid pH to prevent colonization by pathogens. Sebaceous glands in the skin also produce a bactericide to kill invading microorganisms (Golub 1987). Human bites have the potential of causing deep infections because of the high bacterial counts from the mouth (Wise 1987).

The respiratory tract has several defense mechanisms to limit invasion. Nasal hairs and normal flora in the upper respiratory tract help prevent colonization. Phagocytic cells in the alveoli of the lung destroy and remove small infectious particles that could potentially cause damage and infection to the lung (Youmans et al. 1986). The alimentary tract (digestive system) also has several defensive mechanisms. Normal flora of the mouth and large intestine help to prevent colonization by pathogens. And the highly acidic pH of the stomach kills most microbes as they pass through the digestive system.

In the genitourinary tract, the prostatic fluid in males contains bactericidal substances. The frequent flushing action of urine also helps to control microbial populations in the urethra. The normal flora in the female vagina consists primarily of lactobacilli that break down glycogen (a polysaccharide) to form acid. The acidic pH prevents colonization by most pathogens (Youmans et al. 1986).

The eye limits microbial growth by the flushing action of tears. Tears also contain lysozyme, which plays a considerable role in resistance to infection by destroying the cell walls of some bacteria (Youmans et al. 1986).

VIII. Inflammatory Response

The body also has a specific defense mechanism called inflammation, which is a protective response of the tissues of the body to irritation and injury. It is characterized by several events. First, blood flow changes. The blood vessels dilate and allow an increased blood flow to the site of injury, which causes redness and heat. Increased permeability of blood vessels, caused by the chemical histamine, allows fluid to escape into the tissues (Serefin 1987), causing the swelling and pain. Inflammation, because of its combination of effects, is usually protective against infection.

IX. Internal Defense Mechanisms

The human body also has internal defense mechanisms. These are the body's defenses that react against specific microbes. Extracellular parasites are the most susceptible to serum antibody produced by the body's humoral (fluid-producing) response. Facultative and obligate intracellular parasites are more susceptible to cell-mediated immunity. The body also has a third internal defense mechanism, called phagocytosis, which is a nonimmune defense.

A. Humoral Immunity

In humoral immunity, lymphocytes, which are a portion of the white blood cells, are processed into B-cells, either in the bone marrow or in the lymph nodes along the intestinal tract. Antibodies are produced when B-cells are stimulated by a foreign substance called an antigen. The antigen (on an invading microbe) is presented to a B-cell by a macrophage and binds with receptors on the surface of the B-cell. The specific B-cell becomes activated by the antigen and rapidly divides to form a large group of cells.

This mechanism, where B-cells are stimulated, is known as clonal selection (Davis 1986). It is a mechanism of antibody production. The activated cells of this clone will carry out two functions: some become plasma cells and actively secrete antibody for days and die, while others become memory cells, which live for years and respond more rapidly and forcefully should the same antigen appear at a future time (Golub 1987).

There are two ways immunity to infection may be obtained by antibodies, either actively or passively. Active immunity is the production of a specific antibody in response to the presence of a microbe or its products. Active immunity may be obtained by direct infection of the disease or by vaccination. Passive immunity occurs when protective antibodies are transferred from an actively immunized animal to a non-immunized one. A good example of passive immunity is antibodies that are transferred from mother to fetus across the placenta. Colostrum, which is the mother's first milk, is rich in antibody and can also passively transfer immunity to a child (Herscowitz 1985).

Antibodies have several functions to aid the body in the fight with infection. One function is toxin neutralization. Some poisons produced by bacteria can be neutralized by antibodies. Antibodies are also able to attach to microbes and promote phagocytosis by aiding in the process of attachment. They may also bind to microbes and prevent their attachment to epithelial surfaces, thus not allowing them to establish and cause disease (Bellanti 1985; Getzoff 1987; Geyson 1987).

B. Cell-Mediated Immunity

Intracellular parasites are more susceptible to the cell-mediated immunity (CMI). Cell-mediated immunity is the result of thymus-derived lymphocytes (T-cells) and macrophages (Silberner 1988). When activated, these cells are very effective at attacking facultative and obligate intracellular parasites. Cell-mediated immunity is primarily the result of T-cells, which are sensitized by contact with a foreign antigen. An antigen (an invading microbe) is presented to the T-cells in the lymphoid tissue by a macrophage. That specific T-cell becomes activated and rapidly divides to form effector cells. Some effector cells are cytotoxic T-cells that migrate to the site of invasion and destroy foreign cells on contact. Some effector cells are delayed hypersensitivity T-cells that migrate to the site of invasion and produce lymphokines, which are a type of bactericidal. In certain types of infection, macrophages accumulate in large numbers at the site of infection. This response is called a granulomatous response and may lead to formation of a nodule or swelling in the tissue (Bass 1985; Bellanti 1985).

C. Phagocytosis

Phagocytosis (destruction of bacteria by phagocytic blood cells) is a non-immune internal defense mechanism. Phagocytosis is usually carried out by cells called neutrophils and macrophages. Neutrophils are the most important and are produced in the bone marrow. They survive only a few days and contain enzymes and antimicrobial substances. Macrophages are found in the tissues and may live for weeks or months. Neutrophils and macrophages marginate on the walls of blood vessels adjacent to a site of inflammation. They undergo diapedesis and squeeze between endothelial cells (cells that line blood vessels) to enter damaged tissue. The phagocytic process can be divided into two stages. The first is attachment of a phagocyte to a pathogenic microbe. However, if a bacterium has a capsule, this will interfere with attachment. Ingestion follows attachment, and the microbe is exposed to the digestive enzymes and substances contained within the phagocyte (Bellanti 1985; Golub 1987; Langman 1989).

X. Summary

Most of us don't spend much time thinking about the immune system, and that's because it usually functions well. Not so for David, the boy who spent twelve years in a germ-free plastic bubble. David was born with SCID (severe combined immunodeficiency disease) and couldn't produce the cells that are needed to protect the body from disease-producing organisms. A treated bone marrow transplant was given by his sister, but unfortunately, it was infected and caused him to develop cancer. The infection hadn't caused this difficulty in his sister because she already had a functioning immune system when she was exposed to the cancer. A well-functioning immune system permits us to live in a world that is filled with all sorts of disease-causing agents (Mader 1988).

My research has shown me just how complex and fascinating the human body is. There is no other system on earth that is able to repair itself and automatically fight off disease as efficiently. The study of immunity is really the study of host-bacterial interactions. The outcomes depend on factors that allow one or the other to win the battle. It's up to you and your body to win the fight. The most common type of immune malfunction is caused by aberrations in lifestyle: physical overexertion, malnutrition, stress, alcohol, and drugs, all of which lower your resistance and allow pathogens to invade your body (Miller 1986; Klurfeld 1993). The immune system preserves our existence, but we must do our part to not allow disease that "window of opportunity."

REFERENCES

Bass, A. B. Unlocking the secrets of immunity. Technology Review. 8:62-65; 1985.

Bellanti, J. A. Immunology II. Philadelphia: W. B. Saunders; 1978.

Davis, L. Unlocking secrets of antibody binding. Science News. 130:134; 1986.

Getzoff, E. D. Mechanisms of antibody binding to a protein. Science. 235:1191–1197; 1987.

Geyson, H. M. Chemistry of antibody binding to a protein. Science. 235:1184–1191; 1987.

Golub, E. S. Immunology: A synthesis. Boston: Sinauer Associates; 1987.

Herscowitz, H. Cell-mediated immune reactions. 2d ed. Philadelphia: W. B. Saunders; 1985.

Klerfeld, D. M., editor. Human nutrition: A comprehensive treatise, Vol 8, Nutrition and immunology. New York: Plenum Press; 1993.

Langman, R. E. The immune system. New York: Academic Press; 1989.

Mader, S. S. Human biology. Dubuque, IA: Wm. C. Brown; 1988.

Miller, J. A. Keeping a step ahead of immunity. Science News. 129:182; 1986.

Quarnberg, T. [Interview with Dr. Andy Anderson, Professor of Biology, Utah State University]. 1988 April 25.

Serafin, W. E. Current concepts: Mediators of immediate hypersensitivity reactions. New England Journal of Medicine. 130:30–35; 1987.

Silberner, J. Second T-cell receptor found. Science News. 130:36; 1986.

Sommers, H. Indigenous microbiota. Youmans, G. P. et al. eds. The biological and clinical basis of infectious disease. 3d ed. Philadelphia: W. B. Saunders; 1986: p. 110–145.

Wise, H. Man bites man. Hippocratic. 100:93; 1987.

Wyss, O. Microorganisms and man. New York: John Wiley and Sons; 1971.

Youmans, G. P. et al. The biological and clinical basis of infectious disease. 3d ed. Philadelphia: W. B. Saunders; 1986.

SOCIAL SCIENCE ETHNOGRAPHY

(Source: Mass Communications course at Texas Tech University, 1995. Used by permission.)

Red Raider Romances
by Lee Guyette

The following study was conducted at the Red Raider Club in Lubbock, Texas. The study is a brief survey of the nonverbal communication displayed in this particular club. The following observations were made by me not only in the recent few days, but also over a seven-month period in which I worked as a cocktail waitress there. I made my observations from the standpoint of a nonperson/waitress and from the person/female customer. The Red Raider Club is a Country and Western club that caters primarily to a crowd of people between the ages of 25 to 50. It is for the most part a blue-collar, lower-middle class crowd.

Body Types, Shapes, and Sizes

Attractiveness:

A majority of the people, both male and female, seemed only average in appearance. There were a few exceptionally attractive males and females, and they did seem to get preferential treatment; for example, the attractive men were turned down less when they asked a woman to dance, and the attractive women were asked to dance more frequently.

Body Image and Appearance:

Many of the individuals were slightly overweight. They did not seem to be very aware of or satisfied with their bodies. Their body concept seemed low. In the more attractive individuals, the reverse was true. The attractive individuals were more aware of their

364

bodies; they noticed what they were doing with their bodies, and they smiled more and seemed in general more comfortable with themselves. I did notice that the less attractive people seemed to worry less about their unsightly bodies as they became intoxicated.

Body Messages:

Most of my subjects were definitely endormorphic, and they certainly seemed viscerotonic. Most of the men were slightly overweight. There were women as tall as six feet and men as short as five feet. Nearly all my subjects were white. Perhaps 2 percent were Hispanic and there were no blacks. Many of the men had beards and moustaches, perhaps to indicate masculinity. Most of the women wore their hair either long and curly or short and straight.

Clothing and Personal Artifacts

Function of Dress:

The main function of dress in this club was cultural display more than comfort or modesty. Nearly all of the subjects of both sexes wore jeans. The men wore Wranglers and most of the women wore designer jeans. Chic, Lee, Wrangler, Sergio, and Vanderbilt were the most commonly worn for the women. A few women wore western dresses. I did not see any man not wearing cowboy boots and most of the women also wore cowboy boots. A few women wore high-heeled shoes. All of the women wearing dresses wore heels. Most of the people, both female and male, wearing jeans and boots also had their names on the back of their belts. For the men, it was their last names on the belt; for the women, their first names.

Communication Components of Dress:

It is difficult to say whether or not these people were intentionally or unintentionally communicating messages through dress. They all seemed to communicate their preference for western dress. They did not wish to communicate, however, that they were from a lower socioeconomic background by wearing western dress. Although this conception has changed in recent years, it still is thought that lower-middle-class people wear western clothes.

Personality Correlates of Dress:

It is extremely difficult to assess personality types of a large group just from their clothing styles. However, I did notice that most of the women in dresses were there with dates. I also noticed that women wearing red western blouses danced more frequently. For the most part, both men and women dressed conservatively. The colors were usually solid black, brown, and white for the men, and red, purple, or blue for the women.

Perception of Dress:

Most of the people were dressed in the conventional stereotype of western dress. Indeed, it was almost as if there were an unspoken dress code. The young attractive girls, wearing red and purple blouses with ruffles, tight jeans, boots, belts, and wearing their hair long, seemed to be thought the sexiest and most likeable. They were asked to dance more frequently than any others. The young attractive men with beards and moustaches wearing black or white western cut shirts seemed to be the most popular with the women. No one wore very much jewelry of any kind. A few women had small earrings or hair barrettes. Nearly everyone smoked cigarettes continuously. I saw no pipes or cigars.

The Effects of Dress:

The main effect I observed was that everyone seemed able to identify with each other and feel a sense of belonging to the group because of their similar style of dress.

[Researcher goes on to describe behaviors observed according to the following categories: body movements and gestures; facial expressions and eye behavior; responses to environment; personal space, territory, and crowding; touching behavior; voice characteristics; taste and smell; culture and time.]

Discussion

I feel that the nonverbal communication that I have described may be representative of lower-middle-class America in Lubbock, Texas. The nonverbal communication described in this report may illustrate lower-middle-class values: the tendency to be slightly overweight in both sexes; the conservative, traditional, western-style dress; the traditional use of male/female regulators and posture; the over-control of masculine expressions of emotion and the lack of control in feminine emotional expressions; the environment, with its tacky chairs and dirty carpet; the use of territory by the men; the fact that women have no true territory, personal space, or value (the women are treated as possessions and property, and they have only as much value as they are granted by men); the way in which the men have absolute control over when and how they will be touched, but the women have very little to say about when or how the men will touch them; the way the women plead with soft cooing pitch at the end of their voice or remain silent while the men speak loudly and uninterruptedly; the use of substandard speech; the accepted deception on the part of the males; the overwhelming smell of tobacco and liquor and stale urine in the restrooms; the taste of cheap wines, beer, and whisky; the time being measured by the sets the band plays. All of these things are often associated with lower middle classes. Women and men may be poorly educated and thus rely on tradition and myth. I felt that the nonverbal communication that I observed was representative of this particular subculture.

INTERPRETIVE ESSAY

(Source: English course at Utah State University, 2000. Used by permission.)

Jim as a Romantic
by Stephanie J. Owen
English 2010

The Romantic Age took place in Western Europe between the years of 1780 and 1850. It was an age which emphasized the importance of the individual. The use of the imagination and the emotions were considered necessary for the discovery of deep, hidden truths (Knoebel 260) in the Romantic quest for the "ideal state of being" (Miller 383). These truths were thought simple, based on the moral behavior of man (Knoebel 260).

The completion of the Romantic Age in 1850 did not end the characteristics, beliefs, and sensibilities that accompanied the age, however. Fifty years after the end of this period, Jim, the main character of Joseph Conrad's book *Lord Jim*, was described within the book as "excessively romantic" (Conrad 416). After listening to the story of his life, Stein, another character in the book, claimed, "I understand quite well. He is romantic" (212). In trying to explain how a romantic person viewed the world and what he must do to live happily within the world, Stein used a metaphor which I believe is fundamental to understanding Jim's behavior, both his failures and his successes, throughout the book. He stated, "A man that is born falls into a dream like a man who falls into the sea. If he tries to climb out into the air … , he drowns. The way is to the destructive element submit yourself, and with the exertions of your hands and feet in the water make the deep, deep sea keep you up" (Conrad 214). I believe that Jim's romantic characteristics induced his failures when he tried to escape from that which surrounded him and his successes when he submitted himself to his dream, to his ideal response to his environment.

The Romantics placed a strong emphasis on the value of imagination (Knoebel 260). Jim, too, was very imaginative. As Marlow, the main narrator of the book, stated, "He was a poor gifted devil with the faculty of a swift and forestalling vision" (Conrad 96). He often imagined himself in the positions of the heroes of books that he had read and believed that, when the necessity arose, he would be able to act in the manner which he imagined. He felt that his imagination had prepared him for any danger which might occur (6). This type of imagination ruled his life throughout the first half of the book; he lived more within his dream life than in reality. In the second part of the book, though, Jim began to realize his dreams. In Patusan, Jim acted heroically on several different occasions, often because his imagination helped him to discover the best method to approach a difficult matter. He lived very much as one of his fictional characters would live (Martin 205).

Another aspect of the Romantic Movement was the value it placed on individualism. Each person was considered to have importance, and variation was considered to be beneficial (Miller 383). Jim again proved to be romantic in the value that he placed on individuals. Throughout most of the book, however, the only individualism that he understood was his own, as Conrad expressed through the omnipotent narrator; "his thought was contemplating his own superiority" (23). In Patusan, however, Jim began to value the lives of others. He cared deeply for the lives and happiness of the Patusans, and he involved himself in their politics to help assure their freedom. Because he had learned the value of individual expression, he may have placed more value on Gentleman Brown's life than he should have. He had learned, however, that one individual should not necessarily judge another.

Jim also displayed a similarity with the Romantics in his wide range of emotions. The Romantics felt that emotions were important for true understanding of self, and

367

their works continually expressed a high emotional content (Knoebel 260). Jim may not have fully understood his emotional swings, but Marlow certainly noticed them. He claimed, "Your imaginative people swing further in any direction, as if given a longer scope of cable in the uneasy anchorage of life" (Conrad 224).

Immediately after having jumped off of the Patna, Jim's unhappiness and guilt were strong enough to have nearly driven him to suicide. However, another equally strong emotion, his anger at the others in the boat, prevented him (118). As Chester explained, "[He] takes it to heart" (165). After the inquiry, his inability to forget his extreme guilt caused Jim to continually run away from any incident or situation which might heighten his feelings of unhappiness. After finally having arrived in Patusan, Jim began to succeed, and his happiness and pride reached the same levels as his guilt and discomfiture had previously.

The imagination, individualism, and emotionalism already described were, for the Romantics, the basis and means for the discovery of deep, hidden truths (Knoebel 260). They thus rejected materialism (Miller 383) and the morals of their time period (Knoebel 260) in deference to humanitarianism and efforts to reform the world. They sought after "ideal states of being" (Miller 383). I believe that Jim's feelings of superiority and his constant search after heroism were a result of his own desire to idealize his own "state of being." He did have the sense of moral obligation and correctness that was characteristic of the Romantics, but he occasionally failed in his actions. According to Stein, the way to discover truth was to "follow the dream" (Conrad 215), and several times throughout the book, Jim did "follow the dream" to which his imagination, his individualism, and his emotions led him. In those times, he immersed himself "in the destructive element" (214), and then he succeeded. He failed only when he forgot to "follow the dream."

Jim made three major mistakes throughout his career as both a seaman and a leader of Patusan. In my opinion, each of these failures was caused, directly or indirectly, by some aspect of his romanticism which emerged when he attempted to "climb out" of the dream rather than submit himself to it. 'Jim's jump from the Patna, his inability to hold a job after the inquiry, and his misjudging of Brown were all actions which resulted from his uncontrolled romanticism. His first failure was, of course, his desertion of the pilgrims on the Patna when he jumped into the little boat to join the other officers. The strict moral code of the society in which Jim lived required that he remain on the ship with the passengers until it sank, and his own sense of honor demanded the same (Epstein 232). He had had no intention to participate in the despicable act of desertion, but just as the others were about to leave, the ship shifted and "his … imagination … evoked for him all the horrors of panic, the trampling rush, the pitiful screams, boats swamped, all the appalling incidents of disaster at sea he had ever heard of" (Conrad 88). He became immediately afraid of facing that scene and jumped into the boat. His imagination, always such a comfort and considered by many to be such an asset, had betrayed him and his dreams of glory. Instead of preparing him to perform heroic acts as he had believed it would, it forced him to run away from duty. Jim attempted to save his own life, contrary to his desire and dream. He failed himself because he attempted to escape that which was dangerous rather than remain, as he had desired, on the ship and bring himself glory.

After the Patna incident, Jim was forbidden to work on the sea. Attempting to help him begin his life anew, Marlow found him employment. Jim's romantic values, however, caused him to become an unreliable employee. Whenever he knew his employers had learned of his involvement in the Patna incident, Jim refused to face them. He allowed his guilt to drive him away rather than remain and attempt to face his reputation, and he did not immerse himself in the situation in which he lived. His obvious rejection of materialism in favor of respect was very romantic, and he was extremely concerned about his image, his appearance to others (Martin 204). He preferred to run away from the dream of regaining his lost honor rather than to submit to living his life with people who knew of the crime that he had committed, despite the materialistic comfort he had with those people. He would not admit his failure to himself (Stevenson 241), and whenever he felt that those around him were judging him to be less than he believed himself to be, he left his job.

The third major mistake that Jim made in the novel was his misjudging of Gentleman Brown. This mistake, also, had a romantic basis. Jim's romantic dreams had finally come true; he was living as the hero that he had always believed himself to be. He had not, however, forgotten his extreme sense of guilt over his desertion. When he first met Brown, he despised him as a coward, but Brown immediately set up relations between them by saying, "Let us talk … as equals" (Conrad 381). When Jim told him that he deserved to starve in the woods, and Brown asked if Jim really deserved any better, Jim was reminded of his own guilt. Brown then emphasized that guilt by saying that he would like to die but he could not desert his men in such a bad predicament, thus reminding Jim of his own desertion of duty (392). Jim therefore identified Brown with himself, and, because of his own dreams of greatness and the memories of his own failings, he felt that he could not condemn Brown to death. He convinced Doramin and the other elders to allow Brown to go free at the cost of his own life if Brown betrayed their trust. This error of judgment was a result of Jim's high value of the individual. He felt that he had no right to condemn a man to death. Since Brown had also appealed to their similarities (Reichard 548), he remembered his own guilt and felt that if Brown deserved to die, then he probably did, too. Allowing Brown another chance may have seemed to be a heroic and generous action, but in doing so, Jim was again attempting to "climb out" of the responsibilities of his dream. Because of the memory of his own past failings, he was not submitting himself; he was not behaving as his dream characters would.

Although Jim's romanticism caused him much misery, I believe that it was the source of many of his successes as well. When he stopped trying to escape his past and began to behave according to his dream, he became the hero that he wanted to be. Each of his three main failures was followed by a success, caused by different aspects of his romanticism. After having jumped from the Patna, he attended the inquiry of the incident rather than run away. His continual running away from employment was rectified by his succeeding and remaining in Patusan. The act of freeing Brown, allowing him to kill several Patusans, was corrected by his going to Doramin and sacrificing his own life.

A reader can hardly keep from admiring Jim's giving up his life to "follow the dream" at the end of the novel, but Conrad seems almost to condemn rather than support the action. This condemnation raises the question of whether or not Jim's romantic characteristics could be considered his tragic flaw. I personally prefer to view Jim's death as a success, as a final proof that he was capable of controlling his own destiny and a final atonement for all of his mistakes, but I do recognize that his romanticism, his submission "to the destructive element," actually did destroy him. This is the question with which Marlow struggled and with which each reader must also struggle when studying Conrad and *Lord Jim*.

Works Cited

Conrad, Joseph. *Lord Jim*. 1920. New York: Oxford UP, 1989. Print.

Epstein, Harry S. "*Lord Jim* as a Tragic Action." *Studies in the Novel: Northern Texas State* 5 (1973): 229–247. Print.

Knoebel, Edgar E., ed. "Romantic Poetry." *Classics of Western Thought: The Modern World*. New York: Harcourt, 1988. Print.

Martin, Joseph. "Conrad and the Aesthetic Movement." *Conradiana* 17 (1985): 199–213. Print.

Miller, James E., Jr., et al., eds. "The Romantic Age." *England in Literature*. Glenview, IL: Scott/Foresman, 1976. Print.

Reichard, Hugo M. 'The Patusan Crises: A Revaluation of Jim and Marlow." *English Studies* 49 (1968): 547–552. Print.

Stevenson, Richard C. "Stein's Prescription for 'How to End the Problem of Assessing Lord Jim's Career.'" *Conradiana* 7 (1975): 233–243. Print.

HUMANITIES RESEARCH PAPER

(Source: English course at Utah State University, 2005. Used by permission.)

Heidi Blankley
Professor Kristine Miller
British Novel
2 April 2005

Ending the Violence

Pat Barker, a contemporary British author and winner of the prestigious Booker Prize, writes novels about England during the war years (Middlemiss). In *Regeneration*, Pat Barker "examines the treatment of shell-shock victims at Edinburgh's Craiglockhart hospital during World War I" (Perry 44). Although Barker's novel is mainly about the acculturation of shell-shock victims from World War I, it is more concerned with the larger issue that lurks behind the battle scenes: gender stereotypes. Barker suggests that the violence created by adhering to the masculine stereotype—that men are brave warriors and not nurturers—is not merely a social problem, but a mythical, psychological obstacle, the effects of which are seeping into all facets of life. If humans are ever to recover from the violence, Barker thinks we must analyze the root of the violence and come to terms with our destructive behavior toward the environment, other species, and one another.

In chapter 4, a relatively bizarre scene occurs which forces the patient, David Burns, to realize he can exert influence on the violence surrounding him. Burns boards a bus that takes him away from the hospital at Craiglockhart into the countryside. There he comes into contact with a tree that reeks of death, "The tree he stood under was laden with animals. Bore them like fruit" (Barker 38). Burns's first impulse is to give in to fear and run from the grotesque tree, but Barker has a different plan in mind for Burns. Instead, Burns faces his fear head-on and unties the animals:

> When all the corpses were on the ground, he arranged them in a circle round the tree and sat down within it, his back against the trunk. He felt the roughness of the bark against his knobby spine. He pressed his hands between his knees and looked around the circle of his companions. Now they could dissolve into the earth as they were meant to do. (Barker 39)

This scene is so strange and so grotesque that it forces the reader to question Barker's motives for including it. The scene Burns stumbled upon becomes a reflection of the war; the animals represent the hundreds of decaying soldiers. The inhumane hanging of the animals suggests that the soldiers are dying for an inhumane and unnatural purpose. Just as this scene is unnatural in its placement of the animals, so are the massive murders involved with the war (Miller).

Furthermore, the circle Burns makes with the decaying animals resembles the cyclical pattern of history; humanity has spawned war after war, apparently without learning anything from its own violence. As the creator of the circle and also the one who sits within it, Burns recognizes that he is both a physical perpetrator of violence and a psychological victim of it. He copes with this paradoxical situation simply by revising gender stereotypes. As he steps into the circle and returns the animals to the earth, he takes on the qualities of a nurturer, a role contradictory to the masculine stereotype. However, although Burns might wish to remove himself from the situation, from his contributions to the war and violence in general, he is still a part of it, the "white root" of it (Barker 39).

What Barker is trying to accomplish with this scene is to show that no matter what gender, we are a part of the recurring historical pattern of violence, whether it is toward humans or other creatures. The only way to get out of the circle, as Burns does later in his dream about the scene he had witnessed, is to see ourselves inside the circle: "He folded his arms across his face and … began drifting off to sleep. He was back in the wood, outside the circle now, but able to see himself inside it" (Barker 40).

Another character, Rivers, also displays his sensitivity to the destruction around him. Rivers, modeled after a real-life doctor, is shown by Barker to be a humane and sensitive man (Perry 44). In chapter 13, a bumblebee is trapped inside a room where Craiglockhart officials are holding a meeting. Rivers is unable to concentrate on the meeting and keeps scanning the windows, trying to find the bee because "the noise was unreasonably disturbing" (Barker 132). When he finally finds the insect, he "fetch[es] a file from the desk and, using it as a barrier, guide[s] the insect into the open air" (Barker 132). When he turns back into the room, he finds "everybody, Burns included, staring at him in some surprise" (Barker 132-33); judging from this reaction, we can assume that Rivers's response to the bee is an abnormal one. Perhaps the others in the room were unaware of the bee's presence, or if they were aware, maybe they would have acted like "bloodthirsty little horrors" (Barker 172), smacking the bee with the file instead of rescuing it.

Through his action, Rivers transcends the masculine stereotype, which is why his action is met by surprise from the other men. The release of the bee might simply be symbolic of Rivers's escape from Craiglockhart—for at the end of this chapter, he takes some time off for sick leave. But this connection seems too obvious. Barker is once more forcing the reader to question gender stereotypes. By releasing the bee instead of smashing it, Rivers becomes Barker's ideal human. He is a man with the capacity to nurture not only other men but nature as well. In this instance, he represents the balance, a human being acting on natural instinct to save another creature, without questioning his own motives.

Throughout her novel, Barker plays with the myth of regeneration. Typically (in American mythology), the myth of regeneration involves a male character who seeks to escape the bonds of his old life. To do so, he retires from civilization into the purity of wilderness and, after a while, is reborn a newer, wiser man who is more in tune with himself and his surroundings. Although the wilderness in *Regeneration* is civilized, Burns and Rivers try to use the wilderness in the same way. Burns returns to his native home in Suffolk hoping to recuperate from the psychological trauma he experienced in the war. Burns invites Rivers to join him there, hoping Suffolk will have the same invigorating effect on Rivers. Barker's idea of regeneration appears to apply to violence in general, to the war, and to gender roles. Early in the novel, Rivers has an insightful revelation about gender roles:

> He distrusted the implication that nurturing, even when done by a man, remains female, as if the ability were in some way borrowed, or even stolen from women.…
> If that were true, then there was really very little hope. (Barker 107)

If women are the only ones who can be considered nurturers, if men are permanently locked into the role of brave warriors, and if neither females nor males have the capacity to extend the boundaries of these roles, then there is little hope that the psychological trauma of war can be overcome. There is also little hope that the cycle of violence will ever cease, because the masculine gender stereotype depends on war and violence for the man to prove himself as a brave warrior, while the female stereotype depends on wounded soldiers to nurture. The result of clinging to these stereotypes is a perpetual cycle of violence that extends past the war and into the physical qualities of the environment. If the stereotypes are left unquestioned, the cycle of violence will continue, and neither men nor women will be able to recover from the violence.

However, in chapter 15, Barker illustrates a remedy for the destructive cycle of violence with a brilliant metaphor:

> Rivers knew only too well how often the early stages of change or cure may mimic deterioration. Cut a chrysalis open, and you will find a rotting caterpillar. What you will never find is that mythical creature, half caterpillar, half butterfly, a fit emblem of the human soul.… No, the process of transformation consists almost entirely of decay. (Barker 184)

Barker reveals that the only way to abolish war and all the violent behavior equivalent to war is to internalize those traits which are perceived as inherently masculine and inherently feminine—to view the soul as a combination of butterfly and caterpillar, enclosed in the delicate chrysalis of the earth. War is a transition period, a devastating event which can lead to the positive transformation of social roles, if we let it.

In her article on women's fiction, Pykett suggests that "Pat Barker, like a number of other recent women writers, does not interrogate or deconstruct history … but rather she seeks to recover and reclaim the past on behalf of those who have been silenced and marginalized by history" (75). In this novel, the shell-shock victims are those who have historically been silenced. Barker gives them a voice in *Regeneration*. Through them, she suggests that it is possible to heal society if we cease adhering to the stereotypical male and female gender roles. What we need in order to solve the trauma of war and to prevent future violence are not heroes or warriors, but a reconsideration of gender, a restructuring of the rules so that men may reveal their "feminine" sensitivity without being typecast as effeminate, homosexual, or motherly.

Works Cited

Barker, Pat. *Regeneration*. New York: Plume, 1993. Print.

Middlemiss, Perry. Homepage. 1 Jan. 1997. Web. 15 Mar. 2005.

Miller, Kristine. Class notes and personal interview. 10 Mar. 2005.

Perry, Donna. *Backtalk: Women Writers Speak Out*. New Brunswick, NJ: Rutgers UP, 1993. Print.

Pykett, Lyn. "The Century's Daughters: Recent Women's Fiction and History." *Critical Quarterly* 29.3 (1987): 71–77. Print.

MODELS FOR NON-SCHOOL SETTINGS

INVITATIONS

Sample 1: Formal Invitation

The Salt Lake City Arts Council
requests the pleasure of your company
at a reception in honor of
Dr. Patricia Moore
on the occasion of her retirement
on Saturday, March fifth
from 7:30 to 8:30 p.m.
at The Little America Hotel
920 South 600 East Street

R.S.V.P. 555-5555 by March 2

Sample 2: Formal Dinner Invitation

Mr. Peter Poole
requests the pleasure of your company
at a dinner in honor of his daughter
Janet Poole
on the occasion of her graduation
on Tuesday, May eighth
at seven o'clock
at his home
400 Treetop Lane
Sacramento, California 12346
R.S.V.P. 555-5555 by May 2

Sample 3: Formal Invitation to an Anniversary Open House

The children of Mr. Robert Peterson and Dr. Joan Peterson
extend to you an invitation to attend
an open house in celebration of
the Peterson's Golden Anniversary
on Saturday, August 16, at 6:00 p.m.
at the Moose Lodge
1000 Gardenia Street
Athens, Ohio

R.S.V.P. 555-5555 by August 2

Sample 4: Invitation to a Halloween Celebration

It's pumpkin time! We are inviting ghosts, goblins, and all other friends in disguise to a Halloween costume party. Come to our crypt at 1600 Center Street, October 31, at 8:00 p.m. We will supply the cider, refreshments and fun! RSVP (555-5555) before the cats shriek, the dogs howl, and other scary things go bump in the night!

Sample 5: Invitation to a Valentine's Ball

The Colonial Country Club announces its annual Valentine's Sweetheart Ball February 14, at 9:00 p.m. in the Ft. Worth Hotel ballroom. The Bar J Wranglers will once again provide the music. Dress is semiformal and the cost is $25.00 per person. Light refreshments will be served. There will be a cash bar. Please RSVP 555-5555 by February 10.

ANNOUNCEMENTS

Sample 1: Business Anniversary Announcement

You are invited to help us celebrate 20 years of printing service to the residents of Monroe County. We are happy to be the number-one printing company in both sales and service for the county. It's something we have worked hard to accomplish. Please drop in at 4000 Spring Street during the month of July to enjoy summer refreshments and meet our printing team. While you are there, remember to register for our big August giveaway.

Sample 2: Change of Business Address Announcement

I am writing to thank you for your career advice during my job search and to let you know that I have been offered the position of Regional Manager for Database Industries.

As you may know, Database Industries employs over 500 people locally. Of the businesses that offer software products, Database is by far the largest.

One of the things I've learned in this transition is the importance of staying in touch with friends and business associates. Therefore, I wanted to give you my new address and telephone number, with the hope that I will have an opportunity to be of assistance to you and your company.

(Give your name, new address, and phone)

Again, I want to thank you for your help and encouragement. I look forward to staying in touch with you.

Sample 3: Mandatory Meeting Announcement

RE: Company-wide safety meeting

Please plan to attend a special meeting for all employees tomorrow at 1:00 p.m. in the break room.

We are in the process of establishing safety policies for all employees. Managers are requested to bring copies of all accident reports for the last two years.

Sample 4: Announce a Broken Engagement

Susan and I wish to let you know that we have broken our engagement and will not marry, as previously announced. We are both comfortable with this decision.

Thanks for your understanding.

Sample 5: Formal Birth Announcement

Paul and Katrina Dattage announce the birth of their beautiful baby daughter who joined their family March 18, weighing 7 pounds, 6 ounces, and measuring 19 inches.

The family expresses appreciation for the support of friends and the excellent care from the medical staff at General Hospital.

Sample 6: Death Announcement to Friends and Family

We are sorry to inform you that our grandfather Parker passed away last Sunday from complications following open heart surgery. He had been experiencing chest pains for several weeks and the surgery was intended to alleviate the problem.

Following his wishes, we held a graveside service with his children and grandchildren at the Parker family plot in the City Cemetery. Grandmother Parker is doing well and would appreciate phone calls and letters from her friends and family members.

Sample 7: Graduation Announcement

We are pleased to announce the graduation of our daughter Sylvia from the Music Conservatory, and invite you to join us for an evening of celebration at the Conservatory ballroom on May 2 at 7:00 p.m.

Sylvia is looking forward to her career in music. Along with several other musicians in her graduating class, she will soon begin a performing tour through South America with a chamber music ensemble. We hope you can join with us to give her a good send-off.

Sample 8: Announce a Retirement

It's time to express my appreciation for the great friendships I have had here at Anderson's Implements over the past years. As some of you know, I am retiring at the end of August and plan to move to my old hometown of Watson. I hope to do some writing on the history of that area before all the early residents are gone.

I know the owners at Anderson's have been considering two candidates for my position, and I am positive about them both. Either is qualified to do an excellent job. Whomever is hired will bring a wealth of experience as well as fresh ideas.

Leaving will not be entirely easy for me. I have genuinely enjoyed working with all of our great staff and customers. Please feel welcome to drop in to see me in Watson.

Sample 9: Announce a Class Reunion

It's time to renew old friendships at our Monte High Class of '69 reunion next June, and the organizing committee is in full swing!

The first event will be an informal reception at the Field House on Friday evening, June 14, from 7:00 to 11:00. On Saturday, those interested may sign up for an afternoon of golf or tennis before the dinner dance at the Hunt Hotel that evening at 7:00 p.m.

Please help us by filling out the enclosed questionnaire and returning it to Barbara Moe at 200 Main Street, Montevideo, MN 12345, by February 1. We would like to display photographs and other memorabilia from our school days at the dinner dance, so please plan to bring your favorites. Don't forget to bring along your yearbook.

More information will follow in our next letter. Until then we will appreciate your help in locating addresses for the following classmates: Erica Kanter, Peter Holmes, and Sheila Foster.

Appendix K:
Model Bibliography Styles

AMERICAN PSYCHOLOGICAL ASSOCIATION: APA

The documentation style commonly employed in the social sciences was developed by the American Psychological Association (APA). Detailed documentation guidelines for APA style are included in the *Publication Manual of the American Psychological Association*, 6th ed. (Washington, DC: APA, 2010).

USING THE APA CITATION STYLE

1. Introduce your source using a signal phrase that names its author, immediately followed by the date of publication in parentheses: Jones (1995) states that....

2. Paraphrase or summarize the information from your source. It's best to use direct quotations sparingly. Preferably, recast the source information into your own words. If you do use any words or phrases from the author, be sure to include them in quotation marks and to provide the page number(s), preceded by p. or pp., in parentheses.

3. If you did not name the author in a signal phrase, at the conclusion of your summary insert in parentheses the author's last name, a comma, and the date of publication: (Jones, 1995). For a direct quotation or close paraphrase, also provide the page number(s), preceded by p. or pp.: (Jones, 1995, p. 75).

4. At the end of your paper, list the source with complete bibliographic information on your References page.

APA STYLE FOR IN-TEXT CITATIONS

When you rely on information from sources to support your research or arguments in the social sciences, your readers will want to know who wrote each source and when. APA style therefore requires that you provide that information—the author's last name and the date of publication—in the body of your paper in the form of an in-text citation, which is linked to the References list.

1. Author Named in a Signal Phrase

If the author's name is used to introduce the source, provide the year of publication in parentheses just after the name.

Hacking (1995) covers much that is on public record about multiple personality disorder.

2. Author Named in Parentheses:

If the author's name is not used to introduce the source, provide the author's last name and the year of publication in parentheses at an appropriate place. Include a comma between the author's name and the date of publication.

In antiquity and through the middle ages, memory was a valued skill (Hacking, 1995).

3. Specific Page or Paragraph Quoted

When quoting or directly paraphrasing the author's words, provide a page number (or a paragraph number if the electronic source includes one). Precede the page reference with the abbreviation p. (to cite one page) or pp. (to cite more than one page).

There may be a causal explanation for multiple personality disorder, because "multiplicity is strongly associated with early and repeated child abuse, especially sexual abuse" (Hacking, 1995, p. 73).

If the quotation is from an electronic source that does not have numbered pages, provide the author and year only.

Vault Reports makes the following request on its Web site: "If you work (or have worked) for a company we write about, or you have recently gone through a job interview, please fill out our Survey and tell us about your experience" (1998).

4. Work by Two Authors

In citing a work by two authors, provide the last names of both authors. Use the word and to separate their names in the narrative, but use an ampersand (&) to separate their names in an in-text parenthetical citation.

As Sullivan and Qualley (1994) point out, many recent publications take the politics of writing instruction as their central concern.

5. Work by More Than Two Authors

In the first reference to a work by three, four, or five authors, provide the last names for all authors. In subsequent citations, use the first author's last name and the Latin phrase et al. (for "and others"). When a work has six or more authors, include only the name of the first author, followed by et al., in the first and in all following citations.

Writing becomes less egocentric as the child matures (Britton, Burgess, Martin, McLeod, & Rosen, 1975).

According to Britton et al. (1975), mature writers consider their readers more than themselves.

6. Web Sites

When referring to an entire Web site (as opposed to a specific document or page on the site), it is sufficient in APA style to give the address of the Web site within the text itself. Such a reference is not included on the References page.

Patricia Jarvis's Web site includes a great deal of information about recent archaeological digs in the Great Basin (http://www.asu.edu/~students).

APA Style for Bibliographic Footnotes and Endnotes

The APA discourages use of content notes—they can distract readers from the flow of the text. Content notes should be included only if they enhance or strengthen the discussion:

- Make only a single point in each note.
- Number notes consecutively throughout the text, using a superscript number.
- List the notes on a separate Notes page at the end of the text.

APA Style for the References Page

You need to provide your readers with an alphabetical listing of all the works you used as sources. This References list should appear at the end of your paper. The purpose of the References list is to help readers find the materials you used in writing the paper, so the information in it must be complete and accurate. List sources alphabetically by the last name of the author, using letter-by-letter alphabetization. When no author is given, alphabetize by the first word of the title, excluding *A, An,* or *The.* Type the first word of each entry at the left margin. Indent all subsequent lines of the same entry five spaces, or 1/2 inch. (This is called a hanging indent.) Double-space the entire list, both between and within entries.

Book by One Author

Hacking, I. (1995). *Rewriting the soul: Multiple personality and the sciences of memory.* Princeton, NJ: Princeton University Press.

Book by Two or More Authors

Hindelang, M. J., Hirschi, T., & Weis, J. G. (1981). *Measuring delinquency.* Beverly Hills, CA: Sage.

Book by a Corporate Author

National Commission on Excellence in Education. (1984). *A nation at risk: The full account.* Cambridge, MA: USA Research.

Book with an Editor

For an edited book, provide the editor's name in place of an author's name. Include the abbreviation Ed. (for "Editor") or Eds. (for "Editors") in parentheses immediately following the editor's name.

Peterson's (Eds.) (2004). *Peterson's four-year colleges* (35th ed.). Lawrenceville, NJ: Thomson Peterson's.

Chapter or Selection from an Edited Book

To cite a particular chapter or selection in an edited work, start with the author's name, the year of publication, and the title of the selection. Do not italicize the title or enclose it in quotation marks. Next, provide the names of the editors in normal order as they appear on the title page, preceded by the word *In* and followed by the abbreviation Ed. or Eds. (in parentheses) and a comma. End the entry with the book's title (italicized), the inclusive page numbers for the selection (in parentheses), and the publication information.

Kadushin, A. (1988). Neglect in families. In E. W. Nunnally, C. S. Chilman, & F. M. Cox (Eds.), *Mental illness, delinquency, addiction, and neglect* (pp. 147–166). Newbury Park, CA: Sage.

Two or More Books by the Same Author

When two or more entries have the same author, arrange the entries by the date of publication, with the earliest first. If you have two or more works by the same author published in the same year, alphabetize by title and distinguish the entries by adding a lowercase letter immediately after the year: (1991a), (1991b).

Flynn, J. R. (1980). *Race, IQ, and Jensen*. London: Routledge.

Flynn, J. R. (1991). *Asian Americans: Achievement beyond IQ*. Hillsdale, NJ: Erlbaum.

Journals and Magazines in APA Style

A citation of an article in a periodical or a journal follows a format similar to that for a book: Author's Name. (Publication Date). Article title. Publication Information.

- Author's name. As with a book, include the author's last name, followed by first and middle initials.

- Publication date. Include the year and, in some cases, the month of publication, enclosed in parentheses.

- Title of the article. Provide the complete title and subtitle of the article, with only the first letters of the title and subtitle and proper nouns capitalized. Do not italicize titles or enclose them in quotation marks.

- Publication information. Publication information for an article must include several elements:

- Begin with the full name of the journal or periodical, as it appears on the publication's title page, italicized, with all major words capitalized.

- Follow this immediately with the volume number, also in italics. Do not use the word Volume or the abbreviation Vol.

- Next, provide the issue number, if applicable, in parentheses and not italicized.

- Finally, provide the inclusive page numbers for the article. Use the abbreviation p. or pp. with articles from newspapers, but not with articles from magazines or journals.

Article in a Journal

Alma, C. (1994). A strategy for the acquisition of problem-solving expertise in humans: The category-as-analogy approach. *Inquiry, 14*(2), 17–28.

Article in a Monthly Magazine

Include the month, not abbreviated, in the publication date.

Dobson, L. (2006, July/August). "What's your humor style?" *Psychology Today*, 48.

Article in a Newspaper

Provide the complete name of the newspaper (including any introductory articles) after the title of the article. List all discontinuous page numbers, preceded by p. or pp.

Pollack, A. (2006, July 13). Paralyzed man uses thoughts to move a cursor. *The New York Times*, pp. A1, A21.

ELECTRONIC MEDIA IN APA STYLE

The electronic documentation formats found in the *Publication Manual of the American Psychological Association*, 6th ed., were updated in 2010 with new formats for electronic documentation, as in the following examples. When citing electronic media, use the standard APA style to identify authorship, date of origin, title, much as for print material; the Web information is then placed in a retrieval statement at the end of the reference. If you are referencing an electronic version that duplicates exactly a print source, simply use the basic journal reference style for print sources prior to the retrieval statement.

Online Book

Provide any data on the print publication before giving details on where the electronic version can be located.

Aristotle, (1954). *Rhetoric* (W. R. Roberts, Trans.). Retrieved from *The English Server* at Carnegie Mellon University: http://www.rpi.edu/~honeyl/Rhetoric/index.html

Article in an Online Work

Generally, citations for articles in online works follow the same sequence as citations for their print counterparts, followed by the retrieval statement.

Kennedy, B. (2004). Plants and people share molecular signaling system. *Science Journal.* Retrieved from http://www.science.psu.edu/journal/Summer2004/plantsandPeopleSum 04.htm

Women in American history. (2007). In *Encyclopaedia Britannica.* Retrieved from http://www.women.eb.com

Article in an Online Newspaper or on a Newswire

Green, T. (2006, July 10). The Air and Space Museum is falling. *The Los Angeles Times.* Retrieved from http://latimes.com

Article in an Online Magazine

Fantino, J. (2004, March). Crime prevention: Are we missing the mark? *The Police Chief Magazine.* Retrieved from http://policechiefmagazine.org

Document or Full-Text Article Found via a Reference Database

To cite a full-text article you located via a service that your library subscribes to (e.g., *LexisNexis, EBSCOhost,* or *ProQuest*) follow the same format as for its print counterpart. In general it is not necessary to add database information in APA style.

King, M. (2000, July 6). Companies here ponder scout ruling. *Seattle Times*, A1.

Article in an Online Scholarly Journal with Digital Object Identifier

Brumfiel, G. (2006). Planet hunters seek cheap missions. *Nature.* 442 (7098), 6.

COUNCIL OF SCIENCE EDITORS: CSE

Although source citations in scientific papers are generally similar to those recommended by the APA—since scientists also are concerned about how current source material is—there is no uniform system of citation. Various disciplines follow their own styles (e.g., styles developed by the American Chemical Society and the American Medical Society). But many scientists use the guide created by the Council of Science Editors. The information presented here is from the eighth edition of this guide: *Scientific Style and Format, 8th ed.,* (online in cooperation with the Chicago Manual of Style, 2014).

IN-TEXT CITATIONS IN CSE STYLE

The CSE style of documentation offers three alternative formats for in-text citations, each of which is linked to an end-of-paper reference list:

1. The citation-sequence (number) style, in which numbers within the text (assigned based on when the sources are first cited) are used to refer to end references

2. The name-year style, in which in-text references consist of the last name of the author(s) and the year of publication

3. The citation-name style (preferred by the CSE manual), in which an alphabetical reference list is created and numbered, and the number for each source is used within the text, no matter where the in-text reference appears:

Temperature plays a major role in the rate of gastric juice secretion[3]. Recent studies[3,4,8–10] show that antibodies may also bind to microbes and prevent their attachment to epithelial surfaces.

CSE STYLE FOR THE REFERENCES LIST

As in all documentation systems, the CSE's References list must contain all the sources cited in the paper. The title of this page may be References or Cited References. Since the purpose of this list is to help readers find the materials used in writing the paper, information must be complete and accurate.

The following examples reflect the CSE citation-name style, since that is the format most commonly used in CSE-style research papers. List authors with last names first, followed by initials. Capitalize only the first word of a title and any proper nouns. Do not enclose titles of articles in quotation marks, and do not underline or italicize titles of books. Abbreviate journal names of more than one word. Include the year of publication. Cite volume and page numbers when appropriate.

Book by One Author in CSE Style

Kruuk H. The spotted hyena: a study of predation and social behavior. Chicago: Univ Chicago Pr; 1972.

Abercrombie MLJ. The anatomy of judgment. Harmondsworth (Eng.): Penguin; 1969.

Book by Two or More Authors

Hersch RH, Paolitto DP, Reimer J. Promoting moral growth. New York: Longman; 1979.

Book by a Corporate Author

Carnegie Council on Policy Studies in Higher Education. Fair practices in higher education: rights and responsibilities of students and their colleges in a period of intensified competition for enrollment. San Francisco: Jossey-Bass; 1979.

Book with Two or More Editors

Buchanan RE, Gibbons NE, editors. Bergey's manual of determinative bacteriology. 8th ed. Baltimore: Williams & Wilkins; 1974.

Chapter or Selection from an Edited Work

Kleiman DG, Brady CA. Coyote behavior in the context of recent canid research: problems and perspectives. In: Bekoff M, editor. Coyotes: biology, behavior, and management. New York: Academic Pr; 1978. pp. 163–188.

Newspaper Article

Blackman J. Aldermen grill Peoples officials on heating costs. Chicago Tribune. 2001 Jan 16; Sect. 1A:2(col. 3).

Magazine Article

Aveni AF. Emissaries to the stars: the astronomers of ancient Maya. Mercury. 1995 May:15-18.

ELECTRONIC MEDIA IN CSE STYLE

Online Professional or Personal Site

Gelt J. Home use of greywater: rainwater conserves water—and money [Internet]. 1993 [cited 2003 Nov 8]. Available from: http://www.ag.arizona.edu/AZWATER/arroyo/071.rain .html

Online Book

Bunyan J. The pilgrim's progress from this world to that which is to come [Internet]. London: Kent; 1678 [cited 2005 Jan 16]. Available from: http://www.bibliomania.com/0/0/ frameset.html

Article in an Online Journal

Lechner DE, Bradbury SF, Bradley LA. Detecting sincerity of effort: a summary of methods and approaches. Phys Ther J [Internet]. 1998 Aug [cited 2004 Sep 15]. Available from: http://www.apta.org/pt_journal/Aug98/Toc.htm

Article in an Online Newspaper

Roan S. Folic acid may mask vitamin deficiency. Salt Lake Tribune [Internet]. 2003 Aug 7 [cited 2006 Aug 8]. Available from: http://www.sltrib.com/2003/aug/08072003/thursday/ 81868.asp

CHICAGO MANUAL OF STYLE: CMS

The documentation system used most commonly in business, communications, economics, and the humanities and fine arts (other than languages and literature) is outlined in *The Chicago Manual of Style, 16th ed.* (Chicago: The University of Chicago Press, 2010). This two-part system uses footnotes or endnotes and a bibliography to provide publication information about sources quoted, paraphrased, summarized, or otherwise referred to in the text of a paper. Footnotes appear at the bottom of the page; endnotes appear on a separate page at the end of the paper. The Bibliography, like the Works Cited list in the MLA documentation style, is an alphabetical list of all works cited in the paper.

1. Introduce your source using a signal phrase that names its author, with a superscript footnote number following the source information: Jones states that ... [1]

2. Paraphrase or summarize the information from your source. It's best to use direct quotations sparingly. Preferably, recast the source information into your own words. If you do use any words or phrases from the author, be sure to put them in quotation marks.

3. Format your footnotes (listed on the page on which the source was cited) or endnotes (typed in a consecutive list at the end of the paper before the bibliography) according to the CMS format.

4. At the end of your paper, list the source with complete bibliographic information on your Bibliography page.

5. Indicate original source words and phrases with quotation marks. The best research papers use direct quotations sparingly as support for their own ideas and integrate those quotations smoothly. A signal phrase alerts the reader that a direct quotation follows; the quotation marks show exactly which words and phrases are being quoted. Long quotations are formatted using indentation rather than quotation marks. When students get into trouble by borrowing words and phrases without attribution to a source, it is very often the result of sloppy note-taking. Your notes should accurately record source information in your own words, and you should be able to tell at a glance when looking at your notes which information is from which source and on what page that information is located. Careless copying and pasting of text from the Internet can also result in unintentional plagiarism.

CMS Format for In-Text Citations

In the text, indicate a note with a superscript number typed immediately after the information that is being referenced. Number notes consecutively throughout the text.

In *A History of Reading*, Alberto Manguel asserts that "we, today's readers, have yet to learn what reading is."[1] As a result, one of his conclusions is that while readers have incredible powers, not all of them are enlightening.[2]

CMS Format for Notes

If you are using footnotes, put each note at the bottom of the page on which the reference occurs.

Space down four lines from the last line of text, and position the footnote at the bottom of the page. Single space within each note, but double space between notes if more than one note appears on a page.

If you are using endnotes, put the notes in a consecutive list.

Begin a new page at the end of the paper. Type the title Notes at the top of the page, centered; do not use quotation marks. List the notes in consecutive order, as they appear in the text, and numbered correspondingly. Double-space all notes, both within and between entries.

The other details of formatting are the same for both footnotes and endnotes.

Indent the first line of each note, using the paragraph indent.

Use a number that is the same size, and is aligned in the same way, as the note text. Do not use a superscript. Follow the number with a period and a space.

Begin with the author's name, first name first, followed by a comma. Then provide the title of the book (italicized) or article (in quotation marks). Finally, provide the publication information.

For books, include (in parentheses) the place of publication, followed by a colon; the name of the publisher, followed by a comma; and the date of publication. Follow the closing parenthesis with a comma and the number of the page you are citing.

For articles, include the title of the periodical (italicized), followed immediately by the volume number; the issue number, preceded by a comma and the abbreviation no.; the date of publication (in parentheses), followed by a colon; and the page number. Following are examples of notes:

1. Alberto Manguel, *A History of Reading* (New York: Viking, 1996), 23.

2. Steven Brachlow, "John Robinson and the Lure of Separatism in Pre-Revolutionary England," *Church History* 50 (1983): 288–301.

[In subsequent references to the same source, it is acceptable to use only the author's last name, a shortened version of the title, and a page number.]

3. Manguel, *History of Reading*, 289.

[The abbreviation *ibid.* (in the same place) is used to refer to a single work referenced in the immediately preceding note. If the page numbers are different, include the page number as well.]

4. Ibid., 291.

5. Ibid.

FOOTNOTES FOR BOOKS IN CMS STYLE

Book by One Author

6. Iris Murdoch, *The Sovereignty of Good* (New York: Schocken Books, 1971), 32–33.

6. Murdoch, *Sovereignty*, 33. [short form]

Book by Two or Three Authors

[List the authors' names in the same order as on the title page of the book.]

7. John Sabini and Maury Silver, *Moralities of Everyday Life* (New York: Oxford University Press, 1982), 91.

8. Anne S. Goodsell, Michelle R. Maher, and Vincent Tinto, *Collaborative Learning: A Sourcebook for Higher Education* (University Park, PA: National Center on Postsecondary Teaching, Learning, and Assessment, 1992), 78.

Book by More Than Three Authors

[Use the abbreviation *et al.* after the first author's name; list all authors in the accompanying bibliography.]

9. James Britton et al., *The Development of Writing Abilities* (London: Macmillan, 1975), 43.

9. Britton et al., *Development*, 43. [short form]

Book by a Corporate Author

10. American Association of Colleges and Universities, *American Pluralism and the College Curriculum: Higher Education in a Diverse Democracy* (Washington, DC: American Association of Higher Education, 1995), 27.

Book with an Editor

11. Jane Roberta Cooper, ed., *Reading Adrienne Rich: Review and Re-visions, 1951–1981* (Ann Arbor: University of Michigan Press, 1984), 51.

12. Robert F. Goodman and Aaron Ben-Ze'ev, eds., *Good Gossip* (Lawrence: Kansas University Press, 1994), 13.

Book with an Editor and an Author

13. Albert Schweitzer, *Albert Schweitzer: An Anthology*, ed. Charles R. Joy (New York: Harper & Row, 1947), 107.

Chapter or Selection from an Edited Work

14. Gabriele Taylor, "Gossip as Moral Talk," in *Good Gossip*, ed. Robert F. Goodman and Aaron Ben-Ze'ev (Lawrence: Kansas University Press, 1994), 35–37.

15. Langston Hughes, "Harlem," in *The Norton Anthology of African American Literature*, ed. Henry Louis Gates, Jr., and Nellie Y. McKay (New York: Norton, 1997), 1267.

Article in a Reference Book

[The publication information (city of publication, publisher, publication year) is usually omitted from citations of well-known reference books. Include the abbreviation s.v. (*sub verbo*, or "under the word") before the article title, rather than page numbers.]

16. Frank E. Reynolds, *World Book Encyclopedia*, 1983 ed., s.v. "Buddhism."

17. *Encyclopedia Americana*, 1976 ed., s.v. "Buddhism."

Introduction, Preface, Foreword, or Afterword

18. Jane Tompkins, preface to *A Life in School: What the Teacher Learned* (Reading, MA: Addison-Wesley, 1996), xix.

Work in More Than One Volume

19. Arthur Conan Doyle, *The Complete Sherlock Holmes*, vol. 2 (Garden City, NY: Doubleday, 1930), 728.

Government Document

20. United States Federal Bureau of Investigation, *Uniform Crime Reports for the United States: 1995* (Washington, DC: GPO, 1995), 48.

FOOTNOTES FOR ARTICLES IN CMS STYLE

Article in a Journal Paginated by Volume

21. Mike Rose, "The Language of Exclusion: Writing Instruction at the University," *College English* 47 (1985): 343.

Article in a Journal Paginated by Issue

22. Joy S. Ritchie, "Confronting the 'Essential' Problem: Reconnecting Feminist Theory and Pedagogy," *Journal of Advanced Composition* 10, no. 2 (1989): 160.

Article in a Monthly Magazine

23. Douglas H. Lamb and Glen D. Reeder, "Reliving Golden Days," *Psychology Today*, June 1986, 22.

Article in a Weekly Magazine

24. Steven Levy, "Blaming the Web," *Newsweek*, April 7, 1997, 46–47.

Newspaper Article

25. P. Ray Baker, "The Diagonal Walk," *Ann Arbor News*, June 16, 1928, sec. A.

Abstract from an Abstracts Journal

26. Nancy K. Johnson, "Cultural and Psychological Determinants of Health and Illness" (PhD diss., Univ. of Washington, 1980), abstract in *Dissertation Abstracts International* 40 (1980): 425B.

ELECTRONIC MEDIA IN CMS STYLE

The Chicago Manual of Style covers formats for electronic media thoroughly, integrating its coverage of electronic documentation formats with coverage of print citations. In general, electronic sources are cited much as print sources are cited. The URL is listed at the end of the citation. CMS points out that dates of access are of limited usefulness because of the changeable nature of electronic sources and suggests using the date of access only in fields in which the information is particularly time-sensitive, such as medicine or law. If an access date is needed, place it in parentheses following the URL, as in this example from an online law journal:

27. Ruthe Catolico Ashley, "Creating the Ideal Lawyer," *New Lawyer*, April 3, 2003, http://www.abanet.org/genpractice/newlawyer/april03/ideal.html (accessed July 20, 2003).

Online Professional or Personal Site

28. Academic Info, "Humanities," 1998–2000, http://www.academicinfo.net/ index.html.

Online Posting

Archived source addresses are given separately from any other addresses in citing listserv messages. The date of posting is the only date given:

29. Janice Walker, email to Alliance for Computers and Writing mailing list, April 16, 2006, http://www.ttu.edu/lists/acw-l/2006.

Computer Software

To cite computer software, start with the title and then include the edition or version, if any. Next, give the name and location of the organization or person with rights to the software:

30. A.D.A.M.: Animated Dissection of Anatomy for Medicine, Version 2.0, Benjamin Cummings/Addison-Wesley and A.D.A.M. Software, Inc., Reading, MA. Online Book

31. Vernon Lee, *Gospels of Anarchy and Other Contemporary Studies* (London: T. Fisher Unwin, 1908), http://www.indiana.edu/~letrs/vwwp/lee /gospels.html.

Article in an Online Professional Journal

32. Peter Appelros, "Heart Failure and Stroke," *Stroke* 37 (2006): 1637, http:// stroke.aha.journals.org/current.shtml.

Article in an Online Magazine

33. David Glenn, "Sherry B. Ortner Shifts Her Attention from the Sherpas of Nepal to Her Newark Classmates," *The Chronicle of Higher Education*, August 8, 2003, http://chronicle.com.

Article in an Online Newspaper

34. Heather May and Christopher Smart, "Plaza Legal Battle Revived," *The Salt Lake Tribune*, August 7, 2003, http://www.sltrib.com/2003/Aug /t08072003.asp.

CMS FORMAT FOR BIBLIOGRAPHY PAGE

The style for Bibliography entries is generally the same as that for works cited entries in MLA style. Follow the formatting conventions outlined for MLA in this appendix when creating a Bibliography page.

MODERN LANGUAGE ASSOCIATION: MLA

The Modern Language Association (MLA) documentation style has been adopted by many writers in the fields of language and literature (Joseph Gibaldi, *MLA Handbook for Writers of Research Papers,* 7th ed., New York: MLA, 2009).

Using the MLA Citation Style

1. Introduce your source using a signal phrase that names its author: According to Jones, …

2. Paraphrase or summarize the information from your source. It's best to use direct quotations sparingly. Preferably, recast the source information into your own words. If you do use any words or phrases from the author, be sure to include them in quotation marks.

3. At the conclusion of your paraphrase, summary, or quotation, insert in parentheses the page number on which the information was found, followed by a period: (332).

4. At the end of your paper, list the source with complete bibliographic information on your Works Cited page.

MLA Style for In-Text Citations

When you rely on information from sources to support your arguments in the humanities, your readers will want to know who wrote each source and where it can be located. MLA documentation therefore requires that you provide that information—the author's last name and the page number where your source information can be found—in the body of your paper in the form of an in-text citation, or parenthetical citation, which is linked to the Works Cited page. Following are some guidelines for incorporating parenthetical citations in the text of your research paper.

Author Named in a Signal Phrase

If you introduce a paraphrase or direct quotation with the name of the author, simply indicate the page number of the source in parentheses at the end of the cited material.

Attempting to define ethnic stereotyping, Gordon Allport states that "much prejudice is a matter of blind conformity with prevailing folkways" (12).

No page number is necessary when an entire work is cited or for unnumbered Web pages. (Note that titles of independently published works are underlined.)

Conrad's book *Lord Jim* tells the story of an idealistic young Englishman.

The *World Wildlife Federation's* Web site has links to many helpful sites about the environment.

Author Named in Parentheses

If the author's name is not used to introduce the paraphrased or quoted material, place the author's last name along with the specific page number in parentheses at the end of the cited material, before the end punctuation. Do not separate author and page number with a comma.

> When Mitford and Peter Rodd were first engaged, "they even bought black shirts and went to some Fascist meetings" (Guinness 304).

Multiple Sentences Paraphrased

Indicate every instance of paraphrased or summarized material. If an entire paragraph is taken from a single source, mention the author's name at the beginning of the paragraph and cite the page numbers where appropriate.

> As Endelman shows, the turbulence of the interwar years—"political agitation, social discrimination, street hooliganism" (191)—culminated in the formation of the British Union of Fascists. He states that anti-Semitism "was common enough that few Jews could have avoided it altogether or been unaware of its existence" (194).

Work by Two or Three Authors

Include the last names of all the authors (the last two connected by and) either in the text or in the parenthetical reference. Because the following references are to entire works, no page numbers are necessary.

> Goodsell, Maher, and Tinto write about how the theory of collaborative learning may be applied to the administration of a college or university.

> We need to think daily about the implications of our future liberation (Eastman and Hayford).

Work by Four or More Authors

In citing a work by four or more authors, either provide the names of all the authors or provide the name of the first author followed by the abbreviation et al. ("and others").

> In *The Development of Writing Abilities*, the authors call writing that is close to the self "expressive," writing that gets things done "transactional," and writing that calls attention to itself "poetic" (Britton, Burgess, Martin, McLeod, and Rosen).

or

> In *The Development of Writing Abilities*, the authors present a theory of writing based upon whether a writer assumes a participant or a spectator role (Britton et al.).

Work Cited Indirectly

If possible, take information directly from the original source. Sometimes, however, it is necessary to cite someone indirectly, taking material from a quotation in another source—particularly in the case of a published account of someone's spoken words. To indicate an indirect quotation, use the abbreviation qtd. in (for "quoted in") before listing the source.

High school teacher Ruth Gerrard finds that "certain Shakespearean characters have definite potential as student role models" (qtd. in Davis and Salomone 24).

Electronic or Online Source

When information is from an electronic medium, usually the entire work is referenced. In such cases, incorporate the reference to the work within the sentence by naming the author of the source (or the title, if no author is listed) just as it is listed on the Works Cited page. No parentheses are needed when an entire work is cited.

One of the features of *The Encyclopedia Mythica* Web site is its archive of cultural myths, such as those prevalent in Native American society.

Andy Packer's homepage lists a number of links to *Star Wars* Web sites.

MLA STYLE FOR BIBLIOGRAPHIC FOOTNOTES AND ENDNOTES

Generally, footnotes and endnotes are not used in the MLA style of documentation. Notes may be included, however, to refer the reader to sources that contain information different from that given in the paper. In the text, indicate a note with a superscript number typed immediately after the source that is referred to. Number notes consecutively throughout the text. With the endnote style, all of your notes appear together at the end of the paper, on a new page titled "Notes" that should be placed just before the Works Cited list. "" With the footnote style, the footnote is positioned at the bottom of the page on which the reference occurs. Most word processing programs will automatically generate footnotes and place them on the correct page.

Use a note to cite sources that have additional information on topics covered in the paper.

[1] For further information on this point, see Barbera 168, McBrien 56, and Kristeva 29.

[2] For an additional study of Smith's fictional characters, see Barbera's *Me Again*.

Use a note to cite sources that contain information related to that included in the paper.

[3] Although outside the scope of this paper, major themes in the novel are discussed by Kristeva and Barbera.

Use a note to cite sources containing information that a reader might want to compare with that in the paper.

[4] On this point, see also Rosenblatt's *Literature as Exploration*, in which she discusses reader response theory.

MLA STYLE FOR THE WORKS CITED PAGE

You need to provide your readers with a complete and accurate alphabetical list of all the sources used in your paper so that they can readily find these sources if they wish to do so. This list, usually called Works Cited, should appear at the very end of your paper. (The list may also be called References, Literature Cited, or Works Consulted. If you include works that were useful to you in your research but not directly cited in your paper, the list should be called Bibliography. A bibliography that includes brief summaries of the works is called Annotated Bibliography.)

Formatting the Works Cited Page in MLA Style

List sources alphabetically by the last name of the author, using letter-by-letter alphabetization. When no author is given, alphabetize by the first word of the title, excluding *A, An,* or *The.* Type the first word of each entry at the left margin of the page. Indent all subsequent lines of the same entry five spaces, or 1/2 inch. (This is called a hanging indent.) Double-space the entire list, both between and within entries.

Print Books in MLA Style

A citation for a print book has four basic parts: Author's Name. Book Title. Publication Information. Medium.

- Author's name. For books, monographs, and other complete works, include the author's full name as given on the title page—start with the last name first, followed by a comma; then put the first name and middle name or initial, followed by a period.

- Book title. After the author's name, give the complete title of the book as it appears on the title page (underlined), followed by a period. Important words in the title should be capitalized. Include the subtitle, if there is one, separated from the title by a colon.

- Publication information. Indicate the place of publication, followed by a colon (if several cities are listed, include only the first one); the publisher's name as it appears on the title page, followed by a comma; and the date of publication from the copyright page, followed by a period.

- Medium. Indicate the medium of publication, such as Print or Web.

Book by One Author

Diamond, Jared. *Collapse: How Societies Choose to Fail or Succeed.* New York: Penguin 2005. Print.

Book by Two or Three Authors

Fiorina, Morris P., Samuel J. Abrams, and Jeremy C. Pope. *Culture War? The Myth of a Polarized America.* New York: Longman, 2005. Print.

Book by More than Three Authors

Britton, James, Tony Burgess, Nancy Martin, Alex McLeod, and Harold Rosen. *The Development of Writing Abilities*. London: Macmillan, 1975. Print.

or

Britton, James, et al. *The Development of Writing Abilities*. London: Macmillan,1975. Print.

Book with an Editor

Barbera, Jack, and William McBrien, eds. *Me Again: The Uncollected Writings of Stevie Smith*. New York: Farrar, 1982. Print.

Chapter or Selection from an Edited Work

Rushdie, Salman. "Chekov and Zulu." *The Longman Anthology of British Literature: The Twentieth Century*. Ed. David Damrosch, Kevin J. H. Dettmar, and Jennifer Wicke. 3rd ed. New York: Longman, 2006. 2989-98. Print.

Two or More Works by the Same Author

Alphabetize entries by the first word in the title. Include the author's name in the first entry only. In subsequent entries, type three hyphens in place of the author's name, followed by a period.

Rose, Mike. *Lives on the Boundary: A Moving Account of the Struggles and Achievements of America's Educationally Underprepared*. New York: Penguin, 1989. Print.

———. Possible Lives: *The Promise of Education in America*. Boston: Houghton, 1995. Print.

Print Journals and Magazines in MLA Style

A citation for an article in a periodical follows a format similar to that for a book:

Author's Name. "Article Title." Publication Information. Medium.

- Author's name. As with a book, include the author's complete name as listed either in the journal's table of contents or at the beginning of the article itself. For multiple authors, use the order of names shown in the journal.

- Article title. Use the complete title of the article as listed in the journal's table of contents. Enclose the title in quotation marks.

- Publication information. Complete publication information for a source from a periodical includes several elements.

For an article in a journal, the entry should include the name of the journal itself, the volume and issue numbers, the date of publication, and the inclusive numbers of the pages on which the specific article appears.

For an article in a newspaper or a magazine, the entry should include the name of the periodical, the date (formatted as day month year: 22 June 2006), and page numbers for the entire article. (If the article is not on consecutive pages, provide only the first page number followed by a plus sign: +.)

Medium. The publication medium comes last.

In Works Cited entries for sources from periodicals, use of accurate punctuation and formatting is critical. Punctuation helps readers identify the kind of information being provided. The journal title should be underlined; the date should be enclosed in parentheses; a colon should follow the date and precede the page numbers. For all scholarly journals, include both the volume and issue number.

Article in a Scholarly Journal

Cooper, Marilyn J. "Bringing Forth Worlds." *Computers and Composition* 22.1 (2005): 31–38. Print.

Article in a Magazine or Newspaper

Carryrou, John. "How a Hospital Stumbled Across an RX for Medicaid." *Wall Street Journal* 22 (June 2006): A1+. Print.

An Unsigned Article

If an article has no known author, begin with its title, alphabetizing the citation by the first major word of the title on your references list.

"What You Don't Know about Desktops Can Cost You." *Consumer Reports* (Sept. 2002): 20–22. Print.

Electronic Media in MLA Style

Because electronic sources tend to be less permanent and subject to fewer standards than printed works, readers need more information about them than is required for print sources. The *MLA Handbook* points out that citations for electronic publications may need to include information in addition to the three parts (author, title, publication data) typically used for print sources in order to accurately describe the electronic publication and how to access it. Thus a citation for an electronic source may have the following five parts:

1. Author's or site creator's name
2. Title of the document
3. Information about a corresponding print publication
4. Information about electronic publication
5. Publication medium and access date

Because electronic information can be changed quickly, easily, and often, access information is especially important. The version of a Web site available to your readers may be different from the one you accessed during your research. It is wise to print out or save to a disk the electronic source on the day you access it so that you have an accurate record. In its guidelines for electronic style, the MLA acknowledges that not all of the information recommended for a citation may be available. Cite whatever information is available.

An Entire Internet Site

Pew Center on Global Climate Change: Working Together. (2006). Pew Center on Global Climate Change. Web. 15 June 2006.

Online Book

Woolf, Virginia. *The Voyage Out*. London: Faber, 1914. EServer. Ed. Geoffrey Sauer. (2003). U of Washington. Web. 1 June 2003.

Online Periodical Article

Sheikh, Nabeela. "True Romance." *Jouvert: A Journal of Postcolonial Studies* 7.1 (2002): North Caroline State U, Coll. of Humanities and Social Sciences. Web. 23 Mar. 2003.

Article in an Online Scholarly Journal Found Via a Journal Database

Rosenthal, Angela. "Raising Hair." *Eighteenth-Century Studies* 38.1 (2004): 1–16. *Project Muse*. Web. 14 May 2006.

Article Found Via a Library Subscription Service

Bozell, Brent L. III. "Fox Hits Bottom—Or Does It?" *Human Events* 57.4 (2001): 15–. *Academic Search Premier*. Web. 15 Oct. 2002.

Appendix L: Twenty Common Grammar Gremlins and How to Fix Them

1. What is a sentence fragment?

A sentence fragment is a grammatically incomplete sentence. To be a complete sentence, there must be a subject and predicate. Furthermore, a complete sentence may not begin with a subordinating conjunction or relative pronoun that is disconnected from the main clause.

> No sentence fragments. [Faulty. Missing the subject.]
> You should not write sentence fragments. [Corrected.]

> The man in the hat. [Faulty. Missing the predicate.]
> The man in the hat is the conductor of the band. [Corrected.]

> Because we aren't interested in the property. [Faulty. Begins with a subordinating conjunction disconnected from a main clause.]
> Because we aren't interested in the property, we are not going to make a bid. [Corrected]

2. What is a comma splice?

A comma splice results from joining two independent clauses together with a comma instead of using a period and a new sentence. Comma splices can regularly be seen in informal writing. However, they are not acceptable in academic or professional writing.

> Don't join two sentences with a comma, it is not good grammar. [Faulty. Two independent sentences joined by a comma.]
> Don't join two sentences with a comma. It is not good grammar. [Corrected]

3. What is a run-on or fused sentence?

A run-on or fused sentence is similar to a comma splice in that it puts together two independent clauses without punctuating them correctly.

> Avoid run-on sentences they are hard to read. [Faulty. Two independent sentences without proper punctuation.]
> Avoid run-on sentences. They are hard to read. [Corrected]

4. What is a misplaced modifier?

When a writer places a modifier at a distance from the word it is modifying or uses a modifier that does not have a clear referent, the result is a confusing sentence. Check modifying phrases and clauses in your writing to make sure they have been placed close to what they are modifying and that they are not dangling without a clear referent.

Individuals place ads in the newspaper when they want to sell personal property frequently. [Faulty. Modifier far from referent.]

Individuals frequently place ads in the newspaper when they want to sell personal property. [Corrected]

The driver of the speeding car received a ticket from the officer showing no remorse. [Faulty. Who is showing no remorse?]

The driver of the speeding car, showing no remorse, received a ticket from the officer. [Ambiguity corrected.]

A motion picture company frequently, after it shows a movie in the movie theatres, makes the movie available on subscription services such as *Netflix*. [Faulty. Modifier interrupts the sentence.]

After it shows a movie in the movie theatres, a motion picture company frequently makes the movie available on subscription services such as *Netflix*. [Corrected]

Writing carefully, dangling participles are to be avoided. [Faulty. Dangling participle without a clear referent.]

When writing carefully, authors avoid dangling participles. [Corrected]

5. Is there a problem with splitting an infinitive?

Some grammarians object to constructions that place a modifier between the elements of an infinitive phrase, such as *to go*. A phrase with the infinitive split would be *to swiftly go*. However, others feel that it is alright and perhaps sometimes even preferable to split an infinitive when it makes the meaning clearer: *to boldly go* where none have gone before.

It is incorrect to ever split an infinitive in formal writing. [Faulty. Adverb *ever* splitting the infinitive phrase *to split*.]

It is incorrect ever to split an infinitive in formal writing. [Corrected]

6. Should I use *its* or *it's*?

Many writers confuse *its* (possessive form of *it*) with *it's* (contraction for *it is*). This mistake is easy to make if you are not paying attention because your spell checker will not catch it. Do a search/find for *it* to check your own work and correct this error.

Reserve the apostrophe for it's proper use and omit it when its not needed. [Faulty. Wrong use of both.]

Reserve the apostrophe for its proper use and omit it when it's not needed. [Corrected]

7. Should I use *that* or *which*?

The relative pronoun *that* may only be used with restrictive relative clauses, that is, those clauses that restrict the meaning of the clauses they modify. The relative pronoun *which* is more versatile and is grammatically correct in either restrictive or non-restrictive clauses. However, it is important to be consistent in your writing, so many writers choose to use *that* for restrictive and *which* for non-restrictive.

> Always use the relative pronoun, which is needed in your sentence. [Faulty. Restrictive clause would be clearer with *that*.]
> Always use the relative pronoun that is needed in your sentence. [Corrected]

8. Should I use *who* or *whom*?

The relative pronoun *who* is another one that causes confusion for writers who may wonder, "Should I use *who* or *whom*?" You need to look carefully at how the pronoun is functioning in the sentence in order to decide which one is correct. *Who* is the subjective case and *whom* is the objective case. If the pronoun is taking the place of the subject, use the subjective case, *who*. If the pronoun is taking the place of the object, use the objective case, *whom*.

> Who are you going to believe when it comes to correctness? [Faulty.]
> Whom are you going to believe when it comes to correctness? [Corrected.]

Whom is the object of believe and *you* is the subject: You are going to believe *whom*?]

9. How do I make clear what a pronoun refers to?

Another pesky pronoun problem comes when you have multiple nouns and pronouns in one sentence. You should take care that it is clear which noun the pronoun refers to. You should also be consistent with your pronouns and not shift point of view in one sentence (e.g., from second to third person).

> Mark and John were not able to go camping with his father. [Faulty. Unclear what *his* refers to.]
> Mark and John were not able to go camping with John's father. [Corrected.]

> A writer must not shift your point of view or change their pronouns. [Faulty. Writer shifted from second person *your* to third person *their* in the same sentence.]
> Writers must not shift their point of view or change their pronouns. [Corrected.]

10. How can I avoid sounding sexist?

Writers need to take care not to use language in a way that stereotypes gender roles through careless use of examples or word choices.

The woman doctor was assisted in the surgery by the male nurse. [Faulty. Gender stereotypes.]
The doctor was assisted in the surgery by the nurse. [Corrected.]

Everyone should pay attention to his language so he doesn't seem sexist. [Faulty. Generic use of the male gender pronoun.]
Writers should pay attention to their language so they do not seem sexist. [Corrected. Using the plural writers is a way to correct the sexist pronoun reference.]

11. How do I use irregular verbs like *drink* correctly?

Sometimes informal speech makes use of irregular verb forms. If you are not sure of what form of a verb to use, it is a good idea to consult a dictionary.

Steer clear of incorrect forms of verbs that have snuck into the language. [Faulty.]
Steer clear of incorrect forms of verbs that have sneaked into the language. [Corrected. *Sneaked* is the more formal past participle, although *snuck* is now listed as an alternative in many dictionaries.]

12. How do I use *would* and *could* correctly in conditional sentences?

Sometimes you will see the construction *would of* when the person actually meant *would have*. Similarly, use *could have* instead of *could of*.

If the writer would of paid attention, he would of written the sentence correctly. [Faulty.]
If the writer would have paid attention, he would have written the sentence correctly. [Corrected.]

Peter could of used a good editor. [Faulty.]
Peter could have used a good editor. [Corrected.]

13. When do I use *sit* or *set*?

These two little words are frequently confused by writers. *Set* is the transitive verb, that is, it takes an object: to set something (an object) somewhere. *Sit* is the intransitive verb meaning *to be seated*: please sit down.

Please don't set on the couch all day instead of doing your chores. Rather, sit your play station aside and get to work. [Faulty.]
Please don't sit on the couch all day instead of doing your chores. Rather, set your play station aside and get to work. [Corrected.]

14. When do I use *lie* or *lay*?

These two words are also frequently confused. The word lay takes a direct object and means "to place something": I will lay the wreath on the grave. The word lie means "to recline": I intend to lie down after supper.

You should never lie newspapers on the dining room table after you've read them. Besides, I think you should lay down for a nap now. [Faulty.]

You should never lay newspapers on the dining room table after you've read them. Besides, I think you should lie down for a nap now. [Corrected.]

15. How do I make sure verbs agree with their subjects?

Subject–verb agreement means that subjects and verbs should both have the same number, whether that is singular or plural. That is, if the subject is singular, then the verb in the same sentence must agree with it and also be singular. Confusion often comes when a subject is a compound—that is, it refers to two or more things. Most compound subjects have a plural sense and thus take a plural form of the verb.

Verbs has to agree with their subjects. [Faulty.]
Verbs have to agree with their subjects. [Corrected. Both plural.]

Rafting and hiking is my favorite activity. [Faulty.]
Rafting and hiking are my two favorite activities. [Corrected. Plural verb.]

16. How do I use *good* or *well, bad* or *badly, less* or *fewer, can* or *may* correctly?

Some adverbs and adjectives cause confusion. In such cases, you just need to memorize which is which in order to be correct. Here are some examples:

When I feel well, I write good. [Faulty. *Well* is an adverb that describes a verb; and *good* is an adjective that describes a noun.]
When I feel good, I write well. [Corrected.]

In order not to be a badly writer, write all adverbial forms correct. [Faulty. *Badly* is an adverb: to write badly. *Bad* is an adjective: a bad writer. *Correct* is being used as an adverb to modify *write*: write correctly.]
In order not to be a bad writer, write all adverbial forms correctly. [Corrected.]

Margaret had less problems and fewer anxiety than her sister. [Faulty. Use fewer with count items and less with noncount items.]
Margaret had fewer problems and less anxiety than her sister.

Can I go to the store with Jimmy? No, you cannot. [Faulty. Use may when making a request; use can in the sense of "is able": I can lift 50 pounds.]
May I go to the store with Jimmy? No, you may not. [Corrected.]

17. How can I avoid being redundant or wordy?

A common problem with writers in school and at work is wordiness. Writers use extra words in order to sound more important or knowledgeable. However, wordiness can backfire: your readers may find you pretentious or confusing if you write with too much repetition.

Also, too, never, ever use repetitive repetitious redundancies. [Faulty.]
Do not repeat yourself. [Corrected.]

18. How can I put items in parallel form?

The rule to remember is that items parallel in meaning should also be parallel in form. That is, when you are linking items using *and, but, or, nor,* check to make sure the items are all in the same form (all verbals, all phrases or clauses, etc). Similarly, if you are listing items in a series, they should be parallel in form.

> We enjoy listening to music and to dance. [Faulty.]
> We enjoy listening to music and dancing. [Corrected.]

> To write clearly, be sure to resist hyperbole, do not use clichés, and you should never generalize either. [Faulty series.]
> To write clearly, do not use hyperbole, clichés, or generalizations. [Corrected.]

19. How can I avoid the most common apostrophe errors?

The most common apostrophe error is an error of commission. That is, many people put in apostrophes for a simple plural where they are not needed. The apostrophe is used to indicate possession, not simple plurals.

The confusion with plural possession comes in deciding where to place the apostrophe. You need to learn to form possessive plurals by memorizing the following rule: Add an apostrophe alone when the plural word ends in *-s* (the Jones' car, the Red Socks' star hitter, my friends' notebooks); add an *-'s* when the plural form does not end in *-s* (the men's overcoats, the children's books, the geese's feathers).

> On your mailbox, avoid the apostrophe for *The Normans'*. [Faulty. Simple plural, not possessive so no apostrophe needed.]
> On your mailbox, avoid the apostrophe for *The Normans*. [Corrected.]

> My parent's friends often participate in demonstrations. They are passionate about womens' rights. [Faulty. Parents and women are both plural possessives.]
> My parents' friends often participate in demonstrations. They are passionate about women's rights. [Corrected.]

20. How can I avoid the most common quotation mark errors?

The most common quotation mark error comes with end punctuation and quotation marks. Remember, in American English, the end punctuation always comes within the closing quotation marks. The only exception is for so-called "block" quotations which are indented from the margins. [Note: This rule is different for British English, which typically places end punctuation outside of the quotation marks.]

> A journalist once observed, "Everyone in academe knows that it's a jungle out there, not a grove". [Faulty.]
> A journalist once observed, "Everyone in academe knows that it's a jungle out there, not a grove." [Corrected.]

> Do not overuse exclamation points and ""quotation" "marks"!!!" [Faulty.]
> Do not overuse exclamation points and quotation marks. [Corrected.]

Index

Note: (ill.) indicates photos and illustrations.

409

417

419